Unspeakable Images

Unspeakable Images

Ethnicity and the American Cinema

EDITED BY

Lester D. Friedman

UNIVERSITY OF ILLINOIS PRESS
Urbana and Chicago

This book is printed on acid-free paper.

Library of Congress Cataloging-in-Publication Data

Unspeakable images : ethnicity and the American cinema / edited by
Lester D. Friedman.
    p.   cm.
  Includes bibliographical references.
  ISBN 0-252-01575-4 (cl.). — ISBN 0-252-06152-7 (pb.)
  1. Minorities in motion pictures.   2. Ethnicity in motion
pictures.   3. Motion pictures—United States—History.
I. Friedman, Lester D.
PN1995.9.M56U57   1991
791.43'6520693—dc20   90–39869
                                                              CIP

*For my three favorite movie companions—
my stepsons Dan and Tom Walter and my son Marc.*

Whatever is unnamed, undepicted in images,
whatever is omitted from biography,
censored in collections of letters,
whatever is misnamed as something else,
made difficult-to-come-by, whatever
is buried in the memory by the collapse of
meaning under an inadequate or lying
language—this will become, not merely
unspoken, but unspeakable.
>   —Adrienne Rich
>   "It Is the Lesbian in Us . . . ."

They have the power of description and we
succumb to the pictures they construct.
>   —Salman Rushdie
>   *The Satanic Verses*

Contents

Acknowledgments

Any anthology represents the collective ideas, hard work, and persistent energy of many people. The contributors of these original essays all proved wonderfully receptive to editorial suggestions and never displayed the slightest hints of ego or annoyance. One could not ask for a better group of professional colleagues, many of whom I now consider friends. My parents, as usual, gave me their support, encouragement, and love, as did my wife Carolyn and my friend Delia Temes. Bonnie Legnetto typed large portions of the manuscript with skill and speed, and Sharon Osika-Michales provided invaluable secretarial assistance.

Much of this book was completed while on sabbatical leave from the SUNY Health Science Center, Syracuse, for which I thank John Bernard Henry, president, Donald Goodman, dean/provost, and Mary Jayne Schneider, chair of the Liberal Arts and Sciences Department. Bill Nichols was an early and valuable advocate of this proposal. At the University of Illinois Press, Lawrence Malley enthusiastically encouraged the project, Richard Wentworth provided extremely helpful advice as it progressed, Mary Giles edited the manuscript with style and sensitivity, and Karen Hewitt tendered much needed technical and emotional assistance. Finally, David Desser's sharp eyes made editing a much easier process. Their creative suggestions and practical support made this book possible.

Two people deserve special mention for helping me complete this anthology. Denise Stevens of E. S. Bird Library at Syracuse University proofread the chapters and offered valuable suggestions. Michael Kaplan, a graduate film major in the Art Media Studies De-

partment at Syracuse University, was an able, articulate and sensitive assistant from the inception of the project until its completion.
Every teacher should be blessed with such a student.

The following sources supplied stills for this book: Museum of
Modern Art Film Stills Archive, Jerry Ohlinger's Movie Material
Store, Edison National Historical Site, Ontario Film Institute, Orion
Pictures, Paramount Pictures Corporation, George Eastman House,
Lincoln Center, Cinemateca of the Museum of Modern Art (Rio de
Janeiro), Third World Newsreel, Movie Star News, *Playboy* Maga-
zine, and Ciné-Affiches (Montréal).

Introduction

Some time ago, I received a cryptic note from an old friend. "Dear Les, see what you've started! Soon we'll have scholarly books and articles about the image of the Hare Krishnas in film." Inside his message rested a carefully folded advertisement for a book detailing how American movies depict the Catholic church. My friend's comment initially made me laugh, but further reflection led me to consider the direction of my own research. I, like others intellectually intrigued and emotionally moved by ethnic issues, had published an "image of the ——— " book; mine concerned Jews, but various scholars wrote about Native-Americans, blacks, Hispanics, Asians, Arabs, East Europeans, Russians, Germans, Italians, and others. In fact, the long list of citations Allen L. Woll and Randall M. Miller collect in *Ethnic and Racial Images in Film and Television* (1987) bibliographically summarizes the vast amount of work done in this field of inquiry, particularly during the 1980s.[1]

As I glanced at the "image-of" works that dot my office bookshelves, I wondered if we who spend our time researching and writing about ethnicity had not, perhaps unwittingly, ghettoized ourselves. In our zeal to stake our claims on neglected fields of study, many of us seemed like homesteaders trapped in a typical ranchers versus sodbusters Western plot. We fenced off parcels of our chosen academic or ethnic turf, set up barbed-wired barriers to keep out poachers with "inauthentic" voices and to sustain our own authority of experience, carefully tilled and nourished the garden of ideas we planted, and waited patiently for other academic settlers to join our now-expanding community of thinkers. Throughout the process of claiming, cultivating, protecting, and populating this fertile land, we proudly trumpeted our differences. America, for us, was not a melting-pot belief system that boiled out foreign strains of thought and replaced them with the values of white, Christian, heterosexual men. Our movie classics preached an assimilationist, often racist and sexist, philosophy, but from the 1960s onward pictures appeared far less neat and orderly, far less willing to jettison ethnic values in the name of greater Americanism. Yet in our eagerness to examine the particular we lost sight of the relationships among the many. We were so busy constructing walls that we forgot about bridges.

Writing about images was certainly a necessary and vitally important first step in sensitizing our colleagues, as well as the general public, about the pervasiveness of ethnic issues in the cinema. Yet such explorations inevitably focus on value-ladened judgments of authenticity and elusive concepts of realism. Discussion of these issues, claims William Boelhower, is actually a "pseudo-discourse, a pathetic anthropology."[2] In fact, these judgments create at least three persistent dilemmas.

You're Too Much/Not Enough

The first dilemma revolves around what degree of cultural blandness robs a film figure of group heritage and what degree of ethnic characterization turns him or her into a caricature. How, for example, does one determine the acceptable level of blackness for a character, a spectrum that runs from Sidney Poitier to Superfly? Such considerations inexorably lead to questions of stereotyping, arguments about what elements of a group's culture should and should not be represented on the screen. The problem continually plagues performers strongly associated with specific ethnic groups, be they Barbra Streisand, Bill Cosby, Jay Silverheels, or Richard Loo. Most ethnic interest groups, for example, the ADL or the NAACP, although somewhat loath to admit it, simply want positive portraits of their constituencies on the nation's movie screens. More realistically, they settle for equal representation: every machinegun-weilding mafioso murdered should be counterbalanced by a kindly yet courageous Italian policeman. Such problems prove most explosive when a director or writer portrays members of his or her own culture in a manner other group members find offensive, such as Francis Ford Coppola's Italian criminals in *The Godfather* films,

Woody Allen's continual portrait of American Jews, or Spike Lee's "wannabes" in *School Daze*.

You're Being Divisive

The second dilemma asks if, by foregrounding American ethnic differentiation, one undermines American national unity. Until the late 1960s, most scholars viewed ethnic affiliation as an emotional vestige of a romanticized past, a feeling as outmoded as the horse and buggy and destined for a similar fate. Such was not the case, but the question remains, Does drawing attention to one's Old World ethnic roots fracture U.S. society by stressing our differences and downplaying our similarities? Some fear such emphasis on a group's non-American culture inevitably encourages racism and discrimination. Thus, for example, Robert Alter argues that viewing everything through a prism of ethnicity constricts rather than expands our vision, and Meg Greenfield claims that ethnic paranoia threatens the health of our politics.[3] My own experience confirms the powerful presence of this syndrome within segments of the movie business. I surveyed some two hundred Jewish filmmakers about how their ethnic heritage affects their artistry. Many refused to participate, and several attacked my research as "divisive" because it "segregated" Jewish directors from the rest of the industry. The very first response I received harshly accused me of providing ammunition for anti-Semites simply by pointing out that a large proportion of directors in Hollywood are Jewish.

You're Not One of Us

This dilemma questions who possesses authority to write or to depict a group. Can only members of an ethnic group speak authentically about issues concerning that group? Adhering to a position that, in *Beyond Ethnicity*, Werner Sollors labels "biological insiderism," some writers and filmmakers argue that outsiders can never produce films of worth or commentaries of value about a particular ethnic group because they necessarily view it only through their inherently dissimilar, different-from-the-group value system.[4] When majority group members evaluate the work of minority group members, the results are at best simplistic misreadings and at worst cynical misappropriations. Edward Said forcefully demonstrates this position in *Orientalism* (1978), an analysis of Western discourse on the third world.[5] But less sweeping questions arise closer to home. Should, for instance, Thomas Cripps (who is white) write about films that feature back performers? Should white directors such as Clint Eastwood (*Bird*) and Steven Spielberg (*The Color Purple*) direct pictures that speak directly to the black experience?

The search for authenticity and the reliance on realism remain the twin goals of most books and articles which attempt to confront the history of ethnic images in the American cinema, yet few of these works even confront—much less solve—the dilemmas.

Thinking about my previous work and these dilemmas led me to consider another area of film research initially dominated by discussions of images but which ultimately incorporated issues beyond the constricting concerns of authenticity and realism: feminism. After all, both the scholarly community and the popular consciousness invariably link ethnic group members and women together under the often amorphous rubric of "Other." Early feminist writing often concerns itself with the concepts of authenticity and realism, as do books about ethnicity. Unlike some of the intriguing, if rather esoteric and abstract, subjects that attract film scholars, both feminism and ethnic studies resonate far beyond faculty disputations; they have immediately perceivable and long-term effects on those both inside and outside the ivy-covered walls of academe. It occurred to me that some instructive connections could be made between ethnicity and feminism, both as elements in the cinema and as academic disciplines.

The history of feminist criticism's evolution in the academy proves particularly interesting when juxtaposed to the state of ethnic studies in colleges and universities. It is easy to recall when commentators hailed books like Marjorie Rosen's *Popcorn Venus* (1973), Molly Haskell's *From Reverence to Rape* (1974), and Joan Mellen's *Women and Their Sexuality in the New Film* (1974) as the finest examples of feminist criticism. All were, of course, works dealing with how the American cinema portrayed women during various decades, analyzing their image as presented on film. Next came several books about women who made movies, such as *The Work of Dorothy Arzner* (1975) edited by Claire Johnston, and Sharon Smith's 1975 guide to female filmmakers, *Women Who Make Movies*. In addition, such journals as *Take One, The Velvet Light Trap,* and *Film Comment* devoted special editions to women and film during the early seventies. These publications drew general and academic attention to an important area of film history, one almost totally ignored by the earlier generation of cinema scholars.

With the founding of *Jump Cut* in 1974 and *Camera Obscura* in 1977 the field of feminist criticism possessed its own journals. Finally, theory caught up with practice in books such as Patricia Erens's *Sexual Stratagems* (1979), Mary Ann Doane, Patricia Mellencamp, and Linda Williams's anthology *Re-Vision* (1984) and Teresa deLauretis's *Alice Doesn't: Feminism, Semiotics, Cinema* (1985). These works dramatically revealed the theoretical sophistication of a new generation of film scholars, a group of thinkers for whom the image-oriented works of Rosen, Mellen, and Haskell represented an extremely limited approach to a very complex series of issues. As the Doane, Mellencamp, and Williams anthology sums up this evolution, the process that began with studies of images, moved to discovering a lost history of women artists, evolved to the introduction of new critical theories and methodologies, and finally emerged as an accepted academic field that produces its own scholars: "feminist film criticism has become a vital area of research and debate . . . . [and] is in a unique position to challenge traditional academic discourse."[6]

Looking at this evolution of feminist criticism as a paradigm of how ethnic criticism might develop, we immediately note that most current thinking exists in the earliest phase. In this stage ethnic groups demand equal access to the symbolic order, that is, the large number of books detailing the changing image of various ethnic groups in Hollywood films. Such a beginning is crucial but limited. The second phase—discovering a lost history of ethnic artists—will, I think, progress somewhat differently for ethnic scholars than it did for feminists. My hunch is that film researchers will not necessarily unearth forgotten ethnic creators; rather, they will go back and explore how ethnicity functions in the work of artists already prevalent in cinema history. So, for example, an understanding of the Jewish background of Ernst Lubitsch might allow us to see his film differently that we have previously. Likewise, we have yet to uncover the cultural and ethnic forces that influence directors as diverse as George Lucas, Peter Weir, Ridley Scott, John Cassavetes, Paul Schrader, and Brian DePalma. As of now, however, few books or articles attempt to examine ethnicity as a force behind the camera, either in the lives of creative artists or in the economics of the American film industry.

This anthology represents the first attempt to encourage thinking and research about ethnic issues and the American cinema in the third phase: an introduction of critical theories and methodologies. It seeks to build some bridges without totally ignoring the walls.

These essays, therefore, explore the concept of ethnicity not only as it narrowly relates to various nationalities, colors, and religions, but also as it intersects with different ways of perceiving the world, of ordering our experiences, of interpreting our culture, of analyzing our artworks, and of living our lives. Such a broad conception of ethnicity rests on a belief that all categories of classification represent a cultural construction; it also recognizes that all modes of interpretation are, in and of themselves, ideological positions that seek to order our interpretations of experiences, both inside and outside the text, via a predetermined, hierarchical spectrum of responses that runs from good to bad, from higher to lower, from correct to incorrect, from acceptable to invalid. As such, the analysis of symbolic systems (including, of course, film) becomes crucial to any understanding how our society organizes, sustains, and validates various positive and negative notions of ethnic differentiation.

To that end, I have divided the book into two parts, each relating ethnic issues in the American cinema to other disciplines, conceptual theories, or critical positions. Essays in the first part examine how incorporating ethnicity into even the most traditional modes of film analysis—historical, auteurist, genre—forces us to reconsider, and ultimately to reformulate, the elements we include and those we ignore when employing these methodologies. Far from dissipating the effectiveness of such critical tools, the infusion of ethnic issues makes them more flexible, more inclusive, and more responsive to the world which surrounds them. Essays in the second part relate broad areas of critical thought—cultural studies, ethnography, postmodernism, psychoanalysis, feminism, class studies—to ethnicity, analyzing where each intersects and how each amplifies the other. Here, ethnicity functions not simply as one among the many components which comprise interpretive strategy, but rather as an independent critical methodology which, however variegated, can illuminate any text. Each chapter is structured similarly in that it begins with a broad issue, explores the author's central concerns and establishes his or her perspective, and demonstrates the author's position via an analysis of specific films. Thus, each chapter contains both theory and criticism, both abstract arguments and concrete examples. My own introduction seeks to give readers a general overview of ethnicity, relating cinema studies to ideas in sociology, anthropology, psychology, and literary criticism.

Several essays in Part 1 situate ethnic issues within a historical framework. Charles Musser focuses on film comedy from the mid-

1890s to 1930, analyzing the tensions (creative and otherwise) that sprang from the ethnic melting pot-pressure cooker of American cities. In particular, he pays close attention to Edison's early pictures as examples from the silent era and those of the Marx Brothers and Eddie Cantor as examples of early sound comedies. Ian Jarvie researches how representative Hollywood stars from 1932–51 were of the nation's actual ethnic makeup. His on-screen and off-screen evidence indicates that our top stars did not represent an ethnic mosaic, but rather an anti-ethnic image of America. Finally, Sumiko Higashi divides her chapter into two sections: an attack on the ahistoricity of most film criticism and the marginalization of ethnicity, and a contextualized study of Cecil B. DeMille's fascinating silent picture *The Cheat*. By summarizing the historical data necessary to decode the film's subtext, Higashi demonstrates how the film visually represents commonly accepted conceptions of ethnicity, gender, and class at a critical moment in American history. Paul Giles examines how ethnicity plays a crucial yet often ignored part in the work of two seemingly diverse film directors and ranges far beyond facile one-to-one connections between specific references in a film and that film director's cultural background. Using John Ford and Robert Altman as his examples, Giles explores how a residual strain of Catholicism influences the final shape of these artists' texts. Such an analysis goes far beyond iconic representation, as Giles transforms religious ideology from a metaphysical to a materialist context to illuminate these directors' films.

The two final essays in Part 1 show how typical film categories must be reinterpreted once ethnic issues enter into the analysis. Claudia Springer employs two established genres, the action-adventure picture set in the third world and the reporter film, as examples of how Western culture scrutinizes other ethnic cultures. Such films testify to the multiple levels of meaning produced by manipulating conventions and realizing the role of ethnicity within mainstream cinema. Mark Winokur uses contemporary comedies to highlight a tragic paradox of modern life: while American society sanctions the disappearance of blacks in life, it celebrates the success of blacks on film. With particular emphasis on the comedies of Eddie Murphy, Winokur describes "passing" as Hollywood's strategy of racial compatibility, one that perpetuates the fiction that America has solved its race problems while it simultaneously denies depictions of true empowerment. Springer and Winokur encourage us to incorporate ethnic issues into our traditional, usually Structuralist, analysis of standard film genres.

In Part 2, Ella Shohat maintains that, like issues of gender and class, issues of ethnicity are revelant to virtually all films, not only those where the presence of such issues appear on the text's surface. In particular, she investigates the musical for the presence or absence of marginalized groups, even in films which feature all-white casts but reveal the supressed Other through music and dance. Robert Stam explores the relevance of Bakhtin's conceptual categories for the theorization of ethnic representation in the cinema. His essay helps formulate a more nuanced, dynamic, and multidimensional model for the analysis of ethnic representation. Gina Marchetti employes cultural studies as a methodology for dealing with ethnic issues present in one mainstream (*Year of the Dragon*) and one independent (*Mississippi Delta*) film. Such an approach allows readers to look at ethnicity as more than a self-evident and self-contained category; instead, it becomes subject to the dynamics of class, race, gender, and other variables. Robyn Wiegman, focusing on class and gender in several mainstream, commercial pictures, demonstrates how the black female body functions in the circuit of cultural negotiation over black power. Her writing combines both Marxist and feminist concerns filtered through the lens of ethnicity.

The next group of essays relate ethnic issues to various theoretical positions and critical methodologies from different disciplines. Vivian Sobchack explores the representation of cultural meanings of ethnicity in contemporary American cinema, paying particular emphasis to how ideas of postmodernism redefine our ethnic concerns. To illustrate her contentions, she reads *Zelig, Moscow on the Hudson*, and *The Brother from Another Planet* as films which simultaneously affirm and deny the cultural value of the so-called melting-pot mentality. Paul Cowens employs insights from social psychology, particularly social cognition theory, to offer a taxonomy of films in which ethnicity plays a role. His approach posits an active role for the spectator, analyzing how audiences differ as a function of ethnic, cultural, or racial affiliations. David Desser uses Freudian psychology to examine how American silent films represent the on-going cultural dynamic during the early years of the cinema. Paying particular attention to Jewish filmmakers, he articulates the struggle at the heart of ethnic America at this time. In the final essay, Ana Lopez challenges the commonplace assumption that classic Hollywood cinema either stereotypes minorities or simply ignores them. Instead, she portrays Hollywood as an "ethnographer" of American culture: a producer of multiple discourses that intervene in the socio-ideological struggles of a given historical moment. The moment she selects is the period of America's so-called "Good Neighbor Policy" (1939–47), and she emphasizes the films of Dolores del Rio, Lupe Velez, and Carmen Miranda.

The goal of this anthology is to encourage readers from diverse disciplines to reconsider, and I hope to reformulate, their conception of ethnicity, particularly as it relates to American films. Cinema and its creators should be held accountable for racist and sexist images, those visual representations which have important consequences beyond the classroom and the movie theater. Yet to view ethnicity as a broad, complex, and multilayered concept forces one to range far beyond the scrutiny of images for their authenticity. Conceiving of it as both a theoretical construct and a methodological process, these original essays demonstrate some of the myriad ways ethnic analysis offers entrances into texts, connections to other belief systems, relationships to historical periods and events, categories of classification, interactions with different modes of analysis, and models for exploring aesthetic and ideological issues. We hope that the publication of this anthology will mark an important step toward illuminating and engaging with the unspeakable images that for so long have remained shrouded in darkness, and that it will bring into the light of discussion ethnic issues which constitute the body and the spirit of the American cinema.

NOTES

1. Allen L. Woll and Randall M. Miller, eds., *Ethnic and Racial Images in American Film and Television* (New York: Garland Publishing, 1987).

2. William Boelhower, *Through a Glass Darkly: Ethnic Semiosis in American Literature* (New York: Oxford University Press, 1987), p. 132.

3. Robert Alter, "A Fever of Ethnicity," in *America and the New Ethnicity*, ed. David R. Calburn and George E. Possetta (Port Washington: Kennikat Press, 1979), pp. 185–96; Meg Greenfield, "Pluralism Gone Mad," *Newsweek*, August 27, 1979, p. 76.

4. Werner Sollors, *Beyond Ethnicity: Consent and Descent in American Culture* (New York: Oxford University Press, 1986).

5. Edward Said, *Orientalism* (New York: Vintage, 1978).

6. Mary Ann Doane, Patricial Mellencamp, and Linda Williams, eds., *Re-Vision: Essays in Feminist Film Criticism* (Frederick, Md.: University Publications of America, 1984), p. 1.

Lester D. Friedman

1

Celluloid Palimpsests: An Overview of Ethnicity and the American Film

The signs of an ethnic revival, perhaps even an ethnic social revolution, exist all around us. To cite just the most obvious manifestation of this truism, the 1988 presidential campaign pitted against each other two candidates whose ancestors found very different entryways into American society. Yet both these wealthy and powerful men fashioned inspiring Lincolnesque biographies that stressed how each overcame personal hardships to attain Horatio Alger-like success in this land of unlimited opportunities. "History is biography," claimed George Bush when he announced his candidacy for president. The eventual winner of the contest then placed himself squarely in the tradition of those rugged immigrants who trekked westward, telling how he threw all his worldly possessions into an old Studebaker and staked out his oil claim in the wilds of West Texas.

Michael Dukakis began his announcement speech by saying "Today a son of Greek immigrants declares his candidacy for president." The Massachusets governor's subsequent evocation of his family's accomplishments clearly tapped a deep emotional reservoir in the American public and ultimately evolved into one of his most popular campaign themes. This "immigrant mystique," as Meg Greenfield labels it, has become part of the "edifying folklore of American politics" and as such exemplifies a countrywide preoccupation with racial and ethnic roots.[1] Even the comedian Martin Mull's humorous books and television programs about "white people" speak to a WASP yearning for an ethnically defined and differentiated identity.

Such a fascination with our personal ethnic histories sprang to public attention in the late 1960s and early 1970s, dramatically spurred by the insistent, often antagonistic, black power movement. Black demands for ethnic recognition helped legitimize the claims of other ethnic groups for their own individuality. If blacks were beautiful, so too were Jews, and Hispanics, and Asians, as well as the Poles, Italians, and Irish. Taking their lead from proud blacks sporting prominent Afros and wearing colorful dashikis, members of other ethnic groups began to acknowledge and then to celebrate their ethnic symbols and cultural heritages. Soon, it became rather commonplace for communities to hold an annual "Festival of Nations," as immigrants, their sons, and their daughters joined in colorful melanges of ethnic foods, native costumes, artwork, craftsmanship, and stage performances.

Ethnic pride thus grew steadily during the 1960s and 1970s, the desirability of cultural pluralism replacing the earlier goal of total assimilation into the great American melting pot. To be a hyphenated American endowed one with a source of pride, a feeling of uniqueness, and a particular perspective from which to view the often-confusing events of history. It gave one a natural sense of roots, a steady center that would hold amid the passionate intensity and mere anarchy that had been let loose upon the turbulent world of the 1960s and 1970s. Perhaps the most visible national evocation of this persistent trend toward greater ethnic expression was the spectacular 1986 centennial celebration of the Statue of Liberty, a commemoration that exploded with fireworks and tributes to our immigrant heritage.

Celebrations and political campaigns aside, demographic predictions all verify the changing face of our nation's population.[2] The Population Reference Bureau, for example, projects that by the year 2050 slightly more than half of all Americans will be Hispanic, Asian, or black. Before the next century ends, about 40 percent of the nation's workers will be either immigrants who arrived after 1980 or their descendants. According to these projections, the so-called Sun Belt states will contain some of the largest concentrations of nonwhites. By 1990, for instance, more than 45 percent of the children born in Texas and California will be members of a minority group. In California, minorities will collectively constitute a majority of the state's population soon after the turn of the century. By 2035, only 43 percent of Texans will be non-Hispanic whites. Taking these statistical projections into account, the Ford Foundation awarded $1 million to a two-year project, "Changing Relations:

Newcomers and Established Residents in U.S. Communities," headed by sociologist Robert L. Bach and anthropologist Roger Sanjek, the first national study to apply ethnographic research methods to analyze how new immigrants and established residents of widely different cultures and languages relate in six communities.

Such changes in our country's ethnic composition will dramatically affect all our institutions. For example, in the field of higher education, the traditional college-age population of eighteen-to-twenty-four-year-olds will change drastically over the next few decades. By the year 2000, almost 30 percent of this age group will be minorities: Hispanics will increase from 8 percent to 11 percent, blacks from 14 to 15 percent, and other races from 3 to 4 percent. By the year 2050, the minority members included within this eighteen-to-twenty-four-year-old age base will jump to almost 45 percent. In 1950, for comparison purposes, this age group contained only 12 percent minorities, a leap of 33 percent in one century. This demographic revolution will substantially alter not only who attends college but also what is taught to them.

So the often bitter clash over which canons of thought will be taught in our universities pits such traditionalists as William Bennett, Allan Bloom, and E. D. Hirsch, Jr. against scholars who protest the absence of minority and female voices from the core curriculum. Such battles over gender, race, and class represent the clearest example of things to come, as the loud debates over admission qualifications, standardized testing, and curriculum reform remain far from resolved. What is certain, however, is that given these demographic projections once-reticent administrators now seek innovative methods to attract and to retain students and teachers from this portion of society, a segment not so long ago accustomed more to token rather than to affirmative actions. Many hyphenated Americans feel that what comes before the hyphen remains as important an aspect of who they are as what follows it.

Definitions of Ethnicity

With the emphasis on the role of ethnicity in our national and personal lives, not to mention how belonging to (or being assumed to belong to) an ethnic group affects many of our daily interactions, one would think this term's meaning would be obvious. "Ethnic" derives via Latin from the Greek *ethnikos*, the adjectival form of the noun *ethnos* meaning a nation or race. Originally, the word referred specifically to pagans, those people who were neither Christians nor Jews and thus clearly designated as a class of outsiders; eventually, the term broadened to encompass cultural qualities and national or political boundaries.[3] The *Harvard Encyclopedia of American Ethnic Groups*, for example, lists 106 group entries based on fourteen designated features, but its editor still admits "the definition of an ethnic group has been necessarily flexible and pragmatic."

Flexible and pragmatic, indeed. Even a quick glance through the writings of various thinkers who approach the study of ethnicity from different disciplines reveals what a slippery concept it really is. The more one reads, the greater the tendency to agree with United States Supreme Court Justice Potter Stewart who, although he could not clearly define obscenity, still claimed with certitude that "I know it when I see it." With this caveat in mind, let us briefly explore the most important theories on ethnicity proffered by thinkers who come to the field with differing perspectives, an examination that will eventually force us to reexamine some generally held assumptions about how ethnicity has been depicted in the American cinema.

To define ethnicity one logically turns first to the discipline most persistently involved with investigating it: sociology. In 1969, the *Dictionary of Sociology* defined an ethnic group as one "with a common cultural tradition and a sense of identity which exists as a subgroup of a larger society. The members of an ethnic group differ with regard to certain cultural characteristics from other members of their society."[4] The sociologist Milton Gordon, an early researcher in this area, emphasizes three conditions that separate people into discrete ethnic groups: race, religion, and national origin. All of these, he argues, are fundamental to creating a "sense of peoplehood," and he claims that "structural pluralism" (social interaction between members of the same ethnic group) is replacing "cultural pluralism" (distinctive features such as language and customs).[5]

Likewise, Daniel Moynihan and Nathan Glazer conclude that America's melting pot mentality certainly altered immigrant groups, but it did not dissolve them; they, in effect, metamorphosized into a "new social form."[6] Other social scientists like Edward Shils and Clifford Geertz, often labeled "primordialists," argue that such elements as "race" and "religion" provide a fundamental identity around which a distinctive set of cultural attributes adhere over the centuries.[7] Thus for the primordialists, all social interaction must be interpreted with reference to predetermined conditions, those which exist prior to the start of any given social activity. Eventually, according to R. A. Schermerhorn, these memories of a shared historical past become another important component in defining ethnic identity.[8]

Like sociologists, anthropologists explore ethnicity primarily within a cultural context but with some decidedly different slants. Raoul Naroll, for example, defines a tribe or ethnic unit as a group of people whose shared way of life includes distribution of particular traits, territorial contiguity, political organization, language, ecological adjustment, and local community structure.[9] In a similar manner, Ronald A. Reminick concludes that ethnicity is a "highly structured, multi-level human phenomenon with multi-functional significance," one with six distinct parameters: environment, levels of operation, specified set of components, models of the process of ethnic identity change, cause/function set, and functional modes or types of ethnicity.[10]

David Schneider, another anthropologist, focuses on the issue of American kinship as a major cultural system, one which encompasses both nationality and religion. Such a system, he believes, is firmly based on symbols (something which stands for something else) but, he continues, no necessarily intrinsic relationship exists between the symbol and what it symbolizes. Any word, by its very nature, must begin and function as a culturally constructed unit; yet, verbal language is not the sole container of a culture. We communicate with a broad range of cultural signs and symbols, only some of which Schneider classifies as verbal language. From this, Schneider goes on to assert that every "culture-as-constituted can be shown to be organized around a small core of epitomizing symbols."[11]

Among the most influential anthropological work in this field is that of Frederik Barth. He emphasizes that the most important condition in determining ethnic identity is self-ascription, or as he puts it, "those factors which the actors themselves regard as significant."[12] With his heavy stress on personal choice, Barth shifts the emphasis away from the primordialists' focus on internal components (race, religion, national origins, and shared memories) to the maintenance of social rather than territorial boundaries. These he defines as what group members themselves agree about their codes and values. Such boundaries fall into two main categories: overt signals such as dress, language, and foods, and basic value orientations such as standards of morality and excellence. If one claims to be part of an ethnic group and is willing to be treated by outsiders and judged by insiders as such, then one is part of that group. Ethnic groups, therefore, coalesce through self-defined membership. Thus, for Barth, the critical focus shifts from the pre-determined to the situational elements: the "ethnic boundary that defines the group, not the cultural stuff that it encloses."[13]

Some social scientists argue that ethnic group membership results from a predetermined set of objective factors. Others, like Barth, contend that such factors must be augmented by self-ascripted signals and value orientations. Still another group claims that ethnic group membership derives from a purely subjective experience. For example, Max Weber believes that ethnic identity evolves from political needs and thus becomes a matter of a shared common belief, of what he calls "presumed identity." For him, no objective relationship need exist because ethnic group membership is a subjective belief rather than a blood connection. [14] On the farthest extreme of this position, the so-called Symbolic Interactionists claim that ethnic groups are not even natural biological divisions of humanity, but rather temporary alignments of people created by communication channels: ethnic groups simply disappear when people alter their consciousness or change their self-conceptions.[15]

Writers from the field of psychology also struggle to understand ethnic identity, although unlike sociologists and anthropologists, their focus has been more on the individual psyche and its relationship to the group than on tribal interactions. In 1926, Sigmund Freud characterized his own ethnic identity as "the prime bonds," noting that he owed his freedom from intellectual prejudices and readiness to live in opposition to the prevailing beliefs of his time to his Jewish ancestry.[16] Yet Freud's emphasis on repression and sublimation as strategies by which our individual psyches attempt to resolve instinctual conflicts led him to ignore virtually any role that cultural affiliation might play in the formation of personal identity. Only late in his career, as Judith Klein notes, did Freud acknowledge the importance of social and cultural factors in creating the psyche: "What is operating in the superego is not only the personal qualities of these parents but also everything that produces a determining effect upon them themselves, the tastes and standards of the social class in which they live and the characteristics and traditions of the race from which they spring."[17] These "characteristics and traditions" have gradually assumed far greater importance in the work of modern psychotherapists than in the writings and practices of Freud.

Erik Erikson's work, for example, represents a life-long attempt to draw links between individuals and groups (what we now label *psychosocial*), and he often discusses the role ethnic identity plays in such interactions: "Men who share an ethnic area, a historical era, or an economic pursuit are guided by common images of good and evil which assume decisive concreteness in every individual's ego development."[18] Erikson holds that the individual's life-cycle and personal identity inextricably interweave with that of the group: "The term identity speaks for itself in a number of connotations. At one time it will appear to refer to a conscious sense of individual identity; at another to an unconscious striving for a continuity of personal character; at a third as a criterion for the silent doings of ego synthesis; and finally as a maintenance of an inner solidarity with a group's ideals and identity."[19]

To comprehend personal identity, one begins by analyzing how the uniqueness of the individual interacts with the unique values and history of his or her people. Thus, for Erikson, identity "is a process located in the core of the individual and yet also in the core of his communal culture, a process which establishes the identity of these two identities."[20]

Over the last few decades, some psychotherapists have explored the relationship between group cultural identity and personal self-esteem, taking their theories out of the classrooms and into the clinics. Price Cobbs, in 1972, coined the term *ethnotherapy* to describe a clinical model by which he attempted, through group interaction, to change negative ethnic self-images in his patients.[21] Following Cobbs's lead, Joseph Giordano wrote a pamphlet entitled "Ethnicity and Mental Health" stating the case for greater awareness of ethnic factors in mental health programs.[22] Sy Fischer and Rhoda Fischer, who studied family conflicts over three generations in different ethnic groups, suggest that ethnic identity may be unconsciously transmitted:

> Apparently, when the individual is born into a given family he is caught up in a powerful directional current which stems from the basis ethnic-geographical facts of life which characterize the family. His central conflicts are those of a subculture rather than mere reflections of the idiosyncratic problems of the parents. His conflicts express difficulties faced by that segment of the culture in which he is immersed.[23]

In a similar manner, Alvin Poussaint draws on his psychiatric work with black and other minority group patients to conclude:

> the questions of racial and ethnic identity frequently reigns paramount. When it is not a key issue, it is at the very least a peripheral one that needs exploration and clarification . . . . For too long the is-

sue of one's ethnic identity and background has been ignored in the process of psychotheraphy. Too much emphasis was placed on the individual psyche without the proper consideration of one's cultural background and ethnic perspective.[24]

A good example of the work being done in ethnotheraphy is that of Judith Weinstein Klein, a practicing clinical psychologist, whose monograph *Jewish Identity and Self Esteem: Healing Wounds Through Ethnotherapy* provides an apt summation of how some contemporary psychotherapists see personal problems "through an ethnic lens" to define their social context.

For Klein, majority-group and minority-group children all pass through similar developmental stages, but for the latter certain problems become exaggerated because of the child's cultural situation: internalizing a positive self-image, making self/other discriminations, and learning and integrating multiple social roles and group memberships. She concludes, therefore, that the "task of creating an identity . . . for minority children appears to be more complicated and conflictual, especially where the minority group is devalued or regarded ambivalently by the majority culture."[25] Klein even classifies three distinct types of ethnic identifiers:

> The positive identifier who synthesizes good and bad associations with his or her ethnic group; the ambivalent identifier who ascribed both his most valued and most despised traits to Jewishness but never resolved the conflict thus engendered; and the negative identifier who used denial, self-contempt and splitting off to achieve negative distance and to disaffiliate from his or her ethnic group.[26]

Klein and other ethnotherapists see concepts of ethnic identity as a "crossroads issue," one that integrates a person's psychological dynamics with his or her inherited definitions of the self. Such an approach forces one to see problems in a social-historical context, to comprehend the connections between the self and others of the same cultural group, and to feel the benefits of an infinitely expandable extended family.[27]

This admittedly oversimplified presentation of some influential sociological, anthropological, and psychological theories of ethnic identity demonstrates the power and range of this phenomenon. It further highlights the enduring conflict between those who conceive of ethnicity and cultural identity as a predetermined, immutable condition beyond circumstances and rational control, and those who view ethnicity and cultural identity as a self-determined, changeable condition subject to situations and personal taste. In essence, most conceptions of ethnicity negotiate a compromise of varying degrees between these extreme positions, between what Werner Sollors labels "descent" (relations determined for us by blood or nature) and "consent" (relations we choose to accept).[28] Sollors's work represents the clearest bridge between conceptions of ethnicity in the social sciences and artistic incorporations of ethnicity into fictional texts. Although Sollors generally discusses American literary works, using these narratives as his central reference point and theoretical framework, one can easily apply many of his provocative ideas to the American cinema as well.

Sollors sees the central drama of American ideology, identity, ethnicity, and culture as pivoting on the conflict between consent and descent, terms within which he incorporates inherently oppositional belief systems such as Old World hierarchies versus New World freedoms, hereditary qualities versus contractual choices, ancestral definitions versus self-made assertions, blood versus law, nature versus marriage, and heirs versus free agents. The struggles between descent and consent depicted in our national literature demonstrate how a uniquely American culture evolves from non-American pasts:

> Works of ethnic literature—written by, about, or for persons who perceived themselves, or were perceived by others, as members of ethnic groups—may thus be read not only as expressions of mediation between cultures but also as handbooks of socialization into the codes of Americaness. . . . Ethnic literature may thus be read as part of that body of cultural products which tells American initiates and neophytes about, and reminds elders of, "the rites and rituals, the customs and taboos, of this country." . . . In this sense, ethnic literature provides us with the central codes of Americaness.[29]

For Sollors, the most important of these "central codes of Americaness" are the images of exodus and deliverance, newness and rebirth, melting pot and romantic love, jeremiads against establishment figures, and lost generations. All these contribute to new forms of "symbolic kinship among people who are not blood relatives."[30] Sollors appropriates W. E. B. DuBois's use of Emerson's original term *double-consciousness*, saying that ethnic texts invariably speak both to outsiders and to insiders; they mediate between one ethnic group and the rest of America. Paradoxically, then, these works perform two seemingly different functions: maintaining symbolic social distinctions and accentuating common American values. They endow the "diverse population of the United States [with] a shared sense of destiny. . . ."[31]

Drawing upon the ideas of Sollors, William Boelhower approaches ethnicity as a sign system, challenging the prevailing notion of distinctions between ethnic and mainstream writing. "Being American and being ethnic," he claims, "are part of a single cultural framework."[32] Thus, ethnic discourse is American discourse, because "ethnic difference" is an intrinsic part of American identity: "No matter where the American author finally chooses to strike through the pasteboard of American identity," asserts Boelhower, "his questioning always brings him into contact with an ethnic subject, his other self."[33] Of course, ethnic diversity functions nicely in a postmodernist world because it necessarily gives rise to a plurality of different realities: "Ethnic semiosis, then, is a way of thinking differently by thinking the difference, and in the postmodern American framework this may be all the difference there is: a particular form of discourse, of evaluating the agency of the subject, of holding one's ground against the map of national circulation."[34] For both Sollors and Boelhower, therefore, all the components of American culture become palimpsests, tablets upon which are written and rewritten numerous codes and traditions.

Before leaving the world of ethnic American literature so intriguingly reformulated by Sollors and Boelhower, let us briefly examine how two contemporary writers view their status as American authors. Critics usually characterize Norman Mailer as an author who displays little overt evidence of an ethnic sensibility. Yet in *Cannibals and Christians*, Mailer acutely sums up the feelings of the previous generation of ethnic outsiders. A member of a minority group "feels his existence in a particular way. . . . It is the very form or context of his existence to live with two opposed notions of himself." Such a person suffers an "unendurable tension" which surrounds his sense of identity because his emotions are "forever locked in the chains of ambivalence." Minority group members can never allow the outside world to define them, for this leads to insanity; rather, they "must define their nature by their own acts." Yet, perhaps ironically, Mailer argues that these tormented "sons of immigrants" and not those "who were most American by birth and had the most to do with managing America" best describe the real phenomenon of American life, which was "either grand or horrible or both."[35]

Unlike Norman Mailer, who represents the thinking of an earlier generation of outsiders, Calcutta-born author Bharati Mukherjee views her status as a newly minted (February 1, 1988) American in a far less torturous manner. In fact, she demands an expansive literary voice for her immigrant experiences. Mukherjee bemoans the absence of immigrant stories in fiction about these new Americans: "All around me I see the face of America changing. . . . But where, in fiction do you READ of it? Who, in other words, speaks for us, the new Americans from nontraditional immigrant countries? Which is another way of saying, in this altered America, who speaks for YOU?"[36] Part of the problem, she feels, is minimalist writing, which is nativist because it "speaks in whispers to the initiated . . . as though it were designed to keep out anyone with too much story to tell."[37] Describing herself as "chameleon-skinned," Mukherjee argues that modern America's ethnic- and gender-fractured world allows one to enter fictional lives quite dissimilar from one's own. Indeed, in her collection of stories, *The Middleman,* Mukherjee writes of immigrants from Afghanistan and Vietnam, from the Philippines and Sri Lanka, from the Caribbean and Italy, as well as from India. Many of these characters, like Jasmine in the story which bears her name, have "no visa, no papers, and no birth certificate. No nothing other than what she wanted to invent and tell."

But telling a story is only one part of the communication process; the other is having someone who receives it. Proponents of the so-called Reader-Response Theory—which include Wolfgang Iser, Michael Riffaterre, Stanley Fish, David Bleich, and Jonathan Culler— all argue that reading constitutes a dynamic process and, therefore, readers actively participate in the production of textual meaning. Thus, a range of different meanings attest to the diversity of readers, not necessarily to the ingenuity of the author.[38] This radical reevaluation of the role of the reader, of the audience, represents a revolutionary shift in thinking about the literary and dramatic arts; indeed, the reader, rather than the author or the text, assumes the crucial central position in the communication process. He or she becomes the major (sometimes the sole) source of meaning.

Such a clearly subjective process denies both the notion of an objective text whose meanings are available to all readers and a controlling author whose intentions dominate the reader. In fact, reader-response critic Norman Holland claims that individual audience members each respond to a text via his or her own "identity theme," an internal perspective that they project onto texts as well as daily experiences. If this critical theory has even some elements of validity, and common sense dictates that it does, then the meanings we derive from reading a novel or watching a film necessarily emanate from who we are, from our personal identity. Such a conclusion forces us to realize that one's ethnic identity, whether fashioned by consent or descent, must be considered an important component of how one gathers meaning from all texts, even those that contain no overt references to ethnicity.

Ethnicity and the American Cinema

The preceding pages may seem to ignore the central issue of this anthology. After all, what do sociology and anthropology, psychology and literature, Reader-Response Theory and presidential politics tell us about ethnicity and the American cinema? Quite a lot, I would argue. For example, basic differences in fundamental conceptions of ethnic group membership, and consequently ethnic identity, move beyond esoteric disputes when exploring ethnic issues in the American films. These divergent positions highlight the schizophrenia evident in the commercial cinema's treatment of ethnic groups during most of its history. The vast majority of American films, including those made under the studio system and later, appear to be mainly primordialist: they continually depict such predetermined conditions as race, religion, and national origin. To these givens, Hollywood films assign easily recognizable signs (e.g., speech, dress, food choices, and mannerisms) which when taken together function as overt codes that apparently signify divergent ethnic cultures. A mosaic of seeming differences inundates viewers of American films, a virtual collage of skin colors, dialects, foods, mannerisms, and lifestyles.

But by scratching the surface of the vast majority of these films, one plummets to their depths. The basic value orientation, to appropriate Barth's term, remains strikingly similar for most ethnic group members who inhabit American motion pictures. Regardless of race, religion, or national origin, most Hollywood movies superimpose Americaness as a self-ascripting category whose value orientation totally dominates any primordial ethnic conditions. In fact, far from delving into cultural distinctions beyond the most superficial, American movies militantly stress cultural uniformity. Thus, value orientations become ideologically rather than ethnically defined. So while Hollywood films show primordialism and descent characteristics, they preach symbolic interactionism and consent values. According to these films, outward ethnic markings may be predetermined, but inner ethnic values are self-ascriptive.

One of the more obvious examples of this Hollywood tendency is *Gentleman's Agreement* (1947), a big-budget studio production directed by Elia Kazan and written by Moss Hart (based on Laura Z. Hobson's popular novel). The film, which was both a critical and

1.1. Phil Green (Gregory Peck) and his son (Dean Stockwell) in *Gentleman's Agreement*, an example of Hollywood's emphasis on symbolic ethnicity and consent values.

financial success, won Academy Awards for Best Picture, Best Supporting Actress (Celeste Holm), and Best Director. The movie's plot revolves around the activities of a reporter, Phil Green (Gregory Peck), assigned to do a story on anti-Semitism for *Smith's Weekly*. To add drama to his piece, Green pretends to be a Jew, a choice that almost wrecks his romance with his girlfriend Kathy (Dorothy McGuire). After several humiliating and frustrating encounters with prejudice, Green writes his article, patches things up with the newly enlightened Kathy, and receives due praise for his all-American stand against bigotry.

Early in this film, Phil and his son Tommy (Dean Stockwell) discuss what it means to be Jewish (fig. 1.1), and the ensuing conversation reveals the film's ideological position:

> Tommy: What's anti-Semitism?
> Phil: Some people don't like other people just because they're Jews.
> Tommy: Why? Are some bad?
> Phil: Some are, some aren't. Just like everybody else.

Tommy: What are Jews?
Phil: There are lots of different churches. Some people who go
           to them are Catholics. People who go to other churches
           are called Protestants. Then there are others to go to still
           different ones, and they're called Jews, only they call their
           churches synagogues and temples. . . . You can be an
           American and a Protestant or a Catholic or a Jew. Religion
           is different from nationality.

This notion that underneath surface differences, Jews, Catholics, and Protestants (and by extension other minority-group members) all think alike permeates the entire film. It also represents the dominant ideology of the commercial movie industry. In fact, even the overt physical characteristics between ethnic minorities are downplayed, as in a later scene when Phil finally hits on his personal angle for the journalistic expose: "I'll be Jewish. All I've got to do is say it. I've even got a title, 'I was Jewish for Six Months.' [Looks into a mirror.] Hmmm. Dark hair, dark eyes, just like Dave [his boyhood Jewish friend]. No accent. No mannerisms. Neither has Dave. I'll just call myself Phil Greenberg. Ha. It's a cinch." Phil's ruse is spectacularly successful, as neither Jews nor Gentiles discover his charade. This inability to spot cultural differences, combined with scenes like those described above, accurately demonstrate Hollywood's overwhelming endorsement of a melting-pot mentality, one that ignores crucial differences in ethnic identities and blends cultural oppositions into a bland conception of Americanness.

Gentleman's Agreement also provides some insight into how Hollywood films define ethnic identity by depicting two minor Jewish characters who speak about their cultural heritage. First is Miss Wales (June Havoc), Green's secretary, who is also passing as a Gentile, but her masquerade is a permanent rather than a temporary subterfuge. To get her job at the magazine, Miss Wales changes her name from Walofsky and denies that she is Jewish. Such a tactic in the face of overt prejudice may initially strike one as merely prudent or even clever. Later, however, we see Wales has assumed her new role far too well, actually incorporating anti-Semitism into her own thinking. After Green encourages the paper's editor to hire more Jews, Miss Wales actually complains to her boss: "They'll get the wrong kind, too much makeup, too loud clothes, the kikey ones who'll give the rest of us a bad name." When he finally reveals that he's not Jewish and sees her shock, Green accuses Wales of not "believing anyone would give up the glory of being a Christian for even eight weeks." In many ways, Miss Wales stands as a good example of ethnic self-hatred, of the minority member's intense desire to look, act, talk, and be like members of the majority group. She remains, in Mailer's phrase, "forever locked in the chains of ambivalence," because she allows the outside world rather than her inside identity to determine her activities.

A second Jew in the film is the world-famous physicist Professor Lieberman (Sam Jaffe), a character seemingly based on the figure of Albert Einstein. Lieberman represents the evasions of intellectuals who rationalize away their ethnic identities. At a party, he tells Phil and Kathy: "I have no religion, so I am not Jewish by religion. I am a scientist, so I must rely on science which tells me I am not Jewish by race, since there's no such thing as a Jewish type. . . . I remain a Jew because the world makes it an advantage not to be one. So, for many of us, it becomes a matter of pride to call ourselves Jews." Here the film equates cultural identity with simple stubbornness, a cantankerousness that passes for intellectual pride. Given what Lieberman claims, he would cease to call himself a Jew if the world did not make it so difficult to be one. Are there no other reasons for maintaining an ethnic identity? Does a five-thousand-year-old tradition of ethics and religious faith, of artistic and intellectual achievement, hold any appeal for this modern citizen of America? Apparently, with Lieberman's world view, one would have to answer "no." Although unlike Miss Wales, Professor Lieberman refuses to hide his ethnic affiliation, he too remains defined by the perceptions of the majority group. Thus, the film demonstrates Hollywood's conception of what Milton Gordon labels "liberal expectancy": the belief that urbanization, industrialization, and communication modernization will ultimately eliminate ethnic affiliations in favor of universalist identifications. In other words, once we mature we will simply outgrow the artificial distinctions of ethnic identification.

The central Jewish character in *Gentleman's Agreement* is Dave Goldman (John Garfield), Phil's boyhood friend. Again, he represents how Hollywood most comfortably depicts minority-group members: underneath their superficial differences, they feel and think just like the rest of "us." Dave's Americanized values leave little room for his ethnic heritage to emerge. He functions, when bigots leave him alone, quite well in Gentile society, displaying impeccable manners, knowing what wine to order with dinner, and being a combat war hero. About his pal's article on anti-Semitism, Dave tells Phil: "I'm on the sidelines. It's your problem not ours" (fig. 1.2). Your problem, not ours? How hollow this sentiment must

1.2. Dave Goldman (John Garfield), a personification of the American cinema's paean to total assimilation, tells Phil why he's on the "sidelines" for the fight against anti-Semitism in *Gentleman's Agreement*.

have sounded in 1947, the haunting image of six million murdered Jews so freshly branded into the American psyche. If nothing else, Jewish history clearly documents that anti-Semitism, and by extension all other forms of racism, remains one problem that will not vanish if we simply ignore it. But this lesson seems lost on Dave, as well as on Hollywood's filmmakers. Total assimilation preoccupies American film creations like Dave Goldman; they strive to melt silently into American society rather than to maintain any deep sense of ethnic identity. The very fact that Gregory Peck assumes a Jewish persona so easily and so successfully bespeaks volumes for Hollywood's vision of what it means to be Jewish—or black, or Asian, or Hispanic, or Italian, or anything different.

Gentleman's Agreement provides insight into Hollywood's consistent approach to making pictures that focus on minority-group members: the basic problems of all ethnic groups are seen as substantially identical. *Home of the Brave* (1949), for example, is based on a play written by Arthur Laurents about a Jew, yet the protagonist becomes a black in the movie version. *Crossfire* (1947), originally about a homosexual, changes him into a Jew for the screen adaptation. It is questionable whether the problems of blacks are interchangeable with those of Native-Americans, homosexuals, or other minority-group members. Often, as Howard Suber concludes, "ethnicity is little more than a gimmick . . . no more significant than if they happen to be 5'4" in their stocking feet or happen to be just a little bit cross-eyed."[39] The message Hollywood conveys, then, is essentially a simple one. The basic value orientations of a Hispanic, a Jew, a black, or an Asian may have been intrinsically different in another time and in another place. But, in America, unique elements in these ethnically discrete value systems must be discarded if they clash with broad national values. In essence, the movies foster what Herbert Gans calls "symbolic ethnicity": actual ethnic culture values are irrelevant, but ethnic identification retains an emotional aura based on outer symbols. Thus, in Hollywood films, the signifiers remain but the signified has been drastically altered.

The tendency in Hollywood cinema simply to mix and match members from various cultural groups seems particularly strange when one considers the intimate link between ethnic immigrants and American film that created the most dominant movie industry in the world. But, upon deeper reflection, maybe it's not so strange. After all, the ethnic immigrants who dominated the production of films, both as studio heads and creative filmmakers (directors, producers, writers, and performers), as well as the original audiences composed primarily of immigrant movie-goers, shared a belief in the American dream of total assimilation. Israel Zangwill's message in his play *The Melting Pot* spoke directly to them: "America is God's Crucible, the great Melting Pot where all races in Europe are melting and reforming. . . . God is making the American. . . . The real American has not yet arrived. He is only in the Crucible, I tell you— he will be the fusion of all races, perhaps the coming superman."[40] The new immigrants surely did not think of themselves as the progenitors of the "coming superman," but they did want to shed their old identities and be recognized as a "true Yankee."

According to Garth Jowett's social history of American films, the most important component of early movie audiences came from "large urban working class" members who rarely attended live entertainments such as operas, dramas, or even vaudeville shows. The major segments of this population consisted of immigrant workers, for whom the nickelodeons functioned both as entertainment and as guide to the "manners and customs of his new environment." Jowett concludes that the immigrant was the "backbone of support" for the new entertainment medium.[41] Most other film historians agree with Jowett's basic assessment. So, for example, David Cook concludes that "the majority of early filmgoers were untutored laborers, many of them non-English-speaking immigrants, lacking sophisticated verbal skills."[42] Robert Allen claims that early moviegoing was "by no means an exclusive activity of the poor and of the immigrant." But he goes on to note that most movie theaters were located "near large working-class and middle-class populations" and the heavy concentration of nickelodeons on the Lower East Side "indicates that moviegoing was popular among the immigrant population there. . . . "[43]

Because no early surveys summarize and categorize the thoughts of these early immigrant movie-goers, we can only hazard guesses about how they responded to those silent, flickering images on white cast before them. But the crucial point to bear in mind is that what the individual spectator brings to the movie theater will greatly influence how he or she reads and interprets what is projected onto the screen. I have already invoked the insights of Reader-Response Theory to stress the importance of the reader, the film viewer, in the creation of any text's meaning. In addition, many feminist scholars discuss the question of identification between female spectators and film during the viewing process. Such questions, however, need to be asked of all viewers. When Miriam Hansen analyzes the appeal of Rudolph Valentino, she emphasizes female spectatorship, but her discussion incorporates insights beyond the feminine connotations of this star's persona. Valentino's appeal, says Hansen, was that of a "stranger": "Whatever distinguished previous and contemporary male stars from each other, they were all Americans; that is, they did not display any distinct ethnic features other than those that we already naturalized as American. Valentino, however, bore the stigma of the first-generation, non-Anglo-Saxon immigrant—and was cast accordingly."[44] Such statements attest to the growing sophistication of our conceptions of spectatorship.

We are all amalgamated spectators. We define ourselves, and others define us, by gender and by class, by race and by religion, by educational level and by historical period. To assume a forty-year-old black woman in Watts perceives a movie in exactly (or maybe even nearly) the same way as a thirteen-year-old white high schooler in Burlington or a twenty-year-old drifter in Butte defies the dictates of common sense. A filmmaker communicates to his or her audience by employing the culturally accepted iconic codes that characterize our cinema. But after the work is completed, its author simply becomes another commentator on its meaning. A director can tell us what he or she wanted to accomplish, what his or her "intentions" were, but not what the film means to us. Once we realize this fact and begin to research its ramifications more fully, the role of ethnic identity in the viewing process will become much more evident.

Such considerations about the role of ethnic identity in viewing a film remain equally important when discussing the creation of a movie, particularly within the Hollywood studio system. This is not the place to elaborate about the ethnic influences on the Jewish moguls who created and sustained this massive studio system: Jesse Lasky, B. P. Schulberg, Adolph Zukor, Barney Balaban (Paramount); Marcus Loew, Louis Mayer, Irving Thalberg (MGM); Harry, Jack, Albert, and Sam Warner (Warner Brothers); David O. Selznick (Selznick International); Samuel Goldwyn (Goldwyn Pictures); Harry Cohn (Columbia); Carl Laemmle (Universal); and William Fox (Fox Pictures). Their lowly origins varied, but, as with the early audiences who watched their movies, none had to worry about choking on a silver spoon. Louis Mayer, from Russia (fig. 1.3), was a scrap-metal dealer; Samuel Goldwyn, from Poland, a glove salesman; and William Fox, from Hungary, a dressmaker. Carl Laemmle, from Germany, Marcus Loew, the son of Austrian immigrants, and Adolph Zukor, from Hungary, all were former furriers. Harry Cohn, the son of German immigrants, eked out a living on New York City's Lower East Side as a pool hustler and song plugger. Humble origins behind them, these men attained power over their studios that was almost absolute.

Once they achieved success, these men, as much as was possible, buried their immigrant roots, as they ruled over one of America's largest and most influential industries. What united them, as Neal Gabler notes, "was their utter and absolute rejection of their pasts and . . . a ferocious, even pathological, embrace of America." They put their stamp on the American mind; they "colonized the American imagination." In fact, for several generations they defined and transmitted the American Dream, not only for the millions at home but also for countless more whose only view of the United States was cranked out of the studios of these ill-educated but street-wise immigrants. They shared a vision of an America where opportunity and tolerance expanded as limitlessly as the horizons in their Westerns: "Within the studios and on the screen, the Jews could simply create a new country—an empire of their own. . . . They would create its myths and values, its traditions and archetypes. . . . Ultimately, American values can be *defined* largely by the movies the Jews made. Ultimately, by creating their idealized America on the

1.3. Louis B. Mayer, the mogul who ran MGM during Hollywood's golden era, represents those immigrant studio heads who embraced their new country and created an idealized America on the movie screen.

screen, the Jews reinvented the country in the image of their fiction."[45] Their studios' movies promised everyone , even newcomers, a chance to achieve the American dream, but with a steep entry price. To become a true citizen of this new Promised Land, one needed to cast off "foreignisms": religious observances, names, and traditions. Their own lives demonstrated the wisdom of this decision and the vast possibilities for success attainable in this new land. They made the dream flesh.

As ethnic identity plays a key role in the lives, judgments, and perceptions of audience members and studio executives, so it plays an equally important part in the decisions of filmmakers. I will, in the following section, discuss film directors, but by extension all those involved in the creative aspects of moviemaking. Explicit and implicit suppositions, which exist within all national and religious cultures, necessarily affect how the majority views the minority within its midst; of course, it greatly influences how minority-group members learn to perceive themselves as well. Ethnic heritage, therefore, often plays an integral if rarely examined role in creative activity. As the Italian director Federico Fellini observed in an interview with Giovanni Grazzini, "people think of cinema as a camera loaded with film and a reality out there all ready to be photographed. Instead, one inserts himself between the object and the camera."[46]

Elements inserted between the object and the camera are inevitably both conscious and unconscious. They often veer beyond a filmmaker's control, or even understanding. But texts exist only within cultures, and all cultures contain ethnic elements. Because they form a crucial component of society, social and religious ethnic cultures play a vital role in artistic production, regardless of an individual artist's personal beliefs. For example, Paul Gauguin's pictures display a virtual obsession with Christian religious themes and symbols, despite the painter's total rejection of that doctrine and his emphasis on the "savage" elements in his own nature. Every person's cultural heritage powerfully influences his or her identity, viewpoint, imagination, and creativity.

Of course, each person's unique view of the world is fashioned by many other internal and external elements that intersect with ethnicity: age, gender, heredity, historical period, geographical location, family environment, individual psychology, physical traits, and intellectual capabilities. One or two of these elements usually dominate a person's response to any particular situation, but these innate and environmental components all play a role in each individual's own squint at reality. Who we are determines our attitudes toward the world and its inhabitants; who we are defines how we recognize, evaluate, and communicate with others. To invoke the Thomistic adage: "Whatever is perceived is perceived through the character of the one who perceives it."

Although I would not contend that the ethnic component of an artist's identity represents the only determining factor in his or her work, I would argue that such elements have been insufficiently acknowledged and understood by film scholars, historians, and critics. Would not John Ford's pictures have been different if he were not an Irish-Catholic? Could Woody Allen have made the same movies if he were not Jewish? Is Spike Lee's color an important ingredient in his moviemaking? Most people would probably answer "yes" to these questions, but the matter can be complicated still further. Does it matter that Arthur Penn is Jewish, even though few specific references to Jews appear in his works? Put the issue more generally: How might an artist's creation be colored by his or her ethnicity even if the subject matter of a particular film contains no overt ethnic elements? The following analogy can be posited: as a female director does not stop being a woman even when her film is not about overtly feminist issues, so one's ethnic identity and sensibility do not disappear when he or she makes a film about non-ethnic issues.

Finally, even though it is the segment of ethnicity and film most often discussed in previous works, it seems important to pay at least passing attention to the images of ethnic people on celluloid, influential creations fashioned by these artists and studio executives and seen by these audiences. The portraits of ethnic characters in the American cinema constitute a rich and varied tapestry woven by several generations of moviemakers responding to the world around them. Such pictures dynamically depict both the profound impact of ethnic people on American society and that society's perception of the ethnic groups within its midst. Some films help extinguish the darkness of bigotry and ignorance. Others simply mirror long-held prejudices. But whether they explore or exploit their ethnic characters, all these films either implicitly or explicitly show how ethnic groups affect American life and how American life influences its ethnic citizens; it is a two-way process inherent in the first ethnic-American movie as well as in the latest.

As part of a mass-media art form, these films reveal, reflect, and redefine the ever-changing role of ethnic people in American culture by shaping (some would say distorting) the historical movements of these groups into a series of powerful and evocative images that freeze the spirit of an age and allow it to be examined. A discussion of ethnic-American films and characters, therefore, necessarily becomes an exploration of ethnic peoples' historical and cultural problems in America; it demonstrates the ways in which Hollywood attempts to explain, and ultimately, to solve them. As such, these pictures and characters contribute to our conception, our understanding, of America as a nation of ethnic people. Many of the films remain valuable as esthetic objects of worth and beauty; all remain interesting as historical artifacts that help chart the history of ethnic people in the United States. After all, the evolving story of America, from its first inhabitants to its latest arrivals, is the tale of ethnic immigrants.

Conclusion

Although great works of art transcend their age, all works of art are products of their time. *Hamlet*, for example, is as much about Elizabethan England as about personal psychology or twentieth-century America; it reveals aspects of both its maker and its reader. What affects a society necessarily influences its citizens; ethnic culture, in terms of both consent and descent, remains part of a person's private and public identity. No creative endeavor can occur in a cultural vacuum. No artist can be encased in a hermetically sealed environment free from the contamination of his or her era. "Representational images themselves," as Bill Nichols aptly reminds us, "rely upon culturally determined codes."[47] Films, like other art forms, spring from the minds, hearts, and souls of men and women who speak in the language and partake in the activities of their world, even if their participation takes the form of denial, avoidance, and repudiation. Their culture shapes their daily experiences and artistic perceptions. We should always remember the story of the Cree hunter who, when asked to take the judicial oath before testifying in court, responded: "I'm not sure I can tell the truth. I can only tell what I know." So too with artists, with their creations, and with their audiences. We all can only tell what we know.

NOTES

1. Meg Greenfield, "The Immigrant Mystique," *Newsweek*, August 8, 1988, p. 76.

2. All statistics that follow are taken from "A Difference of Degree: State Initiatives to Improve Minority Student Achievement" (Albany: New York State Higher Education Department, July 1987).

3. William Peterson, "Concepts of Ethnicity" in *Harvard Encyclopedia of American Ethnic Groups*, ed. Stephan Thernstrom (Cambridge: Harvard University Press, 1980), pp. 234–42.

4. Wsevold W. Isajiw, "Definitions of Ethnicity," *Ethnicity* 1 (July 1974): 113.

5. Milton Gordon, *Assimilation in American Life: The Role of Race, Religion, and National Origin* (New York: Oxford University Press, 1964).

6. Nathan Glazer and Daniel Patrick Moynihan, *Beyond the Melting Pot: The Negroes, Puerto Ricans, Jews, Italians, and Irish of New York City* (Cambridge: MIT Press, 1963).

7. Edward Shils, "Primordial, Personal, Sacred, and Civil Ties," *British Journal of Sociology* 8 (1957): 130–45; Clifford Geertz "The Integrative Revolution: Primordial Sentiments and Civil Rights in the New States," in *Old Societies and New States*, ed. Clifford Geertz (Glencoe: Free Press, 1963).

8. R. A. Schermerhorn, "Ethnicity in the Perspective of the Sociology of Knowledge," *Ethnicity* 1 (April 1974): 1–13.

9. Raoul Naroll, "Ethnic Unit Classification," *Current Anthropology* 5, no. 4 (1964): 283–312.

10. Ronald Reminick, *Theory of Ethnicity: An Anthropologist's Perspective* (Lanham: University Press of America, 1983).

11. David Schneider, *American Kinship: A Cultural Account* (Chicago: University of Chicago Press, 1980).

12. Fredrik Barth, *Ethnic Groups and Boundaries: The Social Organization of Cultural Differences* (London: George Allen and Unwin, 1969), p. 14.

13. Barth, *Ethnic Groups and Boundaries*, p. 15.

14. Max Weber, "The Ethnic Group" in *Theories of Society*, ed. Talcott Parsons (Glencoe: Free Press, 1961).

15. Schermerhorn, "Ethnicity in the Perspective," p. 2.

16. Sigmund Freud, "Ansprache an die Mitglieder des Vereins B'nai B'rith (1926)," in *Gesammelte Werke*, vol. 16 (London: Imago Publishing, 1941); quoted in Erik Erikson, *Childhood and Society* (New York: W. W. Norton, 1963), p. 281.

17. Sigmund Freud, *An Outline of Psychoanalysis* (New York: W. W. Norton, 1949), pp. 122–23.

18. Harold R. Issacs, "Basic Group Identity: The Idols of the Tribe," *Ethnicity* 1 (April 1974): 20.

19. Erik Erikson, "The Problem of Ego Identity," *Journal of the American Psychoanalytic Association* 4 (1956): 57.

20. Issacs, "Basic Group Identity," p. 22.

21. Price Cobbs, "Ethnotheraphy in Groups," *New Perspectives on Encounter Groups* (San Francisco: Jossey-Bass, 1972), pp. 383–403.

22. Joseph Giordano, *Ethnicity and Mental Health* (New York: Institute on Pluralism and Group Identity, 1980).

23. Seymour Fisher and Rhoda Fisher, "A Projective Text Analysis for Ethnic Subculture Themes in Families," *Journal of Projective Technique* 24 (1960): 369.

24. Alvin Poussaint, jacket notes to Judith Weinstein Klein, *Jewish Identity and Self-Esteem: Healing Wounds through Ethnotheraphy* (New York: Institute on Pluralism and Group Identity, 1980).

25. Klein, *Jewish Identity and Self-Esteem*, p. 57.

26. Ibid., p. 57. Klein notes that some of the trusims that apply to men do not hold true for women. So, for example, low self-esteem is often congruent with religious identification for Jewish women.

27. Ibid., p. 58.

28. Werner Sollors, *Beyond Ethnicity: Consent and Descent in American Culture* (New York: Oxford University Press, 1986).

29. Sollors, *Beyond Ethnicity*, p. 7.

30. Ibid., p. 7.

31. Ibid., p. 259.

32. William Boelhower, *Through a Glass Darkly: Ethnic Semiosis in American Literature* (New York: Oxford University Press, 1987), p. 10.

33. Boelhower, *Through a Glass Darkly*, p. 78.

34. Ibid., p. 143.

35 Norman Mailer, *Cannibals and Christians* (New York: Dell Publishing, 1966), pp. 77, 96.

36. Bharati Mukherjee, "Immigrant Writing: Give Us Your Maximalists!" *New York Times Book Review*, August 28, 1988, p. 1.

37. Mukherjee, "Immigrant Writing," p. 28.

38. For more on Reader-Response Theory see Jane P. Tompkins, ed., *Reader Response Criticism: From Formalism to Post-Structuralism* (Baltimore:

Johns Hopkins University Press, 1980) and Susan Suleiman, ed., *The Reader in the Text: Essays on Audience and Interpretation* (Princeton: Princeton University Press, 1980).

39. Howard Suber, "Gays, Gals, and Goys," *Variety*, January 7, 1979, p. 22.

40. Israel Zangwill, *The Melting Pot*, in *The Collected Works of Israel Zangwill* (New York: AMS Press, 1969), p. 95.

41. Garth Jowett, *Film: The Democratic Art* (Boston: Little, Brown, 1976), p. 38.

42. David A. Cook, *A History of Narrative Film* (New York: W. W. Norton, 1981), p. 37.

43. Robert Allen, "Motion Picture Exhibition in Manhattan: Beyond the Nickelodeon," *Cinema Journal* 16 (Spring 1979): 13.

44. Miriam Hansen, "Pleasure, Ambivalence, Identification: Valentino and Female Spectatorship," *Cinema Journal* 25 (Summer 1986): 23–24.

45. Neal Gabler, *An Empire of The Own: How the Jew Invented Hollywood* (New York: Crown Publishers, 1988), pp. 5–6.

46. Giovanni Grazzini, *Federico Fellini: Comments on Film* (Fresno: The Press at California State, Fresno, 1988), p. 116.

47. Bill Nichols, *Ideology and the Image: Social Representation in the Cinema and Other Media* (Bloomington: Indiana University Press, 1981), p. 26.

Ethnicity: History, Genre,
and Auteurism

2

Ethnicity, Role-playing, and American Film Comedy: From *Chinese Laundry Scene* to *Whoopee* (1894–1930)

I was born, I have lived, and I have been made over. Is it not time to write my life's story? I am just as much out of the way as if I were dead, for I am absolutely other than the person whose story I have to tell.
— Mary Antin, *The Promised Land* (Boston: Houghton Mifflin, 1912), p. xxi.

Love and hate, there it is.
— Mookie to Radio Raheem
in Spike Lee's *Do the Right Thing* (1989)

Ethnic and racial diversity has been a central feature of America's urban experience as long as the country has had cities. In the late nineteenth and early twentieth century, immigrants flooded the nation, their numbers steadily increasing from approximately a hundred thousand a year in 1887 to more than one million in 1907. The year 1896, the first year of commercially successful cinema (i.e., projected motion pictures) in the United States, was also the first time that immigrants from Southern and Eastern Europe outnumbered those coming from more familiar lands to the North and West. This, combined with the internal migration of American-born citizens (black and white) from rural to urban areas, produced an ever-widening cacophony of voices and cultures. This intense encounter with new circumstances produced complex emotional responses. In their political articulations these ranged from a reaffirmation of Old World heritages (including Anglo-Saxon nativism) to a cosmopolitan celebration of democratic pluralism and the opportunity to forge new identities.[1]

The cinema, an increasingly powerful component of the nation's urban-based commercial amusement, flourished in this environment and responded to its imperatives on many levels. With considerable justification, social and cultural historians often portray the movies as a form of mass entertainment which instructed immigrant groups in the values of their new home country and provided them with a common cultural experience that contributed to the erosion of their local, insular cultures. Cinema imposed an essentially assimilationist ideology on its diverse, often immigrant audiences. Neighborhood nickelodeon theaters may have delayed or eased their way into a transethnic and interclass culture or they may have provided a place to counter or deflect the economic and cultural imperatives of capitalism, but these local venues did not and could not provide long-term alternatives.[2]

Those social and cultural historians seeking to explicate the movies' invigorating impact on American culture have resisted arguments that merely see cinema as assimilating these immigrants into the dominant culture. Employing a New Left approach, Robert Sklar pointed to the outsider status of the immigrant producers who came to control the film industry in the 1910s and 1920s. Freed from traditional cultural constraints and having a better understanding of their audiences, they catered to the fantasies and desires of viewers while avoiding excessive doses of genteel nineteenth-century moralism. It was not only the producers, but also performers, directors, and other production personnel who had frequently experienced similar dislocations. Although the cinema was itself a center of ideological struggle, the golden era of the nickelodeons continued to reverberate for another forty years.[3] Roy Rosenzweig argues that the movies forged transethnic unities and created expectations among the working classes that helped mobilize workers during the Great Depression. It encouraged them to demand not just unionization but full power and participation in American society.[4]

The arguments of these left-oriented historians are challenged by a revisionist group who argue that the motion picture industry was peculiarly unconcerned with the needs and desires of their working-class clientele and instead wooed more middle-class and native-born patrons. Theater location and etiquette, ticket price, subject matter and the system of representation suggest the rapid embourgeoisification of the cinema.[5] The cinema, seeking higher profits and improved status, embraced the values of the dominant ideology and almost incidentally imposed them on their captive immigrant, working-class audiences. Another group of scholars has meticulously traced the representations of individual ethnic groups on the screen and generally found these depictions to be problematic and marginal. Their dismay may be occasionally suspended by films benefiting from fleeting conjunctures of historical circumstances, but it is the work of scholars, more than the films, that affirms the integrity and values of the studied group.[6] These two quite different perspectives thus question or overtly challenge arguments that see cinema as a significant support for these least powerful groups.

Explorations of cinema and its relation to ethnicity and class have taken a more theoretically adventurous approach than earlier "images of" Jews/African-Americans/American Indians/etc. analyses. This involves a shift from looking at individual groups with the goal of affirming their identities to a more ironic look at the larger question of ethnic identity itself. Analyzing these films as part of a complex discourse by situating them more firmly within a social and ideational history, they demonstrate that these films are contradictory, "dialogical," and even hopeful.[7] Although films might be made for one group of amusement-goers or intended to be seen in one context, they often acquired unintended and potentially subversive meanings when shown to different types of spectators or in different contexts.[8] Likewise, producers of mass culture cannot simply appropriate subject matter for their own purposes, but must engage the fantasies and experiences of ordinary people. A complex negotiation thus takes place between these diverse levels.[9] Finally, the extent to which the film industry discourse took its working-class and immigrant audiences for granted, and so focused on the wooing of an upwardly mobile, middle-class audience, forces the historian to probe further below the surface and consider why this audience could be "taken for granted." These perspectives return us to the earlier preoccupations of social and cultural historians and compel us to extend our understanding of cinema's relevance to urban immigrants and their children.[10]

To illuminate aspects of cinema's protracted engagement with immigrant, working, or lower-middle-class experience through the third decade of the twentieth century, this investigation takes film comedy as its principal focus. The choice seems appropriate, for humor helped Americans negotiate, question, accept, and sometimes even challenge their situation in an industrial state increasingly dominated by large-scale industrial capitalism. Most important, as Sigmund Freud remarked, comedy has the ability to "evade restrictions and open sources of pleasure that have become inaccessible."[11] It gave voice to pleasures and discomforts that did not, and often could not, find articulation in other forums. Such a probe can help us reconsider and in some cases reposition the framework in which ethnicity and the cinema has been typically discussed.

Oscar Handlin, in his classic study, has argued that "seen from the perspective of the individual received rather than of the receiving society, the history of immigration is a history of alienation and its consequences."[12] We might begin by briefly considering two aspects of this experience. First, immigrants had to cope with the difficult task of forging new identities that matched their new environment. Although some found it possible to exist within the confines of their own ethnic neighborhoods, more typically they had to master a new language, as well as customs and mores. Most took new kinds of jobs. The immigrant was compelled, in short, to become someone else—to become, as Mary Antin suggests, an Other. This meant playing a role—hiding, denying, obscuring, even shedding earlier held, and deeply engrained, identities. It was typically alienating and seemingly unremitting. It also raised crucial questions that put the immigrant on the defensive. Was the self presented to the outside world a "real self" or a false one? And if it was false, was this mask malicious? Would this new self last or would it be discarded like an old suit of clothes? The native-born were never quite sure. Immigrants might change their name, lose their accents, and vote Republican, but their inevitable need to negotiate between two cultures made their allegiance suspect. It was this very fact of role-playing that became part of cinema's core and an essential part of its comedy.

Another crucial dimension of the immigrants' experience, at least in the major cities, was their intense encounter with ethnic difference. For those who once lived in small towns or rural areas, cultural homogeneity had been the norm. Even for those who had lived in more cosmopolitan settings, the mix was different in kind and form. This fresh encounter with racial and ethnic difference threw up a complex of psychological feelings toward others. On one side there was insecurity, fear, anxiety, hatred, and aggression; on the other curiosity, fascination, attraction, desire, and play. These emotions were worked out in lived experience, and yet in many instances could not be expressed or acted upon directly. Again, comedy could be used to tap them.

Ethnic-based comedy has been a feature of American cinema from its beginnings until the present day—for example, Woody Allen's *Zelig* and *Coming to America* with Eddie Murphy. The cycle of films explored in this study, however, culminates with the rich, multiple layering of humor found in *Animal Crackers* with the Marx Brothers and *Whoopee* with Eddie Cantor, both released in the fall of 1930. In different yet overlapping ways, each base their humor on role-playing and the conjunction of diverse ethnicities. Whether we consider Henry Williams (Eddie Cantor) in the role of a fire chief whose hook (his Jewish nose) and ladder (his pueblo-wall scaler) associates Jew with American Indian (fig. 2.1), or the revelation by Ravelli (Chico Marx) that the apparently WASP Roscoe W. Chandler (Louis Sorin) is really the Jew Abie Kabibble from Czechoslovakia, the collisons of ethnic categories release psychic energy. Ethnicity is shown to be a constraint—and a construction—from which characters and audiences can be at least temporarily liberated. Role-playing, which was necessary and typically alienating, could become pleasurable, subversive, and affirming of self.

Ethno-comic Stereotyping and Early Film (1894–1907)

Many of the elements found in *Whoopee* and *Animal Crackers* also appear in one of the first attempts at film comedy. Even the two titles for this brief picture, known as *Robetta and Doreto* or *Chinese Laundry Scene* (1894), suggest some of the possible complexities. During the single twenty-second scene, the Chinaman Hop Lee employs tremendous ingenuity and dexterity to elude the Irish policeman who chases him. These two heavily stereotyped figures are played by the Italian comedy duo Robetta and Doreto, who condensed one of their vaudeville routines then being produced at Tony Pastor's in New York City for the occasion. Here, as was true in much vaudeville comedy, ethnic stereotypes abound but lack stability as performers assume a series of diverse identities, their stage name perhaps being just one more layering in these constructions.

In crucial respects, *Chinese Laundry Scene* offers a complexity absent from most motion picture comedies made before 1908. Unlike this abbreviated vaudeville routine, film comedies generally eliminated the persona of the actor from consideration. Their simple, one-dimensional characters bore greatest resemblance to those appearing in newspaper cartoons. In fact, these characters were typically appropriated from comic strips, which also provided excellent sources for narrative material and form. Much of the humor of the early film comedies thus relied on audiences' knowledge of narrowly based nonfilmic genres deploying pilfering lazy blacks, dumb Irish maids, unscrupulously savvy Jewish storekeepers, naive Yankee farmers, and bad boys. The loss of such intertextual

2.1 In *Whoopee* (1930), Eddie Cantor is a bundle of ethnic contradictions. The amalgamation of Jew and Native American, suggested by this publicity still, is a key to fully appreciating the film's humor.

references is one reason that these films often seem so unfunny to us today.[13]

Irish Ways of Discussing Politics (1896) was set in a barroom where the heavily drinking Irishmen turn a political discussion into a fistic encounter. *The Finish of Bridget McKeen* (1901) offers an even more uncomplimentary depiction. Played by a man in drag, the Irish maid Bridget has a heavy build and masculine appearance that make her sexually unappealing. She has difficulty starting her coal-burning stove and douses it with kerosene. The stove explodes, and she is blown to smithereens. In the second and final shot, we see a painted backdrop of her tombstone on which is written, "Here lies the remains of Bridget McKeen/Who started a fire with kerosene." This is, of course, an Irish joke, the predecessor of today's Polish jokes. *The Finish of Michael Casey* (Edison, 1901) has a similar outcome, and for similar reasons. Both Bridget McKeen and Michael Casey lack common sense and pay for it. Bridget's stereotypical stupidity is also apparent in *How Bridget Served the Salad Undressed* (Biograph, 1900). Asked to serve the salad undressed (that is, without dressing), she takes her clothes off before bringing the salad into the dining room where the WASP family has gathered for its evening meal. The joke is based on verbal confusion and miscomprehension that consistently plagued immigrants who had not yet mastered the intricacies of the new language.

One of the earliest filmic depictions of a Jew, *Cohen's Advertising Scheme* (Edison, 1904), is remarkable in that the Jewish businessman combines charity and smart business in a single gesture. With business slow, the store owner gives a coat to a tramp: on its back is an advertisement, "Go to I. Cohen's for Clothing." Instead of carrying a placard for an hourly fee, the tramp displays the advertisement for free but stays warm in the process. Much of the humor is derived from the complementary, beneficial nature of this exchange between two comic stereotypes.[14]

The knack for clever, even deceptive business moves is evident in *Cohen's Fire Sale* (Edison, 1907), which focuses on a Jewish milliner whose merchandise is inadvertently taken away by a garbageman and ends up on a city dumping barge. The shopkeeper recoups his investment by starting a fire in his store and covering the damage with insurance. He benefits still further by a fire sale, which quickly clears the store of imperfect goods. (fig. 2.2a, b). The story is based on the stereotypical Jewish businessman—astute but unprincipled, someone who can turn misfortune to his own advantage—for whom fire is "our friend" and the fire company "our enemy." The

2.2. Cohen tries to sell his damaged goods without success but later enjoys a landmark business in *Cohen's Fire Sale* (1907), an early film which relies on highly specific ethnic stereotyping.

story of *Cohen's Fire Sale* is quite simple and clearly depicted, but character motivation, narrative logic, and audience comprehension of a few key pieces of information—for example, that a piece of paper is an insurance policy—relies on this highly specific stereotyping. What is particularly noteworthy given the normal endings of tramp and Irish comedies is that Cohen is not chastised for his transgression at the film's end.[15] This is not always the case, at least in similar, slightly later comedies featuring Jewish stereotypes; sometimes he is too smart for his own good. Yet the fact that his crime goes unpunished may suggest that Jews are getting away with something—that is, "getting away with murder."

These uncomplimentary comic caricatures of recent immigrant groups operated within a wider system of comedy in which nonimmigrants were not spared. The rube or Uncle Josh character, for example, was a country bumpkin who comes to the sophisticated city and gets taken. In *How They Do Things on the Bowery* (Edison, 1902), this native-born American hick is outwitted by a New York prostitute who steals his money after giving him a Mickey Finn. One of the most important characters in American early comedy, the tramp, had a nonethnic identity determined by other traits—notably his socioeconomic status. The tramp is an outcast who must pay for his refusal to conform to the norms of proper society. In *Weary Willie Kisses the Bride* (Edison, 1904), the vagabond sneaks a kiss and is thrown off the train for his audacity. Such beatings end virtually every tramp comedy of the period.

These films strongly reflect the values characteristic of urban popular culture and specifically of the predominantly WASP urban filmmakers who produced them. The sophisticated metropolitan male—the kind of man who might frequent Koster and Bial's Music Hall—is the unstated ideal. Certainly the married man who is neither strong nor wise enough to rule his household and preserve his independence is often lampooned (*If You Had a Wife Like This*, Biograph, 1907; *The Suburbanite*, Biograph, 1905). And yet even he could easily become a butt of ridicule through the stereotype of the confirmed bachelor.

The question then arises, Are there any comic characters that do not embody more or less undesirable traits, that are not negative examples but rather encourage viewer identification? There is one critical exception: the "bad boy." Delinquent youths appear constantly in American and European early film comedies. In Edison's *The Terrible Kids* (April 1906), two boys disrupt a neighborhood's routine with the help of their dog, "Mannie." Every scene is a variation on a mischievous prank. Mannie "jumps onto the Chinaman's back, seizes his queue and drags the poor chink to the ground."[16] Several women, a bill poster, and an Italian apple vendor with a pushcart are also victims. Eventually the annoyed adults turn pursuers and capture the two pranksters with the help of the police. At the film's end, as the boys are driven to jail in the police van, Mannie opens the van door and the boys escape.

Audiences were expected to identify and sympathize with the youngsters. In Selig's *When We Were Boys* (1907), two older men reminisce about their youthful, carefree days—the film cutting back and forth between present and past. According to the catalog description for *The Terrible Kids*, "The antics of the kids, the almost human intelligence of 'Mannie' and the narrow escapes from capture, are a source of constant amusement and are sure to arouse a strong sympathy for the kids and their dog."[17] While such boys generally seem WASPY and middle class, such background is not explicit. Whatever their ethnic or class origins, children at least could escape the fate of adult comic stereotypes and presumably grow up to avoid undesirable behavior, ethnicly marked or otherwise.

Within this framework and as part of a larger repertoire, the depiction of any one group could lose much of its sting. Rather than being expressions of nativist sentiment (or being necessarily or only so), they offer a point of view that urges accommodation to the dynamism of urban life. A Bergsonian model of comedy can be appropriately applied to these films.[18] Comedy is a social gesture that chastises those who do not conform to certain "societal norms." Undesirable characteristics of recent immigrant groups are identified or assigned and then lampooned: they are among the group's various "inelastic" traits to be rid of. These comedies thus had a strong assimilationist impulse. In fact, John Higham argues that the 1900–1907 period saw nativism at its nadir as Americans felt optimistic about their ability to accommodate and incorporate diverse immigrant groups. In this context even J. Stuart Blackton's anti-Semitic caricature of Cohen in *Lightning Sketches* (1907) was tempered by the rapid transformational quality of his drawings. This ability to turn easily and quickly one representation into another was emblematic of life for the American immigrant. It was as if these quick-sketch artists (typically native- or English-born men such as Blackton, Windsor McCay, Robert F. Outcault, and George Darling) were demonstrating the process in a more playful mode to those still assimilating—engaging the repetition compulsion in the process. Immigrants could only fully embrace American individualism by freeing themselves of ethnic traits, by constructing a new identity. Assimilation was thus closely linked to American individualism.

These films, and the wider system of stereotyping on which they depended, created difficulties for immigrants in more subtle and oblique ways than by simply denigrating their ethnic group or heritage. These stereotypes posited certain identities and divided immigrants into categories which they did not necessarily choose or readily fit.[19] Jews came from diverse backgrounds and might have more in common with non-Jews than with each other—nor were they all shopkeepers or astute businessman. Italians came from culturally distinct regions and spoke diverse dialectics; they thought of themselves as Sicilian or Neopolitan. The Irish were sharply divided between Protestant and Catholic, yet these differences were ignored. Categorizations put immigrants in double binds that were not of their making. Stereotypes associated them with certain kinds of behavior, but then told them to shed that behavior. The very characteristics that seemed to define one as belonging to an immigrant group were those considered undesirable. Immigrants and their children were assigned a role to play and then told not to play it. Yet to lose their uncouth qualities meant losing an important aspect of their identity. Certainly this was one aspect of alienation, but also one area for potential comic contradiction in the immigrant experience. To expose these stereotypes as nothing but constructions could be liberating. For example, when Bridget is blown sky high in *The Finish of Bridget McKeen*, the exaggerated period of time it takes her body to return to earth is so long that the entire film is reduced to farce; the denigrating force could be turned on its head.

As was true with so much of early cinema, the circumstances in which a film was seen did much to determine audience reaction and meaning. The films were made initially for vaudeville audiences which were, as Albert McLean, Jr, points out, "not prepared to initiate the Italian or the Slav directly into the American way of life."[20] These audiences had, at least to a considerable extent, moved outside the confines of their own ethnic cultures. Embracing the ideology of assimilation, Jews and Irish might find *Cohen's Fire Sale* and *The Finish of Michael Casey* funny rather than offensive. After all, were not Cohen or Casey similar to Uncle Josh and many others in their failure to shed lamentable characteristics? Of course, those resisting or not yet fully initiated into the process of assimilation were less likely to be amused, but we can suppose that exhibitors could judge their audiences and avoided these films when they were

likely to offend. Nevertheless, like vaudeville, American cinema before the nickelodeon era was not particularly well suited for appealing to newly arrived immigrant working-class groups.

If these early representations of immigrant groups were not
necessarily as offensive as we might at first assume, their one-
dimensional characterizations suggest that other comedy forms, notably live performance, provided a more complex and far-reaching
engagement with the alienation of imposed stereotypes. Ethnic cross-
dressing in vaudeville was evident in *Chinese Laundry Scene* but, as
Tom Gunning has pointed out, traces of this can be found in one
other short film, *Levi and Cohen, Irish Comedians* (fig. 2.3, Biograph,
1903), which shows two Jewish comedians ineptly ribbing the Irish
with their comic routine.[21] The audience greets their gags with rot-
ten eggs and vegetables. The pelting of these performers could have
appealed to audiences' anti-Semitism, but it more immediately affirmed what McLean argues was a basic tenent of vaudeville. The
stage Irish, German, or Jew should not be allowed to become a simple object of ridicule in the hands of crude performers.[22] If anything, the comedy affirms the importance of effective role-playing—
in everyday life as well as on the stage. Jewish vaudeville star
George Fuller Golden adopted a brogue and the persona of Irishman Casey and became one of the foremost comics at the turn of
the century. Role-playing was thus elevated to the role of play, of an
easily assumed and discardable mask.

These ethnic representations might be explored from one other
perspective, in light of the people who actually made the films.
Although the actors who played these characters have remained un-
identified, something is known about the films' production personnel. While it is true, as Sklar has stated, that "before 1910 the movies
were as completely in the hands of respectable, established Anglo-
Saxon Protestant Americans as they were ever to be,"[23] the ethnic
diversity of this group should not be minimized. Although several
important turn-of-the-century film companies based in New York
City were owned by WASPs,[24] two other significant centers of motion
picture activity were Philadelphia, where Siegmund (Sigmund)
Lubin was active, and Chicago, where William Selig operated. Lubin was a Jew turned Quaker whose daughter married a Lowry,
who was Pennsylvania Dutch.[25] Selig appears to have had a somewhat similar background.[26] Jews were thus involved in the industry
from its very early stages, resisting the hegemony of New York
WASPdom.

Even in the pre-nickelodeon era, Jews and WASPS occasionally
worked together. The Edison Company hired James (Jacob) Blair

2.3. *Levi & Cohen, Irish Comedians* (1903): ethnic "cross-dressing" which affirms the importance of effective role-playing.

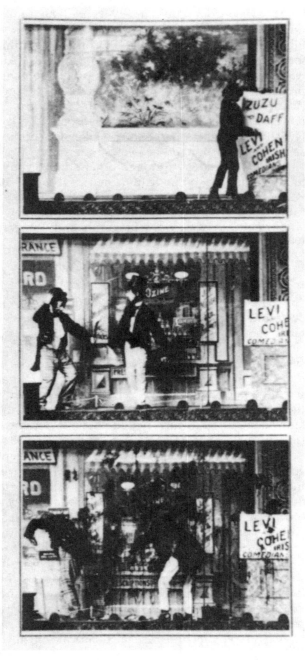

Smith away from Lubin in 1901, and he remained with Edison through 1904. Max Aronson, otherwise known as G. M. (Broncho Billy) Anderson, worked for Edison, Vitagraph, and Selig before forming Essanay with George Spoor in 1907 (Anderson owned 49 percent of the stock).[27] The Edison production chief Edwin S. Porter probably involved Smith and Anderson in the production of *Cohen's Advertising Scheme*. They had left the studio by the time of *Cohen's Fire Sale*, suggesting some of the reasons why Porter's treatment of Jewish storekeepers had shifted. Likewise, Lubin's staff included a substantial portion of non-Jews, for example, John Frawley and Arthur D. Hotaling. Although other ethnic groups were less visible in the industry, William Martinetti, who was Italian, worked for Porter as a scenic designer from 1903 onward, and the Lebanese cameraman Arthur C. Abadie was another longtime Edison employee.[28] In fact, only Biograph and Vitagraph had near lily-white hiring policies.

Downplay, Role-play, and Byplay (1908–27)

The years from 1906 to 1908 witnessed several events that had profound implications for cinema's representations of ethnicity. First, the appearance and proliferation of storefront theaters made cinema a form of mass entertainment and a mass communication system.[29] The size and diversity of audiences increased tremendously. New immigrants became a key component of cinema's expanding patronage. Moreover, films were being rotated through theaters on a daily basis so that exhibitors had little or no advance knowledge of what they would show. It became difficult or impossible to avoid pictures that might offend specific types of audiences.

Cinema's new presence as a form of mass entertainment made ethnic groups more sensitive to the way they were represented on the screen. For example, the manager of the Lyric Theater in Providence, Rhode Island, received a comedy, *Murphy's Wake*, in which Murphy comes home drunk, fights with his wife, and fakes suicide. At his wake, everyone gets drunk, and when Murphy helps himself to the liquor the party breaks up. Irish filmgoers in nearby Pawtucket were so outraged when they saw the picture that they threatened to destroy the Lyric if it was not banned. Mayor McCarthy of Providence intervened, saw the show, and banned the film. As he explained to the manager, "My friend, allow me to say that you are perpetuating a gross and criminal libel upon a time-honored custom among decent people . . . a deliberate insult to a respectable race."[30] Such occurrences emphasized the need for more cautious portrayals of recent immigrant groups. Although newly offensive film stereotypes faded only slowly, particularly in comedy, egregious representations were often followed by protest.[31]

More caution was necessary in the representation of ethnic stereotypes for another, interrelated reason. As John Higham has demonstrated, Anglo-Saxon nativism had begun to revive and would continue to grow into the 1920s.[32] Negative stereotyping increasingly suggested that ethnic and immigrant groups could not be incorporated by the nation. Their meaning had, in effect, flipped. One noteworthy attempt to reverse the ebbing tide of cosmopolitan pluralism was Israel Zangwill's play *The Melting Pot*, which opened in Washington, D.C. on October 5, 1908 with President Theodore Roosevelt and many of his cabinet in attendance. In this ghetto drama, the young Jewish immigrant musician David Quixano and the aristocratic Russian Vera Revendal find themselves falling in love. This mutual attraction, their mutual longing, triumphs over past nightmares and prejudices—even the discovery that her father has led a Russian pogrom that killed the musician's family. In fact, this very gulf between them, the basis for hatred in the Old World, becomes the basis for attraction in the New. As Werner Sollers makes clear, this is not an assimilationist text in the pejorative sense of the term and in the sense that the short comedies discussed previously had an underlying assimilationist ideology. Neither loses nor seeks to suppress his or her ethnic identity. The eventual product of this union will be something new, something specifically American—and an American very unlike the old-line genteel WASP who at one point seeks Vera Revendal's hand.[33]

In more modest ways, the film industry made similar gestures toward its burgeoning immigrant audiences. Two 1908 Biograph melodramas represented Lower East Side Jews in a sympathetic light (*Old Isaac, the Pawnbroker* and *Romance of a Jewess*) even though, as Patricia Erens points out, company personnel lacked firsthand experience of ghetto life. A 1911 romance, Vitagraph's *One Touch of Nature*, picks up on the theme of Jewish-Christian intermarriage. As in many similar films to follow, the parents break with their children over their marriage but reconcile with the birth of the grandchild. Interethnic attraction and anxiety are confronted openly; romance and the freedom to chose one's own way triumph, but not without a struggle.

Ethnicity generally retained only a muted presence in silent film comedies of the 1910s and 1920s. Consider the leading comedians of the slapstick tradition. Buster Keaton regularly played native-born Americans *(Steamboat Bill, Jr.)* and mid-nineteenth century figures *(Our Hospitality, The General)*; Harold Lloyd, who goes from the country to the city in *Safety Last*, was another native American; and Laurel and Hardy's eccentricities have nothing directly to do with ethnicity. Only Charles Chaplin maintained a slight measure of ethnic ambiguity. Like Stan Laurel, Chaplin was English, and *The Kid* was even set in his homeland. Although his uniform was the standard costume for the American-born tramp of the 1890s and nothing overtly contradicts this WASP identity before *The Great Dictator* (1940), his curly dark hair and other attributes allowed viewers to confuse him for a more Mediterranean type. Thus, in *The Pawnshop* (1916), Chaplin's interest in the daughter of a pawnbroker who apparently is Jewish does not raise the issue of ethnic transgression. An immigrant in *The Immigrant* (1917), Charlie nonetheless lacks any clear ethnic identity. This is part of his "universality" which appealed to, and affirmed the experience of, diverse immigrant groups.[34] Intertitles are in conventional English and never suggest foreign accents. The comic tramp had been essentially nonethnic from his first appearances in motion pictures, a tradition that even Chaplin did not break, but merely softened.

The renewal of nativism and the rise of the nickelodeons coincided with a third and initially unexpected development that had profound implications for the ways cinema addressed immigrants struggling with the torturous process of forging new identities in the course of their daily lives. To a considerable extent, its very manifestation was due to the interest of the nickelodeon audiences. The motion picture industry rapidly and with unprecedented intensity—in comparison to other entertainment industries such as vaudeville and the legitimate theater in America and the motion picture industry overseas—developed a star system. As early as 1908 spectators eagerly sought the identities of the actors on the screen—"the Biograph girl" (first Florence Lawrence, then Marion Leonard and Mary Pickford), "the Vitagraph girl" (Florence Turner), and "the Kalem girl" (Gene Gauntier). They not only constructed fantasies around these players, but also enjoyed the ways that they played a wide range of roles, including diverse ethnic roles. On a weekly and even semiweekly basis they could see their favorite stars assume some new identity. In this respect, motion pictures proved the ideal entertainment for working-class immigrants. The movies provided them with an alternative to the alienation and struggle experienced while constructing a new world during the course of their everyday lives. The nickelodeons with names such as

Bijou Dream, Star, and Wonderland transformed an ordeal into play, desire, and fantasy. This constant effort to construct or re-shape the self was naturally not limited to immigrant groups, but it is they who experienced it in particularly intense form. Perhaps most of all it was the Jews who had struggled with these adjust-ments, not only upon their arrival in the United States but also in their European homelands. It is hardly a surprise then that they, more than any other group, viscerally understood the motion pic-ture business. Robert Sklar has suggested that the Jews' outsider status enabled them to escape genteel moralizing, Lary May points to the particular conjunction of skills and economic circumstance that propelled them into the industry in disproportionate number, but this additional pyschocultural dimension would seem no less important to understanding their success.[35] It was with the opening of the early nickelodeons and even more so with the rise of the star system that Jews came to the foreground in the film industry. And it was from that moment that American cinema began its precipi-tous climb to world domination.

During this same period a supra-ethnic comedy emerged in which role-playing within the diegesis achieved crucial centrality. Chaplin again serves as a useful starting point, for his films provide innumerable examples in which his tramp persona assumes a mask or expediently adopts new identities. In *The Tramp* (1915), for exam-ple, he pretends both to work as a farmhand and to join the malev-olent vagabonds—only subsequently to reveal his principled stand against work and thievery. In *The Pawnshop* (1916), he playfully de-stroys a clock while running through a repertoire of guises.[36] In *The Idle Class* (1921), his identity is constructed, to his surprise and much against his will, by well-to-do vacationers. He is invited into their abode, and one insists that he is her husband. When he fails to live up to these impossible expectations, he is thrown out.[37] The very way in which Chaplin's gentleman tramp appeared in new sit-uations and in new guises from film to film confronted the struggle of fitting in—but turned it to comic ends.

The pleasures and some of the dangers of role-playing became the subject of one early feature-length romantic comedy dealing with ethnicity, *Young Romance* (1915). This Jesse Lasky film was pro-duced by Cecil B. DeMille and directed by George Melford from a script by William C. deMille. Its very production involved an interethnic collaboration. According to one reviewer, the film "for-ever silences the claim that refined comedy cannot be conveyed via the screen." It was an American comedy that displayed "the spark-ing, exuberant bubbling humor of our own country, condensed and trebly distilled and an everlasting provocation to hearty laughter."[38] The picture is loosely based on a well-known O. Henry short story, "Transients in Arcadia" (1904), in which Harold Farrington and Heloise D'Arcy Beaumont meet in a hotel and fall quickly in love. This elite interethnic love affair has an unexpected ending when both confess their charade and reveal their true identity. She is Mamie Siviter, Jewish, and a sales girl; he is James McManus, Irish, and a bill collector. O. Henry thus explores this conjunction of dissembling and working-class, immigrant life. Ethnic difference did more than add spice to the class-based stew: it provides a social basis for the comedic twist. It is an unexpected ending but not an arbitrary one.[39] As with *The Melting Pot*, here attraction and union in no way mean assimilation to the dominant WASP culture. If anything, it is immigrant, working-class solidarity in opposition to the ruling elites they briefly impersonate.

On an overt level the filmmakers chose to avoid O. Henry's interethnic byplay, assigning Irish names (Nellie Nolan and Tom Clancy) to both lovers. (With the nation's shifting mood, overt depiction of such an interracial romance might have shifted the comedy's center in ways that the filmmakers preferred to avoid.) Despite their names and background, however, neither character displays the slightest trace of Irishness, avoiding completely the old stereotypes. In many respects these young lovers have already successfully assimilated and learned the lessons of the early comedies. Moreover, the parts of the Irish-American protagonists are played by actors of WASP descent, Edith Taliaferro and Tom Forman.[40] The assimilationist impulse is contained within the creation of character. Identification with character means identification with the effacement of ethnicity. The daily conditions of role-playing are reversed. Instead of immigrants seeking to lose their ethnic markings and assimilate, native-born performers assume ethnic identities—and yet do so without simulating specific qualities that would associate them with that group. This strategy embraces the ideology of ethnic effacement even as it pragmatically faciliates identification by a range of ethnic audiences who could more readily identify with the process and product of assimilation than with a character whose attributes were not only foreign but also perhaps those of an antagonistic group.

Yet when we scratch the surface, something more complex begins to emerge. *Young Romance* daringly explores the liberating possibilities of role-playing even as it finally attempts to contain its implication, as one might expect of a Hollywood film.[41] Both Nellie and

Tom, unknown to each other, work in the same large department store, where they serve middle-class and often quite wealthy customers. Here, they assume the necessarily false mask of politesse when waiting on the condescending and self-absorbed. Yet the film soon reveals that their economic need to play a role can be applied elsewhere and become psychically liberating. The boring routine, rather than deaden these attractive ingenues, encourages fantasy. They have never met, but each decides, after reading a magazine story of noble adventure, to live out his or her fantasy of becoming a member of the leisure class, if only for a week. Although each experiences perilous moments, both successfully cross class barriers in disguise and are accepted, not only by each other but also by the elite groups with which they socialize.

The couple's role-playing deftly, and with a light touch, resurrects the issue of interethnic attraction found in O. Henry's "Transients in Arcadia." She becomes Ethel van Dusen—Dutch, blue-blood stock, and he is Robert de Vignier—suggesting French origins (their initials v. D. and d. V. are simply reversed to emphasize their symmetry). Language and culture pose no problems. Tell-tale family ties are avoided. Class if not ethnic distinctions are more apparent in their roommates, peripheral characters who remain behind. As with the short story, the film explicitly embodies the up-scale identification with screen characters that typified much movie-going. The film plays with distinctions of class in ways that encourage acceptance of one's lot (they really are happier back at the local soda fountain than in the hotel restaurant) yet simultaneously make the possibilities of upward mobility seem readily attainable. The young couple is an attractive *tabula rasa* for whom we can readily posit a successful future.

The dissemblings of the young couple can be compared to those of Count Spagnoli, the con artist who kidnaps Nellie Nolan, thinking she is the van Dusen who inherited a large sum of money. Like the young couple, he too assumes the role of an aristocrat. But rather then trying to pass for a WASP, he retains and so affirms his ethnicity. He is older, his disguise is longstanding (we never learn his real name), and his motivation morally reprehensible. Most interestingly, the part is played by a Spanish actor (Ernest Garcia). Ethnicity is redoubled with the villain, while the protagonists emphasize ethnicity's malleability by the contradictory signals of, for example, the heroine who is Irish passing as New York old-line Dutch but played by someone of WASP/Sephardic Jewish extraction. The ingenues' appealing lightness, their ability to assume different guises as actors as well as characters, contrasts to Spagnoli's heaviness. The effacement of ethnic identity is shown to be a positive achievement, even as the ability to act out new roles becomes a source of pleasure. Yet it is precisely the Spagnoli character, a collection of undesirable traits associated with ethnic groups symbolized by the Black Hand or the Mafia, that most recalls the early film comedies and will be taken up by Chico, in fact by all the Marx brothers, in *Animal Crackers*.

Young Romance embraces the homogenization and role-playing evidenced by its characters on yet another level: a Hollywood studio, Los Angeles exteriors, and the Pacific shoreline represent New York City and the Maine coast. Again, there is a similar challenge and pleasure in carrying out this deceit. Although carefully chosen vistas never overtly undercut this sleight-of-hand, the scenes lack New York's edge. Another film released that same month contained similar fakeries—Southern California passing for South Carolina and whites in blackface trying to pass for African-Americans. Griffith's *The Birth of a Nation*, however, lacked the humor and cosmopolitan vision of *Young Romance*.

If *Young Romance* was released during the first year that feature-length silent films dominated American production, *Abie's Irish Rose* (Famous Players/Paramount, directed by Victor Fleming in 1928) came during the last year of real commercial viability. These bookends reveal the small but significant shifts that had occurred in the post-World War I era. The 1928 film, set in New York City, was based on a play by Ann Nichols that achieved unprecedented success, first on the West Coast and then on Broadway; its New York premiere of May 23, 1922, came a year after the Immigrant Restriction Bill had become law and in the very month of its first renewal.[42] Like *Transients in Arcadia* and *One Touch of Nature*, Nichols's comedy centers on a Jewish-Irish Catholic romance, here between Abraham Levy and Rosemary Murphy. The couple marry and are promptly disowned by their respective parents, until the lure of grandchildren (twins) forces the recalcitrant patriarchs to accept the new state of things (fig. 2.4). The play's Broadway run ended on October 22, 1927, after 2,327 performances—a world record. Earlier that year, Famous Players-Lasky had bought the motion picture rights for $300,000 plus a percentage of the gross, estimated to be worth $1 million.[43]

Family discord is postponed at one point as Rose poses as a nice Jewish girl, Rosie Murphesky, role-playing performed with great awkwardness. The young lovers, having fought in World War I and become fully Americanized (that is, Anglo-Saxonized), are not

2.4 The two patriarchs (J. Farrell MacDonald and Jean Hersholt), surrounded by clashing symbols of Jewish and Christian faith, begin the process of reconciliation in *Abie's Irish Rose* (1928), where much of the comedy results from one ethnic group's discomfort with the customs of the other.

adept at assuming disguises. Much of the humor comes about through the discomfort of one group with the symbols and customs of the other. Yet both Rose and Abie are so cleansed of ethnicity's internalized cultural and psychological specificity—Abie is played by Charles "Buddy" Rogers and Rose by Nancy Carroll—that these differences ultimately seem hollow. Rogers's persona made it easy for gentiles to identify with Abie while Jews, through the very act of identifying with Abie, had assumed an assimilationist stance that made this marriage easy to accept. In complete contrast to *Young Romance*, the couple's inability to fake their persona is a true sign of their assimilation and their identity as *real* Americans, the fires of the war heating Nichols's version of the melting pot.

Abie's Irish Rose's obvious, sometimes even exaggerated, depiction of ethnic difference in customs and the secondary characters is promptly muted by its "universal messages of racial amity, its firm faith that all roads and creeds lead to love and but one Omnipotence."[44] It reasserts fading notions of Anglo-Saxon inclusiveness and ultimately finds safety in sentimentality. To be doubly sure, the filmmakers sanitized the original play of its more problematic slapstick elements and so turned a "farce comedy" into a more "tasteful" comedy-drama.[45] The same basic elements found in *Young Romance* reappear but are reconfigured. The principals no longer carry out their fantasies by entering the elite world in disguise. Despite the democratic leveling of their wartime experiences, Abie and Rose are from the upper or upper-middle classes. Ethnicity is represented more explicitly, but also more superficially. The story's connection with real immigrant experience has become attentuated; the still rarely fulfilled desire for the elusive Other has been made more concrete but also kept at a safer distance.[46]

Young Romance and *Abie's Irish Rose* carefully balance these revelations of pleasure with warnings of the dangers involved, such as parental rejection and the possibility of exposure and humiliation. Both films have a sweetness that easily becomes cloying. Their respective breakthroughs to comic pleasure are so qualified and contained that one might expect that they could readily serve as the object of comic lampooning by a more vigorous slapstick tradition. And in different ways, they did. *Miss Fatty's Seaside Lovers* (Keystone, 1915) is an obvious burlesque of *Young Romance*. Roscoe "Fatty" Arbuckle in the Edith Taliaferro role assumes a disguise all right—that of a woman. She/he is chased by three young men, all of whom are interested in her/his money although put off by Fatty's grotesque size. Social mores and aspirations of upward mobility come in for ludicrous ridicule. The comedy, however, follows a pattern noted by Mark Winokur: eccentricity of character replaces ethnic caricature.[47] *Abie's Irish Rose* was not parodied so systematically, but the tradition of vaudeville comedy and slapstick, nevertheless, blasted its sugar-coated look at love, tolerance, and interracial understanding. Just as this vehicle found its first success on the stage, so too did the anarcho-comic response.

Early Sound Comedy: The Return of the Repressed

Ethnic difference was more readily foregrounded in live theatrical performance than in silent film comedy, a fact that had multiple determinants. First, as Robert Snyder has noted, stage material could more readily be shaped to specific audiences, making it easier to avoid offending patrons.[48] That is, live theater is not mass entertainment and so does not suffer from the resulting contraints. Second, because the cinema had become the dominant form of theatrical entertainment, vaudeville and even Broadway needed to tap subject matter underutilized by the movies. Ethnicity was one such readily available subject.[49] Finally, as Patricia Erens among others has noted, the live stage featured the spoken word (all the more significantly so since motion pictures could not), which is highly sensitive to cultural distinctions and nuances. Thus the original 1922 play version of *Abie's Irish Rose* was performed with heavy ethnic accents which were absent from the screen intertitles. In short, the film industry's need to downplay ethnic difference was facilitated by the lack of synchronous recorded sound just as theater was well suited for exploiting what the cinema had marginalized and repressed. This was not without contradiction, however, since the theater provided the film industry with one of its principal sources of material. But this double bind seemingly performed an inoculatory function, a film's content was authorized by its previous stage rendition.[50] Nevertheless, a whole area of live performance involving slapstick verbal humor did not make it to the screen until the arrival of recorded synchronous sound.

In a polyglot city such as New York language was (and is) problematized, often becoming the focus of discourse—thus the Marx Brothers and Eddie Cantor. Both acts had worked their way up from vaudeville to Broadway by the mid 1920s. Although successful comedians, their verbal and ethnic humor made them ill-suited for silent film. Some of the Marx Brothers appeared in the silent comedy *Humorisk* (1920), presumably a parody of *Humoresque* (1920 directed by Frank Borzage), a hit motion picture melodrama set in the Jewish Lower East Side. Unlike its inspiration, *Humorisk* failed, and negative and print were eventually either lost or destroyed.[51] Eddie Cantor made several film appearances but again the results were disappointing. In the fall of 1928, both he and the Marx Brothers appeared in new theatrical vehicles for their madcap fun—Cantor in *Whoopee* and the Marx Brothers in *Animal Crackers*. Brooks Atkinson began his *New York Times* review of *Animal Crackers* with the kind of rave destined for reprinting in newspaper advertisements: "Here comes the Marx brothers again with their uproariously, slapstick comedy in a new fury of puns and gibes."[52] The *New York Sun* critic Richard Lockridge, tired of incessant musical comedy, was unexpectedly revived by *Whoopee*. "It is all so easy and how one wishes the rest might learn the trick."[53] Florenz Ziegfeld's "trick" was a bevy of WASPY showgirls and Jewish comedian Eddie Cantor.

As Hollywood adapted to sound, it turned to the New York stage for a wider selection of material. Enlisting Cantor and the Marx Brothers was inevitable. The Marx Brothers' first sound film was of their first Broadway musical comedy, *Cocoanuts* (1929). It was shot at Paramount's Astoria studio in their spare time while *Animal Crackers* flourished on Broadway. *Animal Crackers,* also shot at the Astoria studio, avoided some of the pitfalls of the earlier adaptation. Eddie Cantor had made a few brief appearances in sound films, but *Whoopee* was his first large role. Although the film was a careful transcription of the New York musical comedy, the production occurred in California where co-producer Samuel Goldwyn was based. *Animal Crackers* (August 1930) and *Whoopee* (September 1930) finally appeared in cinematic form a year after the Wall Street crash. Both somewhat cautious adaptations of stage originals opened to large audiences and positive reviews in New York City.[54]

Whoopee and *Animal Crackers* are quintessential New York come-dies that take the city's ethnic, social, and cultural milieu as their subject and ridicule *Abie's Irish Rose* in the process. *Animal Crackers* makes a direct reference to the Nichols play and film. There is some verbal confusion over the sentence "get a writ of habeas corpus" which lawyerish Groucho directs at the Chico who, unfamiliar with the term, hears something like "get rid of Habea's corpse." Groucho (sarcastically): "Didn't you ever see Habeas' corpus." Chico: "No, but I saw Abie's Irish Rose." So the play is compared to a dead corpse and left for others to eulogize and bury. Moreover, *Animal Crackers* has its own Abie—Abie the fish peddlar, who is a satiric inversion of the character played by Buddy Rogers—a Jew appear-ing to be a WASP rather than a WASP appearing to be a Jew. Nichols's homilies are challenged by comic aggression which confronts ethnic animosity, attraction, and confusion as well as the problematics of assimilation and upward mobility. Role-playing is brought back with a vengeance; the sugar coating is corroded by acerbic wit.

Whoopee relates to *Abie's Irish Rose* through theme, subject matter, and genre history. Werner Sollors has traced the genealogy of inter-racial romance in nineteenth-century American theater, beginning with the Pocahontas story which first appeared on the stage in 1808 *(The Indian Princess; or, La Belle Sauvage)*. *Abie's Irish Rose* con-tinued this tradition as Jewish-Christian romances replaced their Indian-white predecessors by the early twentieth century, revitaliz-ing the genre in the process. The substitution of Jew for Indian was simple, particularly when figures such as Congressman Oscar W. Underwood condemned the new immigrants for the mixture of Af-rican and "Asiatic" blood coursing through their veins, Jews being of Semitic rather than Nordic origin.[55] By the mid-nineteenth cen-tury, moreover, sentimental Indian plays had already become the object of burlesque. With *Metamora; or, The Last of the Pollywogs* (1847), the Irish immigrant John Brougham ridiculed their conventions and platitudes, using an assault of verbal puns and ethnic substitutions.[56] The remarkable aspect of *Whoopee*, at least in establishing its pedigree, was its ability to revitalize this eighty-year-old genre.

Indian-white and Jew-WASP oppositions structure *Whoopee*, as word play on the title exemplifies. At the start of the film, the cowboys and cowgirls prepare to celebrate a wedding with the western cheer "whoopee." Elsewhere, Cantor sings the urban, sophisticated song "Making Whoopee." The equation of Jew and Indian, a common trope of the period, is made explicitly several times.[57] At the Indian village, Cantor sings a ditty to the tune of "Old Man River": "Old Black Eagle, Old Man Segal": soon after, he calls himself "Big Chief Izzy Horowitz." Again, he poses as an Indian and sells his wares as if he were a shopkeeper on the Lower East Side.[58]

Henry Jenkins has admirably resituated Eddie Cantor's early work within the explicit framework of New York ethnic (particularly Jewish) humor, but the centrality of ethnicity to early Marx Brother comedies still needs to be reassessed.[59] Film historians and critics have been sensitive to the New York-Jewish basis for their humor, but many have argued, either explicitly or by implication, that they never played characters with specifically Jewish identities.[60] Yet in *Animal Crackers*, at least, this misses the fact of their sustained role-playing. The Marx Brothers are Jewish hustlers insinuating themselves into WASP high society, itself shown to be a model of corruption and doubtful respectability, without this elitist group realizing what is happening. This comic premise is an aggressive assault on the exclusionary policies being applied to Jews by WASP-dominated universities, country clubs, and other public and private institutions.[61] Rather than greeting the mounting wave of anti-Semitism with sentimental pleas for tolerance à la *Abie's Irish Rose*, *Animal Crackers* uses ridicule and anger.

Both *Whoopee* and *Animal Crackers*, in their exploration of the love theme, have double romances. In each instance, one centers on a young couple whose eagerly sought marriage is thwarted by some obstacle, whereas the second love affair involves slapstick comedians and is more farcical. The first type of love affair motivates a variety of love-related songs, the second type provides opportunity for verbal puns and wit. The thematic relationship between the two romances is crucial. In *Whoopee*, the first couple, Sally Morgan (Eleanor Hunt) and Wanenis (Paul Gregory), is blocked by the girl's father, who refuses to let her marry someone who is part Indian. Instead, she is made to marry Sheriff Bob Wells. At the last moment, on her wedding day, she refuses to surrender to patriarchy and the law and relies on Henry Williams (Eddie Cantor) to help her escape. Black Eagle, Wanenis' father, also opposes the marriage because of the way whites treat the Indians. Sally Morgan decides she wants to marry Wanenis (keep remembering the Indian-Jew substitution as the plot progresses) anyway, but he refuses, declaring that his acceptance of her sacrifice would make him unworthy. Finally, it is revealed that Wanenis is really white after all; Black Eagle rescued him as a baby. Barriers magically disappear and the couple are united. In the meantime, Wanenis—whom we first encounter dressed as an Anglo—has reembraced Indian life. He is more an Indian at the end of the film than at the beginning but it matters not; societal rules have been satisfied even while they are shown to be empty prejudices.

The second romance is between Henry Williams, a wealthy, hypochondriacal easterner who comes West in search of a cure, and Nurse Mary Custer (Ethel Shutta), who takes care of him even as she woos him. Henry Williams is a knot of ambiguous ethnic identities. He has a WASP's name, and the story line is derived from an Owen Davis play, *The Nervous Wreck*. Yet the character is clearly Jewish—the Eddie Cantor character which audiences knew and loved.[62] Florenz Ziegfeld and Cantor adapted the play and the Henry Williams figure to their own quite different ends. Is he a Jew with an anglicized name or, as he later jokingly declares, a "halfbreed"? Or is Williams a theatrical construct, "the Jewish WASP," a comic contradiction not unlike Chaplin's gentleman tramp. In fact, all three possibilities operate either separately or together. The blonde nurse is much more convincingly Anglo, her last name evoking General George Armstrong Custer, the famed Indian killer. Their final union, while essentially a surrender on Cantor's part, crosses ethnic boundaries and ignores social rules delineated in the complementary romance.[63]

Romances in *Whoopee* are motivated by desire for the Other and for the forbidden. This is also why the disclosure that Wanenis is all white (do we hear all right?) can be so disconcerting. A basis for Sally Morgan's and Wanenis' mutual attraction has been undermined. Perhaps making Wanenis culturally more of an American Indian at the end than the beginning guards against this, but more important, it also exposes the extent to which ethnicity is constructed. *Whoopee* might be compared to *Call Her Savage* (1932), a

Clara Bow melodrama in which Bow plays a half-breed. A product of an illicit affair between a white woman (whose husband cannot comprehend, never mind satisfy, her sexual passions) and a renegade Indian, the daughter cannot grapple with her underlying urges until she learns of her mongrelized identity. Attraction for the Other—racial, gender, and even class—is thus laid bare by the half-breed. Like the mulatto, the half-breed is the product of passion that has broken the bounds of the law.[64] Around such troubling realities of human behavior, it is not unusual to have melodrama and comedy take inverse positions. If *Whoopee* shows racial identity to be a construction, *Call Her Savage* shows that it is immutable, passed from generation to generation without knowledge or choice. Comedy thus ridicules and liberates us from the oppression of societal restrictions, even as melodrama is designed to show the dangers of breaking these same laws.

Spectators could find assimilationist tendencies in *Whoopee*, but the film also affirmed New York's Jewish-American culture and expressed anger at a society that subjects Jews (like Indians) to discriminatory restrictions. Men of power—whether Bob Wells or Jerome Underwood—are the recipients of unleashed anger. Thus, Williams/Cantor tells Underwood that he is Big Chief Rip-Your-Collar. Underwood is puzzled by the name, and so Cantor explains by ripping off Underwood's shirt collar. The comedy unleashes feelings of frustration and anger never allowed to surface in *Abie's Irish Rose*, wherein the long-suffering children wait patiently for their parents to re-own them.

Whoopee, however, is less concerned with comically avenging ongoing humiliations than with tapping pleasures associated with ethnic role-play and interethnic attraction. Ethnic difference and gender difference are similar: opposites attract. *Whoopee* is thus a double romance in another sense—between men and women as well as Jews and WASPs. The hypochondriacal Williams will be cured if he stops treating Mary Custer as a nurse and starts treating her as a lover. His cure proceeds—from his opening rebuff of Miss Custer's advances ("Why do you make overtures to me when I need intermissions") to his later interest in that primeval moment of interracial coupling—the union of Pocahontas and John Smith.

Whoopee mobilizes still other oppositions. The WASP-Jew heterosexual romance plays off an underlying polymorphous perverse sensibility. Several gags and routines involve homosexual attraction, most notably the Underwood-Williams infatuation as they roll on the floor, examining each other's scars. Cantor also assumes a vast array of ethnic identities: an Indian salesman, a Greek cook (Greeks apparently dominated the coffee-shop business in New York even then), and a Negro in blackface. His chameleonlike quality shares many parallels with the Woody Allen character in *Zelig*. As Robert Stam and Ella Shohat have pointed out, Zelig embodies a history in which Jews have often been forced to play "a convoluted game of cultural hide-and-seek in order to avoid being victimized."[65] *Whoopee* is thus an affirmation of diversity and its vicissitudes, a celebration of the dialogic imagination and a burlesque of ethnic and sexual stasis. In short, it embraces the life-generating forces in New York's cosmopolitan culture.

Animal Crackers jokes with many of the same elements as *Whoopee*. At the same time, its angrier edge is more directly connected to the immigrant experience. On the Lower East Side, first-generation Jews and Italians constantly struggled to communicate with each other in a language that neither had yet mastered. With two different accents, there was frequent confusion, frustration, and wacky word-play. Subtle shifts in pronunciation or accent produced unexpectedly different meanings. One pretended to understand, but often did not. And their children, whose ears were more attuned to this city of babble, enjoyed the word-play and used it as the basis for their jokes. Thus Chico and Groucho—the Italian and the Jew— engage in conversation with its slippages and illogicalities. To use one classic example, "viaduct" becomes "why a duck" in *Cocoanuts* (1929). Chico's Italian-accented, fractured English is designed to sow confusion almost anywhere. In *Animal Crackers*, he asks Harpo for a "flash" by which he means flashlight. He knows just what he wants, but Harpo keeps giving him something different—flesh, fish, a flush (as in poker), a flask, and a flute. This failure to communicate hampers their efforts to abscond with the Beaugard painting, and so they are almost caught. The ethnic interfacings of the Lower East Side form the basis for such routines.

Animal Crackers unfolds at a Long Island estate, where Mrs. Rittenhouse (Margaret Dumont), a wealthy widow, is trying to cement her social standing in the elite WASP society with a news-making soirée. Unknown to her, Rittenhouse's special weekend guests are a group of dissembling Jews who assume an array of non-Jewish disguises.[66] These include Captain Jeffrey T. Spaulding (Groucho), who will give an account of his African explorations, and Roscoe W. Chandler (Louis Sorin), an art connoisseur who will unveil his newest acquisition, the $100,000 painting "After the Hunt" by Beaugard. All sport old-English first names (Jeffrey is even spelt

Geoffrey in the society news article that opens the film) and middle initials in elegantly WASPY style (Zeppo appears as Horatio W. Jameson). This concealment is spoofed again near the end of the film as all four Marx brothers form a barbershop quartet and sing "My Old Kentucky Home," while Harpo hovers mute in the background. At the conclusion Groucho announces "this program is coming to you from the House of David," treating it as a radio program. The incongruities of assimilation are mocked but also enjoyed.

Romance is more tenuous in *Animal Crackers* than in *Whoopee*. Both Chandler and Captain Spaulding are interested in marrying Mrs. Rittenhouse for her money (fig. 2.5). They might be seen as competitors for her hand, but as insults and slips of the tongue make clear, they have no genuine romantic interests in her whatsoever. Addressing his hostess, Spaulding calls her Mrs. Rittenrotten and proposes by asking her to wash his socks. The romance that motivates the musical comedy is stymied by absurdly flimsy barriers that prevent the couple's happy union. Arabella Rittenhouse (Lillian Roth), only child of Mrs. Rittenhouse, and John Parker, her painter-fiance, cannot afford to marry: he has sold only two paintings the previous year for $150. The two romances thus stand in opposition. For the naive youths, her money doesn't matter, it almost seems not to exist—why should Parker worry about making a living when all he has to do is marry Arabella. For the older men, money is the only reason to marry Mrs. Rittenhouse. The sickeningly sweet relationship between two WASP ingenues—although Lillian Roth was Jewish, the play employed Alice Wood for the role— is countered by the cynical attraction of the Jew Spaulding for the WASP Rittenhouse.[67]

Marriage is one of the institutions mocked repeatedly over the course of the film. When Spaulding offers to marry both Mrs. Rittenhouse and her matronly rival Mrs. Whitehead (Margaret Irving), they protest that it would be bigamy. Groucho agrees that "It's big of me, too," but abruptly runs off with a bevy of young women, declaring his desire to sow his wild oats before settling down. The legitimacy and propriety of matrimony give way before sexual desire. Interethnic attraction takes still other forms. Harpo's constant chase of a shiksa throughout the film finally ends when Harpo knocks her out with a sleeping potion that he then sprays himself with so he can fall asleep in her arms.

In the Jews' nefarious invasion of WASPdom, almost no one is who he appears to be. Roscoe W. Chandler and Jeffrey T. Spaulding try to pass as Anglos and do a fairly good job. There are moments,

2.5. *Animal Crackers* (1930). Roscoe W. Chandler, a.k.a. Abie the Fish Peddler (Louis Sorin), woos Mrs. Rittenhouse (Margaret Dumont) as Arabella Rittenhouse (Lillian Roth) supervises, in a film directly connected to the immigrant experience.

however, when each man's fraudulent facade is exposed. Captain Spaulding's description of his African trip and his fear of a caterpillar indicate that he has never seen the Dark Continent. Moreover, when guests hail him as an "Explorer" he mishears the word as *schnorrer.* Of course, his misrecognition makes clear that he is exactly that (a beggar or leech) and that he is also Jewish. In fact, the entire weekend subliminally evokes the Old World visits of poor Jews to the dinner tables of their well-to-do brethren which formed part of the charity obligations on the Sabbath.[68]

One of the key moments for reading the Marx Brothers comedies of their most vital period (1929–32) comes when Ravelli (Chico) identifies Roscoe W. Chandler, the sophisticated man of the world, as the former Abie Kabibble from Czechoslovakia—otherwise known as Abie the Fish Peddler (fig. 2.6). Although the assumption of a new name and a new identity at Ellis Island was not unusual, Spaulding and Chandler are con artists. They might be compared to someone like Erich Von Stroheim, who turned himself into a Prus-

2.6. The Professor (Harpo), Roscoe W. Chandler (Louis Sorin), and Ravelli (Chico) in *Animal Crackers*. The two Marx brothers blackmail Chandler, a Jew who is trying to pass as a WASP, thus affirming the immigrant's ability to adapt to the cultural and economic necessities of American capitalism.

sian aristocrat upon arriving in the New World (or like Count Spagnoli in *Young Romance*). Meeting people from the old country thus always threatened to expose the elaborate ruse. "How did you get to be Roscoe W. Chandler?," Ravelli wants to know. "How did you get to be an Italian" is the retort. It is a question Ravelli refuses to answer. (In real life, Leonard "Chico" Marx learned to assume different identities as a way of escaping dangerous situations on the tough streets of polyglot New York.)[69] Again role-playing is emphasized and exposed.

Ravelli's choice of a new identity is perverse because the guise of an Italian immigrant hardly moves him up society's totem pole toward WASP respectability. Rather, it is a gesture of solidarity with another "swarthy race." (His mastery of the Italian accent and stereotypic clothing suggest that Ravelli could have easily created a new WASP identity as have Chandler and Spaulding.) His choice of an Italian persona is a refusal to assimilate. Yet as a musical composer and piano player, he is an Italian immigrant version of the

French composer Maurice Ravel. In a way, his eccentric talents fit his assumed identity (Ravelli can never remember the endings to his piano pieces). He is not, as Arabella Rittenhouse patronizingly mishears and miscalls him, Ravioli. Ravelli, however, is not merely a musician who charges exorbitant fees (he earns $300 a day for not being there); he is also a card shark and blackmailer. He and the Professor (Harpo) quickly force Chandler to purchase their silence so his past will not be revealed.[70]

In large part due to Groucho, a large part of the Marx Brothers' comedy revolving around WASP and Jew has a bitterness that is much closer to the surface than is Cantor's. Groucho's comic insults at Mrs. Rittenrotten may be misogynistic, but they also reciprocate the insults and humiliations that were part of the Jewish immigrant experience.[71] Yet this poses a central question, How were these insults so readily accepted by gentiles, not only in New York but also across the country? The key to such an explanation may be found in Mrs. Rittenhouse's own inability to recognize her guests' real ethnic origins—a failure shared with the whole Long Island crowd. Jews and gentiles may read the film in quite different ways. For people who are not Jews, *Animal Crackers* can be a zany, anarchistic comedy. Thus Groucho's schnorrer can be heard as "snorer"— an association that makes perfect sense because he is carried in on a sedan.[72] Again, the Jewish-centered humor could remain invisible to the uninitiated and be attributed to eccentricity. The film affirms the immigrants' ability to outfox and so adapt to the cultural and economic exigencies of American capitalism.

Mrs. Rittenhouse is not only a gentile, but also a Long Island matron. Although partaking of city life in some respects, she and her circle are linked to nonurban activities; the painting "After the Hunt," part of Abie's smoke screen, depicts the Old World aristocracy whom they seek to emulate. The invasion of the Long Island mansion is not just a Jewish one, but also an urban one. The film will be understood differently whether or not the spectator is from the metropolitan center, especially from New York. Consider Groucho's brief but outrageous parody of O'Neill's *Strange Interlude*. If the spectator is in the know, the spoof is outrageously delightful; if the spectator is not, it is delightfully nonsensical. *Animal Crackers* thus spoke to truly cosmopolitan audiences—not just Jews but those who shared in their cultural experiences, and not just New Yorkers but those who partook of its vital cultural life—over the heads of others.

In the Marx Brothers' and Eddie Cantor's films, ethnicity and outsider status are the focus even as class issues are put aside. Thus the anarchic invasion of the Rittenhouse mansion by Jews can be compared to the destruction of various locales by Charles Chaplin's tramp—for example the well-to-do household in *Work*. Charlie's paste brush keeps hitting the boss in the face, and the house as well as social and marital relations are soon destroyed. Comedic warfare is based on culture and ethnicity in one case, work and class relations in the other. In both, however, the objects of comic aggression are figures of relative power. Although the immigrant experience and the working-class experience are closely intertwined historically, in the period through 1930 and beyond, American film comedians seldom played overtly with both subjects at the same time. In this instance, the Marx Brothers, like Eddie Cantor, forged their comedy in the face of a groundswell of anti-Semitism. Their comic achievement can be found in the depth and range of emotions which they tapped and then unleashed. The fact that their characters are simultaneously "unassimilable" and highly adept role-players is one of their key comic contradictions.

The coming of sound, which put *Whoopee* and *Animal Crackers* on the screen, did not herald a new age in which cinema was sensitive to the joys and trials of ethnicity. As Jenkins has shown, Eddie Cantor's Jewishness, and ethnicity more generally, were virtually eliminated in *Palmy Days* (1931) and his subsequent films. *Whoopee* and other pictures featuring New York theatrical stars, for example Fanny Brice, had not done well outside major urban centers. The need to reshape the performer's image to a national, mass audience meant parting with Yiddishisms and other New York-oriented jokes that did not play in more rural areas.[73]

A somewhat similar, although more gradual and less radical, process occurred with the Marx Brothers. Chico's image as an Italian immigrant and Groucho's role as a shyster were so integral to their comic personas that they were difficult to change entirely—and less necessary. Since their films were much less expensive to make than *Whoopee*, profits came easier. Yet the Marx Brothers' move to Hollywood after *Animal Crackers* resulted in significant shifts. Never again would ethnic interfacing be so explicitly the focus of their humor. The robed professors in *Horsefeathers* look like Hasidic Jews, but the opportunities for such double, incongruous readings become less common. The Marx Brothers' later comedies avoided reference to New York delights such as the Theater Guild, cockroaches, and Al Smith. Rather than parody *Strange Interlude*, which was in the fortieth week of its run when *Animal Crackers* opened, they make fun of gangster films, college pictures, and other cinema genres. From this perspective, *Duck Soup* (1933) becomes somewhat of a disappointment; the word-play and story line have lost most of their ethnic basis.[74] Perhaps this might help to explain its disappointing reception in both reviews and at the box office. If so, its failure ironically forced the group to mellow their angry edge still further. The weakening of comic aggression, the replacement of a special address to cosmopolitan audiences with a special address to movie fans, contributed to the decline of their humor. Ethnicity once again was pushed to the margins of film comedy.

Any treatment of ethnicity and cinema occurs within a larger discourse. After a long history in which diverse ethnic and racial groups have not been equal in the eyes of the law, the United States has finally entered an age that endorses the legal principles of racial equality. Equality and cooperation are expected if not required in many areas of public life, producing a new official vision of the United States of quite recent origin, stemming from the civil rights movement of the 1950s and 1960s. This triumph in the political realm has been one of the key achievements of American society.[75] However much its promises have been contained or undercut by economic and social inequality, this envisions a new status quo, what has been called an ethnic salad bowl.

In film studies the project of liberal humanism has produced a body of impressive literature that has not only sought to document and understand the history of a given group, but also to provide a collective memory that can sustain it. The film-related activities and representations of American Jews, particularly those immigrants from Eastern Europe, have been traced by scholars such as Lester Friedman, Patricia Erens, and Neal Gabler, who have actively elaborated and affirmed this group's identity. Their approach often reinforces difference through a number of strategies: by demonstrating incompatibilities among groups,[76] by emphasizing prejudical or even hostile responses by gentiles, and finally by maximizing achievements within the group.[77]

The model of ethnic pluralism, despite its many positive aspects, contains key internal contradictions that make its position unstable and ultimately untenable. Although its immediate accomplishments have been to reassert and revitalize the identity of their respective groups, its longer term position seeks to make time stand still. The ethnic salad bowl trope imagines a world in which people from diverse backgrounds interact in public spheres and yet affirm their ethnic identities in the private realm, in their socializing but above all in their family life. They are, to use the Glazer-Moynihan term, "unmeltable ethnics."[78] A balance between internal cohesion and external interaction would then result.[79]

The public and private spheres, however, are not nearly as discrete as this model would suppose. Americans find their friends, lovers, and spouses in the realm of school and work more than in a private realm. In a mobile society such as the United States, people often constitute their private sphere from the public. We chose those people with whom we wish to share our private selves. If WASPS, Jews, Irish-Catholics, African-Americans, Japanese, American Indians, and other ethnics are equally acknowledged for their own peculiar cultural, emotional, and experiential differences, then would not others wish to know these differences in a context of greater privacy and intimacy? Might not these differences be, in some respects, of greatest value for someone else? Is the world in which one grew up the world in which one will necessarily wish to remain? The amount of moving that Americans do—and, of course the very fact of immigration—suggests that it is not.

This chapter comes from a perspective that has increasingly emerged out of, and in reaction to, the model of ethnic pluralism. Advocates of liberal pluralism have frequently seen interethnic attraction, intermarriage, and the resulting "half-breeds" as disturbing phenomena that undermine the implicit deal struck in the early 1960s when diverse groups were, in effect, assured that equality in the public world would not result in reckless polymorphous conduct in the private realm. Recent trends for the new (now not so new) immigrant groups show that this is not the case. Forty percent of American Jews are now marrying non-Jews, meaning that four-sevenths of the marriages involving Jews are now interethnic.[80] Interaction in the private sphere has been as compelling as in the public.

As Werner Sollors has argued in *Beyond Ethnicity,* the dislocations and interactions common to immigrant experience often produced a sharp awareness that ethnicity was a construction. Tension exists between descent and consent, between roots and the right to make or reshape the self.[81] In the New World, more than in the Old, the latter has held sway and is seen as a particularly American freedom. Identity is malleable and a site for social, political, and personal struggle. America's ethnic landscape has been in constant flux. Whatever the future, we know that tomorrow it will have a different form than it does today. If change is inevitable, how it changes and to what it changes are open questions—as Spike Lee's *Do The Right Thing* so powerfully suggests. It is in the interactions of desire and fear, love and hate, work and romance, public and private, that this takes place. It is these concerns that Eddie Cantor and the Marx Brothers address with remarkable humor, and they remain vital today.

NOTES

This chapter was originally presented as a paper at the IREX-sponsored conference "New York-Budapest, 1880–1930" in Budapest, Hungary, August 1988. The thoughts and suggestions of the participants were extremely helpful in making further revisions. Henry Jenkins III introduced me to *Whoopee*, Robert Sklar provided essential critical assistance, and Lester Friedman in his editorial capacity perfectly demonstrated the term *mensch*. I am also indebted to Miriam Hansen for frequent discussions and intellectual exchanges. Finally, I would like to thank two people who inspired this discussion: Lynne Zeavin, who was looking for a nice Jewish boy but married me instead, and Robert Sklar, who thought I was a nice Jewish boy and so introduced me to that nice Jewish girl—who was what I was looking for all along.

Sources for the principal films discussed herein are: *Chinese Laundry Scene*, *Cohen's Fire Sale*, and *The Terrible Kids*, Museum of Modern Art; *Cohen's Advertising Scheme*, *Levi and Cohen*, *The Irish Comedians*, *The Finish of Bridget McKeen*, *One Touch of Nature*, and *Abie's Irish Rose*, Library of Congress; *Young Romance*, UCLA Film and Television Archive (and through American Federation of the Arts); *Miss Fatty's Seaside Lovers*, Em Gee Films. *Whoopee* and *Animal Crackers* are both available on video.

1. John Higham, *Strangers in the Land: Patterns of American Nativism 1860–1925* (New Brunswick: Rutgers University Press, 1955), pp. 87, 119, 159.

2. Garth Jowett points out that cinema "acted as a guide to the newcomer on the manners and custom of his new environment," *Film: The Democratic Art* (Boston: Little, Brown, 1976), p. 38. Lewis Jacobs and Roy Rosenzweig suggest that films provided a common cultural experience that transcended ethnic boundaries and, despite the relative constraints on language posed by silence and subtitles, a way to learn English, Lewis Jacobs, *The Rise of the American Film* (New York: Harcourt, Brace, 1939), pp. 77, 155; Roy Rosenzweig, *Eight Hours for What We Will: Workers and Leisure in an Industrial City, 1870–1920* (Cambridge: Cambridge University Press, 1983), pp. 191–221. Both Rosenzweig and Kathy Peiss have considered ways in which the early nickelodeons acted as local centers for community activity, providing a milieu where working-class immigrants could resist some aspects of this assimilationist impulse, Kathy Peiss, *Cheap Amusements: Working Women and Leisure in Turn-of-the-Century New York* (Philadelphia: Temple University Press, 1986), pp. 139–162. James Hoberman has shown how ethnic motion picture theaters were factors in New York City into the 1930s in *Between Two Worlds*, a history of Yiddish cinema (New York: Museum of Modern Art and

Schocken, in press). See also Judith Mayne, "Immigrants and Spectators," *Wide Angle 5,* no. 2 (1982): 32–40 and Miriam Hansen, "Early Silent Cinema: Whose Public Sphere?" *New German Critique* 29 (Winter 1983): 147–84.

3. Robert Sklar, *Movie-Made America: A Cultural History of American Movies* (New York: Random House, 1975); Sklar, "Oh! Altusser!: Historiography and the Rise of Cinema Studies," *Radical History Review* 41 (1988): 11–35.

4. Rosenzweig, *Eight Hours for What We Will,* p. 228.

5. Russell Merritt, "Nickelodeon Theaters, 1905–1914; Building an Audience for the Movies," in *The American Film Industry,* 2d ed., ed. Tino Balio (1976, repr. Madison: University of Wisconsin Press, 1985), pp. 83–102; Robert C. Allen, "Motion Picture Exhibition in Manhattan, 1906–1912: Beyond the Nickelodeon," in *Film Before Griffith,* ed. John L. Fell (Berkeley: University of California Press, 1983), pp. 162–75; Noël Burch, "Porter or Ambivalence," *Screen* 19 (Winter 1978–79): 91–105; Tom Gunning, "Weaving a Narrative: Style and Economic Background in Griffith's Biograph Films," *Quarterly Review of Film Studies* (Winter 1981): 11–25.

6. Donald Bogle, *Toms, Coons, Mulattoes, Mammies, and Bucks: An Interpretative History of Blacks in American Film* (New York: Viking Press, 1973); Thomas Cripps, *Slow Fade to Black: The Negro in American Film, 1900–1942* (New York: Oxford University Press, 1977); Daniel J. Leab, *From Sambo to Superspade: The Black Experience in Motion Pictures* (Boston: Houghton Mifflin, 1975); John E. O'Conner, *The Hollywood Indian: Stereotypes of Native Americans in Film* (Trenton: New Jersey State Museum, 1980); Lester Friedman, *Hollywood's Image of the Jew* (New York: Frederick Unger Publishing, 1982); Patricia Erens, *The Jew in American Cinema* (Bloomington: Indiana University Press, 1984); and Sarah Blacher Cohen, ed., *From Hester Street to Hollywood: The Jewish American Stage and Screen* (Bloomington: Indiana University Press, 1986).

7. In cinema studies these include Robert Stam and Ella Shohat, "*Zelig* and Contemporary Theory: Meditation on the Chameleon Text," *Enclitic* 9, nos. 1–2 (1985); Ana Lopez, "Hollywood as Ethnographer," paper given at the American Studies Conference, Miami, November 1988; and other essays in this anthology.

8. *The Corbett-Fitzsimmons Fight,* intended for male devotees of manly blood sports, was seen by an unexpectedly large number of women who suddenly gained a degree of access to this formerly forbidden world. The bad-boy genre, intended for middle-class native-born men who might nostalgically recall their childhood, was viewed by working-class immigrant youths with the beginning of the nickelodeon era. In this new context, the genre suddenly seemed to turn theaters into schools for crime, Charles Musser, *The Emergence of Cinema: The American Screen to 1907* (New York: Scribner's, 1990). See also Miriam Hansen, *From Babel to Bablylon* (Cambridge: Harvard University Press, 1991).

9. Amusement entrepreneurs must acknowledge the beliefs and desires of their patrons, and often must actively seek to discover them. Although they can select and reshape these values, they cannot simply

impose their own ideological system. See, for example, Robert Snyder, *The Voice of the City* (New York: Oxford University Press, 1989).

10. For an eloquent and astutely argued evaluation of this literature see Hansen, *From Babel to Babylon.*

11. Sigmund Freud, *Jokes and Their Relation to the Unconscious* (London: Hogarth Press, 1960), p. 103.

12. Oscar Handlin, *The Uprooted: The Epic Story of the Great Migrations that Made the American People* (Boston: Little, Brown, 1951), p. 4. Handlin's emphasis on uprootedness and victimization have been tempered by more recent studies that find greater continuities in the move from Old World to New, such as John Bodner, *The Transplanted: A History of Immigrants in Urban America* (Bloomington: Indiana Press, 1985) and Peiss, *Cheap Amusements.*

13. I have purposefully avoided examining representations of non-European racial groups such as African-Americans and Asian-Americans. The unfavorable treatment of blacks may appear similar to the treatment of many European groups, just more extreme, but this qualitative difference was great enough in degree to become a difference in kind. With the barrier to acceptance for blacks and Asians much greater, these assimilationist comedies did not include them. Blacks and Asians were not, except in the most peripheral sense, consumers of popular amusements. They were usually not welcome in vaudeville houses and other theatrical venues catering to whites. In any case, films did not cater to these outcast groups; moreover African-Americans and Asians—unlike Jews, Italians, and the Irish—were effectively excluded from American film production in this period.

14. Both Erens (*The Jew in American Cinema*, p. 30) and Friedman (*Hollywood's Image of the Jew*, p. 21) find this film much more offensive than do I. It is not that their interpretation is "wrong," but that less negative readings are possible or even likely.

15. But neither is he really responsible for his misfortune.

16. *Film Index*, June 23, 1906, p. 9.

17. Ibid.

18. Henri Bergson, "Laughter," in *Comedy* (Baltimore: Johns Hopkins University Press, 1956).

19. Werner Sollors, *Beyond Ethnicity: Consent and Descent in American Culture* (New York: Oxford University Press, 1986), p. 199.

20. Albert F. McLean, Jr., *American Vaudeville as Ritual* (Lexington: University Press of Kentucky, 1965), p. 41.

21. Tom Gunning, presentation at the New York Public Library, 1989; see also Tom Gunning, *Outsiders as Insiders: Jews and the History of American Silent Film* (Waltham: National Center for Jewish Film, Brandeis University, n.d.).

22. McLean, *American Vaudeville as Ritual*, p. 121. This was particularly true at Keith's, the principal outlet for Biograph's film exhibitions.

23. Sklar, *Movie-made America*, p. 33.

24. The American Mutoscope & Biograph Company and American Vitagraph had New York roof-top studios in the late 1890s. Thomas Ed-

ison's Edison Manufacturing Company opened a new indoor film studio in what was then mid-town Manhattan (East 21st Street) in early 1901.

25. Joseph P. Eckhardt and Linda Kowall, *Peddler of Dreams: Siegmund Lubin and the Creation of the Motion Picture Industry, 1896–1916* (Philadelphia: National Museum of American Jewish History, 1984).

26. Although Lary May identifies Selig as a Protestant, his name is commonly Jewish, *Screening Out the Past: The Birth of Mass Culture and the Motion Picture Industry* (New York: Oxford University Press, 1980), p. 251. More research needs to be done on Selig before his background is clearly established.

27. Both anglicized their names when they joined Edison.

28. Miriam Rosen kindly brought Abadie's background to my attention.

29. Raymond DeFleur and Everette Dennis describe mass communication as "a process in which professional communicators use mechanical media to disseminate messages widely, rapidly and continuously to arouse intended meanings in large and diverse audiences in attempts to influence them in various ways," *Understanding Mass Communication* (Boston: Houghton Mifflin, 1981) p. 11. The introduction of a formal release system by the Association of Edison Licensees in the early part of 1908 completed this transformation which ultimately involved changes in methods of representation, film production, exhibition, reception, and distribution. Analyzing the complex interrelated process by which these changes occurred is essentially outside the scope of this study. See David Bordwell, Janet Staiger, and Kristin Thompson, *The Classical Hollywood Cinema: Film Style and Mode of Production* (New York: Columbia University Press, 1986); and Charles Musser, *Before the Nickelodeon: Edwin S. Porter and the Edison Manufacturing Company* (Berkeley: University of California Press, 1990).

30. *Moving Picture World*, May 18, 1907, p. 167.

31. Friedman, *Hollywood's Image of the Jew*, pp. 17–34; Erens, *The Jew in American Cinema*, pp. 33–107.

32. Higham, *Strangers in the Land*, pp. 158–74.

33. Sollors, *Beyond Ethnicity*, pp. 66–74.

34. Because ethnicity as such was downplayed, Chaplin could still appeal to nonimmigrant groups.

35. Sklar, *Movie-made America*, pp. 37–45; May, *Screening Out the Past*, pp. 167–75.

36. For ways in which this scene uses humor to assault the regimentation of the workplace that was part of most immigrants' experience see Charles Musser, "Work, Ideology and Chaplin's Tramp," in *Resisting Images: Radical Perspectives on Film History*, ed. Robert Sklar and Charles Musser (Philadelphia: Temple University Press, 1990).

37. Just as 249 foreigners had been expelled from the United States by the infamous Palmer raids in 1919; *The Idle Class* was the first film that Chaplin began after the Palmer raids (he had gone into production on his previous comedy, *The Kid*, in July 1919).

38. "Young Romance," *Moving Picture World*, February 6, 1915, p. 837.

39. Such unexpected endings seemingly function in ways quite similar to jokes, releasing psychic energy and giving access to the inaccessible.

40. Both names do, however, contain traces of ethnic ambiguity. *Taliaferro* perhaps has Sephardic Jewish origins and seems Italian to the uninitiated. There is a slight chance that Tom Forman could be Jewish. Edith Taliaferro was the sister of Mabel Taliaferro, also a popular leading actress of the period, "The Taliaferros—Sisters and Co-Stars," *Theater*, February 1914, p. 70.

41. See Judith Mayne, "Uncovering the Female Body," pp. 63–67 in *Before Hollywood: Turn of the Century Films from American Archives*, ed. Jay Leyda and Charles Musser (New York: American Federation for the Arts, 1986) for an analysis of this film in terms of gender.

42. " 'Abie's Irish Rose' Opens," *New York Sun*, May 24, 1922, p. 16. Both Friedman and Erens provide the incorrect date of 1924 for the play, which ran for almost six years. In *Strangers in the Land* (pp. 309–16) John Higham points to anti-Semitic claims that the country was being invaded by "unassimilable Jews" as one of the arguments for the law—an accusation which the play clearly challenges.

43. "Adieu by 'Abie's Irish Rose,' " *New York Times*, October 23, 1927, p. 30; "Irish Rose Film Sets Sales Record," *New York Times*, February 27, 1927, p. 30. Anne Nichols was in Los Angeles working on the film adaptation when the play closed. By that date it was claimed that, including road companies and foreign productions, there had been 17,600 performances seen by an estimated eleven million theatergoers. J. Brooks Atkinson, "Obituary," *New York Times*, October 23, 1927, p. 1H. This included runs of fifty-seven weeks in Chicago, twenty-nine weeks in Pittsburgh, twenty-eight weeks in Detroit, and twenty-eight weeks in Cleveland, *Variety*, December 30, 1925, p. 219.

44. "The New Photoplay," *New York Sun*, April 20, 1928, p. 19.

45. " 'Abie's Irish Rose' on Screen Eclipses Record Stage Play," *New York Herald Tribune*, April 20, 1928, p. 14.

46. In *America's Jews* (New York: Random House, 1971) Marshall Sklare suggests that rate of intermarriage between Jews and gentiles remained low in the 1920s, well under 5 percent (pp. 180–209). Between 1908 and 1912, the rate of intermarriage in New York City was just over 1 percent.

47. Mark Winokur, "Improbable Ethnic Hero: William Powell and the Transformation of Ethnic Hollywood," *Cinema Journal* 27 (Fall 1987): 5–22. The emphasis on eccentricities and virtual elimination of ethnic stereotyping is characteristic of Mack Sennett's Keystone comedies, which featured such stars as Slim Summerville, Chester Conklin, Mack "Ambrose" Swain, Ben Turpin, and Arbuckle.

48. Snyder, *The Voice of the City*.

49. Most films dealing with this sensitive subject either were adapted from stage hits or were quickie spin-offs. Thus *Abie's Irish Rose* spawned many film imitations long before it reached the screen under its own name.

50. After only three years of its Broadway run, *Abie's Irish Rose* returned an estimated $5 million to the producer (*New York Times*, May 25, 1924, p. 4). This convinced film industry executives that the subject was likely to make money and pre-testing the market had reduced the dangers of offending large groups of people. Although many critics had attacked *Abie's Irish Rose* viciously when it first appeared on the stage, by 1928 it was accepted as a "classic."

51. Wes D. Gehring, *The Marx Brothers: A Bio-Bibliography* (New York: Greenwood Press, 1987), p. 26.

52. "The Play," *New York Times*, October 24, 1928, p. 26.

53. "Ziegfeld Makes 'Whoopee'," *New York Sun*, December 5, 1928, p. 28.

54. For example, *New York Times*, August 29, 1930, p. 20, October 1, 1930, p. 26.

55. Higham, *Strangers in the Land*, p. 164. That Indians were seen by Mormons, if no one else, as the lost tribe of Israel is just another bizarre intersection.

56. Sollors, *Beyond Ethnicity*, p. 121.

57. Ibid., p. 141–42.

58. Many of these ethnic amalgamations have been enumerated by Henry Jenkins III in " 'Shall We Make It for New York or for Distribution?': Eddie Cantor, *Whoopee*, and Regional Resistance to the Talkies," *Cinema Journal* 29 (Spring 1990): 32–52.

59. Jenkins, " 'Shall We Make It for New York?' "

60. Erens, *The Jew in American Cinema*, p. 133; Friedman (*Hollywood's Image of the Jew*), although not unsympathetic to this viewpoint, briefly surveys other assessments (pp. 65–66); Gerald Weales, who sees *Animal Crackers* as a satire on fashionable celebrities, also misses this crucial point, *Canned Goods as Caviar: American Film Comedies of the 1930s* (Chicago: University of Chicago Press, 1985), p. 79. See also Patricia Mellencamp, "Jokes and Their Relation to the Marx Brothers," in *Cinema and Language*, ed. Stephen Heath and Patricia Mellencamp (New York: American Film Institute, 1983), pp. 63–78.

61. Higham, *Strangers in the Land*, pp. 277–86.

62. Abie was played by a WASP in both the New York play and Hollywood film version of *Abie's Irish Rose*, while the situation was reversed with *Whoopee*, as Williams is played by a Jewish comedian.

63. In all sorts of ways, therefore, violence and seduction, attraction and hatred, death and sex play off each other, with racial difference being the common thread.

64. Michael Rogin, "The Sword Becomes a Flashing Vision," *Representations* 9 (Winter 1985): 150–95.

65. Stam and Shohat, "*Zelig* and Contemporary Theory."

66. This invasion has a self-reflexive quality in that the New York theater had been overrun by a new generation of Jewish patrons, performers, and entrepreneurs.

67. This is not always true; for example, in *Horsefeathers*, all the brothers are attracted to and try to seduce the "college widow" (Thelma Todd).

68. In an intersection that speaks more to continuities in Jewish humor than to specific influences, Groucho/Spaulding is highly reminiscent of the character created by Israel Zangwill in *The King of the Schnorrers* (London: Macmillan, 1893).

69. Harpo Marx with Rowland Barber, *Harpo Speaks!* (New York: Limelight Editions, 1985), p. 31.

70. *Animal Crackers* may also be the ultimate comic deflation of the art world, then still a protected sphere of elitist, nonimmigrant culture (the Beaugard painting renders a scene after a fox hunt). From a parody of Eugene O'Neill's *Strange Interlude* to a weighty if nonsensical discussion on art by Chandler and Spaulding, elitist culture is mocked. Ravel, Ravelli, Ravioli: these different levels of artistry have their counterparts in the different versions of the painting "After the Hunt." The original Beaugard is put on display but is replaced by a meticulous copy by Parker and then a bad imitation by Grace Whitehead, a jealous rival of Mrs. Rittenhouse. In fact the original and Parker's copy are virtually indistinguishable, making us ultimately question the authenticity of Chandler's canvas. And if he really could afford to spend $100,000 on the painting, why would he be anxious to marry Mrs. Rittenhouse and her money? For Harpo (the Professor), who rejects both language and representation, the paintings serve as a blanket and pillow for a night's sleep. Typically, Harpo signs his name with an *X* in *Horsefeathers* (1932)—not simply as the signature of someone who can't write, but as a negation of what is written.

71. The best book-length interpretation of the Marx Brothers' humor is still Freud's *Jokes and Their Relation to the Unconscious*, a conjunction made clear in Woody Allen's opening monologue in *Annie Hall* (1977).

72. A reading I believe I made when first seeing this film as a youth.

73. Jenkins, " 'Shall We Make It for New York?' "

74. For an effort to relate *Duck Soup* to immigrant roots see Mark Winokur, " 'Smile, Stranger': Aspects of Immigrant Humor in the Marx Brothers' Humor," *Literature/Film Quarterly* 13, no. 3 (1985): 161–71.

75. Nathan Glazer, *Ethnic Dilemmas 1964–1982* (Cambridge: Harvard University Press, 1983).

76. Thus, Friedman argues that the breakdown of the interethnic relationship between Alvy Singer and Annie Hall in *Annie Hall* demonstrates that it was "doomed to failure because of their cultural and emotional differences" (*Hollywood's Image of the Jew*, p. 280). That the two actors in this role (Woody Allen and Diane Keaton) were an item off screen and that Allen is now married to and shares parental responsibilities with shiksa Mia Farrow would, however, appear to challenge such a reading. Erens offers a somewhat more sophisticated reading, but one that cannot contemplate the possibility of progeny for binary opposition would give way to a dialectics of reproduction—children.

77. Neal Gabler has almost completely repressed the presence of gentile groups except when anti-Semitic activity is the issue, *An Empire of Their Own: How the Jews Invented Hollywood* (New York: Crown Publishers, 1988).

78. Nathan Glazer and Patrick P. Moynihan, *Beyond the Melting Pot: The Negroes, Puerto Ricans, Jews, Italians and Irish of New York City*, 2d ed. (Cambridge, Mass: MIT Press, 1970.

79. The America-as-a-salad bowl metaphor only works as an image out of time. The lettuce is picked and will wilt. Will not the salad become a compost heap—from which something new will grow? Which perhaps only shows how organic metaphors can become overextended.

80. "In Dual-Faith Families Children Struggle for a Spiritual Home," *New York Times*, August 18, 1988, p. C1.

81. Sollors, *Beyond Ethnicity*, p. 199.

Ian C. Jarvie **3**

Stars and Ethnicity: Hollywood and the United States, 1932–51

> We shall call "ethnic groups" those human groups that entertain a subjective belief in their common descent because of similarities of physical type or of customs or both, or because of memories of colonization and migration; this belief must be important for the propagation of group formation; conversely, it does not matter whether or not an objective blood relationship exists.[1]

How representative were Hollywood stars of the ethnicity of the nation as a whole? It is often presumed that they were not. They certainly did not represent the 10 percent or so of the nation who were black. As far as the other ethnic identities within the nation are concerned, the data are difficult to interpret and easy to exaggerate.

Before presenting data and analysis, preliminary questions of selection and reliability must be addressed. First, there are problems concerning how to use the concepts of stars and ethnicity.

Stars

Who should be classified as a star is far from clear. Consider some criteria of that status such as an icon on a dressing room door. This is a contractual matter between actor and studio; like other contractual matters, for example, a name above the title, were it to be used as a criterion of stardom the result would be to inflate the numbers of stars greatly by the addition of now-unrecognizable names.[2] As an alternative, if the contractual matter of salary were used as a criterion of stardom, that would have the additional shortcoming of making the population of stardom subject to all the unreliability of Hollywood bookkeeping and rumors, as well as excluding big stars in their early and lower-paid years.

If contracts do not provide satisfactory criteria of stardom, what about public acceptance? Sampling public opinion by such means as questionnaires, or the existence and size of fan clubs, would make stardom a simple function of public opinion. Although in the last analysis the public decides whether or not someone is a star, that decision is made at the box office, and its results may not agree with what is said to the researcher. Another route to public opinion is the press. But to accept as a star everyone whom the press names as such is to give undue weight to the views of a small group of journalists. No doubt they try to fathom whom the public has made a star, but tendencies to hyperbole and exaggeration, not to mention optimism and even payola, scarcely make the press a reliable guide. The box office, then, appears to be the best guide.

In addition to the difficulty of deciding whom to classify as a star, questions arise of which stars to study and by what criteria such a selection is to be made. Many writers on stars simply select those who happen to interest them; just as unsatisfactory is to select past stars who are presently remembered and revered. Neither approach generates a representative group, and only a representative group will sustain generalizations about the ethnicity of stars and the latent content of what the star system projected. However, box-office attractions do constitute the sort of representative group necessary.

Ethnicity

Confusion about ethnicity is greater than that over stars. The long history of our ways of categorizing fellow humans—into barbarian and civilized, into races, by cultures—is a melancholy one, for the categories were usually normative. That there has of late been a strong reaction against the judgmental use of ethnic categories is manifest in the current United States census form on which ethnicity is ascribed by self-description—no set of categories being suggested to help or direct the answer. From a social science point of view, this is a very untidy practice. Ethnic self-identity claims employ diverse criteria: general appearance (WASP), surname (Hispanic), religion (Jewish), skin color (black), nationality (Italian-American), hemisphere (Oriental), and language (Creole). Because all categories can be permutated with hyphens, the possibilities are endless.

The census form makes ethnicity subjective. Another approach—which we can call "objective"—is possible. This begins from the idea that ethnicity designates concrete groups with restricted membership and mappable boundaries. Max Weber, the classical authority on the subject, warned, however, that ethnicity disappears during any attempt to define it too closely.[3] Furthermore, he thought the phenomena which were interesting were a political creation of the larger group. Ethnicity was a property of minority groups. Since his time the view has emerged that we are all ethnics. It follows that even the majority group—in this case called WASPs—is an ethnic group. In the period chosen, with few exceptions, stars belonged to the majority WASP group—in fact, in persona, and in screen roles.

In combination the two troublesome notions of stars *and* ethnicity present a number of further difficulties. The stars' ethnic self-description, that is, how they would have described themselves on their census forms, is unavailable. Their public was not surveyed systematically about how they would ethnically classify this or that star. As if these difficulties were not enough, a threefold ambiguity of reference exists. Stars and public might both respond differently depending on whether the question of ethnicity referred to the ethnicity of the *actor* who signs the contract (ethnicity 1 "real"); the ethnicity of the *star* embodied in that actor (ethnicity 2 perceived); or the ethnicity of the *roles* that star played on the screen (ethnicity 3 on screen).

For example, the Austrian-American actor Paul Muni (Muni Weisenfreund) played Italian, Oriental, Mexican, French, and many other roles.[4] Did he have any determinate ethnicity (ethnicity 1) for the public? Did he try to project an ethnicity of his own? He seldom played a Jew, although he might have classified himself as one on the census form. Did his star persona (ethnicity 2) take on the ethnicity of his roles (ethnicity 3), his (real life?) Jewishness, both, or neither? Was he perhaps taken by the public to be ethnically WASP but capable of making himself up as exotics? The case is undecidable for lack of information. It is not crucial because I have cheated: Muni does not make the list created by the box office criteria used herein.

Other out-of-bounds examples would be Mickey Mouse and Donald Duck, as well as Snow White and the Seven Dwarfs. The ethnic classification of the first two presents grave problems, although they seem to me to be WASP.[5] Some books claim these two cartoon characters were "stars," and that Snow White "starred" in one of the most popular films of the year. Be that as it may, their absence from the lists compiled by using my chosen indicators simplifies the matter.

With the foregoing difficulties in mind, my procedure was as follows. Without solving once and for all the problem of who is and who is not a star, assume there were stars. Within the group of those who were stars, focus on the big box-office attractions. To decide their ethnicity, I became the census respondent on their behalf, checking my attributions by running the same stars by an ethnic cross-section of my students (self-identified). In effect there were three census forms to be completed for each person: one for the actor (ethnicity 1), one for the star who is the actor's doppelganger (ethnicity 2), and one for the roles with which the star is associated (ethnicity 3). While I identified the ethnicity of the actor behind the roles (ethnicity 1), this was primarily for background information. What interested me most were the ethnic identification of the off-screen star persona (ethnicity 2) and the ethnic content of the roles themselves (ethnicity 3).

How, exactly, to choose a representative sample of box-office stars? My special interest is Hollywood in its golden age, when its products predominated on world screens.[6] That period ended early in the 1950s with the rapid shrinkage of the American film industry. Sound films are more tractable than silent because more are readily accessible. This focuses a twenty-year period, from 1930 to 1950, and it so happens that a useful reference book provides data from 1932 on.[7] These data are the exhibitors' reports on the ten top-drawing stars of each year, compiled for Quigley publications *Motion Picture Herald*, *Motion Picture Daily*, and *Motion Picture Almanac*. Subject to the same lack of precision as all Hollywood data, these were, however, used to make industry decisions. Fifty-six names appear from 1932–51 (table 3.1). All of the films that these stars made while on the list have been researched and listed in an endeavor to identify the ethnic profile drawn by those roles.

The first glance over table 3.1 creates a few surprises. Names virtually never mentioned by present-day experts on the stars—such as Abbott and Costello (fig. 3.1) and Sonja Henie—feature prominently. Males outnumber females in all but four years.[8] Apart from the child stars, entrants are usually of quite mature age on first appearance in the list. (Because one or two birth dates are in dispute, figures are rough.) The mean age at entry for males is around thirty-six, with a standard deviation of 8+. The mean age at entry for females is 28.5, but if we eliminate the two children, Temple and

Table 3.1. Top Box Office Stars 1932–51

Star Name	Real or Given Name	Age of Entry to List	Where Born	Ethnicity 1 "Real"	Ethnicity 2 Perceived	Ethnicity 3 on Screen	Years on List
Abbott, Bud	William Abbott	46	U.S.A.	WASP	Same	Same	7
Astaire, Fred	Austerlitz, Frederick	36	U.S.A.	WASP	Same	Same	3
Autry, Gene	Same	33	U.S.A.	WASP	Same	Same	2
Beery, Wallace	Same	46/51*	U.S.A.	Irish?	Same	WASP?	5
Bergman, Ingrid	Same	31	Sweden	WASP	Same	Same	3
Bogart, Humphrey	Same	44	U.S.A.	WASP	Same	Same	7
Brown, Joe E.	Same	43	U.S.A.	WASP	Same	Same	3
Cagney, James	Same	36	U.S.A.	Irish	Same	Same	6
Cantor, Eddie	Iskowitz, Edward Israel	41	U.S.A.	Jewish	Same	Same	1
Colbert, Claudette	Chauchoin, Lily Claudette	30	France	French	WASP	Same	3
Cooper, Gary	Cooper, Frank J.	35	U.S.A.	WASP[+]	Same	Same	12
Costello, Lou	Cristillo, Louis	35	U.S.A.	Hispanic	Italian	Same	7
Crawford, Joan	Le Seuer, Lucille	29	U.S.A.	WASP	Same	Same	5
Crosby, Bing	Crosby, Harry Lillis	33	U.S.A.	Irish	Same	Same	12
Davis, Bette	Davis, Ruth Elizabeth	31	U.S.A.	WASP	Same	Same	4
Day, Doris	Kappelhoff, Doris	27	U.S.A.	WASP	Same	Same	1
Dressler, Marie	Koerber, Lila Von	63	Canada	WASP?	Same	Same	3
Farrell, Charles	Same	31	U.S.A.	WASP	WASP	WASP	1

Table 3.1. Top Box Office Stars 1932–51

Star Name	Real or Given Name	Age of Entry to List	Where Born	Ethnicity 1 "Real"	Ethnicity 2 Perceived	Ethnicity 3 on Screen	Years on List
Faye, Alice	Leppert, Ann	26	U.S.A.	WASP	Same	Same	2
Flynn, Errol	Same	30	Australia	WASP	Same	Same	1
Gable, Clark	Same	34	U.S.A.	WASP	Same	Same	15
Garbo, Greta	Gustafson, Greta	27	Sweden	WASP	WASP	WASP	1
Garson, Greer	Same	34	U.K.	WASP	Same	Same	5
Gaynor, Janet	Gainer, Laura	26	U.S.A.	WASP	Same	Same	3
Grable, Betty	Same	26	U.S.A.	WASP	Same	Same	10
Grant, Cary	Leach, Archibald	40	U.K.	WASP	Same	Same	3
Harlow, Jean	Carpentier, Harlean	22	U.S.A.	WASP	Same	Same	1
Henie, Sonja	Same	27	Norway	WASP	Same	Same	3
Hope, Bob	Hope, Leslie Townes	38	U.K.	WASP	Same	Same	11
Johnson, Van	Johnson, Charles Van	29	U.S.A.	WASP	Same	Same	2
Ladd, Alan	Same	31	U.S.A.	WASP	Same	Same	1
Lewis, Jerry	Levitch, Joseph	25	U.S.A.	Jewish	?‡	WASP	1
Loy, Myrna	Williams, Myrna	32	U.S.A.	WASP	Same	Same	2
MacDonald, Jeanette	Same	33/34	U.S.A.	WASP	Same	Same	1
Martin, Dean	Corcetti, Dino	34	U.S.A.	Italian	Same	Same	1
O'Brien, Margaret	O'Brien, Angela Maxine	8	U.S.A.	Irish	WASP	WASP	2

Table 3.1. Top Box Office Stars 1932–51

Star Name	Real or Given Name	Age of Entry to List	Where Born	Ethnicity 1 "Real"	Ethnicity 2 Perceived	Ethnicity 3 on Screen	Years on List
Peck, Gregory	Same	31	U.S.A.	WASP	Same	Same	1
Powell, Dick	Same	31	U.S.A.	WASP	Same	Same	2
Powell, William	Same	45	U.S.A.	WASP	Same	Same	1
Power, Tyrone	Same	25	U.S.A.	WASP	Same	Same	3
Rogers, Ginger	McMath, Virginia	24	U.S.A.	WASP	Same	Same	3
Rogers, Roy	Slye, Leonard	33	U.S.A.	WASP	Same	Same	2
Rogers, Will	Same	56	U.S.A.	WASP	Same	Same	4
Rooney, Mickey	Yule, Joe, Jr.	18	U.S.A.	Irish	Same	Same	4
Scott, Randolph	Crane, Randolph	47/52*	U.S.A.	WASP	Same	Same	2
Shearer, Norma	Same	32	Canada	WASP	Same	Same	3
Stewart, James	Same	42	U.S.A.	WASP	Same	Same	1
Taylor, Robert	Brugh, Spangler Arlington	25	U.S.A.	WASP	Same	Same	3
Temple, Shirley	Same	6	U.S.A.	WASP	Same	Same	6
Tracy, Spencer	Same	38	U.S.A.	Irish	WASP	WASP(?)	10
Wayne, John	Morrison, Marion Michael	47	U.S.A.	Irish	WASP	WASP(?)	3
Webb, Clifton	Hollenbeck, Webb Parmelee	57	U.S.A.	WASP	Same	Same	1
West, Mae	Same	41	U.S.A.	WASP	Same	Same	2
Williams, Esther	Same	26	U.S.A.	WASP	Same	Same	2

Table 3.1. Top Box Office Stars 1932–51

Star Name	Real or Given Name	Age of Entry to List	Where Born	Ethnicity 1 "Real"	Ethnicity 2 Perceived	Ethnicity 3 on Screen	Years on List
Withers, Jane	Same	11	U.S.A.	WASP	Same	Same	2

Sources: Cobbett Steinberg, *Reel Facts* (New York: Vintage Books, 1981); numerous reference books.

*The reference books give differing dates of birth.

†Cooper, like a number of others I have classified as WASP, was Roman Catholic. Some stars, especially Irish and Italian, emphasized their religion as part of their persona.

‡It is unclear whether in his Martin and Lewis days Lewis was recognizably Jewish to the audience.

Withers, and the far from anile Marie Dressler, the mean rises to thirty-three, with a standard deviation of 10+. Public perception is invalid that stars of either sex "made it" very young; many worked primarily in light entertainment with no pretensions to be anything more. Were I more attentive to current critical practice I should also discuss those names not present in the list: the "presence" of significant absences.[9]

It is assumed that readers will know what the listed stars look like. That information, plus their stage name and a general feel for the star persona is all we have to start with; we cannot be familiar with every single film each of these stars made in the twenty-year period. Nevertheless, reviews, stills, and biographies can supplement film libraries, VCR tapes, and memory. On that basis we can proceed to ethnic matters by looking at the evidence of names (s 1), accents (s 2), appearance (s 3), roles and reality (s 4), and their relation to the dream of America (s 5).

Names as Ethnic Signifiers

First, contrary to popular opinion, the WASPishness of the stars was not a disguise. Of the fifty-six star names, forty-four (or possibly forty-five if Marie Dressler is included) were unequivocally WASP (or Roman Catholic) by stage name and real name; seven more were Irish by name; two Italian by stage name (Costello and Martin); Cantor was Jewish by stage name and Lewis, who was Jewish, had a stage name that was not manifestly Jewish. A great many of the

3.1. William (Bud) Abbott (left) the straight man and Louis (Lou) Cristillo (Costello) in a studio portrait that reverses their usual expressions.

stars used their "real" names, or a very close variant thereof, for example, "Gary" instead of Frank J. Cooper. There seems to have been an esthetics of names—"Roy Rogers" rather than Leonard Slye; "Cary Grant" rather than Archibald Leach—that was separate from ethnic disguise because the alteration does not shift the star to another ethnic group. In some cases the surname is a help to the actor's ethnic assignment; especially in black and white movies, nothing in appearance distinguishes, for example, an Irish actor from a WASP.

Lou Costello (Louis Cristillo) may be Italian-American or Hispanic (ethnicity 1), he surely is white, but not likely Anglo-Saxon Protestant. The same goes for Eddie Cantor (Edward Israel Iskowitz, fig. 3.2), who seems to have settled for a stage name more euphonious to the English-speaking audience but still undisguisedly Jewish (ethnicity 1 = ethnicity 2). Beery, Cagney, Crosby, O'Brien, Rooney, and Tracy are all, it seems to me, unmistakably Irish surnames, and those of Catholic Ireland at that. "John Wayne" is not an Irish name, yet its possessor was aggressive in affirming off-screen loyalty to that ancestral connection.

3.2. Edward Israel Iskowitz's stage name (Eddie Cantor) did not conceal his Jewishness, although this was seldom used in his film roles, as witness this publicity image from *40 Little Mothers* (1940).

A fascinating case is that of Tyrone Power (his real name). Both Christian name and surname smack of Eire, the former more than the latter. Undoubtedly much of Power's appeal came from his very handsome face. Whether his Irish descent (ethnicity 1) was apparent to the movie fans who had not read his biography is hard to tell. Usually Power played WASP heroes with appropriate names (ethnicity 3), but he was also one of the handful of top stars who tackled roles which involved a shift of ethnicity (ethnicity 1 and 2 = ethnicity 3). He played Frenchmen twice in 1938 (*Marie Antionette* and *Suez*), a turbaned East Indian in *The Rains Came* (1939), and Hispanics in *The Mark of Zorro* (1940) and *Blood and Sand* (1941). He was not named to the top ten after 1940, and he did not play Latins or exotics at all after that. Whether there is a causal connection and which way it flowed is thus moot.

In addition to euphony, there seem to have been a number of other "esthetic" criteria at work in the choice of names: avoidance of the ordinary and avoidance of the fancy, for example. Myrna Williams became Myrna Loy, Harry Lillis Crosby became Bing

Crosby, and Ruth Davis became Bette Davis,—all cases of lessening the ordinary. Meanwhile, Spangler Arlington Brugh became Robert Taylor, Lucille Le Seuer became Joan Crawford, Harlean Carpentier became Jean Harlow, and Webb Parmelee Hollenbeck became Clifton Webb—all cases of lessening the fancy. However these re-namings came about, they reveal an interesting tendency akin to reversion toward the mean. If the mean is WASP for ethnicity 1 and 2 and the names that go with it, there seems to be a middle ground between ordinariness and uniqueness toward which the name altering tends.

German-American ethnicity was clearly avoided in names: Frederick Austerlitz became Fred Astaire, Doris Kappelhoff became Doris Day, Lila Von Koerber became Marie Dressler, and Charles Van Johnson, presumably Dutch, became Van Johnson. Such disguise needs little explanation beyond noting the vitriolic anti-German sentiments associated with the World War I and revived by World War II.

Also to be avoided were names that are also ordinary words or their homonyms: hence Rogers not Slye, Rooney not Yule, Scott not Crane, and Gaynor not Gainer. No rule is without its exceptions, so, although Leach had to go, its replacement, Grant, is a word, and Gumm was replaced by Garland; no change occurred in Hope or in West.

What can we learn from these name changes? It cannot be concluded that there was consistent concealment of ethnicity by name change among this group of top box-office stars. There was a good deal of name changing, it is true, but for different purposes. Here the limitations of the sample population are evident. No doubt a good many actors and actresses with non-WASP names changed them for that reason alone, a practice that contrasts with present custom, when such names as Mandy Patinkin and Meryl Streep are retained. The selected group showed more complexity; clearly one result of "we are all ethnics now" is that names which proclaim ethnicity are retained.

The third category is composed of names as indicators of role ethnicity. I have noted how Tyrone Power played a number of roles wherein the character's Hispanic surname immediately indicated that he was supposed to be neither WASP nor Irish-American, Power's two possible ethnic identities as actor and star. The three Scandinavians in the list—Bergman, Garbo,[10] and Henie—invariably played characters whose name designated them as foreign, obviating explanation of their retained accents. In compiling table 3.2, I have included the films of the year before the star entered the top-

Table 3.2. Scandinavians as Generically "Foreign"

Film	Character's Name	Character's Nationality
GRETA GARBO		
Inspiration, 1931	Yvonne	French
Susan Lennox, Her Fall and Rise, 1931	Susan Lennox	U.S.
Mata Hari, 1931	Mata Hari	Dutch
Grand Hotel, 1932	Grusinskaya	Russian
As You Desire Me, 1932	Maria (Zara)	Italian
SONJA HENIE		
One in a Million, 1936	Greta Muller	Swiss
Thin Ice, 1937	Lili Heiser	Swiss
Happy Landing, 1938	Trudy Erickson	Norwegian
My Lucky Star, 1938	Kristina Nielson	Norwegian
Second Fiddle, 1939	Trudy Hovland	U.S.
Everything Happens at Night, 1939	Louise	Swiss
INGRID BERGMAN		
Notorious, 1946	Alicia Huberman	German
Arch of Triumph, 1948	Joan Madou	French
Joan of Arc, 1948	Jeanne D'Arc	French

ten box-office attractions list, assuming that they contributed to the achievement.) With the exception of "Susan Lennox," the character names are to be taken as "foreign"—but French, German, and Russian as easily as Scandinavian.

Accents as Ethnic Signifiers

The three Scandinavian stars mentioned previously retained traces of their "foreign" accent even after long residence in Hollywood. It was hard to put them into sound films playing native-born Americans. Their accents were seldom used to designate Scandinavian origin specifically; Bergman and Garbo often played Germans, and sometimes Russians. The same was true of foreign-born stars who did not meet our box-office criteria, for example, Marlene Dietrich, Charles Boyer, Conrad Veidt, Paul Henried, and Louis Jourdan.

Yet there was no consistent policy. Particularly puzzling was the treatment of actors with British accents. Cary Grant and Greer Garson were British-born and so spoken, yet little or no effort was made to limit the parts they played. Some claim that Grant developed a transatlantic accent, but I am skeptical; his accent remained

English, just as Clifton Webb's, however clipped, remained American. The differences were, however, very subtle and the attribution of transatlantic character clearly an effort to explain the combination of ready comprehensibility and hard-to-place. One reason sometimes given in this period for not distributing British films more widely in the United States was that they needed subtitling in certain regions. The evidence of the use of accents in Hollywood tells against such an excuse. To my ears, Errol Flynn never lost his Australian twang, yet time and again he was cast as an American and no explanation was offered of his way of speaking. He is only a single name on the list, but there were other imports not on the list, such as Leslie Howard and David Niven, whose accents similarly were unexplained and unsubtitled.

An incidental point made by other commentators is that sound filmmakers sought players with an enunciation comprehensible to the broadest numbers of people—hence extremely marked accents, such as Boston, Brooklyn, or Deep South were seldom heard from the big stars when the role they played had no regional specificity. Clark Gable made no effort to sound particularly "Southern" in *Gone With the Wind*, and neither did Leslie Howard. Vivien Leigh made an attempt at it, and again in *A Streetcar Named Desire*, in which latter she was not followed by Marlon Brando or Kim Hunter.

As with surnames, accents are not especially good or specific indicators of ethnicity, and they muddle actor, star, and role. Furthermore, because accents are rather bland among most of the stars on the list, tending in most cases toward the Midwest-California speech that has emerged as American Standard, they can now be set aside.

Appearance and Ethnicity

Before we know a person's name, before we hear them speak, they present an appearance to us. Appearance is a marker of limited use to this discussion. When ethnicity centered around "color," appearances were paramount; blacks, Indians, and Orientals were largely identified by their looks ("visible minorities," fig. 3.3). An immediate result of the claim that we are all ethnics now is to displace color as a primary ethnic signifier. Indeed, the bulk of ethnic groupings are to be found within the "white" category. Superstition to the contrary, there is no way of identifying Irish, Italians, Jews, and Scandinavians by appearances. Furthermore, it is rightly thought to be offensive to make any such claim. Without exception,

3.3. A typically unconvincing and no longer funny moment from an Abbott and Costello film, *Pardon My Sarong* (1942). The menacing tribesmen, all white men in blackface, represent typical Hollywood portrayals of "natives" in comedies and adventures, images that now offend ethnic sensibilities.

all of the stars on the list are "white" in appearance, especially insofar as the bulk of their films were in black and white, and the combination of that medium and their make-up would ensure that such subtleties as "swarthiness" would be ironed out. In this period there were leading actors who had an ethnically identifiable appearance, but none has entered the selection. In the 1920s, Sessue Hayakawa was a star, one whose appearance and name clearly identified him as Japanese; the same holds true for Anna May Wong as Chinese in the 1930s. And, of course, only a handful of black actors had recognizable names, and perhaps only Paul Robeson and Lena Horne approached star status.[11]

Ethnic Profiles

In table 3.1, and in the preceding text, a distinction has been made concerning the ethnicity of the actor (ethnicity 1), the ethnic ity of the star's persona (ethnicity 2), and the ethnicity of the screen roles (ethnicity 3). Emerging profiles can be examined under these three headings.

The Actor's Ethnicity

Overwhelmingly, actors and actresses are white, Christian, European, native English-speakers, American-born, and highly assimilated. This last feature is important. Even in cases in which actors had a different ethnic trace, it was not emphasized. These were Hollywood actors, not in Yiddish theater or some other ethnic preserve. The choice to pursue success in Hollywood ensured that, as actors, the roles they would be called upon to play, the sorts of off-screen lives they could pursue, would be those possible in the very strange new community that the movie industry was forming on the West Coast. Although odd in the way of other one-industry towns,[12] Hollywood was in fact tolerant of a good deal of the traditional ethnic diversity that was supposed to be dissolved in the melting pot. Religious practice off-screen, for example, might continue regardless of whether it conformed to some WASP norm. Assimilation was also taking place in another domain, the work that actors were able to do. Hollywood participated in the process of assimilating Americans of diverse origin, not by enforcing Norman Rockwell life-styles at home but rather by projecting and promoting a picture of American culture and society more homogenized than true. I would, however, reject Winokur's view that the transformation of William Powell from ethnic roles to romantic hero "reflects the engineered, mechanized transformation of an actor's character actor status to star and leading man status. It is the local version of a fantasy life that film moguls at Paramount and MGM participated in at wider levels when they created out of the Southern California farms and wilderness a version of a city that they controlled and in which they could then feel at home in as founding fathers and natives. They created from the material of the villain, the ethnic, and the revolutionary a romantic protagonist."[13]

Other demographic features of the list pertain to the male-female ratio, longevity, and age. As was noted previously, most of the stars listed were male. Males also stayed on the lists longer. John Wayne held the record, with twenty-five years, but most of his reigning years fall outside the period under discussion. In the present list the leaders were Clark Gable, fifteen years; Gary Cooper and Bing Crosby, twelve years each; Bob Hope, eleven years; and Spencer Tracy, ten years. The leading woman, Betty Grable (fig. 3.4), also lead ten years on the list.

3.4. Her bleached or "strawberry" blonde hair and fair skin make Betty Grable almost a caricature of the peaches-and-cream, allegedly nonethnic ideal. She was a major box-office attraction at Twentieth Century-Fox for nearly twenty years.

With the exception of the child stars, actors and actresses were of mature age by the time they were declared top box-office attractions. This is rather different from the situation in the silent period, when actresses especially were extremely young, and in the period subsequent to 1951, when the phenomenon of the teen-age star became more common. Although the stars invariably played roles that were younger than their chronological ages, their true age and experience enabled them to play their young parts with a maturity and confidence that assisted in fulfillment of the audience's fantasy. The characters might be young, but they operated in the world with a confidence that many viewers wished they had—or had at that age. This connects negatively to ethnicity: individual qualities, not cultural and ethnic background, accounted for who the actor was.

The Ethnicity of the Star Personae

Actors were carriers of something extra, a particular social status we call the "movie star." One way to model this is to think of the star persona as a doppelganger, a shadow self that is always present but not in all respects identical to the actor and hence not the same person as the actor. Another way to think of it is as a living mask that can be taken to be a person, although it in fact conceals another person beneath. The mask analogy is misleading only in that it tempts us to think of the person wearing the mask as real and the mask as appearance. When our topic is stars, the reverse is the case.

A star persona is, sociologically, a real thing.[14] It is a persona as distinct from the roles played as is the actor playing the roles. A star was a persona created, with or without the cooperation of the actor concerned, by the publicity machine of the studio collaborating with the press, other media such as radio, fan clubs, and word of mouth.[15] A crucial instrument was the studio biography of the star in which fact and fiction were mixed into a factoid, perhaps hinting at lowly ethnic origins, or at lofty ones, or at ordinariness, in a manner calculated to match what were thought to be the lines of appeal and enigma that suited the looks, the publicity campaign, the activities, and perhaps, the roles, the star played or was to play.[16]

In an important theoretical discussion of the content of television, Sari Thomas has argued that such material was designed to send the specific message that although there was room at the top, life there was difficult.[17] It could also be said that the star system in general sent those messages. The promise of stardom to white ethnics was that they too could choose to escape the constraints of ethnicity without giving it up in real life by aspiring to become a star. However, the price could be high if there was a tension: the possibility of confusing the off-screen self (ethnicity 1) with the star persona (ethnicity 2) in cases in which these were different.

The Ethnicity of the Role

Unsurprisingly, and in agreement with the charge of stereotyping so often leveled at Hollywood, most actors and stars most of the time played roles the ethnicity of which conformed to their ethnicity 1 and ethnicity 2. Seldom were their faces and features made up, their accents changed in order to make them change ethnicity. Abbott and Costello always played themselves, and much the same could be said of Bing Crosby, Bob Hope, Shirley Temple, or Sonja Henie, even though they assumed different names in their roles.

There was, then, what the statisticians call good agreement among the ethnicity of the actors, the ethnicity of the star personae they assumed, and the ethnicity of the roles or vehicles in which their star personae were displayed on the screen. Spencer Tracy might play Dr. Jekyll and Mr. Hyde; might play an American flier; might play George Heisler, a German; but in general he did not play Orientals, Italians, blacks, Hispanics, and so on. Much the same was true of Will Rogers, or Clark Gable, or John Wayne. If anything, the male stars in particular seldom strayed far from their ethnic identity (ethnicity 2).

Although its connection to ethnicity is indirect, it may be appropriate here to discuss the frothy nature of so many of the stars' personas and their roles: Shirley Temple (fig. 3.5), Jane Withers, Hope and Crosby, Mickey Rooney (fig. 3.6) Abbott and Costello, Esther Williams, Martin and Lewis, and Sonja Henie were famous for performances in material so lightweight that it has gone almost undiscussed in academic film studies. Their films aimed to be light, amusing, harmless, inoffensive, and to conform politically and sexually to the strictest Hays Code standards. The films represented a WASP America that was carefree and inward-looking. When Abbott and Costello and Martin and Lewis appeared in comedies about the armed services, when Hope and Crosby (fig. 3.7) took the road to all manner of exotic locales, without exception all were filmed on back lots and studio sets that bore as much resemblance to the real world as did blackface vaudevillians to Negroes. Both the realities of their own society and the actual look of the rest of the world could be ignored without damage at the box office. The heavy guns

3.5. Shirley Temple was the most successful of all child movie stars; her fresh-faced look and bubbly manner were indissolubly white, middle-American "cute."

of political and deconstructionist criticism have yet to be turned on this material and its popularity.

Stars' Ethnic Profiles as Dreams of the United States

Because ethnicity was regarded as submerged by the second generation fewer attempts have been made to draw an ethnic profile than one might suspect. The two years shown in figure 3.8 are estimates based on census figures and on surveys. Both presume the black population of the United States to be around 10.5–11 percent. The profile changed very little over the thirty years, certainly not enough to warrant any inferences to the ethnic profile that the stars presented. The principal difference between the profile of the group of stars and the ethnic profile of the country is that the stars' profile is relatively undifferentiated: a number of the countries in the actual profile do not appear at all in the star profile (fig. 3.9). Otherwise the WASP dominance, with strong representation of Irish and Italian, is not excessively discrepant.

3.6. Joe Yule, Jr. (Mickey Rooney) in a studio portrait. Despite his red hair and Irish surname, what he primarily represented on the screen in his years of greatest fame was all-American, small-town "pep."

3.7. Leslie Townes (Bob) Hope and Harry Lillis (Bing) Crosby (*Road to Rio*, 1947) combined comedy and song in the seven *Road to . . .* pictures: picaresque adventures of good-hearted but all-American rogues, often at large in the third world.

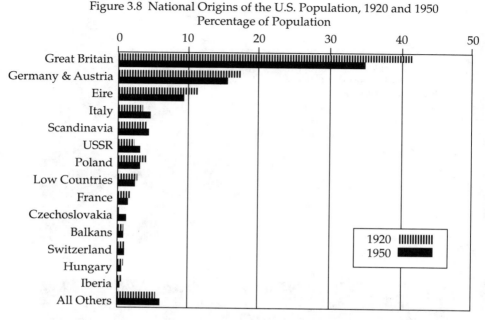

Figure 3.8 National Origins of the U.S. Population, 1920 and 1950
Percentage of Population

Sources: Warren S. Thompson and P. K. Whelpton, *Population Trends in the United States* (New York: McGraw Hill, 1933); J. H. Bonnet, J. Reimer, and M. Serandour *The Population of the United States* (Paris: Masson, 1972).

What should we make of this rather bland, light-skinned, light-entertainment, ethnically-hard-to-differentiate group of top stars? Is it merely that talent and taste happened to coincide in the people who constituted this group? Or is it one of the manifestations of the melting pot: stars who were representative of the majority of the population, true, but who underrepresented and hence obliterated or made invisible the large ethnic differences of the United States? If we incline at all toward the latter view, we are faced with the question of causal connections. Was the ethnic profile of this group of stars the result of the movie industry responding to public prejudice, to its having a favorable attitude only to a certain subset of the possible ethnic types that could appear on screen? Or, did the causation run the other way? Did motion picture companies promote a simplified majoritarian ethnic type? And was this in anticipation of their audience's prejudices? A projection of the moviemakers' prejudices? Or a projection of their aspirations as immigrants making good, wanting to lose their own ethnic distinctiveness?

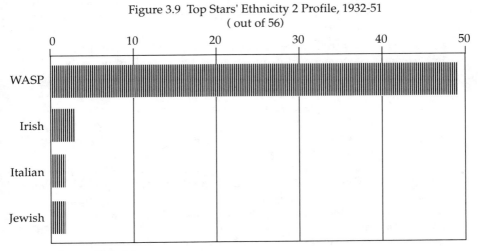

Figure 3.9 Top Stars' Ethnicity 2 Profile, 1932-51
(out of 56)

Source: Table 3.1.

One way to resolve this causal conundrum is to allow that the causal direction probably ran both ways, but that it makes most sense to shift to a functionalist perspective. This focuses attention on the functions stars have for the public and for the movie companies. If sociologists are to be believed, the United States had almost unprecedented pressures toward conformity once ethnically discriminatory immigration legislation was put in place and the vast immigration of the turn of the century slowed to a virtual standstill. Indeed, David Riesman argues that American institutions were creating a new type of personality, the "other directed,"[18] meaning one oriented toward conformity. The period 1932–51 coincided with the height of this social tendency, and also with the height of the movies' influence as the central mass medium shaping the society.[19] Given this drive to assimilate, to press all groups down into the melting pot, it is small wonder that the most popular stars appeared in movies that rarely showed that struggle. What the movies offered were stars who embodied the assimilated ideal.

During the interwar years the movies had become the central mass medium of the United States, central in the sense of being at the center of the society, integrated with its other major institutions such as family, school, polity, and church.[20] Each town had one or more cinemas, which most people attended frequently; movies provided entertainment and news in a manner calculated to be acceptable to the maximum numbers of the population. Occupying such a position, the movies were a force not to reproduce the society as it was, as the Marxists would have it, but a mechanism for projecting the aspirations of the society and hence for moving the society toward what it wanted to be rather than what it was. The public pillorying and virtual cashiering of such stars as Roscoe Arbuckle, Joan Bennett, and Ingrid Bergman for alleged sexual transgressions reveals just how important the movies' role as moral exemplar was taken to be. Stars were examples held up to American youth. They must be blameless. It was also the case, during this period, that American movies rarely engaged in blatant party politics, although Warner Brothers signaled sympathy for Roosevelt, and some studios and executives did a good deal of off-screen organizing. Stars by and large played little or no part in political campaigns. This was explained, I would argue, by the movies' desire to occupy the common ground, to avoid being partisan. Such an aspiration is naive, of course, but more in hindsight than in actuality. At all events, I interpret the party political neutrality as parallel to the ethnic blandness. When overt politics hit the headlines at the 1947 HUAC hearings, the anti-foreign and anti-Semitic flavor of some of the proceedings were not played up in the press, and scarcely surfaced at all on the screen.[21]

In offering the public stars who were role models, types with whom to identify, movies contributed their share to the aspiration that Americans could be free of the ethnic passions, identities, and conflicts of the Old World, unified by being American. The allegiances that Max Weber had identified as ethnic inputs were appearance, religion, language, customs, and political community. *Ethnicity* was his term for consanguinity, either actual or supposed. By coming to the United States, people broke their religious, political, customary, and linguistic ties one way or the other, it was thought. Perhaps it was also thought that in the absence of these religious and other ethnic differences would either count less or in different ways. Appearances, however, were hardly likely to change—or were they? Complexion and physiognomy are what we tend to concentrate upon, but this may be faute de mieux. In the ancestral countries these factors were wrapped in differences of costume, coiffure, decoration, diet, culture, and customary behavior. Most of these latter differences were obliterated in the melting pot of the movies and the movie stars. On and off the American screen men invariably wore trousers and shirts, women dresses or skirts; men's hair was short, women's long; jewelery and face-painting were confined to women; men, women, and children were always seen dining together, at fixed times, at home, eating the same food and using knife-fork, plate-spoon implements; taboos, special modes of cooking, and proper ordering of dishes were not shown; customary behavior regarding the relations of men to women, or parents to children, of comportment in public, were all based on a new model. Whatever ineliminable differences existed were due solely to physiognomy, pallor, and the like and were isolated and hence minimized. A person might be a bit swarthy or short but—provided voice, manner, and costume did not draw attention—there was a hope of blending in.

A striking aspect of this was the stars' mating habits. Whatever their ethnic identity, the stars were shown as autonomous, their family of orientation being a mere matter of background. Their family of procreation, however, was always shown to be built from a free decision to "fall in love" with some other free agent, often another movie star. Such encounters between prominent and visible people could thus be studied closely. The public could watch the process of try-out, disappointment, and eventual success when a marital union was consummated. In the presentation of the qualities that made the union possible and promised success almost none of Weber's ethnic inputs was ever discussed. That the stars might not be co-religionists was the only ethnic factor commented on extensively, especially Roman Catholicism. As Americans, even if sometimes recent ones, the stars spoke the same language, followed the same customs, were perceived as co-sanguinous. Their unions were not arranged by others, not available for comment or criticism by others, and suggestions by, for example, studios that they opposed this or that union were held to be stuffy or interfering.

These marital unions were always predicated on the promise to generate personal happiness and fulfillment, marital goals that would at most seem frivolous bonuses in many traditional ethnic contexts. They might or might not issue in children, but in any case, very few, and these children would be raised to have virtually no ethnic distinctiveness. Furthermore, these unions were disposable and serial. In the event fulfillment was not found, it was appropriate to resume autonomy and dissolve the union, dissolve the family unit, and seek to re-create it with others. Thus was ethnicity to be replaced by an individualism which freed the individual from being hostage to his or her roots in all matters from the food eaten to the major decisions of life. All such were to become matters of individual choice, choice that was virtually always revisable and revocable.[22]

Much the same analysis applies to on-screen representation of courting and marriage customs. Wolfenstein and Leites are greatly struck by how, in the movies of 1946, "American films tend to picture both hero and heroine unbound by family ties. Homeless, in the main jauntily self-sufficient, they make their way through city streets, night clubs, lunch wagons, and hotel rooms until they find each other, and then pass from our view before they settle down to constitute a new family. More than half of the heroes and half of the heroines have no relations. If they do have any they are not likely to have more than one."[23] This, they suggest, reflects the American emphasis on the family you make (procreation) as against the family from which you came (orientation). This emphasis cuts against ethnicity, which emphasizes family of orientation and other ties of background.

Thus far, this analysis of stars and ethnicity has focused on the stars and the public, on how stars behaved in their presentation of self, and on the public reacting with approval or disapproval at the box office. The fifty-six individual stars were products of the star systems, part of the complex movie manufacturing system developed in the United States. Stars were a form of product differentiation and also a form of capital. In investing in them as saleable products, film companies were putting forward a group with the ethnic profile outlined herein. What then of those studios and their personnel, what was their input to the ethnicity of the stars? It is tempting to contrast the ethnic picture in front of the camera with that behind. This is encouraged by the ethnic profile of the early studio heads. In a brilliant analysis, Lary May has shown many reasons why Jews gravitated to the new industry, why they came to prominence after 1914, and why their cultural background created favorable preconditions for them to understand and hence produce what their audiences would enjoy.[24]

But it is important to remember that May deals with early Hollywood until just about the point at which the present survey begins. Quite different evidence is available about Hollywood in the 1930s, and from a rather good source: the work of a social scientist and pupil of Charles Merriam and Harold Lasswell, Leo Rosten, whose book *Hollywood* appeared in 1941. Rosten, himself a Jew, could not be thought insensitive to the issue. Yet he states that "There is a widespread assumption that the movie men are 'foreigners,' and even those of old native stock are believed to have 'Jewish' names. Some of the most important people in the movie hierarchy—Darryl F. Zanuck, Y. Frank Freeman, Sidney Kent, George Schaefer, Eddie Mannix, Joseph I. Breen, William Le Baron, Hal Roach, Cecil B.

Demille—are erroneously believed by many to be of the same faith as the mother of Christ."[25]

He describes with characteristic glee the Christian affiliations of all of these man. Of course, by the time Rosten was doing his research (1939–40), many of the early pioneers May lists had sold out, died, or been retired to chairman of the board—as Mr. Bernstein quipped in *Citizen Kane*. Still, it seems to be Rosten's point that identifying Hollywood power with Jewish moguls was stereotyping. Later in the book, using place of birth as an ethnic indicator (without using the concept), Rosten presents other figures which show differences from those May assembled from the 1920 and 1923 *Motion Picture Directory and Trade Annual*. May had found fourteen of thirty-six producers foreign-born, eighty-three of 290 directors, 235 of 1,011 players, and fifteen of 161 writers.[26] According to Rosten:

> There is a popular impression that most producers are "foreigners." The facts contradict this belief. Out of 132 producers and executives, 82.6 percent were born in the United States, and 17.4 percent were born abroad. If we include 4 Canadian-born among the American born, we find that 85.6 percent of the producers in Hollywood were born in the United States or Canada, and 14.4 percent were born abroad. [A footnote adds that some of the foreign-born were British and Irish, leaving only 8.3 percent born in continental Europe.]
>
> How does the number of foreign-born producers compare to other groups in the movie colony? A much smaller percentage of the producers (17.4) were born abroad than actors (25.3) or directors (28.7), but a larger percentage than writers (13.9). For the four leading professional groups in Hollywood as a whole (555 cases), 78.2 percent were born in the United States and 21.8 percent were born outside our national territory.[27]

Obviously both sets of figures must be used with caution. Being born in the United States does not necessarily imply absence of ethnic traits or desire to affirm them; being born abroad is a questionable indicator of ethnicity. But, as I mentioned previously, pressures to assimilate were such that even the census assumed that ethnicity disappeared after the second generation. Rosten's use of the word "foreigners" suggests his aim was combating nativist criticism of Hollywood as well as anti-Semitic imputations. Furthermore, the position in Hollywood of Rosten's 8.3 percent born in continental Europe is unspecified. Were these men powerful and well placed and hence disproportionately influential, for example?

Two sorts of conclusions are possible. One concerns reflections on the significance of ethnicity in movies; the other is more general, the problems of identifying and hence analyzing ethnicity in movies.

Not for a minute would I deny that the markers of name, country of birth, accent, or appearance are unsatisfactory separately or in combination. To some extent our hand is forced by previous conceptions of ethnicity, in particular its assimilation to minority and to foreignness. Although individual ethnic groups might constitute minorities if considered serially, considered collectively, as in figure 3.8, they are a majority, and an increasing one. Census-takers and sociologists in the past assumed the reality of the melting pot process and thought ethnicity was being eroded. We now know better, and new waves of immigrants are making no pretense of any assimilation that involves alienation from what they see as ethnic roots. The census assumption that measuring who was foreign-born and how many generations had been in America also assumed an ongoing process of obliteration of ethnic distinctness. The emergence of ethnicity that is American, that is, not foreign but does not blend into middle-American or WASP norms, seems to have been unanticipated. Hence we lack useful data for the general population, as well as for the particular patterns of Hollywood.

Thus, most attempts to generalize about ethnicity in movies must be called into question. The old rule of Jewish behind the camera but never in front sounds plausible enough, yet so few of the top box-office stars were Jewish that its suggestion that some concealment of Jewishness went on in front of the cameras is nullified. Furthermore, the rule seems to exaggerate the extent of behind-the-camera Jewishness. In the absence of evidence, impressions are not to be trusted. The actual influence of small numbers of Jews would be easy to exaggerate, both by Jews and by anti-Semites, for their opposite reasons. On-screen the evidence clearly indicates that when seen through its top stars, America did not seem to be an ethnic mosaic. On the contrary, the stars represented a non- or anti-ethnic image of "all-Americanism" which only now, in a time of heightened ethnic sensitivity, looks very odd indeed.

With these cautions in mind, what can be made of the figures? For simplicity's sake assume that both May's figures and Rosten's are correct for the dates given, 1920–23 and 1939–41. It follows that there must have been a gradual change in the unassimilated ethnic profile of the professional groups in Hollywood. It is particularly striking that both May's and Rosten's figures show that writers were the group with the highest percentage of native-born, which suggests, but does not imply, that they had the lowest percentage of unassimilated ethnicity. Those who are tempted by the hypothesis that on-screen WASP Hollywood was the projection of assimilating

Jewish moguls, or assimilating foreign producers, directors, and actors, might find such evidence dismaying. The screen worlds and stories are primarily the responsibility of the writers. Unless we think they were mere marionettes writing to order the dreams of moguls, producers, and directors, it is necessary to re-think the idea that the on-screen world inhabited by the fifty-six stars in this survey is an emblem of Hollywood ethnic attitudes. At the very least, because writers have the highest percentage of native-born, and perhaps therefore the least ethnic remains, the world and the characters they put on the screen represent an idealized America for more people than just immigrants in process of assimilation. This in turn fits with the fact that by 1932–51 the movies were directed toward, as well as representing, mainstream America. To the extent that they simplified America's ethnic profile, it was in the direction that conformed to aspirations as well as dreams.

NOTES

1. Max Weber, *Economy and Society* (New York: Bedminster Press, 1968), p. 389.

2. Despite my search for defensible criteria, I suspect that Table 3.1 contains names that some readers will have difficulty placing, for example, Charles Farrell and Jane Withers.

3. Weber, *Economy and Society*, p. 395.

4. For example, *Scarface, The Good Earth, Juarez, The Story of Louis Pasteur*, and *The Life of Emile Zola*.

5. Both Donald and Mickey, especially the former, seem to me to inhabit a Norman Rockwell world, which, I take it, is basically WASP.

6. The rough boundaries of the golden age are the consolidation of sound (around 1929) and the age of gimmickry and television-induced decline (1952-55).

7. Cobbett Steinberg, *Reel Facts: The Movie Book of Records* (New York: Vintage Books, 1982). Doris Day comments: "The ultimate yardstick of achievement in Hollywood has been the annual poll of theatre owners of America. To be voted by them into the top ten is to enter the celluloid sanctum sanctorum," A. E. Hotchner, *Doris Day: Her Own Story* (New York: William Morrow, 1975), p. 143.

8. It may be that the public does not agree with Stanley Cavell: "One remembers how much of the history of film is a history of the firmament of individual women established there. Individual men, even the greatest, with few exceptions are fads or conveniences by comparison," *The World Viewed* (New York: Viking Press, 1971), p. 48.

9. As happens in Mark Winokur's article, "Improbable Ethnic Hero: William Powell and the Transformation of Ethnic Hollywood," where eth-

nicity is crudely identified with criminality and lower class origins, *Cinema Journal* 27 (Fall 1987):5–22.

10. Garbo's name change did not alter her ethnicity as a star, which always was Scandinavian, so perhaps it was for euphony.

11. Sidney Poitier was a well-known and successful actor, for example, but did not build, so far as I know, a star persona. Entertainers who also worked in movies—Harry Belafonte and Sammy Davis, Jr.—came from the end of the studio era in which Lena Horne flourished.

12. It is important to refer to Hollywood as a one-industry town, and not to Los Angeles. The latter was not at the time, or in any period since, economically or politically dominated by the movie industry.

13. Winokur, "Improbable Ethnic Hero," p. 11.

14. The concept of the star persona is analyzed thoroughly in Donald Horton and R. R. Wohl, "Mass Communication and Para-Social Interaction," *Psychiatry* 19 (1956):215–29. Their article was written just as television was making its impact so they were able to contrast the emerging television star personae with the traditional movie star personae. "Para-social" interaction is their term for interaction between star and public that simulates two-way interaction while being in truth one-way.

15. With the decline of the studio system the star system has, in my view, undergone radical change. It no longer centers on movies and movies alone. This in itself licenses the promiscuous usage of, for example, *The National Inquirer*, which will refer to Vanna White or Lisa Bonet or Wayne Newton as "stars." They are not stars in any sense coherent with those being discussed herein, but then there may be none of these people now because the system has changed.

16. See "Publicity" in Christopher Finch and Linda Rosenkrantz, *Gone Hollywood: The Movie Colony in the Golden Age* (New York: Doubleday, 1979; and Peter Valenti, *Errol Flynn: A Bio-Bibliography* (Westport: Greenwood Press, 1984).

17. Sari Thomas, "Mass Media and the Social Order" in *Inter/Media Interpersonal Communication in a Media World*, ed. Gary Gumpert and Robert Cathcart (New York: Oxford University Press, 1986), pp. 611–27. Thomas pinpoints the myths "there's room at the top," "anyone can achieve," and "it's not so great at the top."

18. David Riesman, *The Lonely Crowd* (New Haven: Yale University Press, 1950).

19. This argument is made in "Explorations in the Social Career of Movies: Business and Religion," in I. C. Jarvie, *Thinking About Society: Theory and Practice* (Dordrecht: Reidel, 1986).

20. From this analysis see Edward Shils, *Center and Periphery: Essays in Macrosociology* (Chicago: University of Chicago Press, 1975).

21. See Karel Reisz, "Hollywood's Anti-Red Boomerang," *Sight and Sound* 22 (1953):132f.

22. Two nonacademic but wonderfully informative and lively source books for all this are Penny Stallings, *Flesh and Fantasy* (New York: St. Martin's Press 1978) and Finch and Rosenkrantz, *Gone Hollywood*.

23. Martha Wolfenstein and Nathan Leites, *Movies: A Psychological Study* (Glencoe: Free Press 1950), p. 101.

24. Lary May, *Screening Out the Past* (New York: Oxford University Press, 1980).

25. Leo Rosten, *Hollywood: The Movie Makers, the Movie Colony* (New York: Harcourt Brace 1941), p. 178.

26. May, *Screening Out the Past*, p. 255.

27. Rosten, *Hollywood*, p. 267.

Ethnicity, Class, and Gender in Film: DeMille's *The Cheat*

The Limits of Poststructuralism

Film studies has acquired legitimacy in higher education in recent years, particularly with the use of poststructuralist models
stressing formal analyses of texts that differentiate contemporary
scholarship from earlier works. As the discipline of film studies
has evolved, certain topics, such as ethnicity in relation to socioeconomic class, have been relatively marginalized while others,
such as gender, have become mainstream. An inquiry into the reasons for the marginalization of ethnicity requires that we discuss
poststructuralism as the dominant research paradigm that has been
useful in legitimating film studies. (Poststructuralism herein must
be construed as a more homogenous current of thought than it is,
in fact.) Further, we need to assess the adequacy of poststructuralism for studying ethnicity and film, a subject that, in my opinion,
ultimately requires a social and historical contextualization of
readings.[1]

Since curriculum generally reflects scholarly trends, a review of
anthologies widely used in theory and criticism courses provides a
convenient starting point. A useful critique of poststructuralism,
labeled "an approach comprising elements of structural, semiotic,
Marxist, feminist, and psychoanalytic thought," appears in Bill
Nichols's introduction to his anthology *Movies and Methods II*. Published in 1985, almost a decade after volume 1, the updated collection is less eclectic than its predecessor and attests to the dominance
of poststructuralist film theorists who communicate with each other

in Frenchspeak or the language of "terrorist semiotics."[2] Aside from exploring the elitist implications of the rhetoric of film critics, Nichols discusses several problems posed by poststructuralism: "the death of the subject" since subjectivity, a textual effect, is constructed in language, and subjects are positioned by the constraints of ideology; the resulting diminution of human agency and the (ir)-relevance of film studies to political agendas and intervention; the inability of poststructuralists to move beyond "discourse as an object of theoretical inquiry"; the problematical relation between text and context; and the overemphasis upon synchronic, that is ahistorical, as opposed to diachronic models.[3]

Subjectivity and Gender

As a way to focus on the complex issues that Nichols raises, I would like to begin by exploring reasons for the centrality of the question of gender (as opposed to ethnicity and class) in film studies. Problems resulting from the articulation of gender will facilitate an understanding of the need to progress beyond formal analyses of texts in relation to subject positioning to a more historically specific view of the film audience. According to the poststructuralist model of subject formation, based on the juncture of Lacanian psychoanalysis and Althusserian notions about ideology, subjectivity is a textual effect or construct. Philip Rosen in yet another anthology composed of poststructuralist readings explains, "the experience of subjectivity is intricately interlocked with the reproduction by a social formation of itself as a 'natural' state of things . . . the production of what exists as 'natural' is the operation of ideology."[4] Consequently, poststructuralists have emphasized film viewing or reception in terms of subject positioning, that is, the ways in which film as a text positions the subject as spectator to receive the dominant ideology. Feminists predictably raised questions of gender in relation to subjectivity because the concept of sexual difference is integral to Lacanian psychoanalysis and to spectator positioning. In a seminal article, Laura Mulvey discusses the gaze of the male spectator in relation to the female body on screen as signifying castration.[5] Since poststructuralist readings of classical cinema render representations of women as fetishized or devalued objects, feminists responded with readings that go against the grain to accent contradictions in the text and also stressed avant-garde or alternative film.

Although the Lacanian underpinning of poststructuralist models used to delineate the subject as spectator provoked feminist critics to raise questions about gender, the spectator remains an abstract textual construct. Assessing feminist criticism, Jane Gaines argues that feminists lost their best argument by ignoring the social, as opposed to the textual, construction of gender.[6] Christine Gledhill pursues the same line of argument in an earlier critique of feminist criticism that has been reprinted in Gerald Mast and Marshall Cohen's anthology. She charges that because women were construed as textual constructs, the result was a "hiatus between women as constructed in language and women as produced by historical, social and economic forces." For example, feminists have had relatively little to say about the intersection of gender with ethnicity and class.[7] In materialist terms, Gledhill is particularly concerned that "the constitutive force of language has displaced the effectivity of the forces and relations of production" and concludes by issuing a call for "some kind of realist epistemology."[8]

British critics at the Birmingham Centre for Contemporary Cultural Studies also argue that focus on subjectivity constructed according to the Lacanian model is ahistorical and has politically conservative implications. Stuart Hall, for instance, asserts that "the premises of historical materialism . . . which attempt to relate ideologies to political and economic practices . . . in specific social formations and in specific historical conjunctures, have been translated onto the terrain of the 'the subject.' . . . The 'politics' of ideological struggle thus becomes exclusively a problem of and around 'subjectivity' in the Lacanian sense."[9] Dave Morley states the same argument in a different vein: text-subject interaction becomes one in which the text is understood as reproducing the Lacanian subject isolated from social and historical structures. Consequently, sociological determinism is displaced by a textual one.[10] British critics are especially concerned about the implications of textual determinism with respect to the possibility of a politics of contestation and opposition.

Ethnicity and the Concept of the Other

Although the language of British critics sounds like French-speak, their critique of the Lacanian model is useful for clarifying why issues such as ethnicity and class in relation to film have been marginalized. In effect, the spectator remains undifferentiated because the poststructuralist concept of the film-goer as spectating subject is divorced from any specific historical context. Further, when ethnicity or class do become pertinent to a reading of film, yet another Lacanian psychoanalytic concept, that of the Other, is deployed. Unlike the Lacanian subject, whose construction in language has been spelled out ritualistically as the preface to formal analyses of texts, the concept of the Other is not as carefully defined and is, in fact, quite vague. Undoubtedly the reason is as follows, according to Anthony Wilden:

> It is not possible . . . to define the Other in any definite way, since for Lacan it has a functional value, representing both the "significant other" to whom the neurotic's demands are addressed (the appeal to the Other), as well as the internalization of this Other (we desire what the Other desires) and the unconscious subject itself or himself (the unconscious is the discourse of-or from-the Other). In another context, it will simply mean the category of "Otherness," a translation Lacan has himself employed. Sometimes "the Other" refers to the parents: to the mother as the "real Other" . . . to the father as the "Symbolic Other," yet it is never a *person*. Very often the term seems to refer simply to the unconscious itself, although the unconscious is most often described as "the locus of the Other." . . . Lacan is more precise about the Other when he calls it the "locus of the signifier" or "of the Word," since he is obviously talking about the collective unconscious without which interhuman communication through language could not take place.[11]

A difficult and inexact concept, the Other has been appropriated by psychoanalytic film critics in generalized ways that emphasize repression and projection. For example, Robin Wood (who rejects the Lacanian reading of Freud) states in a well-known study of horror film that the psychoanalytic significance of Otherness "resides in the fact that it functions not simply as something external to the culture or the self, but also as what is repressed (but never destroyed) in the self and projected outwards in order to be hated and disowned."[12] Film critics have thus labeled corps of out-groups including women, gays, ethnic minorities, socioeconomic classes, rival ideological groups, youth, and cultural subgroups as the Other. But although the concept of the Other is useful, it has serious limitations. Critics employ it as a convenient, catchall category when the delineation of ethnic, class, and gender relations requires greater historical specificity.

As developments in film studies show, scholars have responded to critiques of poststructuralist models by analyzing spectatorship in historical, as well as theoretical, terms. But since film critics have been trained to theorize rather than work with empirical data, their conclusions about the social composition of film audiences during specific historical periods are often tenuous. For example, Miriam Hansen deals with issues of female spectatorship and ethnicity within the context of the twenties in a prize-winning essay about Rudolph Valentino. Disregarding the phenomenon of such stars as Mary Pickford, who appealed overwhelmingly to women during the teens, she asserts that "for the first time in film history, women spectators were being perceived as a socially and economically significant group." She analyzes Valentino's appeal to women with respect to an "oscillation of his persona between sadistic and masochistic positions" and the repression of racial difference. But her claim for a female subjectivity constructed not just textually but historically is insubstantial. References to the New Woman of the Jazz Age are brief and generalized, as opposed to complex psychoanalytic analyses of female spectatorship. Furthermore, discussion of Valentino's ethnicity in terms of the concept of Otherness is quite limited given the virulence of American nativism and racism during the twenties. Was it coincidental that Valentino achieved stardom as a Latin lover during the same years that Italian anarchists Sacco and Vanzetti were unjustly tried and executed? Such questions require a more detailed probing of history. [13]

Film History

Contextualization of readings, as opposed to textual analyses that focus on internal logic or processes, would be useful in clarifying issues about ethnicity both on and off screen. But poststructuralist models render the relation between text and context problematic. As anti-empiricists influenced by Althusserian thought, poststructuralists reject traditional concepts of the relation between knowledge and reality and assert that discourses have no referents. Consider, for example, the epistemological proposition that "there is a sense in which we can never get outside the mind so that we can never attain a direct knowledge of . . . concrete historical reality. . . . The 'real,' insofar as it can be said to exist at all, remains . . . inaccessible to knowledge." [14] Poststructuralist readings that emphasize the textual and intertextual, as opposed to the contextual, thus predictably result in "the windless closure of the formalisms." As a strategy to open the text "onto its *hors-texte*," Fredric Jameson denies that the Althusserian notion of history as an absent cause means that the "referrent" does not exist. Rather, he claims, history is "inaccessible to us except in textual form and . . . our approach to it and to the Real itself necessarily passes through its prior textualization. . . . "[15] But as Jameson demonstrates in a study of a Balzac novel set in the era of the French Revolution and the Bourbon Restoration, his approach to opening up the text requires a more sophisticated knowledge of history in the traditional sense than most critics possess.[16]

Since poststructuralist theory and criticism render the relationship between text and context problematical, critics interested in ethnic and class issues should logically turn to film history. But film history, which has until recently been marginal, has also been influenced by poststructuralism, especially Althusserian Marxism. At first glance, Althusserian or structural Marxism appears antithetical to historical studies. Althusser asserts that individuals are unwittingly constituted as (Lacanian) subjects necessary for the workings of ideology to ensure a reproduction of the relations of production. Consequently, there is little room in history for human agency or the ability of men and women to shape their own destiny. Exercised about the eviction of human agency from history, the British historian E. P. Thompson warns that Althusser's version of history is a "process without a subject."[17] Put another way, "the true 'subjects' of history are no longer individual human actors" but "the 'mode of production,' which refers not only to the economy but to the total combination of 'instances' or 'levels'—economic, political, ideological, and theoretical—which together produce and reproduce themselves and the relations between them." Further, Thompson attacks this Althusserian reformulation of the base-superstructure model in which the forces of production remain determinant only "in the last instance" and the superstructure maintains a "relative autonomy," two concepts that are ultimately incompatible. For Althusser, structural causality has displaced the causal primacy of productive forces.[18]

Althusserian displacement of human agency by mode of production has been influential in the conceptualization of revisionist and materialist film history. To date, much film historical work based on empirical research has focused on aspects of mode of production, namely, the economics of the film industry, the functioning of the studio system, and developments in film technology (sound, color, cinematography, and so forth). But as historiographical critics point out, Althusser's emphasis on mode of production cannot account for change over a period of time or transitions from one mode to another. Not surprisingly, film historians investigating the motion picture industry as mode of production favor synchronic over diachronic models. A monumental history such as *The Classical Hollywood Cinema*, subtitled *Film Style and Mode of Production*, is an example. As Tom Gunning stresses in his review of this work, co-authors Bordwell, Staiger, and Thompson posit a classical paradigm that exhibits amazing stability over a number of decades and absorbs potentially disruptive innovations.[19] Further, the classical cinema appears to be insulated from dramatic political and socioeconomic upheaval occurring in twentieth-century American society. Changes over time, whether in film style or the sociohistoric context of filmmaking, are thus glossed over in this film history.

Bordwell et al. focus on the classical Hollywood cinema, but film historians have been largely attracted to the era of so-called primitive film. The Brighton project, which provided documentation about films dating back to 1900–1906, sparked considerable interest in research about early cinema.[20] Although the resulting studies are significant, they are essentially formalist or textual in that emphasis has been placed upon the evolution of film language, specifically the history of camera placement, editing techniques, lighting effects, and so forth. Since comparatively little research has been undertaken to clarify the relationship between film and society, these studies could be classified as microhistory. Not coincidentally, interest in the development of film language has dovetailed with emphasis upon mode of production as the primary concern of film historians.

Film history, as it has evolved thus far, has limited usefulness for critics studying ethnicity because focus on mode of production or film language leaves little room for a consideration of the broader political, socioeconomic, and cultural context. Assuming defensive postures in a discipline dominated by theorists who are anti-empiricist and ahistorical, Robert Allen and Douglas Gomery devote a chapter in *Film Theory and Practice* to social film history (differentiated from esthetic, technological, or economic film history) as an investigation of production and consumption with emphasis upon the audience; however, their research model is disappointing.[21] A study of Joan Crawford as a product of the studio star system based on Richard Dyer's concept of stardom is chronological but much too generalized. Not much is said about Crawford in specific historical contexts, such as the depression thirties, or about American society outside the studio gates. Consequently, the phenomenon of stardom is isolated from a consideration of the larger culture.[22] For a study of film in relation to ethnicity, social film history beckons as a promising field, but it has to be reconceptualized and documented with use of empirical data amassed and interpreted by traditional historians. Such an eclectic approach may prove insightful for film critics who wish to comprehend the variety and complexity of ethnic experience in pluralist America in relation to film production and reception.

Contextualizing Cecil B. DeMille and *The Cheat*

In *The Political Unconscious*, Jameson argues that an individual text can be grasped as "a symbolic move in an essentially polemic and strategic ideological confrontation between the classes." Consequently, "the reconstruction of so-called popular cultures must properly take place . . . [and] is of a piece with the reaffirmation of the existence of marginalized or oppositional cultures," including those of ethnic peoples and women.[23] Despite the primacy accorded class, Jameson's project of (re)textualization to expose the ideological context opens possibilities for readings of film as texts registering the repression of ethnic groups and women. In fact, historians have repeatedly demonstrated in monographic studies that ethnic and gender issues are interrelated with those of socioeconomic class. Assuming that texts are symptomatic of social reality, I propose to discuss the critical and commercial successes of Cecil B. DeMille during the teens, especially *The Cheat* (1915), as representations of ethnicity, gender, and class at a critical moment in American history. DeMille's prewar films address the political, socioeconomic, and cultural tensions that characterized the early twentieth century much more directly than his later spectacles. But to read these films intelligibly, we need to know the history of the motion picture industry and the Progressive Era as the context within which DeMille won acclaim. Consequently, I will engage in a procedure reversed from that practiced by film critics and summarize historical data necessary to decode the subtext as a way of reading the text.

DeMille's Pre-World War I Films

DeMille's later career as a showman who directed gaudy spectacles has eclipsed his contribution to the advance of early film, especially his role in legitimating film as artistic entertainment for the middle class. With Jesse L. Lasky, Samuel Goldfish (later Goldwyn), and Arthur Friend, DeMille founded the Jesse L. Lasky Feature Play Company in 1913 to produce feature-length films that would attract respectable patrons. In 1916, the Lasky Company merged with Adolph Zukor's Famous Players, a studio with comparable ambitions. During these years, motion pictures were not insignificantly labeled photoplays. As a strategy to draw the middle class to films, the Lasky Company adapted stage plays featuring well-known theatrical performers, negotiated a highly publicized deal to adapt the Broadway productions of David Belasco, and lured to Hollywood Metropolitan Opera soprano Geraldine Farrar, a diva whose adulation had transformed her into an international media star. As director-general of Lasky and Famous Players-Lasky (later Paramount), DeMille capitalized upon his family's connections with the legitimate theater: his father and brother were famous playwrights who had collaborated with Belasco, and his mother had been a successful theatrical agent.

Since DeMille's initial strategy in courting the middle class was to adapt familiar works, seventeen of twenty-five features dating back to the prewar period were adaptations of popular plays, novels, and short stories.[24] At least 50 percent of these prewar films dramatized the interrelated issues of ethnicity, class, and gender, particularly with respect to romantic coupling. As these films were mostly adaptations meant for cultivated patrons, social attitudes expressed toward ethnic and working-class peoples may be interpreted as fairly widespread among the Anglo-Saxon middle and upper classes. Specifically, a distinction is made between white ethnic groups (Germans and Irish) and nonwhite ethnic groups (Indians, Arabs, and Japanese) with respect to the desirability of sexual or marital union. In effect, nonwhite ethnic persons are portrayed as unassimilable in films such as *The Squaw Man* (1914), *The Arab* (1915), and *The Cheat* (1915). DeMille is more ambivalent about Spaniards or Mexicans as depicted in *Rose of the Rancho* (1914) and *Girl of the Golden West* (1915), a Belasco play that became the basis of Puccini's opera, in that intermarriage at the conclusion also means the couple is extruded from society.[25] When Spanish conquistadors are Europeans in contrast to their Aztec victims, as in *The Woman God Forgot (1917)*, romance is possible only after the "native" civilization has been leveled. In films such as *Chimmie Fadden* (1915), *Chimmie Fadden Out West (1915)*, *Kindling* (1915), *The Heart of Nora Flynn* (1916), and *Dream Girl* (1916), the ethnic groups are white, specifically Irish and Dutch, but they are contrasted with Anglo-Saxons in terms of socioeconomic class and lack of cultivation. Although white ethnic groups are not rendered outside civilization, their status is at the bottom of an economic pyramid marked by class stratification. With the exception of the Cinderella ending in *Dream Girl*, which required the disappearance of a destitute and drunken Irish father, class divisions are barriers to romance. Even in a film such as *The Golden Chance* (1915), in which the heroine marries beneath her class but not across ethnic lines, class difference proves ineradicable. From a didactic point of view, a significant aspect of the contrast between white ethnic characters and the Anglo-Saxon rich is that among the latter, several have become selfish and grasping.[26] Wealth during the era of progressive reform is not yet completely displayed in good conscience. Contradictions in the representation of the elite are thus evidence of contradictions in the dominant ideology.

As trade journal literature attests, critics singled out DeMille's early pictures as examples of superior film production and expressed high expectations of Lasky releases.[27] Significantly, only *The Cheat* achieved instant canon status and is available today in a print viewed at retrospectives and in film classes.[28] Since canon formation is a political enterprise, inquiry into reasons for recognition of *The Cheat* as opposed to DeMille's other films should prove enlightening.[29] DeMille's brother William noted in an autobiographical account of his film career that *The Cheat* became "the talk of the year." Yet an examination of trade journals shows that *Carmen* (1915) received far greater publicity, if not critical acclaim, as a result of the screen debut of Geraldine Farrar, whose association with the Metropolitan Opera brought a touch of high culture to film. Lasky claimed that *Carmen* had been "equalled if not surpassed" by *The Cheat*, a film that he billed as "the very best photoplay" his company had produced (fig. 4.1). Samuel Goldwyn wrote in his autobiography that *The Cheat* catapulted DeMille "to the front" and that it was "a first real knockout after a number of moderate successes." Again, trade journal literature and DeMille's financial statements indicate otherwise, although foreign receipts for *The Cheat* were considerably higher than revenues for any of DeMille's earlier films.[30] Possibly William deMille and Goldwyn were influenced by the response of French critics, such as Louis Delluc, whose reaction to *The Cheat* was nothing short of adulation. Although wartime conditions delayed its premiere until later in the teens, *The Cheat* ran for ten months at a theater on the fashionable Boulevard des Italiens.[31] In effect, both Farrar's screen appearance and French critical response to *The Cheat* were momentous events that enabled the Lasky Company to publicize its productions as works of art for middle class patrons.

4.1. Cecil B. DeMille directs Geraldine Farrar, Metropolitan Opera soprano, who became an important film star after her screen debut in *Carmen*.

Unfortunately, critical recognition of *The Cheat* as a virtuosic, artistic achievement is complicated by DeMille's later reputation as a showman, as well as by the inaccessibility of silent films that would provide a basis for comparison. Specifically, film critics and historians have singled out the film for its dramatic use of low-key lighting, especially in a set design with Japanese shoji screens photographed in stunning shot reverse shots with shadowed figures.[32] Although critics had become accustomed to "Lasky lighting" in previous DeMille features, a reviewer claimed that *The Cheat* "should mark a new era in lighting as applied to screen productions."[33] Likewise, historians such as Bordwell, Staiger, and Thompson emphasize the "spectacular low-key arrangements" made famous by the film.[34] Concerned about the chronology of stylistic innovation, Barry Salt observes that *The Cheat* was "not quite so thoroughgoing and extended in its use of low-key arc lighting" as Ralph Ince's lesser-known film, *His Phantom Sweetheart*. Salt does credit DeMille with effective use of shadows in *The Cheat*, but also cites *Maria Rosa*, a vehicle for Farrar that DeMille filmed earlier in 1915.[35] Bordwell, Staiger, and Thompson mention DeMille in conjunction with his cameraman Alvin Wyckoff and his art director Wilfred Buckland, but Salt attributes the lighting in DeMille's film to his cameramen. DeMille himself, however, claimed that he preferred "contrasty" lighting and had to issue special instructions to his camera crew to achieve desired effects. But he always acknowledged Buckland, Belasco's former art director, as a genius.[36] A reading of the script of *The Cheat*, coauthored by Hector Turnbull and Jeanie Macpherson, reveals that lighting effects were carefully thought out in advance. DeMille even penciled in a notation for the use of baby spots for a particular shot and specified color tinting of scenes, an effect that must have had an impact upon viewers but is ignored today as prints in distribution, unlike the original nitrate positive, are in black and white.[37] Since DeMille had a reputation for closely supervising script construction, a process that involved him in endless wrangles with the New York office during the teens, his lighting cannot be attributed entirely to Buckland. In short, DeMille deserves credit for his early reputation as an artistic filmmaker. Incredibly, he made *The Cheat* while simultaneously shooting another film, *The Golden Chance*, due to a hectic production schedule that eased when Lasky merged with Famous Players the following year.

Aside from the dramatic lighting, Salt claims that *The Cheat* achieved its powerful impact by its high ratio of medium shots since parallel action is lacking and the editing rhythm slow. Actually, DeMille moved his camera closer to the actors in his earlier films, and some of the most dramatic shots in *The Cheat* are long shots. Esthetic and technical considerations such as lighting, editing, and mise-en-scène are obviously significant in canon formation, but sociological issues regarding a film's reception are hardly negligible. Unfortunately, most film historians stress the former at the expense of the latter. In fact, *The Cheat*'s canon status cannot be entirely attributed to cinematic effects and divorced from the historical context. As a widely read critic wrote at the time, the melodrama was full of "incisive character touches, racial truths, and dazzling contrasts"; that is, the film deals with ethnicity and gender in a shocking manner that still fascinates.[38] Specifically, the scene that inspires real frisson is one in which a Japanese merchant brands a beautiful white socialite with a hot iron bearing his trademark. Public fascination with *The Cheat* was so great that in a reversal of the usual procedure, the film was adapted for stage in the United States and opera in France (where it was retitled *Forfaiture*) and remade by Paramount during the twenties and thirties.[39] In order to understand the eclat of *The Cheat*, it is necessary to explore developments in American society during the teens, specifically race and gender relations.

American Patricians, New Immigrants, and the "New Woman"

As John Higham has demonstrated in his classic work *Strangers in the Land*, the revival of American nativism that crested in 1914 can only be understood in the context of the social and economic crises of the industrial era. Labor unrest of the late nineteenth century—culminating in the Haymarket riot, the Homestead strike, and the Pullman strike—was especially unsettling for conservative patricians in the Northeast. Gradually, Anglo-Saxon nativists veered toward racism which, in the early twentieth century, intersected with nationalism and became the most important component in nativist ideology. Despite the humanitarian impulse of Christianity and American democracy as promulgated by progressives, themselves divided about immigration, Anglo-Saxon nativists began to differentiate between old and new immigrants. Put another way, racist sentiment usually directed against blacks, Asians, and Native Americans was now channeled toward Europeans, especially Jews and Italians, who comprised a large percentage of the new immigration that peaked in 1907. Discrimination against unassimilable foreigners within had its counterpart in racist nationalistic feeling, as Americans ventured on imperialistic adventure and assumed "the white man's burden" in the Philippines, Hawaii, and Puerto Rico.[40]

Curiously, Eastern patricians, buttressed by eugenicists' concerned about "race suicide" and opposed to birth control, found themselves in alliance with populist xenophobic movements in the South and the West. Southerners intent on white supremacy were threatened by the influx of new immigrants, as well as by blacks increasingly subjected to Jim Crow laws. Western agitation was fueled by reaction to the Japanese and, on the Pacific coast, racism merged with nationalism in hysteria about the Yellow Peril. Japan's stunning victory in the Russo-Japanese War in 1905 threatened Americans invested in an Open Door policy in China and impelled novelist Jack London, a reporter during the war, to preach white supremacy. California legislation segregated Asian students and prohibited the Japanese from becoming naturalized citizens or landowners. Anti-Asian riots erupted all along the West Coast. In 1907, President Roosevelt negotiated the Gentlemen's Agreement with the Japanese government to specify restriction of the immigration of Japanese laborers.[41]

Despite anxiety about unprecedented class and ethnic problems that were channeled into xenophobic feeling, Anglo-Saxons retained their hegemonic status. Concerns about "race suicide," on the one hand, and revolution, on the other, proved to be unfounded. Jackson Lears, who draws upon Antonio Gramsci's and Raymond Williams's concept of cultural hegemony, demonstrates that the northeastern elite exerted a tenacious hold on wealth and power. Arguing that Anglo-Saxons bolstered up selfhood by projecting impulses which they distrusted in themselves onto foreigners (a concept analagous to that of the Other), Lears points out that class revitalization was reenforced by racism. Part of this revitalizing process, a reaction to fears about social decay, was an emphasis upon Spartan cults of "the strenuous life." Outdoor exercise, sports, and military adventure became rituals for self-purification.[42] Writing about a different historical context, Foucault notes that "emphasis on the body should undoubtedly be linked to the process of growth and establishment of bourgeois hegemony." Concerns about lineage, vigor, and hygiene with respect to the body were distinctly related to racism and racist expansion.[43]

Significantly, the bourgeois elite found themselves threatened not only by ethnic peoples and the working class, but also by women in their own households. During the Progressive Era, debate about "the woman question" and the concept of separate spheres for the sexes became vigorous as the suffrage movement revived. As indicated by the endorsement of women's suffrage by the General Federation of Women's Clubs in 1914, the vote had at last become a respectable issue. Later that same year, Margaret Sanger began a long struggle to challenge laws prohibiting women's access to birth control. In effect, native-born, educated, middle-class women had already begun to control their fertility, a development that had profound consequences for their status and role. While married women were generally active outside the home in clubs promoting civic projects, unmarried women increasingly found acceptable employment in professions such as clerical work and teaching. As the historian Nancy Woloch has concluded, "the new woman," who was decidedly middle and upper class and possibly college-educated, hit her stride during the progressive era.[44]

In his study of the northeastern elite, Lears demonstrates that the personal response of individuals in a hegemonic group to perceived threats can have unintended public consequences. For instance, as Anglo-Saxons fretted about "overcivilization" and engaged in quests to reassert manhood, their search for self and authentic experience fused with the emphasis of a growing consumer culture based on immediate gratification. Unwittingly or not, they contributed to the process of self-commodification and the extension of rationalization in modern bureaucracy. Without losing their hegemony, the bourgeois elite facilitated the transition from a producer economy based on the Protestant ethic of self-denial to a consumer economy based on therapeutic ideals of self-fulfillment disseminated by the media, especially the advertising industry.[45] Perhaps another unintentional but useful outcome of this process was the continued subordination of women. Significantly, Protestant notions of character based on personal morality and social engagement were displaced by concepts of personality in a consumer culture.[46] Since women were not to function in the public sphere, character had always been manly; however, once personality became defined in terms of the goods and services available to consumers, women assumed importance. By the turn of the century, the home had become transformed into a unit of consumption and women became consumers par excellence. But though the role of women (especially middle- and upper-class women) in a consumer economy was pivotal, their function was reduced to that of a status symbol attesting to masculine success in the marketplace.

The Cheat: Reading the Subtext

As a director who appealed to the ambitions of the middle class, DeMille has long been credited with influencing consumer tastes in postwar films that rendered conspicuous consumption as spectacle (fig. 4.2). But prewar films such as *The Cheat* and *The Golden Chance* already showcased life among the rich and featured the upper-class woman, splendidly arrayed and coiffured, as the ultimate spectacle. Significantly, Fannie Ward, star of *The Cheat* brought to the film not only her reputation as a legitimate stage actress, but also her persona as a celebrity. Ward's career as an actress had been briefly interrupted by marriage in London to a British millionaire, characterized as "actually rolling in gold," whose death left her a wealthy young widow. She returned to the United States in 1907 "with three maids, two automobiles, five dogs, and a wardrobe that, with her jewels, cost a million dollars." An actress whose lavish apparel was well publicized, Ward published an advice column in which she counseled women about fashion. She suggested, for example, "Express your own personality in every way. And let the world feel you are going to do this because of the individual expression of the clothes you wear."[47] By the time Fannie

4.2. DeMille in directorial garb, with his editor Anne Bauchens and his camera crew, Karl Struss, Alvin Wyckoff, and Peverell Marley.

Ward appeared as a fashionable and flirtatious socialite in *The Cheat*, she had embodied that role in real life. Significantly, the character she plays in the film is introduced in a full frontal shot so that women could see the details of her elegant costume.

A melodrama, *The Cheat* was co-authored by Jeanie Macpherson, the scenarist who would script most of DeMille's Jazz Age films about consumption. Catastrophe results when socialite Edith Hardy (Ward) accepts $10,000 from a Japanese merchant (Sessue Hayakawa) to avoid ruinous disclosure after a stock market gamble in which she loses Red Cross funds raised for Belgian refugees (fig. 4.3). (Significantly, the merchant's ethnic identity and name, Tori, became "Burmese" in a rerelease after Japan became an ally during World War I.) She agrees, of course, to pay the price, but when she later reneges, a violent struggle takes place during which the merchant brands her with the symbol of his possessions, a shrine gate. (The Japanese term for such a gate is *torii*.) Edith retaliates by shooting and wounding her attacker (fig. 4.4) but is shielded by her husband Richard (Jack Dean), who arrives on the scene shortly after her departure and surrenders to police. During a sensational mo-

4.3. In *The Cheat*, Fannie Ward agrees to "pay the price" in exchange for a $10,000 check written by Sessue Hayakawa, the Japanese merchant who remains an unassimilated ethnic Other.

ment at the trial, however, Edith proclaims her guilt and disrobes to reveal the scar that vindicates her action. The sympathetic courtroom crowd, which has become all male in the final shots, erupts in anger and surges forward in a scene recalling a lynch mob. In fact, the script characterizes the situation as a "riot" and has the audience shouting, "Lynch him! Lynch him!" [referring to Tori], and urging men to "right the wrong of the white woman."[48] As noted by a film reviewer at the time, "the wrath of the audience bursts forth with elemental fury and there ensues a scene that for tenseness and excitement has never been matched on stage or screen."[49]

Poststructuralist readings of *The Cheat* based on psychoanalytic models would undoubtedly focus on the woman as spectacle and the Japanese merchant as the Other. Judith Mayne, for example, has concluded, "It is by designating the woman as object of spectacle . . . that order is restored—the guilty punished, the just set free."[50] Despite the ending, DeMille's film remains extremely ambiguous; its subtext regarding social contradictions can be better understood by reference to events of the period as described above. As a

4.4. Ward avenges herself after Hayakawa brands her during a violent struggle in *The Cheat*, a film which became part of the public discourse about white supremacy and the new immigration during the silent era.

representation of the Anglo-Saxon elite enjoined to keep ethnic peoples and women in their place, Richard Hardy exemplifies the ennervated male whose loss of potency so concerned the patricians Lears describes. At the beginning of the film, both Richard and Tori (I will use the Japanese rather than "Burmese" name, Haka Arakau) are introduced as characters seated at their desks. But Hardy, a businessman who has yet to make his fortune, pores over stock market ticker tape in a uniformly lit shot, whereas in a dramatically lit shot, Tori, a wealthy collector, brands an art object with his sign. Despite his name, the Anglo-Saxon stockbroker appears pedestrian in contrast with the Oriental merchant who projects wealth, power, and mystery. According to the bourgeois ethos, however, the business world where men make money is more relevant than the art world where women preside.[51] Although the script describes Tori as dressed in "smart American flannels" for the opening shot, on screen he wears a Japanese robe.[52] Clearly Edith, who is selfish, duplicitous, and irresponsible, is attracted to the merchant, as he is sensual in comparison to her lacklustre husband. Richard eventually regains her by winning a fortune and going to jail to protect her reputation, but he cannot control her headstrong behavior, not even at the trial when she discloses the truth against his wishes. Significantly, the only scene in which Richard commits a violent act takes place when he arrives at the merchant's home shortly after the shooting and breaks down the shoji screen to gain entry. But by then, his wife has already avenged herself and disabled her assailant.

Edith is rehabilitated as a wife despite a narrative rupture in that she has clearly been labeled the cheat, but the Japanese merchant remains unassimilable. Contradicting a title that describes him as part of the Long Island "smart set," he is rarely seen conversing with anyone except the Hardys. A collector of objets d'art, Tori desires Edith, but as becomes evident in the scene in which he brands her, his sexual instincts are brutal. Given California legislation barring Japanese from land ownership and citizenship, the courtroom scene in which Tori and his Japanese servant testify against Richard is hardly credible but essential to the logic of the film. *The Cheat* is a statement about the impossibility of assimilating "colored" peoples, no matter how civilized their veneer, and it warns against the horrors of miscegnation.[53] As DeMille preaches in a cliched intertitle that he penciled on the script, "East is East and West is West, and never the twain shall meet."[54] When the courtroom crowd attempts to attack Tori, it recalls lynch mobs that murdered blacks. Within the context of the early twentieth century, protest against Asians and blacks was also protest against new immigration. In 1905, Congressman Oscar Underwood supported a literacy test for immigrants by claiming that the pure whiteness of the old immigration was being threatened by the mixture of Asiatic and African blood coursing in the veins of Southern Europeans.[55]

As a fallen woman, the heroine of *The Cheat* is rehabilitated through objectification as spectacle, a strategy that reenforces sexual difference. But it could also be argued that the threat of sexual difference, represented by the demands of the "new woman" (a descendant of the vampire) in a materialistic consumer culture, is displaced onto ethnic difference. Scapegoating is a common ploy used against ethnic groups, but even this tactic remains ambiguous. Edith and Tori are enemies by virtue of sexual and ethnic differences; nevertheless, they share an inferior status under white male hegemony. From the beginning of the film, the two are linked in pleasurable pursuits, while Richard is confined to his desk to pay for Edith's extravagance. With respect to visual style, Edith and Tori

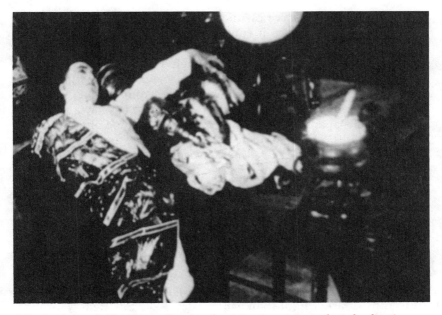

4.5. An injured Hayakawa lies on the tatami mat in a shot duplicating an earlier pose by Ward when she lay wounded after being branded, a visual example of how both characters share inferior status under white male hegemony.

are both characters coded by elaborate costumes, sculptured lighting effects, and medium close-ups. On the night of their assignation, Tori is even more sumptuously arrayed than Edith. DeMille's conception of space is pictorial, a concept perfectly executed through the use of sliding shoji screens as the backdrop of a decor that renders characters as ornamentation. Seduced by luxurious art objects, Edith and Tori are themselves objectified in shots of exotic interiors, as they move laterally in contiguous but fragmented spaces. Perhaps most telling are corresponding high-angle shots of the characters after their violent struggle. Edith collapses and lies diagonally on the floor, the line of her body intersecting with the line of the tatami mat. After clutching her left shoulder, which has been branded, she shoots Tori who, now also wounded in the left shoulder, falls and lies diagonally on the tatami floor (fig. 4.5).

Ambiguity in the strategy of reasserting traditional white male dominance and displacing sexual onto ethnic conflict in *The Cheat* also results from Sessue Hayakawa's riveting screen presence and characterization. Film critics unanimously singled out Hayakawa's subtle acting style, since it contrasted with the melodramatic posturings of Fannie Ward and Jack Dean and rendered the villain a complex character.[56] For example, when Edith appeals to Tori to drop charges against her imprisoned husband by once again offering her body, he responds impassively, "You cannot cheat me twice." Catapulted by the film into stardom, Hayakawa, an actor who had left Japan to pursue a stage career, became one of Famous Players-Lasky's principal male stars. A feature article about the Lasky company in the *New York Dramatic Mirror* listed Hayakawa's name at the top of a roster of the studio's male stars.[57] Despite several productions in which he played heroic, as opposed to villainous, roles, Hayakawa's screen persona undoubtedly remained charged by the brutality of the character he played in *The Cheat*, a part that aroused protest in Japan.[58] Significantly, publicity stories emphasized his bellicose nature and gave detailed descriptions of the ritual of hara-kiri.[59] *Photo-Play Journal* informed readers, "You can 'take it from us,' this popular Japanese artist can scrap. His efficiency in the art of belligerency may be due to his fondness for it. In fact, he'd rather fight than eat any day . . . . Sessue is a formidable rival either at boxing or jui-jitsu (*sic*)."[60] A fan magazine described him as "one of the best actors on the screen . . . but his heart is somewhere out on a battleship, when the big guns are frowning out of the forward turrets." Referring to Hayakawa's education in a Japanese naval academy, the Freudian language of the piece is both amusing and telling. A conclusion states that Hayakawa "in . . . his customs and manners and conversation . . . is American to the finger-tips, but one always feels that . . . there is the soul of some stern old Samurai."[61] Ultimately the Japanese as an ethnic group were unassimilable, not least because Japan's rise to world power status was perceived as a threat to the United States and to Western perceptions of the Orient as feminine.[62] As talk of the Yellow Peril reached its height on the eve of World War I, Homer Lea, California's leading thinker about racial issues, warned the West Coast about Japanese invasion.[63]

Given Jameson's premise that narrative is a symbolic resolution of political and social conflict and an instance of class discourse, a comprehension of film history and the history of the Progressive Era is essential to uncover history repressed as subtext in DeMille's prewar films. With reference to *The Cheat*, contextualization enables present-day spectators to understand that at the time of its release, the film was part of public discourse about white supremacy and the new immigration, as well as debate about the "new woman." Racism emanating from the Northeast and the West and the South, regions with specific racial compositions that created tension, spread across the rest of the country and contributed to xenophobic sentiment directed against immigrants from Southern Europe. The courtroom scene of *The Cheat* can thus be read as a conflation of black, Asian, and Southern European threats to white womanhood and the reassertion of native American manhood, however tenuous, against such threats. The ambiguity pervading DeMille's film is an instance of the contradictions involved in the formulation and reformulation of dominant ideologies, such as nativism, articulated by both patrician and populist elements threatened by socioeconomic developments in the early twentieth century. Since the ethnic and gender conflicts represented in *The Cheat* are far from resolved as the twentieth century comes to a close, the film still retains its power to shock, although in ways modulated by the present.

NOTES

I am indebted to Robert J. Smith for editing various drafts of this chapter, Ronald Gottesman for helpful suggestions, Gordon Beemis and Corinna Haskins for enabling me to view *The Cheat*, and James Card for yet another screening of *Carmen*. I also wish to thank Ned Comstock at Archives of the Performing Arts, University of Southern California; James V. D'Arc and his staff at Archives and Manuscripts, Harold B. Lee Library, Brigham Young University; and Chris Horak and his staff at George Eastman House for their assistance. Research for this chapter, part of a larger project about Cecil B. DeMille, was funded by the National Endowment for the Humanities.

1. From a wider perspective, Russell Reising argues in *The Unusable Past: Theory and the Study of American Literature* (New York: Methuen, 1986): "Recent theorists of American literature tend to minimize . . . social and historical contexts in one or both of two ways. First, they devalue, often suppress, writers and varieties of writing that do reflect interest in a historically determined social milieu. Second, they either deemphasize what social reference exists in the writers and works they study, or they turn them into non- or even anti-referential elements" (p. 34).

2. Rick Altman uses the term *Frenchspeak* in "Psychoanalysis and Cinema: The Imaginary Discourse," *Quarterly Review of Film Studies* 2 (August 1977): 257. Also reprinted in *Movies and Methods II*, ed. Bill Nichols (Berkeley: University of California Press, 1985). Nichols attributes the term *terrorist semiotics* to Dana Polan.

3. Nichols, ed., *Movies and Methods II*, pp. 1–25.

4. See Philip Rosen's "Introduction: Text and Subject," in *Narrative, Apparatus, Ideology* (New York: Columbia University Press, 1986), pp. 155–71, 158.

5. Laura Mulvey, "Visual Pleasure and Narrative Cinema," *Screen* 16 (Autumn 1975): 6–18. Also reprinted in *Movies and Methods II*, ed. Nichols, pp. 303–15; in *Narrative, Apparatus, Ideology*, ed. Rosen, pp. 198–209; and in *Film Theory and Criticism*, 3d ed., ed. Gerald Mast and Marshall Cohen (New York: Oxford University Press, 1985), pp. 803–16. Mast and Cohen's anthology, unlike Nichols's and Rosen's, is more historical and eclectic.

6. Jane Gaines, "Women and Representation," *Jump Cut* 29 (February 1984):25–27. Gaines observes that the rise of psychoanalysis coincided with the academicizing of film study. Also see Julia Lesage's well-known attack against *Screen* (reprinted by its editors) "The Human Subject—You, He, or Me? (or, the Case of the Missing Penis)," *Jump Cut* 4 (November-December 1974):26–27, and B. Ruby Rich, "Cinefeminism and Its Discontents," *American Film* 9 (December 1983):69–71.

7. Teresa deLauretis pointed to *"differences among women"* as exemplified by the black lesbian protagonist in *Born in Flames*, but she made this argument in 1985. See her "Aesthetic and Feminist Theory: Rethinking Women's Cinema," *New German Critique* 34 (Winter 1985):154–75. At the Society for Cinema Studies workshop on teaching held in Montreal in 1987, Mary Helen Washington labeled feminist film theory as racist. See also Jane Gaines, "White Privilege and Looking Relations: Race and Gender in Feminist Film Theory," *Cultural Critique*, no. 4 (Fall 1986): 59–79.

8. Christine Gledhill, "Recent Developments in Feminist Criticism," *Quarterly Review of Film Studies* 3 (Fall 1978):482–83, 492; also reprinted in Mast and Cohen, *Film Theory and Criticism*, pp. 817–45. An updated version appears in *Re-Vision: Essays in Feminist Criticism*, ed. Mary Ann Doane, Patricia Mellencamp, and Linda Williams (Frederick: University Publications of America, 1984), pp. 18–48.

9. Stuart Hall, "Recent Developments in Theories of Language and Ideology: A Critical Note," in *Culture, Media, Language*, ed. Stuart Hall et al. (London: Hutchinson, 1980), p. 159. British critics have been influential in delineating more heterogeneous models of subjectivity.

10. Dave Morley, "Texts, Readers, Subjects," in *Culture, Media, Language*, ed. Hall et al., pp. 163, 173.

11. Anthony Wilden, *The Language of the Self* (Baltimore: Johns Hopkins University Press, 1968), pp. 263–64. For a discussion of woman as the Other, see Simone de Beauvoir's classic *The Second Sex*, trans. and ed. H. M. Parshley (New York: Knopf, 1952).

12. Robin Wood, "An Introduction to the American Horror Film," in *Movies and Methods II*, ed. Nichols, p. 199. An earlier version was published as "Return of the Repressed," *Film Comment* 14 (July-August 1978):27–32.

13. Awarded a prize by *Cinema Journal* (a publication that used to focus on film history), Hansen's article contains impressive footnoting; there are five references to works in women's history but none about the history of the twenties. See Miriam Hansen, "Pleasure, Ambivalence, Identification: Valentino and Female Spectatorship," *Cinema Journal* 25 (Summer

1986):6–32. At the Society for Cinema Studies conference held in Iowa in 1989, Hansen read a paper titled "The Adventures of Goldilocks: Spectatorship, Consumerism and Public Life," an attempt to historicize the female spectator as a consumer. But Hansen did not differentiate in terms of class: women who were consumers were distinctly middle-class because working-class women had little or no disposable income.

14. Steven B. Smith, *Reading Althusser* (Ithaca: Cornell University Press, 1984), pp. 83, 71–72. Althusser's "Ideology and Ideological State Appartuses," in *Lenin and Philosophy and Other Essays*, trans. Ben Brewster (New York: Monthly Review Press, 1972) has been influential among film critics.

15. Fredric Jameson, *The Political Unconscious: Narrative as a Socially Symbolic Act* (Ithaca: Cornell University Press, 1981), pp. 42, 35.

16. Jameson can also be vague about infrastructural change when referring to the system of capitalism during specific historical periods. For relevant debate about literary theory, see Gerald Graff, who argues in *Literature Against Itself* (Chicago: University of Chicago Press, 1979) that "The fact that meanings in general are products of artificial sign systems does not necessarily discredit the enterprise of inquiring into the reference of these meanings to nonlinguistic states of affairs" (p. 22). Reising agrees that "derealization of literature is symptomatic of much contemporary critical thought and should be understood, in part, as indicative of contemporary aesthetic trends" (Reising, *The Unusable Past*, p. 36). Likewise, Andreas Huyssen points out that French poststructuralist theory lost its political edge when transferred to the United States but that "the aestheticist trend within poststructuralism itself . . . facilitated the peculiar American reception"; he notes that "the politically weakest body of French writing . . . has been privileged in American literature departments over more politically intended projects. . . ." See Huyssen, "Mapping the Postmodern," *New German Critique* 33 (1984):34–35.

17. See E. P. Thompson, *The Poverty of Theory and Other Essays* (New York: Monthly Review Press, 1978), pp. 147, 165, 189. Also see debate about his polemic in *People's History and Socialist Theory*, ed. Raphael Samuel (London: Routledge and Kegan Paul, 1981), pp. 376–408.

18. Smith, *Reading Althusser*, pp. 22, 74, 157–73, 187–91. Also see Gregor McLennan, "Philosophy and History: Some Issues in Recent Marxist Theory," in *Making Histories*, ed. Richard Johnson et al. (Minneapolis: University of Minnesota Press, 1984), pp. 146–47. McLennan argues that "structural causality is conceived by Althusser as 'mode of production' " and that this concept, aside from being useless in explaining transition between modes, results in the diminution of human agency and history becoming static.

19. David Bordwell, Janet Staiger, and Kristin Thompson, *The Classical Hollywood Cinema: Film Style and Mode of Production* (New York: Columbia University Press, 1985); Tom Gunning, *Wide Angle* 7, no. 3 (1984): 74–77. Gunning has written a persuasive theoretical justification for a diachronic

study in his disseration, "D. W. Griffith and the Narrator System: Narrative Structure and Industry Organization in Biograph Films 1908–1909," Ann Arbor: University Microfilms International, 1986, forthcoming as *D. W. Griffith and The Origins of American Narrative Film* (Urbana: University of Illinois Press).

20. Roger Holman, ed., *Cinema 1900–1906*, 2 vols. (Brussels: Federation Internationale des Archives du Film, 1982).

21. Robert C. Allen and Douglas Gomery, *Film History: Theory and Practice* (New York: Alfred A. Knopf, 1985). Allen and Gomery assert that "there is a world that exists independently" of the investigator and base their methodology on Realism, a theory that "takes as its object of study the structures or mechanisms that cause observable phenomena." But their discussion of philosophy of history and historiography is oversimplified. For a useful critique, see Richard Allen's review in *Wide Angle* 8, no. 1 (1985):56–58.

22. Allen and Gomery, *Film History*, pp. 172–86. See Mary Beth Haralovich, "Film History and Social History," *Wide Angle* 8, no. 2 (1985): 4–14 and Richard deCordova's review in *Camera Obscura* no. 18, pp. 146–54. The spring 1989 issue of *The Velvet Light Trap* contains some articles that deal with film history within a wider social context.

23. Jameson, *The Political Unconscious*, pp. 80–86. See also William C. Dowling, *Jameson, Althusser, Marx* (Ithaca: Cornell University Press, 1984), pp. 140–41.

24. DeMille quickly exhausted the concept of adaptations and increasingly turned to original screenplays in the middle teens.

25. Ramerrez, a.k.a. Dick Johnson, the outlaw hero of *Girl of the Golden West*, is the Anglo leader of Mexican outlaws in Belasco's play, which is decidedly racist; such distinctions are difficult to ascertain in DeMille's adaptation. See David Belasco," The Girl of the Golden West," in *American Melodrama*, ed. Daniel C. Gerould (New York: Performing Arts Journal Publications, 1983), pp. 183–247.

26. As mentioned in various studies, melodrama was initially a form of entertainment for the lower classes and the poor were often characterized as victims of the privileged. DeMille was thus working within established conventions. See Martin Meisel, *Realizations: Narrative, Pictorial, and Theatrical Art in Nineteenth-Century England* (Princeton: Princeton University Press, 1983), chap. 8.

27. For the teens, I have examined *Motion Picture News* and *New York Dramatic Mirror* at George Eastman House in Rochester, N.Y., and *Moving Picture World* at the Academy of Motion Picture Arts and Sciences, Margaret Herrick Library, Beverly Hills, Calif. (hereafter cited as AMPAS).

28. I am writing about *The Cheat* rather than some other DeMille film because a print was readily available.

29. Janet Staiger, "The Politics of Film Canons," *Cinema Journal* 24 (Spring 1985):4–23.

30. William deMille, *Hollywood Saga* (New York: E. P. Dutton, 1939), p. 139; "Mr. Lasky Says 'The Cheat' Is Greatest Play," *Moving Picture World*,

December 4, 1915, p. 1857; "Fanny Ward in 'The Cheat,' " *Moving Picture World*, December 18, 1915, p. 2206; Samuel Goldwyn, *Behind the Screen* (New York: George H. Doran, 1939), p. 82; interview with Cecil B. DeMille, Autobiography Files, Box 5, folder 1, Cecil B. DeMille Collection, Brigham Young University, Harold B. Lee Library, Provo, Utah (hereafter cited as BYU; box and folder numbers have been rearranged).

31. Louis Delluc, "Les cinéastes: Cecil B. DeMille," *Cinéa*, July 21, 1922, p. 11; *Homenaje a Cecil B. DeMille*, Filmoteca Nacional de España, Para IV Semana Internacional de Cine Religios en Valladolid (April 1959).

32. DeMille also cut from exterior to interior shots on opposite sides of the same wall and emphasized the theme of cheating in *Girl of the Golden West*, a film made approximately a year before *The Cheat*.

33. "Miss Ward Puts Aside Stage Mirth for Screen Emotion," *Motion Picture News*, December 25, 1915, p. 69.

34. Bordwell, Staiger, and Thompson, *Classical Hollywood Cinema*, pp. 224–25.

35. Barry Salt, *Film Style and Technology: History and Analysis* (London: Starword, 1983), pp. 139, 146, 148.

36. Box 5, *Squaw Man* folder 6, and Box 3, Biography folder, Cecil B. DeMille Collection, BYU.

37. Script of *The Cheat*, Cecil B. De Mille Collection, University of Southern California, Archives of the Performing Arts, Los Angeles (hereafter cited as USC). Turnbull is always credited as author of *The Cheat*, but both the script and credits of the film show that Macpherson was co-scenarist.

38. Salt, *Film Style*, p. 172; Julian Johnston, "The Shadow Stage," *Photoplay* (March 1916):102.

39. Scripts of the remakes show that the shocking idea of miscegenation was progressively diluted so that the villain becomes an Indian and then white. Scripts of *The Cheat* (1921 and 1933), Paramount Collection, AMPAS.

40. John Higham, *Strangers in the Land: Patterns of American Nativism 1860–1925* (1963, repr. New York: Atheneum, 1981), pp. 113–57.

41. Higham *Strangers in the Land*, pp. 158–75; John Higham, *Send These to Me: Immigrants in Urban America* rev. ed. (Baltimore: Johns Hopkins University Press, 1984), pp. 50–53; Richard M. Abrams, *The Burdens of Progress 1900–1929* (Glenview: Scott, Foresman, 1978), p. 111.

42. T. J. Jackson Lears, *No Place of Grace: Antimodernism and the Transformation of American Culture 1880–1920* (New York: Pantheon, 1981), pp. 1–58, 98–117.

43. Michel Foucault, *The History of Sexuality*, vol. 1 (New York: Pantheon), pp. 122–27.

44. Nancy Woloch, *Women and the American Experience* (New York: Alfred A. Knopf, 1984), pp. 245–49, 269–303.

45. Lears, *No Place of Grace*, pp. xi–xx.

46. Richard W. Fox, "Character and Personality in the Protestant Republic 1850–1930," paper delivered at SUNY Brockport, April 1988. Also see

Warren Sussman's " 'Personality' and the Making of Twentieth-Century Culture," in *Culture as History: The Transformation of American Society in the Twentieth Century* (New York: Pantheon, 1984), pp. 271–85.

47. Fannie Ward Scrapbook, Robinson Locke Collection, Library and Museum of the Performing Arts, Lincoln Center, New York (hereafter cited as LMPA)

48. Script of *The Cheat*, Cecil B. DeMille Collection, USC.

49. "Two Lasky Features," *Moving Picture World*, December 25, 1915, p. 2384.

50. Judith Mayne, "The Limits of Spectacle," *Wide Angle* 6, no. 3 (1983): 6–9; since this article appears in an issue about feminism and film, not surprisingly Mayne is more interested in how *The Cheat* constructs gender as opposed to ethnicity.

51. Remy A. Saisselin, *The Bourgeois and the Bibelot* (New Brunswick: Rutgers University Press, 1984), p. 80.

52. Script of *The Cheat*, Cecil B. DeMille Collection, USC.

53. In 1916, a serial titled *The Yellow Menace* was very popular at the box office and novelized for publication in daily installments in newspapers. A Chinese villain named Ali Singh, played by a white actor, leads a conspiracy against anti-alien legislation in episodes with such titles as "The Mutilated Hand" and "The Poisonous Tarrantula," see the *New York Dramatic Mirror*, August 12, 1916, p. 25. Publicity stories about Margaret Gale, the featured actress, emphasized themes of miscegenation by describing a Chinese prince who courted her while she was filming in Hong Kong. See Margaret Gale Scrapbook, Robinson Locke Collection, LMPA.

54. Script of *The Cheat*, Cecil B. DeMille Collection, USC.

55. Higham, *Strangers in the Land*, p. 164.

56. In *Stage to Screen* (New York: DaCapo Press, 1949), A. Nicholas Vardac credits DeMille as a director who brought a new "realism" in acting to the screen and cites *The Cheat* without noting the contrasting acting styles of the stars (p. 218). James Card notes that DeMille was loyal to the concept of a stock company and consistently inflicted upon his audience bad performances by members of his ensemble, conversation with James Card, Rochester, N.Y., July 1988.

57. *New York Dramatic Mirror*, October 28, 1916, pp. 35–36.

58. "A Romance of Nippon Land," *Motion Picture Classic* (December 1916) in Sessue Hayakawa Scrapbook, Robinson Locke Collection, LMPA. Tsuru Aoki, Hayakawa's wife, co-starred with him in a number of features that dwelled upon the theme of miscegenation. Hayakawa left Lasky and organized his own production company, Haworth, in 1918; his silent film career declined in the early twenties. In 1957, he returned to public attention in his role as a Japanese officer in *Bridge on the River Kwai*.

59. *Photoplay* (November 1917) in Sessue Hayakawa Scrapbook, LMPA.

60. *Photo-Play Journal* (May 1918) in Sessue Hayakawa Scrapbook, LMPA.

61. Harry C. Carr, "Sessue the Samurai," *Motion Picture Classic* (January 1919) in Sessue Hayakawa Scrapbook, LMPA.

62. A deconstruction of Puccini's *Madama Butterfly* (adapted by the composer from a turn-of-the-century Belasco play), David Henry Hwang's award-winning *M. Butterfly* emphasizes the West's characterization of the East as feminine and rape as a Western ritual. As the only Asian nation to imitate Western industrialization and imperialist expansion, Japan violated characterizations of the East as feminine and has thus been labeled barbaric. For comment regarding the effiminacy of the Asian hero, see Julia Lesage, "Artful Racism, Artful Rape," *Jump Cut*, no. 26 (1981): 51–55, also reprinted in *Jump Cut: Hollywood, Politics, and Counter Cinema*, ed. Peter Steven (Toronto: Between the Lines, 1985) and *Home Is Where the Heart Is*, ed. Christine Gledhill (London: British Film Institute, 1987), pp. 235–54.

63. Richard Hofstadter, *Social Darwinism in American Thought*, rev. ed. (1944, repr. Philadelphia: University of Pennsylvania Press, 1955), pp. 190–91.

The Cinema of Catholicism:
John Ford and Robert Altman

"If the anthropological study of religious commitment is underdeveloped," Clifford Geertz has written, "the anthropological study of religious non-commitment is non-existent."[1] While scholars of the Ancient World have no hesitation in analyzing the influences of religious myth upon the plays of Aeschylus and Euripides without themselves believing in the literal existence of the gods of Mount Olympus, critics of contemporary art have too often neglected the significance of ways in which religious forces operate in a culturally materialist (rather than theological) sense. There are various historical reasons for this: the initial dominance of genteel Christian critics, the subsequent violent rationalist reaction, and the consequent intellectual divisions between physical *or* metaphysical, materialist *or* religious. But it is becoming increasingly recognized that this polarity represents a false antithesis: whatever the status of one's spiritual beliefs, it is important also to examine how particular religious cultures influence (often unconsciously) the production of specific texts. As Robert Phillip Kolker has written, contemporary film criticism needs "not merely to reduce film to abstract generic patterns, but to open up the sealed spaces and weave together the loose ideological pieces of film, literature, television (advertising, religion, photography, painting, politics)—our entire cultural discourse—in order to find out what in the world we are talking about."[2] To discuss the influence of Roman Catholicism upon the films of John Ford and Robert Altman is not in any sense to classify them as "Catholic" filmmakers, but simply to point out that a residual strain of Catholicism is one component (among others) which influences the final shape of their texts.

Whereas the old auteurist theory proposed by the *Cahiers du cinéma* group of the 1950s insisted upon the autonomous vision of an individual author, analysis of religious ethnicity in film traces the text back to a cultural matrix which informs it. This cultural matrix is not, of course, purely biographical: Ford and Altman's work is—to use an Althusserian term—interpellated within the structures of consciousness produced by Catholicism, however much these individuals may (or may not) have consciously distanced themselves from religion in their everyday lives.[3] And yet it is the subtlety and unpredictability of the way Ford and Altman negotiate this cultural inheritance which makes their films so much more interesting than those old stereotypical representations of Catholicism in American movies where Catholicism becomes a synonym for mother-fixated gangsters and devotees of outsize pizzas.

The theoretical pattern I am proposing operates in the same way for any other artistic medium: a contemporary critic should not neglect Shakespeare's modes and institutions of production, but that does not mean he or she should therefore treat Shakespeare's plays as being equivalent to those of Thomas Kyd, for whom the modes of production were very similar. The most enduring authors dismantle banal stereotypes and rearrange the cultural terrain in what Wolfgang Iser called "unexpected combinations," thereby inviting an audience to share an apprehension of how material (and, in this case, religious) forces can have covert and immaterial psychological effects.[4] For Ford and Altman, religion becomes not some grand explanatory "Metanarrative," in Jean-Francois Lyotard's hostile phrase; rather, they represent it as a transformed and amorphous idiom of consciousness which is perpetuated, as Michael Fischer said of ethnicity generally, "through processes analogous to the dreaming and transference of psychoanalytic encounters."[5] And the depths of these perceptions are not shared by most filmmakers; authors are not autonomous, but nor are they all equally valuable.

It is important to note first that the whole idea of iconography occupies an ambiguous place in American culture and was treated with great suspicion by the Puritan heritage emerging out of the seventeenth century. In her book *The Interpretation of Material Shapes in Puritanism*, Ann Kibbey quotes John Calvin as scorning "The incomparable boon of images, for which there is no substitute, if we are to believe the papists. . . . Whatever men learn of God from images is futile, indeed false," Calvin went on: "We see how openly God speaks against all images, that all who seek visible forms of God depart from him." Kibbey suggests that Calvin conceived of Catholic visual art as being in opposition to the living icons,

Protestants themselves, who constituted the proper visual art of Christianity: "literal-minded realism" and a concentration upon the common stuff of quotidian reality were considered superior to Papist icons which tended to lead in the direction of superstitious ritual and fetishistic adoration.[6]

It is not coincidental that the growth of the cinema in the 1910s and 1920s coincided with a famous cultural rebellion against Puritanism; and indeed in popular mythology of the time the equation between films and Catholic ritual became commonplace: moviehouses were known as "cathedrals," with the darkened auditorium and organ music (for silent films) all adding to the atmosphere of liturgical devotion. On the other side of the same coin, James Fenimore Cooper's pastoral idealization of *The Pioneers* (1823) significantly employs the word *film* in a derogatory sense to imply unwelcome interference and illusion: "it may be humbly hoped that the film which has been spread by the subtleties of earthly arguments will be dissipated by the spiritual light of Heaven."[7]

Bearing in mind this difference in emphasis between Protestant spirit and Catholic icon, it is interesting to note that both Ford and Altman conceive their films primarily in visual terms. As Tag Gallagher has said, Ford's pictures give the impression of being "aliterary" in origin, of depending more upon images than words (Gallagher contrasts Howard Hawks, whose films rely more upon the dramatic script); whereas Altman himself has said that he sees a film as "closer to a painting" than to a literary text.[8] As Werner Sollors has pointed out, we must beware of establishing oversimplified dichotomies whereby Catholicism identifies itself only in contradistinction to a mythically homogeneous American Protestant "mainstream" which never actually existed.[9] But in fact the cinema of Ford and Altman, although grounded upon Catholicism, nevertheless distinguishes itself by its very interrogation of any such concept of ethnic purity. Rather than the complacent pizza-laden plenitude of imaginary origins, Ford and Altman's cinema examines the way images emanating from a specific religious culture become relocated within the complexities and ambiguities of the secular world.

John Ford's biography clearly testifies to his intense involvement with the Catholic church. Ford's father was born in Galway and immigrated to Portland, Maine; Ford himself was in his youth a member of the Knights of Columbus, and like his father a lifelong active supporter of the I.R.A.[10] His nephew, John Feeney, actually became a priest, eventually presiding over the multiple masses which smoothed Ford's passage from this world to the next, and indeed the film director died with rosary beads in his hands.

Within Ford's movies, overt representations of Catholicism in both its social and political aspects are not hard to find: *Mary of Scotland* (1936, fig. 5.1) outlines the melancholy history of Mary Stuart following the Stuart-Catholic party line whereby Mary herself never stoops to a scheming thought; *The Informer* (1935), from a novel by Liam O'Flaherty, portrays the cowardly betrayal of Sinn Fein by one Gypo Nolan (Victor McLaglen) who turns informant so he can claim reward money from the police and emigrate to America; *The Fugitive* (1947), from Graham Greene's novel *The Power and the Glory*, focusses on a vagrant priest (Henry Fonda) reenacting the ritual of crucifixion as he flees from oppressive anticlerical authorities in Mexico. Ford called *The Fugitive* his only "perfect" film, and in this opinion he differs interestingly from his critics, most of whom find the film's unusually abstract, expressionistic, and highly ritualized style to be at odds with the more squalid and credibly human world of Greene's novel.[11] Ford, however, remained devoted to the picture: it is as if the film constituted for him an idealized masque, a revelation and apotheosis of the spirit in a world from which mundane human tensions have (temporarily) been erased.

One of the important things about Ford's more celebrated films, though, is that this sense of apotheosis—which shines through unobstructed in *The Fugitive*—comes into significant conflict with a more recognizable human environment, so that dialogues are established between worlds of spirit and matter, plenitude and loss. Loss, in fact, is a central theme of Ford's work: the emphasis falls on how green *was* my valley, as in the 1941 film of that name. In *The Quiet Man* (1952, fig. 5.2), John Wayne's Sean Thornton yearns to reinsert himself into the small Irish community from which his family has been exiled, and he recommends himself to Mary Kate by participating in Catholic church services, to which he is also a stranger. *The Quiet Man* is not so much a sentimental film as a film about how such sentimentality operates: Thornton explains to the Widow Tillane that ever since he was a boy "Innisfree has been another word for Heaven to me"; but although the lush green cinematography on one level validates Thornton's idyll, he (and the viewer) soon come to realize that life with Maureen O'Hara's cantakerous Mary Kate will consist of anything other than easy pastoral nostalgia. Mystification in Ford tends to be accompanied by demystification: plenitude disappears even as it is inscribed.

5.1. Heroic martyrdom: Katharine Hepburn as the Catholic queen in *Mary of Scotland*, one of John Ford's overt representation of the social and political aspects of Catholicism.

5.2. John Wayne's Sean Thornton pays homage to his Catholic roots in *The Quiet Man*, a film depicting an American's yearning to reinsert himself into the Irish community from which his family has been exiled.

The process is akin to what William Boelhower has called "ethnic semiosis," whereby the inevitable displacement and absence of ethnic origins lapses into the circulation of signs rotating around the chimera of an imaginary center.[13] In *Rio Grande* (1950), Victor McLaglen, Ford's perennial good-hearted Irishman here impersonating "Sergeant Quincannon," comically pauses to genuflect before the altar while rescuing a small girl from a bullet-ridden church in Mexico. In the jungle of *Mogambo* (1953), Ava Gardner's Eloise Kelly suddenly takes time off from her stalking of Clark Gable to confess her sexual misdemeanors to a priest. The point is not that these are not "genuine" expressions of religion, but rather that they are both unexpected, and hence both trading off an incongruity between the emblem of piety and an unsympathetic outer world surrounding it. Whereas in *The Fugitive* the psychology of the priest is comfortingly externalized by the formalized cinematography, in most of Ford's other films spiritual impulses find themselves colliding with a careless secular world. It is this sense of disjunction that helps to bring about the idea of martyrdom which echoes throughout Ford's cinema, not only in religious contexts (*Mary of Scotland*) but also in the celebration of wartime heroics (*The Battle of Midway, They Were Expendable*) and in other dramas of social life (*Seven Women*): nobility of spirit interacts uncomfortably with what is mundane and materialistic. This interest in martyrology also helps to lure Ford's sympathies in the direction of Confederate armies: in his references to the Civil War in *The Horse Soldiers* (1959) and elsewhere the fated imminent demise of the South seems to be one of the qualities attracting Ford's attention.

Ford was also drawn toward the South in reaction against what his films take to be the mean and cerebral narrow-mindedness of the centers of federal power. In *Rio Grande*, Wayne's Kirby York complains bitterly about the State Department's ignorance of local conditions and its failure to provide him with enough troops to combat the Indians. In *Fort Apache* (1948), the same Wayne character comes into conflict with Henry Fonda's Owen Thursday, a theoretician of war who hankers after the politesse of the military academy and plans his assaults on the Comanches along the lines of battles fought back in 1221. When the Irish-American soldier Michael O'Rourke takes Thursday's daughter off riding within range of the Comanche camp, he is scorned by Thursday as behaving like an "uncivilized Indian."

Boelhower has traced a dichotomy in the theory of American identity between the universalizing structures established by the Enlightenment, which sought to impose a rational grid upon the land, as opposed to those ethnic, aleatory, and therefore oppositional energies implied by Indian culture: "a mobile, shifting semantics, a performative discourse that made no sense outside of its own local context."[14] If we follow this pattern, it is not hard to see how Ford identifies his own Irish Catholic ethnicity with the Indians' traditional role of disenfranchised outsiders. Indeed, toward the end of his life, Ford himself stated: "More than having received Oscars, what counts for me is having been made a blood brother of various Indian nations. Perhaps it's my Irish atavism, my sense of reality, of the beauty of clans, in contrast to the modern world, the masses, the collective irresponsibility. Who better than an Irishman could understand the Indians, while still being stirred by the tales of the U.S. Cavalry? We were on both sides of the epic."[15]

Ford's Catholicism becomes a lower-case catholicity, a delight in ethnic cross-fertilization which disrupts the rigidly dualistic mentality associated with Puritan culture. *Cheyenne Autumn* (1964) resists the reification of Indians as the "Other" in its depiction of the

Cheyennes' flight from Oklahoma to the Yellowstone country; and *The Grapes of Wrath* (1940) shows similar empathy with outsiders forced into the experiences of displacement and exile. Ford drew a parallel between *Grapes of Wrath* and the Irish famine of the 1840s, which started off the large-scale emigration from Ireland to America.[16]

At the same time, it is essential to recognize that the idiom of problematic outsiderhood enjoyed by Indians is not something which could satisfy Roman Catholic culture in the United States. The central paradox of American Catholicism is its aspiration toward universalism—"holy Catholic, apostolic and universal Church"—in a country where it has traditionally represented a minority interest. In historical terms, this paradox produced considerable theological controversy in the early decades of this century around the issue of "Americanization": Catholic thinkers debated whether the church should maintain its separation from mainstream American ideals, or whether it would be best served by moving toward integrating itself within the dominant patterns of American cultural life.

The arguments on both sides were intense and wide-ranging and cannot be dealt with fully herein. Essentially, clerics with more conservative or separatist tendencies (such as Archbishop John Hughes of New York and later Michael Corrigan, Bernard McQuaid, and Anton Walburg) were staunch advocates of parochial education and other forms of dogmatic orthodoxy, and they feared that the integrity of the church would become compromised by a too free and easy interaction with the secular optimism and commercial framework of the United States. On the other hand, more "liberal" prelates such as James Gibbons and John Lancaster Spalding wanted American Catholicism to emerge out of the constrictive confines of its oppositional ghetto and play a more central role in the development of American society. Gibbons and Spalding thought the church would never reach its full potential for growth in the United States if it remained locked into the role of a refuge for impoverished immigrants seeking escape from the pressures of harsh Protestant materialism.[17]

The point is that American Catholicism in the early twentieth century was developing ambitions to expand its sphere of influence in a way that more localized Indian cultures were not, and these conflicting pressures, between an inheritance of alienation on the one hand and an impulse toward assimilation on the other, led Ford to take that double-edged attitude toward American mythologies which he himself recognized when he said "We were on both sides of the epic." The reference here, of course, is to subconscious cultural forces which operate in a subliminal way, as in Fischer's model of transference. However it is partly because of his ethnic and religious background that the notion of the *frontier* in Ford becomes a self-reflexive trope indicating a radical ambivalence toward an American society where he, as an Irish Catholic, lives on the border.

The frontier in Ford's cinema, then, is not only a geographic place, but also a psychological state of mind. Throughout his films we see an emphasis on the establishment of shared myths and community feeling: the weddings, the burials, and the frequent renditions of "Shall We Gather at the River." These are the "sacramental" moments, engineered by deep focus and wide-angle shots and embodying the full potential of comic ritual, that rhythm Susanne Langer describes as "heightened vitality, challenged wit and will, engaged in the great game with Chance."[18] Indeed, it is one of the extraordinary aspects of Ford's pictures that they possess an uncanny ability to mythologize events even as they record them, so that the action seems to be taking place on two different levels at once.

At the same time there is a knowingness about how such myths are often invented specifically to serve the needs of a particular community: in both *Young Mr. Lincoln* (1939) and *Fort Apache* a double perspective operates whereby the image Henry Fonda will bequeath to posterity becomes more important to him, and to us, than his incarnation as an individual person. This myth-making process is even more explicitly foregrounded in *The Man Who Shot Liberty Valance* (1962), whose initial shot of a puffing steam-train introduces the film's central smokescreen whereby the legend that it was James Stewart's Stoddard rather than John Wayne's Doniphon who disposed of Lee Marvin's dastardly Valance enables Stoddard to embark upon his popular career as a senator and help transform the wilderness of the West into a garden. It is the fact that myth is intertwined with knowing irony in Ford's cinema that produces, as McBride and Wilmington note, an "odd synthesis of anarchism and authoritarianism which makes his work equally attractive to those on both extremes of the political spectrum." Order is balanced against anarchy to produce films which, in their ambivalence, verge toward becoming parodies of the American Western genre.[19] Ford's American Catholic sensibility, posed equivocally on the frontier of social conformity, produces films which are both inside and outside the myth of the pioneering West: the ethnic expression here becomes a formalistic ambivalence.

This merging of romanticism and irony is reflected in the mise-en-scène of Ford's cinema, both in that frequent disjunction of perspective—whereby an interior space or charmed circle (a church, a dance, or a home) is played off against an all-encompassing sense of wide-open space surrounding it—and also in Ford's preference for neutral, distancing shots rather than over-the-shoulder angles which might invite an audience to identify with one individual character. In *The Searchers* (1956), we do not look *with* John Wayne at the Indians, we look *at* Wayne looking at the Indians. Characters are positioned within a structured space and become components of the landscape from which they emerge. In this sense, the vast rocks of Monument Valley operate as an essence around which the individual characters circulate as accidents, temporary embodiments of a changeless theme ("You said that tower over there looked like a cathedral back in Santa Fe," says Sandy to Travis on the journey westward in *Wagon Master*.) The way in which Ford tends to use the same actors over and over again reinforces an idea of mere personal identity becoming tangential to wider issues of repetition and ritual.

As Northrop Frye points out, this form of ritual, which can contain and overcome an individual tragedy within itself, is most closely associated with the genre of comedy, whose etymological origins—Greek *komos*, revel or feast—indicate the traditional affiliation between comedy and social harmony.[20] In comedy, attention tends to be deflected away from personal suffering and focused instead upon the functioning of the group as a whole. Not for Ford the existentialist individualism of *High Noon*; rather, Ford's films subvert individual dignity and propose an idiom of what we might call ontological burlesque, something which becomes fundamental to Ford's perception of human existence in the world. This ontological burlesque is intimately linked to Ford's residual Catholicism. G. K. Chesterton, a more theologically minded Catholic, expressed this same sensibility when discussing cinema in *As I Was Saying* (1936):

> merely lowbrow films seem to me much more moral than many of the highbrow ones. Mere slapstick pantomime, farces of comic collapse and social topsy-turvydom, are, if anything, definitely good for the soul. To see a banker or broker or prospering business man running after his hat, kicked out of his house, hurled from the top of a skyscraper, hung by one leg to an aeroplane, put into a mangle, rolled out flat by a steam-roller, or suffering any such changes of fortune, tends in itself rather to edification; to a sense of the insecurity of

earthly things and the folly of that pride which is based on the accident of prosperity. But the films of which I complain are not those in which famous or fashionable persons become funny or undignified, but those in which they become far too dignified and only unintentionally funny.[21]

Chesterton's emphasis is intently metaphysical: he believes the reversals of comic farce epitomize how all humans are on the same level in the sight of God, which is why slapstick is, in his view, "good for the *soul*" (my emphasis). Ford shares this cast of mind: one hardly sees a conscious theological impulse in those rough-and-tumble whisky-drinkers scattered through his films who link his cinema with the Irish-American vaudeville tradition of the nineteenth century; but these ragamuffins always operate as a threat to the pretentiousness of those "far too dignified" characters (in Chesterton's phrase) who believe in their own elective superiority. One classic confrontation of this kind is in *Donovan's Reef* (1963), where John Wayne, impersonating the Irish soak Michael Patrick Donovan, mocks and finally quite literally up-ends Elizabeth Allen's Bostonian snob. Likewise, in *Seven Women* (1966), the more earthy Dr. Cartwright (Anne Bancroft) witnesses the psychological breakdown of the narrow-minded Protestant missionary Miss Andrews (Margaret Leighton), who babbles on irrelevantly about the sins of fornication and uncleanliness when the more urgent issue of plague is gathering about her. The wandering burlesque troupes in *My Darling Clementine* (1946) and *Wagon Master* (1950), which produce parodic versions of Shakespeare and other plays, could be seen in this light as offering self-reflexive comments upon Ford's cinematic enterprise as a whole. In *Clementine*, Granville Thorndyke's company proceeds from "The Convict's Oath" (a "Blood Chilling Drama") to a jokey version of *Hamlet*, with Thorndyke's recitation of Hamlet's famous soliloquy seeming to lampoon that nervous Protestant spirit by which the Dane was agitated.

In Ford's movies, then, everything is brought down to the same irredeemably comic level. As Ford himself said toward the end of his career, "I feel I'm essentially a comedy director, but they won't give me a comedy to do": although we should qualify this by adding that Ford's films always reveal the comic elements immanent within any given situation.[22] As Constance Rourke has noted, this burlesque sensibility is characteristic not only of American humor, but also of the American national spirit generally, with its inclination to overturn the Old World vices of pomp and pretentiousness. Ford's predilection for deflation is also especially appropriate to the psychology of the West, whose vast landscapes dwarf and ridi-cule the more formalized and genteel manners of the Eastern Seaboard.[23]

Ford's lingering Catholicism is also a significant component in this cultural matrix. In 1831, de Tocqueville's traveling companion Gustave de Beaumont contrasted Protestant and Catholic congrega-tions in America by remarking that while the Protestants generally originated from the same social rank or class, Catholic parishes would receive indiscriminately people from all classes and condi-tions in society.[24] The bulk of these Catholics were recent immi-grants and so tended to be lower-class anyway, of course, but de Tocqueville himself advanced a theological as well as a sociological explanation for this phenomenon. Protestantism, he said, was de-signed to foster independence, whereas Catholicism stressed hu-man equality:

> In the Catholic Church the religious community is composed of only two elements: the priest and the people. The priest alone rises above the rank of his flock, and all below him are equal. On doctrinal points the Catholic faith places all human capacities upon the same level; it subjects the wise and ignorant, the man of genius and the vulgar crowd, to the details of the same creed . . . reducing all the human race to the same standard, it confounds all the distinctions of society at the foot of the same altar, even as they are confounded in the sight of God.

Because of this emphasis upon human equality, de Tocqueville des-ignated Catholics "the most democratic class in the United States."[25] But of course their conception of democracy was not merely a polit-ical idea; it was, as Chesterton similarly noted, an intuition of the theological irrelevance and indeed farcical nature of human distinc-tions *sub specie aeternitatis*. It is this sense of the ridiculous which Ford's cinema also shares, a commitment to ritual which involves an ascetic undermining of human vanity. For Ford, burlesque becomes a moral imperative.

Although Robert Altman shares some of Ford's characteristics, he is more elusive to analyze in terms of the Catholic patterns in his work. Altman was born into a Catholic family in Kansas City in 1925 and educated at Jesuit schools, but unlike Ford he is an apos-tate, having left the church about the same time as he joined the army in 1943, and according to most critics, "Religion never affected his life very much."[26] Certainly the religious culture is more sub-dued in his films, except perhaps for *M*A*S*H* (1970), which makes

5.3. Robert Altman's parody of the Last Supper in *M*A*S*H*. Here, the Holy Eucharist is equated to sexual potency.

fairly clear analogies between the church and the army. As Altman said later: "Catholicism to me was school. It was restrictions; it was things you had to do. It was your parents. It was Mass on Sunday and fish on Friday. And then when I got out of that I got into the army. It was the same thing—you had to have a pass to get out."[27]

Thus *M*A*S*H* satirizes oppressive military systems by comparing them to oppressive systems of religion: the mock version of "Onward Christian Soldiers" signifies how the army attempts to equate itself with Christianity as an institution demanding loyalty and obedience, but in *M*A*S*H* both forces fail miserably. Altman's compulsion is to lampoon religion itself as much as the U.S. army. When the Painless Pole finds himself the victim of sexual impotence and plans to commit suicide, Catholic priest Dago Red worries anxiously about whether or not he is allowed to give absolution to a man about to end his own life; but this vexed question happily proves redundant as the Painless Pole's vital member enjoys a "mock resurrection" when Jo Ann Pflug's Lieutenant Dish comes on the scene.[28] *M*A*S*H* also includes a parodic version of the Last Supper, where the Holy Eucharist becomes equated with sexual potency (fig. 5.3). The scene's gleeful profanity operates on the Joyce-ian principle whereby satire of religion often implies an obsession with the forms and meanings of the religion being satirized.

This loss and absence of religious belief is a theme which manifests itself explicitly in two of Altman's later films. In the 1978 science-fiction world of *Quintet*, Paul Newman's Essex finds himself stranded in an ice-age city presided over by the autocratic figure of "Saint Christopher" (Vittorio Gassman). St. Christopher wears crucifixes, mumbles Latin prayers, and harps on about "the geometric shape of the universe" which he declares to have five stages—birth, maturing, living, aging, and death—with an empty "void" at the center. He advises Essex to while away the time in this godforesaken city by playing the game of quintet, the pattern of which reflects St. Christopher's gloomy image of life. Quintet is indeed compulsory in this city: "limbo" has been redefined as the name of a zone on the quintet playing-board. St. Christopher, who believes "Hope is an obsolete word," is a high priest of the metaphysical vacuum which surrounds this desolate arena—his cassock is white rather than black, as if to mirror the frozen wastes outside. Newman's Essex finally decides to reject these rigid structures, however, and at the end of the film leaves the city to set out on a lone voyage "north," opting for the more dignified and heroic gesture of self-extinction. As in *M*A*S*H*, religion in *Quintet* connotes oppression and suffocation and produces the kind of environment toward which the only appropriate response is rebellion.

In *Come Back to the Five and Dime, Jimmy Dean, Jimmy Dean* (1982), based upon a play by Ed Graczyk, Altman's interrogation of the psychological complexities of belief moves into a more equivocal area. The film rotates around the myth of James Dean, which swiftly becomes conflated with the martyrdom of Christ: a song asking "Must Jesus Bear the Cross Alone?" plays under the opening sequences, together with pictures of Dean and Christ, and one image of Dean later appears to be bleeding, like Christ crucified. The scene takes place at a reunion of "The Disciples of James Dean" twenty years to the day after the star's fatal accident, with the past lives of these Texas "Disciples" being acted out behind a two-way mirror. Sandy Dennis's Mona suffers from what Cher's Sissy calls a "Mona Magdalene" complex: Mona believes she was the chosen "from everybody else to bring his child into this world"—Dean's child, that is, not Christ's. She is decidedly reluctant to face up to the fact that the night she spent twenty years ago was with a local lad who recommended himself because of a physical resemblance to Dean. "Believing is so funny isn't it," muses the cranky old storekeeper Juanita (Sudie Bond), "when what you believe in doesn't even know you exist." Dean, like God, is an absent deity, a shadow who haunts their lives without ever revealing himself. Juanita herself is a Bible-belt fundamentalist cherishing the image of her late husband Sidney hobnobbing in heaven with the Almighty, but Jo (Karen Black) destroys her illusion by uncovering how in fact Sidney was an alcohol-sodden wretch who kept a bottle under the counter and died of a decayed liver. Juanita finds her world-view shaken: "I wonder why it was that my God turned away from me like that?" "I just think," replies Sissy, "that there's so many people in the world nowadays that it's hard for him to give the personal attention that he used to." As a special concession to relieve some of the divine burden, Sissy reveals that "I don't pray no more, I gave it up for Lent."

Just as Christianity in *M*A*S*H* and *Quintet* is represented as foolishly authoritarian, so Altman commented that he saw *Come Back to the Five and Dime* as an attempt "to undo this God thing, to find out the truth. I don't like the idea of superstars—they're an excuse for the masses not to think about their own problems."[29] But the paradox in this film is that the characters continue urgently to seek some form of belief, which has become an emotional and psychological necessity long after any rational justifications for such belief have evaporated. Indeed, much of Altman's cinema has focussed upon ways in which popular myths or media legends might operate as surrogate systems of communal faith in a postreligious era. James Dean was in fact also the subject of Altman's first film, a documentary made in 1957, and he has presented Robin Williams self-consciously cherishing his media stardom in *Popeye* (1981), and Dick Cavett playing himself as a famous chat-show host in *Health* (1982).

Altman's best-known celebration of secular ritual is *Nashville* (1975, fig. 5.4), where the audience's attention is directed toward such corporate mythologies as the institution of country and western music, the race for the presidency, and the impending Bicentennial celebrations. Significantly, all these public images are filmed in Altman's characteristic style, that is, refracted and reproduced through glass doors, mirrors, advertisements, and television newscasts. *Nashville* is not so much interested in defining these icons as in apprehending how they are perceived when modulated into the wider world. These myths of society become explicitly equated with the rituals of Catholicism when the film focusses upon several statues of Madonnas in the bedroom of Sueleen Gay (Gwen Welles), an

5.4. The celebration of secular ritual in Altman's *Nashville*, as the institution of country and western music becomes another example of corporate mythologies.

apprentice country singer who worships Ronee Blakley's Barbara Jean and tries (ineptly) to emulate her idol, practicing her imitative act in the dressing-table mirror. During the movie, we also look in on Catholic, Baptist, and Black Revivalist church services. Sacred symbols of old merge into sacred symbols of the new, as secular society becomes apotheosized. Caught up within these redemptive mythic structures, the characters eulogize their own loss of individual freedom: "You may say/That I ain't free/But it don't worry me" runs the film's final song. Altman's frequent trick of sudden jump-cutting at unorthodox moments, with its consequent defiance of the conventional logic of narrative, implies how any dramatic closure will be avoided here, and how the epic institution of "Nashville" will simply roll on and on.

As Fredric Jameson has pointed out, in any textual narrative the "formal processes" become "sedimented content in their own right . . . carrying ideological messages of their own, distinct from the ostensible or manifest content of the works"; and as the ideology of religion is no exception to this rule, it is crucial to recognize

how a residual element of cultural Catholicism is embedded in the
formalistic patterns of Altman's movies, as much as in the "manifest content" of statues of Christ and the Virgin Mary.[30] The idea
of ritual dominates *A Wedding* (1978), not only in its analysis of
marriage and representation of the Episcopalian Brenner and
Italian-American Catholic Corelli families, but also in its visual composition which is designed to twin everything with its contrary.
Dino Corelli (Desi Arnez, Jr.), the groom, has a twin sister; a shot of
men rushing for the lavatory is intercut with a shot of women rushing for the lavatory; the symbolic rebirth of marriage is twinned
with the adjacency of death, as the aged Mrs. Sloan (Lillian Gish)
chooses this celebration as an appropriate place in which to expire.
The film describes an interpenetrating simultaneity depriving characters of individual dignity by a process of comic fissure which
twins everybody with his or her neighbor in a ritual of consumption
and excretion, life and death. As the Brenner bedrooms all have
mirrors over the walls, the reduplication of these characters in
the glass acts as a formal correlative to this sense of splitting and
entwinement.

These "formal processes" also rise out of a culture of Catholicism: Catholic philosophers have generally stressed the significance
of "analogy" and the "analogical imagination," the "key to the resemblances of all things," as providing "a metaphysical explanation
of the structure of existence, indeed of all that exists."[31] This concept, deriving ultimately from Aristotle and Aquinas and popular-
ized after the World War II by Catholic thinkers such as Jacques
Maritain and William F. Lynch, holds that each part of God's creation exists in a state of continuous interaction with the essential
whole, or "Primal Cause" as Maritain puts it.[32] In the "analogical
order," says Lynch, we find an "*interpenetration* of unity and multiplicity, sameness and difference."[33] It is a reworking of Aquinas's
argument in the *Summa Theologicae* about how the existence of
earthly accident is always contingent to God's essential Being, so
that any terrestrial incarnation can always be referred back to the
divine center by means of what Maritain called the "infinite mirrors
of analogy."[34] According to Catholic thought, the opposite to this
analogical is the *univocal* imagination, that Romantic or solipsistic
cast of mind which "wishes to reduce and flatten everything to the
terms of its own sameness." Another term which has become associated with the univocal idea is *angelism*, the doomed attempt on
humanity's part to elevate itself to the status of a quasi-divine being
by aspiring to "shut himself off in solitude from man and God in
order that he may stand brilliantly on his own."[35]

Now, it is by no means my intention to suggest that Altman's films carefully follow the dictates of Neoscholastic dogma, but this system of thought, transferred from a theological to a culturally materialist context, affects the work of Altman in the same way as it affected the fictions of James Joyce, Luis Buñuel, and other Jesuit-educated lapsed Catholics. Just as *A Wedding* formalistically and thematically emphasizes analogies and resemblances among heterogeneous groups of people, so the central theme of *Brewster McCloud* (1970) is the communal nature of social life, the necessary sharing and indeed interchangeability of human characteristics. In this film, the hero's Faustian ambitions and efforts to fly are burlesqued by a system of analogies between birds and human beings, so that a series of linguistic and conceptual puns is established whereby human and animal behavior becomes interchangeable. The lecturer on ornithology (René Aubjerjonois, who begins visually to resemble a bird himself) orates on how "among forms of behaviour which show great stereotypes are those that have to do with care of the body surface," and the frequent interruptions of bird droppings are mirrored by Suzanne's (Shelley Duvall's) discussion of how she gets diarrhea whenever she eats Mexican food.

Indeed, scatology plays a dominant role in the movie: there is even a plan at one point to call in a "scatologist" from the University of Houston to help the Texas police solve the murders which in fact Brewster (Bud Cort) has been committing. The scatology signifies here a desire to pour dirt on everybody: everything is spoofed and debunked—even the police lieutenants are deprived of their Steve McQueen-esque glamour and reduced to reading "Captain America" comics—for Altman's film is designed to demonstrate how American society forms one mad mutually interdependent circus, whose components are all punningly entwined. This is why Brewster crashes dead at the end; by attempting to fly, he was aspiring to transcend the communal funhouse, whose social unity is celebrated at the beginning of the film by a version of the Stars and Stripes.

In *M*A*S*H*, the ubiquity of sexual desire invalidates the army's supposedly higher purpose; in *Brewster McCloud*, it is the universality of bodily functions which links the social fabric together. In the terminology of Catholic theology, Brewster is a univocal character who, despite himself, becomes assimilated within an analogical order. This analogical order is explicitly illuminated in one scene in which Brewster has taken Suzanne's car by mistake, confusing it for his, whereupon he notes that she has a statue on the windscreen exactly resembling his own. "That's the Virgin Mary," replies

Suzanne. "That used to be really popular a long time ago." In *Brewster McCloud*, the universalism of religion has transformed itself into the universalism of scatology, sexuality, and media mythologies (appropriately the temple in a Houston amusement park has been renamed the "Shirley Temple"), but the emphasis is still upon what is "popular" and accessible to the whole of society. The romantic hero finds himself trumped by the infinite mirrors of analogy.

For Altman, as for Ford, comedy becomes a moral imperative. Just as Chesterton deemed "comic collapse" to be "good for the soul," so Lynch declares comedy to be the most ethical of artistic forms: "It gets below all the categories within which the most of life is spent and destroys the most of these categories (the rich, the proud, and might, the beautiful, the style, the Joneses) in its descent. . . . Comedy is perpetually reminding the uprooted great man that in some important sense he was once, and still is, a bit of a monkey."[36] Or, as Altman himself once put it, "Can you find somebody who isn't somewhat of a fool?"[37]

The Long Goodbye (1973) perfectly illustrates this Catholic thesis of the "analogical order" being the "home of the comic," especially in its depiction of the sorry plight of Sterling Hayden's blocked writer Roger Wade.[38] *The Long Goodbye* is, as Pauline Kael remarked, a veritable *Finnegans Wake* of the media world, piling allusion upon allusion: the figure of Elliott Gould's Phillip Marlowe (fig. 5.5) recalls many earlier screen characters, from Humphrey Bogart onward; Marlowe's final comic waddle back through the alley after murdering Lennox (to the strains of "Hooray for Hollywood") echoes both *The Third Man* and the ending of many Chaplin movies; for his portrayal of Dr. Verringer, Henry Gibson is intertextually trading off his role in the 1960s' television comedy "Rowan and Martin's Laugh In," and so on.[39] However, this "bisociative" technique, as Alan Karp has called it, does not constitute merely a tricksy collection of cinematic *hommages*, but induces a universe of moral reflection, emphasizing the same kind of mirroring and interchangeability that we saw in *Brewster McCloud*.[40]

The Long Goodbye is constructed upon Maritain's "infinite mirror of analogies," and although Hollywood has superseded God as the Prime Cause, nevertheless the oscillation here between essence and accident (Hollywood archetype and its contemporary existential incarnation) is a fictional replication of those philosophical structures recommended by the Jesuits. Instead of an analogical order between human and divine, Altman posits an analogical order between human and Hollywood. And it is just this world of analogical reflec-

5.5. Elliott Gould as representative of Altman's "bisociative" technique in *The Long Goodbye*, a film displaying the Catholic thesis of the "analogical order" being the "home of the comic."

tion from which Roger Wade attempts to escape: "I'm a man cannot stand confinement," thunders Wade with the kind of crazed, phallic romanticism which refuses any acquiescence in human limits ("When a writer can't write," he says, "it's like being impotent"). Wade is another version of Brewster McCloud, someone determined to dominate and overhaul the world in his own outsize person, but his individualism turns to frustrated alienation, and then to suicide as Wade drowns himself in the Pacific Ocean. Even in his death, however, Wade is deprived of sublimity: when he sets off into the ocean, it is in a remote corner of the frame, while the camera focusses on Marlowe conversing with Wade's wife in the foreground. Even in this grand gesture of suicide, Wade still finds himself compromised by the mirrors of irony. Wade is in fact only reflecting the fate of Norman Maine, who took a terminal stroll into the sea in *A Star Is Born*.

Roger Wade is a prime example of the "univocal" or "angelic" mind posing as the exclusive interpreter of an uncertain world and attempting to translate the energy of the human will into a form of infinity. The comic and parodic structure of Altman's film, however, denies Wade his cherished romantic singularity, and instead places Marlowe in his traditional role of moral arbiter. Whereas Wade attempts to eradicate analogical irony, Marlowe thrives upon it. Because he knows he is only playing a role in an old movie which has been acted out before, Marlowe does not trouble himself with internalized psychology ("Do you ever think of suicide, Marlowe?" Wade asks. "Me, I don't believe in it," replies Marlowe). He contents himself with the surfaces of Los Angeles and with witty impersonation of the parts he has to play. While Wade attempts to accommodate the universe to his private dreams, Marlowe seems to welcome his fragmented self and his incarnation as the secondary accident of some primary, preexistent essence.

None of this, of course, is to imply that Altman should be seen as a "Catholic" filmmaker in the narrow sense. Indeed, there is a double deconstruction of theology at work here. First, Altman exploits the cultural patterns of Catholic thought without paying any attention to the metaphysical origins by which these patterns are supposedly sanctioned. Second, even the moral imperatives established by this cultural idiom are in fact codes deriving from one particular and limited ideology. Lynch asserts that the analogical imagination is "right" and the univocal imagination "wrong," but there is no attempt to make such ethical judgments in this analysis: we are concerned simply with how these fictions of theology have worked their way into Altman's imagination.[41] Compare Lynch's prospectus for "what makes a playwright"—"He should know a great deal, and this in terms of his own blood stream, about the dance and ritual in the oldest and widest senses of these terms . . . He should be a man who delights in the coronation of a queen or the inauguration of a President, who delights generally in a public style of life for man. He should know history and not think that his private mind can alone create a theatre. . . . "—with Altman's insistence on filmmaking as: "a collaborative art. I set a boundary line and framework, but I don't try to fill it all in. If I tried to put in the middle of it everything that was in my imagination, it would be simply that. It would be a very sterile work. So I try to fill it with things I've never seen before, things that come from other people."[42]

Like John Ford, Altman opens out his films to the wide screens of ritual and areas of public belief which expand beyond his own personal concerns. Both Ford and Altman veer toward analogical universalism in their work, the paradox being that these universalist tendencies can be related back to a specific cultural inheritance. Altman is indeed a director who "delights in . . . the inauguration of a President," as we see not only from *Nashville* but also from the HBO television series "Tanner '88," created jointly by Altman and Jules Feiffer, which charts the progress of a fictional candidate during the 1988 presidential contest.

One consequence of this representation of politics as ritual is that the mode of Altman's fictions is, characteristically, disinterested irony rather than polemic or satire. For example in Altman's film *Thieves Like Us* (1974), as Leonard Quart has noted, the depression of the 1930s is never invoked as a cause for the behavior of the outlaws Bowie and Keechie.[43] In the original 1937 Edward Anderson novel, their criminality is blamed on an inequitable social system; in Nicholas Ray's 1949 version of the story, Bowie and Keechie emerge as sanctified loners, tense and brooding rebels without a cause who devote themselves to protest against the world of social convention. But while Ray's version is protestant, Altman's is catholic, for Altman's thieves are antiheroic comedians content to play games of bank robbery in parody of the institutionalized thievery they see around them (as T-Dub says, "them capitalist fellows are thieves like us").

Altman's Bowie (Keith Carradine) and Keechie (Shelley Duvall) violate the first principles of a successful criminal career by deliberately seeking publicity and delighting to read about their own exploits in the newspapers. Whereas Nicholas Ray's characters scrupulously alienate themselves from the world, Altman's thieves desire to infiltrate society and become celebrities: they listen to tales of "Gangbusters" and the "International Secret Police" on the radio and validate themselves by their proximity to this glamorous model. *Thieves Like Us* represents another example of Altman's universalism: omnipresent throughout the mise-en-scène are the modern Madonnas of Coca Cola advertisements—even the Mississippi State Penitentiary sign is flanked by Coca Cola motifs—and, true to their interpellation within these corporate structures, all of Altman's characters dutifully respond by calling for ice-cold Cokes.

This absence of a social polemic in *Thieves Like Us* can also be located within the context of Catholic theology. One of the reasons Catholicism favors a ritualistic universalism is that as a creed it pays relatively little attention to the problem of human ugliness or evil. The Puritan sensibility is much closer to the old Manichean notion of evil being equally as powerful a force as good; but Thomas Aquinas observed that "the existence of *all things* derives from divine beauty" (my emphasis) because evil, according to Aquinas, betokens nothing more than a lack of the appropriate divine harmony and does not constitute any form of autonomous energy. As Maritain summarizes the argument: "There are things deprived in some respect of due proportion, radiance, or integrity, but in which Being still abounds, and which keep on pleasing the sight to that very extent. For a pure intellect, everything is a kind of spatio-temporal number, as Pythagoras saw it."[44]

Likewise, for Altman, the foolish or the stupid or even the immoral are essential numbers in a wider geometric pattern. In *Thieves Like Us*, he is not so interested in opposing capitalists to proletariat as in demonstrating the resemblances of these two groups, how they are both part of the same all-inclusive system. In *Nashville*, Haven Hamilton's dim-witted song about how the United States "must be doing something right to last two hundred years" is hilarious, but not necessarily satirical.

Altman deconstructs American myths and implies how they are brought into being, but, as he stated in a 1976 interview, he does not seek to annul these categories: "My attitudes and my political statements . . . aren't nearly as harsh as people seem to think. When *Nashville* came out, there was this wild reaction: 'Oh, what a terrible view of America!' It's a view of America, all right, but I don't agree that it's terrible. I'm not condemning America." He went on to say that he opposed "complacency" and "the feeling that any way we do things must be the right way."[45] But that is a

long way from what Robert Phillip Kolker deems Altman's "fundamentally desolate vision," his "bitter observation of domination and
passivity, of assent to ritual and assumption of cultural myths," or
from James Monaco's assertion that "Altman's people are univer-
sally addicted to an American mythos . . . to which their own reality never measures up. Altman doesn't seem to want to let them
take action, and that is a major and unavoidable criticism of the theory of his work."[46]

Such criticism may be valid enough in its own way, but it does
not seem to recognize its own culturally specific origins, nor the
culturally specific ethos of Altman's cinema. Rather than confronta-
tions of good and evil, the primary concern of Altman's films is to
delineate landscapes of community and ritual where events unfold
with a random contingency which is never purely aleatory, but
rather imbued with a sense of zany inevitability, as the hazards of
existence are reflected back by the "infinite mirrors of analogy" to
an essential whole.

This political ambiguity is one aspect linking Altman's cinema
with John Ford's work. Ford's acknowledgment of how he was "on
both sides of the epic" is reproduced in Altman's stance as "simultaneously contemptuous and in love with his America," as Quart
puts it.[47] There is a specific social context for this, insofar as Ford's
films operate within forms of gentle parody, poised in that familiar
American Catholic way between the pressures of assimilation and
the pressures of alienation, and this is a pattern which Altman's
pictures take up as well. But there is also a transformed theological
context, as both Ford and Altman reject the dialectic of good and
evil, opting instead for an all-embracing universalism. Their styles
of filmmaking, with a heavy emphasis on ritual and a consequent
tendency to disrupt and dislocate the solipsistic vision of any one
individual character, function as a corollary to this thematic impulse. The frequent dances and hymn-singing in Ford's films can be
seen as a parallel to the overlapping dialogue and almost continuous use of panning in Altman's work: both directors describe wide-
open landscapes where characters merge and do indeed "overlap,"
bound together as contingent components of secular (and, in Ford's
case, religious) myths.[48] Altman once said "it's an impression . . .
of total character and total atmosphere that I am in. What happens
because of what." Both that sense of totality, and also the idea of
things existing not as isolated objects but in terms of their relation
to one another ("What happens because of what") are crucial to the

work of Ford as well as to that of Altman.[49] Both filmmakers secularize the Catholic conception of analogy, which emphasizes resemblances between disparate entities. As a result, they both discover a moral imperative in the form of comedy, whereby social distinctions are obliterated, as the idiom of burlesque ensures everybody comes to resemble everybody else in the sight of that entity that Derrida would term (God).

This appearance of a religious heritage in Ford and Altman's work does not in any way marginalize their status as "American" artists. As Werner Sollors has argued, distinctions between "ethnic" and "American" artists have historically tended to be far too simplistic. Just as the work of Eugene O'Neill, Carl Sandburg, Vladimir Nabokov, and many other "American" authors possesses a latent ethnic component which coexists simultaneously with American idioms, so in the cinema of Ford and Altman we can perceive residual forms of religious ethnicity operating in subtle and "unexpected combinations" which materially affect the texts' final shape. Catholicism does not provide any underlying "explanation" of these filmmakers' work, but a religious ideology, often transformed from a metaphysical to a materialist context, is, for Ford and Altman, one force which illuminates their vision.

NOTES

1. Clifford Geertz, "Religion as a Cultural System," in *Anthropological Approaches to the Study of Religion*, ed. Michael Banton (New York: Praeger, 1966), p. 43.

2. Robert Phillip Kolker, "On Certain Tendencies in American Film Criticism," *American Quarterly* 38 (Summer 1986):332.

3. See Louis Althusser, "Ideology and Ideological State Apparatuses (Notes Towards an Investigation)," in *Lenin and Philosophy and Other Essays*, trans. Ben Brewster (New York: Monthly Review Press, 1972).

4. Wolfgang Iser, *The Act of Reading: A Theory of Aesthetic Response* (Baltimore: Johns Hopkins University Press, 1978), p. 61.

5. Jean-Francois Lyotard, *The Postmodern Condition: A Report on Knowledge*, trans. Geoff Bennington, Brian Massumi, and Regis Durand (1979, Manchester: Manchester University Press, 1986), p. 34; Michael M. J. Fischer, "Ethnicity and the Post-Modern Arts of Memory," in *Writing Culture: The Poetics and Politics of Ethnography*, ed. James Clifford and George E. Marcus (Berkeley: University of California Press, 1986), p. 196.

6. Ann Kibbey, *The Interpretation of Material Shapes in Puritanism: A Study of Rhetoric, Prejudice, and Violence* (Cambridge: Cambridge University Press, 1986), pp. 45, 49.

7. James Fenimore Cooper, *The Leatherstacking Tales, I* (New York: Library of America, 1985), p. 128.

8. Tag Gallagher, *John Ford: The Man and His Films* (Berkeley: University of California Press, 1986), p. 465; Judith M. Kass, *Robert Altman: American Innovator* (New York: CBS-Popular Library, 1978), p. 21.

9. Werner Sollors, *Beyond Ethnicity: Consent and Descent in American Culture* (New York: Oxford University Press, 1986), pp. 26–39.

10. Gallagher, *John Ford*, pp. 26, 29.

11. Joseph McBride and Michael Wilmington, *John Ford* (New York: Da Capo, 1975), pp. 9–11.

12. Gallagher, *John Ford*, p. 234.

13. William Boelhower, *Through a Glass Darkly: Ethnic Semiosis in American Literature* (New York: Oxford University Press, 1987), p. 132.

14. Boelhower, *Through a Glass Darkly*, pp. 46, 63.

15. Gallagher, *John Ford*, p. 341.

16. Peter Bogdanovich, *John Ford* (London: Studio Vista, 1968), p. 76.

17. See, among many other discussions, James Hennessey, *American Catholics: A History of the Roman Catholic Community in the United States* (New York: Oxford University Press, 1981), pp. 180–210.

18. Susanne Langer, *Feeling and Form: A Theory of Art* (New York: Charles Scribner's Sons, 1953), pp. 348–49.

19. McBride and Wilmington, *John Ford*, p. 21.

20. Northrop Frye, *Anatomy of Criticism* (Princeton: Princeton University Press, 1957), p. 175.

21. G. K. Chesterton, "About the Films," in *Authors on Film*, ed. Harry M. Geduld (Bloomington: Indiana University Press, 1972), p. 113.

22. Gallagher, *John Ford*, p. 269.

23. Constance Rourke, *American Humor: A Study of the National Character* (1931, repr. Garden City: Anchor-Doubleday, 1955), p. 232.

24. John Tracy Ellis, *American Catholicism*, 2d ed. (Chicago: University of Chicago Press, 1969), p. 60.

25. Alexis de Tocqueville, *Democracy in America*, vol. 1, ed. Phillips Bradley (1835, repr. New York: Knopf, 1945), pp. 300–301.

26. Gerald Plecki, *Robert Altman* (Boston: Twayne, 1985), p. 1.

27. Alan Karp, *The Films of Robert Altman* (Metuchen: Scarecrow Press, 1981), p. 5.

28. Les Keyser and Barbara Keyser, *Hollywood and the Catholic Church: The Image of Roman Catholicism in American Movies* (Chicago: Loyola University Press, 1984), p. 190.

29. Quoted in Robert Self, "Robert Altman and the Theory of Authorship," *Cinema Journal* 25 (Fall 1985):8.

30. Fredric Jameson, *The Political Unconscious: Narrative as a Socially Symbolic Act* (Ithaca: Cornell University Press, 1981), p. 99.

31. William F. Lynch, *Christ and Apollo: The Dimensions of the Literary Imagination* (New York: Sheed and Ward, 1960), p. 149.

32. Jacques Maritain, *Creative Intuition in Art and Poetry* (New York: Pantheon-Bollingen Foundation, 1953), p. 127.

33. Lynch, *Christ and Apollo*, p. 141.

34. Maritain, *Creative Intuition*, p. 128.

35. Lynch, *Christ and Apollo*, pp. 107, 80.

36. Ibid., pp. 91, 97.

37. Kass, *Robert Altman*, p. 230.

38. Lynch, *Christ and Apollo*, p. 108.

39. Pauline Kael, "Movieland—The Bums' Paradise," in *Reeling* (Boston: Little, Brown, 1976), p. 187.

40. Karp, *Films of Robert Altman*, p. 45.

41. Lynch, *Christ and Apollo*, p. xiii.

42. Ibid., p. 182; Altman quoted in Jonathan Rosenbaum, "Improvisations and Interactions in Altmanville," *Sight and Sound* 44 (Spring 1975):92.

43. Leonard Quart, "On Altman: Image as Essence," *Marxist Perspectives* 1 (Spring 1978):121–22.

44. Maritain, *Creative Intuition*, p. 164.

45. "The Playboy Interview: Robert Altman," *Playboy* 23 (August 1976):55.

46. Robert Phillip Kolker, *A Cinema of Loneliness: Penn, Kubrick, Coppola, Scorsese, Altman* (New York: Oxford University Press, 1980), pp. 323, 338; James Monaco, *American Film Now* (New York: Plume-New American Library, 1979), p. 326.

47. Quart, "On Altman," p. 118.

48. Commenting on Altman's use of panning, Michael Tarantino has estimated that there are no more than twenty static shots in the entire 111 minutes of *The Long Goodbye*. Michael Tarantino, "Movement as Metaphor: *The Long Goodbye*," *Sight and Sound* 44 (Spring 1975):98.

49. Kass, *Robert Altman*, p. 21.

Comprehension and Crisis: Reporter Films and the Third World

For something to be seen, it has to be looked at by somebody, and any true and real depiction should be an account of the experience of that looking. In that sense it must deeply involve an observer whose body somehow has to be brought back in.

—David Hockney[1]

It is the superstructure of Western beliefs and values in the field of information which is principally in crisis.

—Anthony Smith[2]

A phenomenon that exemplifies the crisis in "Western beliefs and values in the field of information" that Smith cites is the emergence of a series of films that combine two established genres: the action-adventure genre set in the third world and the reporter-film genre. These films draw on a tradition of newspaper-reporter films—for example, *The Front Page* (1931), *Picture Snatcher* (1933), *Five-star Final* (1931), *His Girl Friday* (1940), *Front Page Story* (1954), *Front Page Woman* (1935), and *All the President's Men* (1976)—to center on a journalist who investigates a situation, typically increasing his or her knowledge as the narrative progresses. Interpretation becomes a central thematic concern as the reporter tries to make sense out of a confusing situation. Action-adventure films—for example, *Raiders of the Lost Ark* (1981), *Green Ice* (1981), *High Road to China* (1983), *Never Say Never Again* (1983), *Octopussy* (1983), *Indiana Jones and the Temple of Doom* (1984), *Romancing the Stone* (1984), *Hotel Colonial* (1987), and *Firewalker* (1987)—contribute the convention of placing a Western, usually male, protagonist in the center of third-world settings. The mise-en-scène surrounds him with cliched signifiers of the third world as mysterious, inscrutable, exotic, sensual, corrupt, and dangerous.

What results from the generic hybrid is a narrative pattern that combines adventure with investigation, all revolving around an outsider who interprets an unfamiliar location: *The Year of Living Dangerously* (1982), *Last Plane Out* (1983), *Under Fire* (1983), *The Killing Fields* (1984), *Salvador* (1985), *Cry Freedom* (1987), and *Deadline* (1987). These films, which I will call third-world investigation films, typically position the spectator in the role of cultural outsider by virtue of techniques that encourage identification with the reporter protagonist. On one level the films are about problems of cross-cultural interpretation, dramatized by the reporter's struggle to understand events taking place in a foreign culture; but more important, they are concerned with constructing white Western male subjectivity. Because they revolve around the theme of interpretation, the films are unavoidably about constructing the self; as James Clifford reminds us, "Interpreters constantly construct themselves through the others they study."[3] We project our own personal concerns onto whatever we interpret, and our interpretations are influenced by our prior assumptions as we strive for self-knowledge.

Jacques Derrida characterizes the subject as "being implicated in the game, of being caught by the game, of being as it were from the very beginning at stake in the game."[4] Jacques Lacan provides a psychoanalytic explanation for any interpreter's inevitable self-projection onto the object of study in his essay appropriately titled, "Of Structure as an Inmixing of an Otherness Prerequisite to Any Subject Whatever." Lacan argues that "the fading subject yearns to find itself again by means of some sort of encounter with this miraculous thing defined by the phantasm. In its endeavor it is sustained by that which I call the lost object. . . . "[5] It is not unusual now for ethnographers to acknowledge explicitly that they are implicated in their interpretations as a result of the structures they impose on their objects of study. Claude Levi-Strauss, as Derrida shows in his essay "Structure, Sign, and Play in the Discourse of the Human Sciences," described his interpretations of mythology as, to some extent, myths themselves, for they were always informed by his attempts to create order and coherence and influenced by assumptions he held in his position as interpreter.[6]

Ethnographic accounts that, unlike Levi-Strauss's, make claims to authoritative objectivity no longer go unchallenged. In addition, discussions of ethnicity have abandoned the traditional narrow focus on minority ethnic groups, or on cultures deemed exotic by Western anthropologists, to encompass all humanity, including the ethnographer's own ethnic group. As Clifford notes, "Now ethnography encounters others in relation to itself, while seeing itself as other."[7] Even whiteness, as Richard Dyer has shown in his essay, "White," in *Screen*,[8] and Martin Mull has explored humorously in *The History of White People in America*,[9] lends itself to analysis as an ethnic group. In the nineteenth century, white Western self-analysis was disguised only thinly in the literary concern with the innocent abroad who is transformed through exposure to a foreign land. Third-world settings are catalysts for self-knowledge in these texts, perhaps best exemplified by Joseph Conrad's *Heart of Darkness*, and what the Western protagonist sees around him is often a metaphor for qualities he must confront and deal with in himself.

When we understand that constructions of the ethnic Other are linked inextricably to constructions of self-identity, it becomes apparent that in third-world investigation films it is the journalist's ethnic identity at stake. From the moment he arrives in a new location, he is confused by strange, often dangerous, sights and sounds. By emphasizing confusion, the films create desire for knowledge and for the authority it bestows. Underlying the narratives is the assumption that self-identity will follow from comprehension, implying that the reporter will find himself when he understands the confusion surrounding him, that he will define himself in opposition to the Other. Such narratives of self-discovery, of course, appear across disciplinary boundaries and modes of representation. For example, they have been called "fictions of learning" in ethnography[10] and "stories of apprenticeship" in literature.[11]

To establish the reporter's initial unformed and unsettled identity, the films destabilize subject positioning by constructing the foreign culture as chaotic and violent, with the camera primarily adopting the reporter's disoriented point of view. In *Salvador*, as soon as Richard Boyle (James Woods, fig. 6.1), and Dr. Rock (Jim Belushi) drive into El Salvador from the north, they encounter military brutality against civilians—including a sudden, horrifying execution—and are violently seized and taken prisoner. The soundtrack plays a crucial role in creating confusion, with screams and shouts in Spanish intensifying the impact of chaotic events. *Cry Freedom* begins with a violent nighttime attack by the South African military on a black settlement. Likewise, *Under Fire* opens with a violent skirmish between government troops and rebel soldiers in Chad. Its introduction to Nicaragua includes a grenade exploding in

6.1. Richard Boyle (James Woods) is poised to snap a photo in *Salvador:* a film that destablizes subject positioning by constructing foreign culture as chaotic and violent.

a nightclub near the journalists' table and, shortly after, Russell Price (Nick Nolte) taken prisoner by brutal policemen. *The Killing Fields* stages a massive explosion in a busy Phnom Penh street near where the journalists sit at an outdoor cafe. *Last Plane Out* introduces instability with an opening sequence of Sandinista rebels in Nicaragua shooting a farmer and his wife who refuse to hand over their young son. In *Deadline*, as Don Stevens's (Christopher Walken) car approaches Beirut, a bomb explodes loudly nearby. All of these opening sequences create a sense of helplessness in the face of unpredictable violence.

To put the audience in the reporter's position in relation to his confusing surroundings, frequent shots from his point of view encourage sharing his observation of the new location. Often, the country and its people are framed by the window of a car as the reporter drives (or is driven) through the landscape, watching from a sheltered remove. However, cars do not always protect the reporter from violence in the film. In *The Year of Living Dangerously*, Guy Hamilton (Mel Gibson) and Billy Kwan (Linda Hunt) are forced to leave their car in the middle of an anti-American demonstration, where they are attacked by angry demonstrators. In *Under Fire*, when Alex Grayson (Gene Hackman) leaves his car to ask a group of soldiers for directions, they shoot him. In *Deadline*, Don Stevens is driven through Beirut blindfolded, denied the conventional privileged sight provided by a car. Typically, what the gaze observes in the films is seductive and mysterious and steeped in violence.

Not only is the violence designed to destabilize the reporter and spectator, but it is also a projection of the reporter's repressed desires onto the ethnic Other. To heighten the aura of seductive danger, the films consistently introduce a character who individually embodies the culture as a whole and evokes the reporter's simultaneous attraction and confusion. The object of the reporter's fascination is usually a woman—either Western or non-Western—but is occasionally a non-Western man (for example, in *The Killing Fields* and *Cry Freedom*), representing Otherness in its different guises—based on gender and ethnicity—for a white Western male subject. Typically, the reporter attempts to stabilize his identity by befriending or romancing the Other, but his attempts to get to know her or him are initially thwarted, and the narratives often withhold information, making the Other the enigma that propels the narrative. At the same time that the reporter investigates the political situation he is assigned to cover, he also investigates the woman or ethnic Other, asking other characters about them and sometimes searching for them.

6.2. Sydney Schanberg (Sam Waterston) and his translator and guide Dith Pran (Haing S. Ngor) interview Cambodians in *The Killing Fields,* another film that introduces an ethnic Other to embody a foreign culture.

His search also represents a search for the self. After projecting his desires onto the Other, the reporter feels incomplete without her or him and seeks to attain wholeness through unity with the object of desire. In *Deadline,* for example, Don Stevens, a special correspondent sent on short notice from Paris, where he was covering fashion shows, to Beirut, where he is covering war, spends most of the narrative trying to clear up his confusion about the identity and loyalties of a woman who seems to play an important role in political events. *The Killing Fields* involves Sydney Schanberg's (Sam Waterston) long-distance search from New York for Dith Pran (Haing S. Ngor) who is held prisoner in Cambodia (fig. 6.2). Guy Hamilton, in *The Year of Living Dangerously,* tries repeatedly to reach Jill Bryant (Sigourney Weaver) by telephone, and when she refuses to take his calls, attends social events solely for the purpose of encountering her. In the other films as well, as long as the individual object of fascination and the culture as a whole defy access, subject positioning remains unstable. The narrative goal is to comprehend the unfamiliar and overcome inconsequentiality and thereby create a newly defined and stable ethnic, cultural, and gender identity defined as white, Western, and male in relation to the third-world Other.

When the Other is a woman, the camera participates in the narrative investigation by scrutinizing both her body and the setting.[12] *The Year of Living Dangerously, Salvador,* and *Under Fire,* in particular, emphasize photographic scrutiny of the woman. In *Under Fire,* Russell Price repeatedly photographs Claire Sheridan (Joanna Cassidy). In one sequence, after they have made love for the first time, he stands above her and photographs her nude back as if it were a landscape. Alex Grayson, Sheridan's former lover, learns from the photos that she has slept with Price, connecting photographic with physical possession. In *The Year of Living Dangerously,* a revealing conflation of woman and land occurs in a conversation between Western reporters. One reporter announces, "I've secured me a portion of Indonesia," to which another responds, "So have I; she's waiting for me up in my room." The first reporter continues, "A beachhead of tranquility, a private domain, a haven: I have taken me a bungalow." Here in succinct form, and with a dose of irony that comments on its own discourse, the film conflates a woman and the third-world terrain and reveals a Western male desire to possess both.

When the Others are defined by ethnicity and are male, there is less voyeuristic scrutiny of bodies that conflates them with the landscape, but it is not altogether absent. In the pre-credit sequence in *The Killing Fields,* for example, Dith Pran is conflated with Cambodia as Schanberg describes how he grew to "love and pity" Cambodia over a close-up of Dith Pran's face. In *Cry Freedom,* Steve Biko (Denzel Washington) merges with a tree the first time we see him. Shot from Donald Woods's (Kevin Kline) point of view, Biko is obscured by the tree's leaves and by the glare of bright sunshine in Woods's eyes. *Cry Freedom* differs from the other films in that the reporter is at home in the location he interprets; he is a white South African learning about South Africa. However, he is taken by Biko to an unfamiliar location, a black township, that functions filmically in relation to the ruling white South African culture like a third-world location in relation to the United States or Europe in other third-world investigation films.

In these films the protagonists do not fear making a commitment, but rather being neglected. Their greatest fear, it seems, is that they might be unable to understand, much less control, events around them. What they seek, then, is confirmation, or to put it in a Lacanian perspective, a mirror. They need to be recognized, even ad-

6.3. Two romantically involved American journalists (Nick Nolte and Joanna Cassidy) seek shelter from gunfire during the Nicaraguan revolution in *Under Fire* as the politically uncommitted reporter invents a new self by aligning with an individual and a cause.

mired, in order to reexperience the mirror stage of development when, as infants, they acquired a unified sense of self by recognizing their reflection and imagining that everything in the world would respond like a mirror to reveal their presence. The reporters' desire is a narcissistic one for constant affirmation of self in everyone and everything they see. Rather than fear that their voyeurism will be detected and their gaze returned, they fear that it will not be returned.

Although the reporters are usually politically and romantically uncommitted when the films begin, like Russell Price behind the shield of his camera, they gradually invent a new self by aligning themselves with an individual and a cause. In *Salvador*, Richard Boyle proposes marriage to Maria (Elpedia Carrillo) and increasingly supports the El Salvadoran rebels. In *Under Fire*, Russell Price gets close to Claire Sheridan and to the Sandinistas (fig. 6.3). In *The Killing Fields*, Sydney Schanberg speaks out in opposition to U.S. policy in Southeast Asia as a result of his friendship with Dith Pran. In *The Year of Living Dangerously*, Guy Hamilton woos Jill Bryant and becomes more sympathetic to the communists. In *Cry Freedom*, Donald Woods becomes Steve Biko's friend and a supporter of the Black Consciousness Movement led by Biko. In *Last Plane Out*, Jack Cox (Jan-Michael Vincent) romances Maria (Julie Carmen), but, in a departure from the pattern, he supports his old friend President Somoza from the beginning and retains his loyalty even after he learns that Maria is working with the Sandinistas.

A common feature of the films is that, in their attempt to define the reporter's new-found subjectivity, they diminish the threat posed by the initially aloof woman or the man from another ethnic group. When the character is a woman, the reporter typically becomes romantically involved with her, simultaneously possessing her body and her "story," making her transparent. He finds assurance that she wants, and perhaps even needs, him. Thus, the films equate women with responsibility and assign them the stereotypical role of redeeming irresponsible men. Guy Hamilton seduces the aloof and reluctant Jill Bryant, and even after he betrays her confidence, they reunite at the airport to flee Indonesia together at the end of *The Year of Living Dangerously*. Richard Boyle convinces the skeptical Maria to marry him by agreeing to give up alcohol and other women and go to confession in *Salvador*. Jack Cox wins over the Sandinista fighter Maria so that she allows him to board the final plane leaving Nicaragua even though her Sandinista friends are determined to capture him in *Last Plane Out*. Unlike the other films, in *Under Fire* Claire Sheridan does not resist Russell Price; however she does conform to the role of representing moral obligation by encouraging Price to support the Sandinistas. *Deadline* never establishes a romantic relationship between Don Stevens and Sarah, but, in conventional fashion, she urges him to support a cause.

In *Cry Freedom* and *The Killing Fields*, where the Other is male, the reporter is not overtly romantically involved with him (although *The Killing Fields* is more explicit than most other buddy films about a homoerotic attraction between the two men), but any danger he poses disappears. In *Cry Freedom*, Steve Biko is at first presented from Donald Woods's white racist point of view as a threat, but by the end Biko has proven to be, as Woods states, "more moderate and more intelligent than you believe." After Biko is killed, he is internalized by Woods, who hears Biko's voice speak to him in internal diegetic voice-over, allowing Woods to become Biko's spokesman and diminishing any threat Biko might have posed as a separate, autonomous subject (fig. 6.4). In *The Killing Fields*, Dith Pran is never presented as a threat, but his allegiance to Schanberg is emphasized during their separation, while Pran is undergoing

6.4. Donald Woods (Kevin Kline) attends an anti-apartheid rally in *Cry Freedom,* an example of how using a white spokesman for black causes diminishes the threat of blacks as separate, autonomous subjects.

Khmer Rouge "reeducation," with Pran's voice-over addressing his observations to "Sydney." Pran's loyalty to Schanberg is sealed by their highly emotional reunion at the film's end.

Although the films establish white male dominance by removing the threat posed by the gender or ethnic Other, some of them are less certain about Western cultural dominance. In two of the films, *Salvador* and *Last Plane Out,* where the reporter becomes romantically involved with a local woman rather than with another Westerner, he is unable to bring her to the United States. He cannot control the difficulties that arise from their cultural differences. Three of the films in particular acknowledge that their own generic discourse on cultural power is problematic. *Under Fire, The Year of Living Dangerously,* and *Deadline* raise questions about the reporter's ability to interpret an unfamiliar culture without first having a thorough knowledge of how historical contexts have informed current events. In so doing, they take on one of the most hotly contested issues in international relations, the media's dissemination of information.

Critics perceive it as a colonial legacy that international news has been dominated by reports provided by only four large Western news agencies: Reuters, Agence France-Presse, Associated Press, and United Press International.[13] Anthony Smith explains that the news agencies arose during the nineteenth century as a result of competition among imperial powers to establish news networks throughout their dominions. He elaborates: "It was no accident . . . that the same nations which controlled physical transportation around the globe and which thereby maintained contact with their centres of trade and other colonies, also constructed the first news networks to sell information to the world's newspapers."[14] Criticism stems in part from the agencies' sensationalistic coverage of third-world events: "The agencies have a long history of sensational reporting of the Third World. . . . From the 1890s it seemed that the more distant parts of the globe were permanently subject to violence and drama; the East was constantly ablaze with revolt and carnage; Central America was wracked with picturesque revolution while Africa was the province of romantic jungle explorers."[15]

Largely as a result of years of sensationalistic reporting, photographic images of death and violence in the third world, as Cuban author and critic Edmundo Desnoes has pointed out, are "prey to a whole range of distortions and ideological readings" by North American observers.[16] In an analysis of how Western news reports have sensationalized and distorted events in the Islamic world, Edward Said relates the problems posed by media coverage to larger, more pervasive issues: "Between them, the activities of 'covering' and 'covering up' Islam have almost eliminated consideration of the predicament of which they are symptoms: the general problem of knowing and living in a world that has become far too complex and various for easy and instant generalizations."[17]

Typically in third-world investigation films, the reporter "covers" a location on the basis of what he sees; visual perception is invested with explanatory power. In the Western tradition, sight, the privileged sense, is granted the power to reveal the truth. According to Walter J. Ong, our technological culture is marked by an "addiction to visualism," and ocular vision has become "an analogue for intellectual knowledge."[18] A quotation from Bernard Lonergan provided by Ong states concisely why the analogue is inadequate:

> Now, if human knowing is to be conceived exclusively, by an epistemological necessity, as similar to ocular vision, it follows as a first consequence that human understanding must be excluded from human knowledge. For understanding is not like seeing. Understanding

grows with time: you understand one point, then another, and a
third, a fourth, a fifth, a sixth, and your understanding changes several times until you have things right. Seeing is not like that, so that
to say that knowing is like seeing is to disregard understanding as a
constitutive element in human knowledge.

A further consequence of conceiving knowing on the analogy of
the popular notion of vision, is the exclusion of the conscious subject.
Objects are paraded before spectators, and if the spectator wants to
know himself, he must get out in the parade and be looked at. There
are no subjects anywhere; for being a subject is not being something
that is being looked at, it is being the one who is looking.[19]

Moreover, what is suppressed in the correspondence between seeing and knowing is that interpretations are produced in cultural,
historical, and personal contexts and are always shaped by the interpreter's values. Observers who interpret foreign cultures without
thorough study of how history has shaped current events will more
than likely produce interpretations that reflect their own cultural
presuppositions and personal desires.[20]

The journalist in third-world investigation films typically relies
on vision to understand; the more he sees, the better he is able to
achieve what the film presents as the correct interpretation. The
films confirm the reporter's perceptions by constructing characters
who are immediately identifiable as good guys or bad guys on the
basis of their physical appearance, speech, and gestures.[21] As a reporter charged with explaining what he sees, or as a photojournalist, he also often relies on images—photographs and videotapes—
that he collects. When the films present the photojournalist's
photos as if they provided unmediated access to the truth, they perpetuate what Desnoes calls a lie: "all photojournalism contains a
trap. Constant pressure and a leveling effect inhibit the creative development of artists who work for the news. The iron cast deceives
us with its uniformity. Press photographers always find themselves
obligated—consciously or unconsciously—to photograph things in
a mediocre, uniform style to insure that the observer's eye never
discovers the secret: that photography is a lie, with everything depending on an individual photographer's focus and point of
view."[22] When the conventional third-world investigation narrative
suggests that seeing results in understanding, and that images reveal and transmit the correct interpretation, they privilege vision
in the quest for truth, thereby substituting immediacy for analysis
and eliding contradictions and complexities that are not readily
apparent.

Deadline, Under Fire, and *The Year of Living Dangerously,* however, express skepticism about this conventional generic discourse and complicate the relationship between seeing and knowing. There are suggestions in the films that images do not correspond to reality, that truth does not lie on surfaces, that images construct meaning according to their interpretive contexts, and that images are not a neutral record of events but have political ramifications of their own. Although they fail to investigate their own reliance on images and leave cinematic mechanisms unexamined, the three films criticize photography and video, a photojournalist's primary tools, and problematize the reporter's desire to establish his identity by gaining authority over his surroundings.

Deadline begins by doubting the ability of a special correspondent to arrive on the scene and understand a complex situation. Although the film has a recuperative ending that reduces the confusion to a matter of mistaken identities, several sequences emphasize the failure of vision—and the "vision" of a camera—to bring about comprehension and, by extension, self-discovery. The film's first section emphasizes special correspondent Don Stevens's isolation from Beirut after his arrival there. He remains holed up in a hotel that houses other Western journalists, drinking in the hotel bar, relaxing on his bed, sunbathing at the side of the pool, and refusing to enter the city to gather information for his reports. While Stevens is ensconced in the hotel, there are frequent shots of television monitors playing video reports of violence in Beirut in contexts that emphasize their formulaic nature. In one sequence, Stevens provides clichéd commentary to accompany his cameraman's video, and after the cameraman quits in disgust at Stevens's detachment, Stevens borrows old outtakes of street violence from another journalist to use in his next report. Beirut is absent in the early part of the film except in the self-consciously mediated footage seen on video monitors. The figurative blocked vision that results from television mediation is emphasized with a false eyeline match that cuts from a shot of Stevens at night peering through his hotel room window's venetian blinds after he hears gunfire outside to a close-up of a video monitor showing violence in the streets, which a zoom-out reveals to be taking place the next day after a temporal ellipsis. Stevens can only see what his prior experience has made recognizable to him: images that have been technologically mediated and constructed on the basis of Western journalistic conventions.

The film gradually transforms Stevens from passive and detached to an active participant, but his actions prove futile because he has not fully comprehended the intricacy of the situation or his own inconsequentiality. He learns that the Christian Phalange intend to attack a Palestinian neighborhood, but when he warns Palestinians in the streets, they mock him and reject his warnings. Confined in a locked room, he overhears, but does not see, the nighttime massacre when the Phalange indeed attack. Although Stevens is prevented from seeing the attack when it occurs, the following morning he gets exclusive video footage of the carnage because he is on the inside while other reporters are barred from entering the neighborhood. The recuperative switch to a stock story of rivalry between journalists limits the film's critique of the media, but it remains skeptical of the reporter's ability to take charge and transform events by subordinating them to his new-found identity. Stevens's attempt to establish his indispensability by saving the Palestinians proves futile. He remains superfluous to Beirut's conflicts and ends up wandering through a refugee camp.

Under Fire both enacts and critiques the convention of a Western protagonist's self-discovery in a third-world location. Photojournalist Russell Price is transformed into a participant-observer committed to Sandinista victory in Nicaragua (fig. 6.5), but he simultaneously learns that he cannot control the consequences of his own decisions and actions; his subjectivity does not control events. Price's dilemma is presented largely through the film's sustained interest in representation, the basis for photojournalism and the photojournalists' way of relating to their environment. The film makes images its subject matter by indicating that they are not politically neutral and construct meaning according to the contexts in which they are interpreted.

From the beginning, even before Price is introduced, his subjective point of view is made obvious by freeze frames: black and white stills that interrupt the narrative flow to show that a photo is being taken. (*Cry Freedom* opens with the same technique, but it does not subsequently pursue the implications of image-making.) During footage of fighting among rebels on the ground, some riding elephants, and a government helicopter in Chad, Africa, in 1979, individual shots are frozen in black and white and we hear a camera click before the return to color film. The sequence ends with a series of stills, and the last one, a low-angle shot of an elephant and its rider being shot at from a helicopter hovering directly above them, is in color and cropped on either side, revealing an additional level of mediation. Throughout the sequence there is no reverse-angle shot that would reveal the photographer behind the camera,

6.5. Russell Price (Nick Nolte) is caught in street fighting in *Under Fire*, both an enactment and critique of the Western protagonist's self-discovery in a third-world location.

but the freeze frames leave no doubt that there is human as well as technological mediation at work; someone is choosing where and when to take each photo. The next shot, after a temporal ellipsis to a village setting, answers the enigma by showing photojournalist Russell Price adorned with cameras around his neck. Later his elephant photo makes the cover of a news magazine and Price is congratulated by his colleagues at a poolside in Managua, where the photo becomes nothing more than an interesting composition and an impressive photographic credit.

The process from profilmic event to photograph to signifying image with the potential to alter events becomes a central thematic interest of the film. Sandinistas convince Price to photograph their dead leader, Rafael, as if he were alive. The photo has a series of results, some unexpected, indicating that the significance of an image lies in how it is interpreted and that images have the power to cause events. In effect, images are events. As expected, Price's photo of Rafael inspires Sandinista fighters. An unexpected result is the reappearance in Managua of Alex Grayson (Gene Hackman), a former foreign correspondent turned network anchorman in the United States, whose return to Nicaragua ultimately results in his death at the hands of Nicaraguan soldiers. His murderer's identity is revealed by photos of the shooting taken by Price, disproving Somoza's claim that Alex was killed by Sandinistas. This time, Price's photo reveals and transmits the truth, unlike his photo of Rafael.

In a sense, then, Price has vindicated himself with his photos of Alex's death. Yet even the photo of Rafael does not technically lie. It accurately depicts the profilmic event: Rafael seated at a table with Sandinistas standing on either side. The photo itself states nothing about Rafael's condition. It is only the observer who assumes that someone seated at a table is alive. A line spoken by Claire Sheridan takes on new significance: "Things aren't what they seem." Yet another result of Price's photos from the Sandinista hideout is that they allow a mysterious Frenchman with CIA connections, Jazy (Jean-Louis Trintignant), to steal them and use them to identify Sandinistas targeted for assassination. In fact, despite his attempts to establish himself as a Sandinista supporter, Price has been used by both sides simultaneously: his photographs were staged by the Sandinistas for their purposes and used by Jazy for his. Price learns that his decision to snap a photo is not always innocent and its consequences are beyond his control, but he nonetheless shares responsibility for those consequences. A photo is also far less transparent than he believed, conveying meanings and propelling events depending on how the viewer wants to respond. Price's desire to project his interpretation onto events and images proves impossible.

Under Fire subsequently persists in confusing and destabilizing Price. When fighting between Sandinistas and government troops erupts throughout Managua, Price is driving a car in the city accompanied by Alex. Even though they are close to their hotel and know the area, Price gets hopelessly lost. He comments that everything looks different, and he cannot find his way. The film suggests Price can have only a superficial familiarity with the city after his relatively short visit, and even though Price's photo makes him a central causal agent in Nicaraguan events, his centrality results from events largely unknown to him and manipulated by others. He is only a pawn in a much larger, and more contradictory, game. The film even comments on the irony of the Western tendency to prioritize the presence of Westerners in the third world. A Nicaraguan nurse says to Claire after Alex has been killed: "You know the man who was killed? 50,000 Nicaraguan have died. Perhaps now Americans will be outraged at what is happening here. . . . Maybe we should have killed an American journalist 50 years ago."

The Year of Living Dangerously revolves around a new foreign cor-respondent's attempt to establish himself and gain the respect of his colleagues. The film shows that the reporter's desire for recognition (a desire to redefine himself as a highly respected journalist) influ-ences the way he perceives and interprets and ultimately leads to his failure to penetrate superficial appearances. Unlike most third-world investigation films, *The Year of Living Dangerously* sets up a perspective that observes the visiting journalist—Guy Hamilton of the Australian Broadcasting Service—who is judged unwelcome. Billy Kwan states in voice-over, "You're an enemy here, Hamilton, like all Westerners. President Sukarno tells the West to go to hell, and today Sukarno is the voice of the Third World." When Hamil-ton is insulted by gun-toting youths in Djakarta's slums, Billy reas-sures him: "Don't take it personally; you're just a symbol of the West." It is Kwan (who is half-Chinese and half-Australian, and therefore another foreigner in Indonesia), not Guy Hamilton, who is granted the privilege of voice-overs that reveal his thoughts, partic-ularly his thoughts about Hamilton. Kwan's scrutiny of Hamilton is part of the film's suggestion that all ethnic insiders and outsiders simultaneously scrutinize each other.

At one point, the film crosscuts between Hamilton's and a palace guard's eyes in extreme close-up, each searching the other's eyes for some revelatory sign. Eyes become one of the film's primary motifs, foregrounding the process of observation and interpretation. When Billy decides to befriend and assist Hamilton ("despite your na-ivete") he announces, "We'll make a great team, old man. You for the words, me for the pictures. I can be your eyes." Hamilton, how-ever, consistently resorts to Western cliches when reporting on con-ditions in Indonesia, drawing on superficial metaphors and getting carried away by the rhythm of his prose, as Jill Bryant points out to him when she characterizes his reports as melodramatic. He sees, and describes, only as he has learned in the West. Furthermore, he uses the situation in Indonesia narcissistically to further his ambi-tions, especially when he chooses to file a report on confidential information provided by Bryant, despite the damage filing it could do to her and to Indonesian politics.

When Billy feels that Hamilton has betrayed him by placing his career above personal loyalty, he chides, "I made you see things. . . . I created you," making the link between Hamilton's identity and the way he perceives the world. After Billy dies, Hamilton's capacity to see and interpret is severely impaired, both literally and figuratively. Soldiers try to prevent him from entering a government building, and when Hamilton ignores them, one

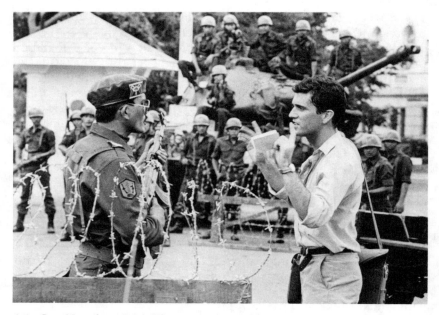

6.6. Guy Hamilton (Mel Gibson) confronted by a military road block during the Indonesian civil war in *The Year of Living Dangerously,* a film emphasizing the inability of Western reporters to understand events in another culture simply by observing them.

strikes him in the eye with a rifle (fig. 6.6). Hamilton retreats with a detached retina, his bandaged eye indicating that he has lost the vision provided by Billy and reinforcing the notion that he can only see what he is prepared to see. Indonesia is now closed to him; he has come full circle to the beginning when he was unwelcome. (Hamilton's assistant, Kumar, says, "Billy Kwan was right. Westerners do not have answers anymore.")

The Year of Living Dangerously consistently emphasizes Hamilton's inability to understand events in Indonesia by simply observing them. The film suggests that the reporter, who epitomizes the ideal of detached observation, fails when confronted with an alternative reality. As Carolyn A. Durham writes, "Weir associates a visual theory of knowledge with Western individualism. Although Guy believes that his traditional linkage of scientific objectivity with journalistic practice allows him to see reality as it really is, free from the interference of personal of cultural assumptions, in fact, he projects images of a profound subjectivity in which he reflects and

6.7. Hamilton strolls through Djakarta with Billy Kwan (Linda Hunt), his photographer and guide in *The Year of Living Dangerously,* Peter Weir's critique of the illusion of journalistic neutrality.

sees only his own self."[23] When the film ends by whisking the nearly blinded Hamilton off to the airport and putting him on a plane out with Bryant, the cliche of a last-minute escape is both a trite convention and an acknowledgment that the reporter has failed; he is incapable of comprehending the complexities behind surface appearances because he insists on clinging to the illusion of journalistic neutrality at the same time that he is motivated by self-interest.

However, even Billy Kwan interprets incorrectly. Kwan's function as interpreter of Indonesia proves not only inadequate but also manipulative (fig. 6.7). Through Kwan, the film links the voyeuristic urge with a narcissistic urge to control. Kwan organizes his thoughts about people he knows into typewritten files, typing: "Here on the quiet page, I'm master. Just as I'm master in the darkroom. . . . I shuffle like cards, the lives I deal with." Kwan attempts to control people's lives on the typewritten page, in the darkroom, and in life. As a photographer, he subscribes to a visual theory of knowledge and uses his photographs to manipulate others, but he fails to account for people making their own choices independently of his desires.

The Year of Living Dangerously goes further in its critique of the subject's desire to objectify what is observes into a fixed, determinate meaning. Kwan shows Hamilton his shadow puppets and explains that if he wants to understand Java, he has to understand how the sacred Indonesian shadow play evades any conclusive meanings: "You must watch the shadows, not the puppets. . . . In the West we want answers for everything. Everything is right or wrong, good or bad. But in the puppet play, no such final conclusions exist." Kwan's statement is borne out by the narrative's inconclusive treatment of Indonesian politics: there are no clearcut distinctions between right or wrong, good or bad. Billy Kwan's own attempts to find workable answers fail and prove to be based on his need to control. The puppet play also serves as a metaphor for film; both cast light and shadow on a screen, and in both, it is up to the viewer to construct meaning. Rather than investigate the film medium itself, *The Year of Living Dangerously* examines the multiple interpretations elicited by photographs. Like the puppet play, photos in the film are understood on the basis of interpretive conventions and cultural conditioning. Billy explains how Indonesians interpret the puppet play, and politics, as a balance of the left with the right, whereas Westerners look for conclusive answers. As an example of the Western urge to categorize, a Western photographer holds up his photo of a bare-breasted Indonesian woman and says, "Beauty among the squalor. I did that with a 200mm." Reporters jokingly debate whether the photo is pornography or art, and Kwan responds mockingly, "If it's in focus, it's pornography; if it's out of focus, it's art."

Although photos of Indonesia's poor in the film elicit feelings of sympathy from the viewer, they also extend the theme of multiple and illusory meanings that evade clearcut explanation. Billy Kwan photographs everything, especially faces, and the walls of his bungalow are plastered with photos of his friends and of deformed and impoverished Indonesians. We frequently see them in close-up from Kwan's point of view as he contemplates them. When Guy Hamilton asks why Kwan doesn't exhibit them, Kwan responds, "I don't care about the photographs. I care about the content. I'm not very aesthetically minded." And yet there is no simple transparent relationship between the photos and their content. One of Sukarno, for example, is actually Billy dressed to resemble him. Billy has literally projected himself into that photo, a process not significantly different from the way he and others project their own personal concerns into all of his photos and into all that they see.

The film's frequent return to the same photos of Kwan's walls, each time suggesting new interpretations, is reminiscent of the Soviet filmmaker Lev Kuleshov's experiments with editing in the 1920s. Kuleshov edited the same shot of a man's neutral face with a series of different shots, and discovered that audiences interpreted the man's expression differently according to the context provided by each preceding shot.[24] In *The Year of Living Dangerously,* Hamilton stares at Kwan's photos of Jill Bryant at different times, and each time the photos suggest different connotations arising from his latest encounter with her. Likewise, a photo of the woman and child supported by Kwan takes on new meaning, seen from Kwan's point of view, after the child has died. The photos do not offer up a single meaning, but reflect whatever the viewer projects onto them, just as Indonesia reflects back to the Western reporters whatever they are prepared to see, and just as any foreign culture becomes a mirror to ethnic outsiders who have no knowledge of historical complexities and therefore cannot see anything but their own cultural assumptions.

We can expect to see the continued release of third-world investigation films, texts recapitulating and reworking the theme of a white Western male identity crisis played out against a backdrop of ethnic, gender, and cultural Others. The films will most likely be as varied as those discussed in this chapter, but also as uniform: adhering unself-consciously to established conventions, a seamless representational style of realism, and a tradition that equates seeing with knowing. As a body, third-world investigation films are testimony to the multiple levels of meaning produced by manipulating conventions within the limitations of mainstream cinema, where things simultaneously are and are not what they seem.

NOTES

1. David Hockney, as quoted by Laurence Weschler in "A Visit with David and Stanley, Hollywood Hills 1987, " in *David Hockney: A Retrospective,* ed. Maurice Tuchman and Stephanie Barron (New York: Abrams, 1988), p. 85, and reprinted in *Film Comment* 25 (July-August 1989):53.

2. Anthony Smith, *The Geopolitics of Information* (New York: Oxford University Press, 1980), p. 172.

3. James Clifford, "Introduction: Partial Truths ," in *Writing Culture: The Poetics and Politics of Ethnography,* ed. James Clifford and George Marcus (Berkeley: University of California Press, 1986), p. 10.

4. Jacques Derrida, "Structure, Sign, and Play in the Discourse of the Human Sciences," in *The Structuralist Controversy: The Languages of Criticism and the Sciences of Man*, ed. Richard Macksey and Eugenio Douato (Baltimore: Johns Hopkins University Press, 1970), p. 248.

5. Jacques Lacan, "Of Structure as an Inmixing of an Otherness Prerequisite to Any Subject Whatever," in *The Structuralist Controversy*, ed. Macksey and Douato, p. 194.

6. Jacques Derrida, "Structure, Sign, and Play in the Discourse of the Human Sciences," ibid., pp. 247–65.

7. James Clifford, "Introduction: Partial Truths," in *Writing Culture* ed. Clifford and Marcus, p. 23.

8. Richard Dyer, "White," *Screen* 29 (Autumn 1988):44–64.

9. Martin Mull and Allen Rucker, *The History of White People in America* (New York: Putnam, 1985).

10. James Clifford, "On Ethnographic Allegory," in *Writing Culture*, ed. Clifford and Marcus, p. 108.

11. Susan Rubin Suleiman, *Authoritarian Fictions* (New York: Columbia University Press, 1983), p. 65.

12. I have written an essay that focuses specifically on the conflation of women and the landscape in third-world investigation films, "Reporters, Women, and the Third World in 1980s Film," *Phoebe: An Interdisciplinary Journal of Feminist Scholarship, Theory and Aesthetics* (Fall 1989):88–92. There is also a tradition in 35mm still photography of photographing nude women's bodies as if they were landscapes, for example Bill Brandt's (British, 1904–83) close-ups of parts of women's bodies.

13. Smith, *The Geopolitics of Information*, p. 73. Perhaps the most highly publicized response to the inadequacy of agency coverage was the New International Information Order, a program proposed by United Nations representatives from third-world countries in the middle 1970s to counteract Western media domination of international news.

14. Ibid., p. 74.

15. Ibid., p. 79.

16. Edmundo Desnoes, "The Death System," in *On Signs*, ed. Marshall Blonsky (Baltimore: Johns Hopkins University Press, 1985), p. 40.

17. Edward W. Said, *Covering Islam* (New York: Pantheon Books, 1981), p. xii.

18. Walter J. Ong, *Interfaces of the Word* (Ithaca: Cornell University Press, 1977), pp. 126, 123.

19. Bernard Lonergan, "Consciousness and the Trinity," a talk given in the spring of 1963 at the North American College in Rome, and reprinted in Ong, *Interfaces of the Word*, pp. 121–22.

20. John Carlos Rowe analyzes the limitations of eye-witness accounts in "Eye-Witness: Documentary Styles in the American Representations of Vietnam," in *Cultural Critique 3*, ed. Rick Berg and John Carlos Rowe (Spring 1986):126–50.

21. Susan Rubin Suleiman explains that characters are "constructed by amalgam" when they are assigned qualities and physical attributes to substantiate value judgments on their philosophical-ideological outlooks, creating an implied link between what they believe and how they look and act, in *Authoritarian Fictions*, pp. 188–90.

22. Edmundo Desnoes, "The Photographic Image of Underdevelopment," *Punto de Vista*, Havana 1967; trans. Julia Lesage and reprinted in *Jump Cut* 33 (February 1988):76.

23. Carolyn A. Durham, "The Year of Living Dangerously: Can Vision Be a Model for Knowledge," *Jump Cut* 30 (March 1985):6.

24. For a discussion of "the Kuleshov effect," see David Bordwell and Kristen Thompson, *Film Art: An Introduction*, 2d ed. (New York: Knopf, 1986), p. 207.

Black Is White/White Is Black: "Passing" as a Strategy of Racial Compatibility in Contemporary Hollywood Comedy

Jokes, even if the thought contained in them is non-tendentious and thus only serves theoretical intellectual interests, are in fact never non-tendentious. They pursue the second aim: to promote the thought by augmenting it and guarding it against criticism.

—Sigmund Freud[1]

How can one chart the effects of the culture on its marginal members? Although we can easily assert that, in an earlier period of American history "the minstrelsy era really took off at the same time as the abolition movement,"[2] the 1980s seemed too complex to make any easy formulations. Under the Reagan administration, blacks and other minorities experienced a gradual erosion of the civil rights gained and consolidated in the fifties and sixties: immigration laws requiring passes, English-only initiatives, increased corruption in the judiciary system in the North as well as in the South, and designer vigilantism. At the same time, the 1960s' ocean of prosperity, in which even blacks were able to swim, began to dry up, leaving minorities gasping at the margins. As a consequence, blacks in the 1980s were, as a group, less educated, poorer, and died in greater numbers than ever before. While even feminists could be proud of certain real and probably permanent, although insufficient, gains in, for example, the academy, blacks continued to drop out of college before graduation at an enormous rate. Cuts in social spending and, more generally, the disappearance in America of the heavy industries in which many urban blacks traditionally made their way into the middle class, were responsible for even more misery than would otherwise be visible.

What has any of this to do with comedy, which, although satirical and biting in other countries, is here evasive and sophomoric?
Contemporary American comedy evades realistic treatments of social issues, opting instead for escape from these issues. Compare
Rules of the Game (1939), with its complex treatment of class decay
and class relation, or *Traffic*'s (1971) avant garde comedy of industrial society, with such mainstream American entries as *The Golden
Child* (1986), *Beverly Hills Cop* (1984), or *48 Hours* (1982). How is
the comic-book plot of *The Golden Child* a realistic depiction of race
relations in the United States? How can we discuss the screwball
comedy plot about lovers of disparate backgrounds imposed on *48
Hours* as a strategy for racial harmony, other than as an ironically
conceived solution having more to do with Leslie Fiedler's romance
between the white man and his "dusky lover" offered in *Love and
Death in the American Novel* than as the laissez-faire realism the film
purports to offer?[3]

No easy connection can be made between black life and black
screen representation. We cannot, for example, unproblematically
assert that traditional black stereotypes are back in fashion. Although it was always a complex phenomenon, doing black stereotypes before World War II was comparatively easy: Uncle Tom, Zip
Coon, Mammy, and the Pickaninny were all easily recognizable.
Then came civil rights, the social problem films of the 1950s and
1960s—for example, *Pinky* (1949), *Guess Who's Coming to Dinner*
(1967), and *Imitation of Life* (1959)—and the gradual, begrudged entry into the Hollywood mainstream via exploitation and a few legitimate roles. However, even in the late 1970s James Monaco could
assert that "the roles have multiplied perhaps ten-fold, but the old
stereotypes survive to be joined by new ones."[4]

In order to formulate a model that will allow more specific discussion of contemporary black film roles, let us, on the strength of
two observations about society, make one assumption about film.
The observations are that the integration of blacks as equal participants in society remains an official but elusive goal, and the absence
of black representation in film is one manifestation of that problem.
The very safe neopsychoanalytic assumption is that any existent
representation of blacks will have an enormous amount of social energy cathected onto it. That the bulk of this representation should
occur in comedy is an indication of the strength of the attempt to
avoid the representation of an enormously difficult subject. It also
suggests a canny ability to sublimate some of this social energy
and anxiety toward the secondary "desire" to recreate a difficult

problem as easily soluble, in other words to recreate race relations as useful insofar as they militate toward humor.

Of course humorous solutions are *fantasy* resolutions of incongruous oppositions. But, as Freud asserts, those fantasies are no less really desired for being fantasies. The "thought" that contemporary films about race embody is the desire that blackness cease to exist, that it be replaced with at most a white version of who and what blacks are. Blacks should be replaced by humans—as humanity is whitely defined. Or, if erasure is impossible only because, were everything white, the page and screen would be blank—the only threat greater than difference is sameness—then borders should be set up, distance maintained, time stopped at about 1947. The lack of black representation in most American film genres is complemented by a reactionary message in the one genre in which blacks make a significant appearance. The resolutions to issues of race proposed by such films as *The Jerk* (1980) and *Beverly Hills Cop* and *Who Framed Roger Rabbit* (1988) should not be dismissed because they are comic. Their plots offer strategies that should be examined as seriously as they are intended. And, of course, the strategy of using comedy as the largest forum for the representation of race ought also to be examined. Race relations as comedy is the contrived de-resolution of a problem into a number of discrete moments of pleasure.

Blackground

The dominant contemporary problem has been to accrue a mere sufficiency of representations of blacks in film. This problem is in part corporate: the white-dominated means of production tends to exclude not just positive but all representations of blacks in film: "We're simply missing from the product."[5] In a way, this is the most extreme criticism of the film industry possible. But the longevity of this practical problem offers itself as both caused by and indicative of another, theoretical dilemma. The white film establishment does not know which is more politically correct (and so bankable): to portray blacks as middle class, or to represent the economic poverty of black life in America. The first option—for example, television's "The Cosby Show"—neglects significant representation of the disenfranchised and smacks of tokenism; the second option too often, as in *The Color Purple* (1985), denies the possibility of positive role models in its depiction of black male rage and impotence.

These limits in representation encourage a kind of iconographicization of the black image, which, in critical discussion, leaves its creators susceptible to the charge of stereotyping. Once the culture as a whole has opted for this reduced version of representation, it becomes possible to see the behavior of even the most complex film characters as stereotypical. The otherwise astute Donald Bogle, for example, characterizes the radicalized, militant blacks of *Putney Swope* (1970) as "supercharged athletes, as high-powered sexual beings, as loud-mouth do-nothings. Instead of picking at any genuine Black follies to prove his point, the director chose to satirize the lies, myths, cliches, exaggerations."[6] Even Spike Lee in *She's Gotta Have It* (1986) can be characterized as Zip Coon, however perfectly aware we may be of the degree to which Lee is an ironized, individuated character.[7]

Especially in mainstream commercial films, one feels the effect of what, in a different arena, Edward Said refers to as *Orientalism*, the tendency of the hegemonic culture to read and represent the ethnic Other as a projection of the kinds of impulses the culture is afraid of acknowledging, but fascinated by, in itself.[8] Black portrayals will be unacceptable as long as they are created by white administration and money because they represent the mainstream's view of the ethnic and, as such, are always crypto-anthropological in nature, always one culture pretending an objective definition of another. In a white hegemony, black depictions will always be readable as stereotypical.[9]

Still, the Reagan years spawned a visible, if token, Republican black middle class that American film has decided is representative and "real." This class is small. Much of it is spurious—blacks *not* voting as Democrats through a disillusionment with the increasing conservativeness of that party. But, in the portrayal of positive black role models, this new black middle class (with some adjustment in party affiliation) figures heavily in films and television shows as different as "The Cosby Show," *Jumpin' Jack Flash* (1986, fig. 7.1), and *She's Gotta Have It*. This class is the most attractive for Hollywood to represent as interesting because it offers the most hope of allowing black roles that evade stereotyping. As *Hollywood Shuffle* (1987) correctly charts, black *ficelles*—street people, muggers, and pimps— still inhabit film as foils to Clint Eastwood and Charles Bronson. The classic versions of stereotypes exist as well, even if, like the black East German Pullman porter in *Top Secret* (1984), the stereotype is parodic. But this "crossover" middle class offers the fewest overt problems in representation because, whatever its ambivalence in relation to black identity, it presents blacks as potential leads for narratives within Hollywood formulas (e.g., the screwball comedy)

7.1. Whoopie Goldberg, an example of Hollywood's portrayal of the new black middle class, in *Jumpin' Jack Flash*.

that traditionally rely on some form of economic independence as a pre-condition for interesting activity.

The representation of blacks as unproblematically successful extends to the actors as well as the roles. There seem to be more successful blacks in films now than at any time since the significant black independent industry of the twenties and thirties. While the reality of blacks in the marketplace and society has worsened in the last ten years, more popular black (comic) leading men are in film— Eddie Murphy, Arsenio Hall, Bill Cosby, Richard Pryor, and, marginally, Robert Townsend and Spike Lee. But this individual success has an at best ambiguous status: American film is guilty of the same tokenism as the culture. *While American society has sanctioned the disappearance of the black in life, it celebrates the success of the black on film. Mainstream black film in American under the Reagan administration became a way to unwrite the history of blacks in America in the eighties.*[10]

Only incidentally a survey on the progress of the ethnic stereotype in the 1980s, this chapter will examine the way in which Hollywood "gets away" with representing disappearance as its reverse. Although the commonsensical perception is probably correct that racist stereotypes exist in more subtle versions of the Mammy, the Pickaninny, and others, I will instead discuss certain comic techniques used in an ideologically focused manner on a less-discussed character: the light black passing as white.

The old comedy technique of parody, and the new comedy technique of doubling, have as their offshoots a kind of passing as a member of a different race in certain films of the late 1970s and 1980s. Certain mainstream films use a version of passing to present their stars for token inclusion into the essentially white society those films depict. The black actor passes in a white role, the white actor in blackface. This dual displacement allows a safe filmic nondiscussion of the place and origin of blacks in America. One sees a reactionary dialogue in these comedies that both echoes and precedes a particular rewriting of American history as including only those blacks who are really white—success, upward mobility, and virility defined as white—and exclusion of blacks who are black.

Of course, the resistance to seeing these fluffy films as serious is explained by the extremity of the message. The reactionary assertion of the films must be acknowledged if the films are to be taken seriously. So they are not taken seriously. Nevertheless, in the case of these comedies, we should probably take the advice of an acute commentator of humor to "assume of all these anecdotes with a logical facade that they really mean what they assert for reasons that are intentionally faulty."[11]

White on Black

It is in itself significant that in the 1980s the overwhelming number of black leads were still comic. And among the most interesting abilities of the black lead is his imitative ability. In the 1970s Richard Pryor starred in a number of films in which he was disguised in one way or another. The Swank distributors' blurb describes Pryor in *Which Way Is Up* (1977) as a "farm worker, his father and a hypocritical preacher." The most poignant moment, though, comes in a film released at the beginning of the 1980s. In *Stir Crazy* (1980), in order to escape from prison, Pryor (the comic of the mournful countenance) has to wear clown makeup: a black man in prison escapes by wearing whiteface. This is oddly metaphorical for the racial thematics of 1980s' films.

Like Pryor in *Blue Collar* (1978), some comics play various versions of working-class, blue-collar blacks. Or, like Pryor in *Car Wash* (1976), they make forays into parodic versions of wealthy blacks.

But black stand-up comics like Arsenio Hall, Whoopi Goldberg, and Eddie Murphy play multiple roles that have to do with making it as affluent white-collar workers, or even wealthy princes, in such films as *Jumpin' Jack Flash* and *Telephone* (1987) and *Coming to America* (1988).

These actors tend to have a wider range of roles that come to define the comic black actor as being about role-playing. Even *Hollywood Shuffle* is in part about the ability of the lead to play a number of roles—the detective, the jive dude, and the movie reviewer (à la Siskel and Ebert). The strategy of the film is a standard catharsis—to act out the roles one fears becoming is to exorcise them from one's personality. Robert Townsend's self-conscious, ironic use of jive roles is supposed to be an exorcism of their power to persuade. Yet we are left with a film in which such roles are still, as always, portrayed as stereotypically comic, if self-consciously so.

The frequency with which actors play multiple roles within a film indicates a tendency to thematize role-playing. Playing a number of roles indicates the actors' understanding of those roles and what they mean. But playing them ironically also means a certain detachment from them, a space that prevents a complete identification of the actor with his or her role. If Goldberg's pretending to be a street person or junkie means that she could not really be one of these characters, what does Eddie Murphy's pretending to be a policeman in *48 Hours* or a customs inspector in *Beverly Hills Cop* mean?

Further, the need to prove that these roles could belong to them, even ironically, means that the roles are not perceived as automatically possible to them. The fact that, as a group, black actors have to prove their fitness for such roles is itself proof that they are not yet accepted as belonging. Northrop Frye's sense of the disguised hero entering the green world for the solution to the conundrum postulated at the beginning of the play as his life has, in the contemporary portrayal of blacks in a white society, a more insidious meaning.[12] The traditional hero enters and leaves the forest, taking something or someone significant with him. But the black lead can never leave the green world; he is defined as already having everything of value he needs, with the exception of freedom and money of course, always available on white corporate America's terms. Orlando enters the Forest of Arden to find Rosalind, whereas Eddie Murphy goes to Beverly Hills to solve a murder. Orlando leaves Arden with Rosalind; Murphy leaves with the hotel bathrobe he has stolen. Murphy and his sidekick—fair, blonde Lisa Eilbacher—are, as Don Lockwood constantly asserts about his relation to Lena La-

7.2. Eddie Murphy as a white man in *Coming to America*. The thematic testing of the comic is part of an exclusionary ideology in which the very ability of some blacks to play white roles is the proof that not all blacks can play these roles, that some blacks are somehow special.

mont, "just good friends." No simulated cunnilingus as in *Romancing the Stone* (1984) for the lead couple here.

Testing is always by its very nature exclusive: not everyone passes, and only a few do well. If one actor is proficient enough to play a variety of middle- and lower-class roles, then he is always so at the expense of a number who are not. The thematic testing of the comic is part of an exclusionary ideology in which the very proof of the ability of some blacks to play more or less white roles is also the proof that not all blacks can play those roles, that these blacks are somehow special (fig. 7.2). Like middle-class black America, these actors are token. They carry the unfair but inevitable burden for both the right and left of accounting for their success when others are left behind. Even in *Hollywood Shuffle* the hero is shown making a choice to leave Hollywood as a choice toward family; the family, and personal connections of the star, are partially responsible for his not making it.

The tendency of black comics to imitate black stereotypes and white mannerisms to the same end can be seen most clearly in certain Eddie Murphy vehicles. Although imitation of whites was always part of stock-in-trade of Zip Coon, the difference is that Eddie Murphy is better than his white counterpart (fig. 7.3). Zip Coon was always a poor imitation of the white dandy. The central scene of *48 Hours* is Murphy's entrance into the bar as a fake police officer in order to procure information from the customers. Murphy gets his

7.3. As in *Beverly Hills Cop*, the primary job of Eddie Murphy in *The Golden Child* is to care for the nonblack.

information, behaving in the best tradition of the kind of white officer who sent him to jail. We admire the uncanny excellence of his ability to identify with the aggressor in this film; technique replaces theme as focus of our attention. Murphy is much better, more deft and competent, than his white accomplice, Nick Nolte.

If anything, Nolte is the hulking, inarticulate, slightly confused and stupefied animal—the negative, more or less self-conscious projection of the kind of character the film chose not to make Murphy. He is the white accomplice who is more stereotypically black than Murphy, further muddying the types while allowing them to persist. The pairing of Murphy and Nolte is a reworking of the screwball formula fantasy in which the antagonists are found to have affinities that take precedence over social and class differences. Only here, the affinities have racist rather than sexist undertones.

In *Trading Places* (1983), we are early given a sense of how Murphy will come to play a black playing a black. Even the plot of the film is about race and the problem of getting the black man into white America as unobtrusively as possible. In order to settle a bet about the comparative influence of heredity and environment, a black beggar is placed in a position of luxury and responsibility by two cretinous bigots. Throwing a party in his new, luxurious digs for his old, lumpenproletariat (largely black) friends, Murphy ultimately ejects them, careful for the furniture they are misusing as he had misused it in a previous scene. The film does not punish him for his abandonment of his friends. In fact, while exorcising the poor black in him, he is made to seem liberal in contrast to the villains of the film, two of whom sport pictures of Reagan and Nixon on their desk, and one of whom is reading a copy of G. Gordon Liddy's *Will*.

At the beginning of the film Murphy pretends to be lame and blind in order to beg; he sways like Ray Charles while sitting on a little cart like Porgy's, doing two imitations at once. At the end of the film he pretends to be a black national, perhaps a U.N. member, with parti-colored caftan and a vaguely British-colonial accent. He is a black man in blackface, pretending to be black, a fair representation of the classic minstrel paradox. It is blackness passing as itself, wearing the face it is forced to take, re-representing itself as its larger audience conceives of it.

In *48 Hours*, Murphy's portrayal of a black con man is equally ambiguous; it is parodic—we know that although he is a black man with a gun he will not really kill anyone important. His gun has no bullets, his badge is phony. But the parody is an indication that Murphy will, in classic Hollywood style, go from one side of the law to the other. If audiences enjoy him, he will, like Cagney, Bogart, and Gable, go from outlaw to cop in one jump, simultaneously reinforcing two traditional Hollywood assertions: class knows no racial distinctions—police and criminal inhabit different sides but the same milieu—and ethnics are the best policemen themselves. Like the Italian "Little Caesar" who becomes Dr. Ehrlich, or the Irish "Public Enemy" who becomes everyone's favorite G-man, Axel Foley becomes the ethnic who goes straight, leaving behind his old neighborhood in the process.

Beginning with shots of urban street life made fashionable in this comedy cycle by *The Blues Brothers* (1980), *Beverly Hills Cop* announces itself as a film about black urban life. However, the film very quickly moves to its title location. *Beverly Hills Cop* is careful to show that the villains against whom Axel Foley fights are white. Further, the lead heavy—Maitland—has close-cropped blonde hair and steely, blue-grey eyes. Steven Berkoff plays Maitland as more than merely authoritarian: he is epicurean, quietly cold, and sartorially fascist in the best parodic neo-Nazi style.

Again, as in *48 Hours*, much of the comedy depends on imitation and "faking." The imitations multiply like the epiphanies in *Ulysses*: Foley pretends to be a *Rolling Stone* reporter in order to get a room at the Beverly Hilton, an effete homosexual in order to get into a restaurant to confront the villain, a customs agent to explain his presence in a "secured" area. He is constantly explaining his presence as a black man, explaining to the valet at a stylish restaurant that his car looks so damaged because of its treatment the last time he ate there. He also pretends to be a black-marketeer, a truck driver from Buffalo, and a florist delivery person.

This need to explain Murphy/Foley's presence derives from the fact that he is the only significant black man in the film. (As an entry in the detective-thriller genre, the film does of course contain a minor black heavy and cops.) He must not only justify his presence in the haunts of the very white, but also must show that, as a symbolic presence, he contains the whole range of possible black behaviors, ironized and simplified, within his own personae. He has to account for his absence from the black urban milieu in which we first see him by carrying its stereotypes with him.

Murphy/Foley must be serious about the comic parts. He is in an oddly liminal position: the imitations are parodic, but coming as a part of the plot, the diegesis, he is dependent on them in order to get him into positions and places of power. Unlike, for example, Groucho Marx, who does not care whether or not anyone believes his roles, and who subsequently never tries to be anything other than a lecherous, middle-aged, self-parodic Jew, Murphy/Foley must convince the other players that he is who he pretends to be. His is a modernist stance disguised as a postmodernist stance because it is functional playing, not merely a laughing into the abyss. What ought to be merely comic routines, and were in his "Saturday Night Live" skits, are in fact teleological.

Murphy's characters pretend to positions of power rather than actually inhabit them. His job at Duke and Duke (*Trading Places*) is the result of a momentary whim; it ends as quickly. His gun in *48 Hours* is not, until the end of the film, loaded. Even in *Beverly Hills Cop*, where he is given a status as a member of a police force, that power is negated by taking him out of his area of jurisdiction. The negation becomes in fact a part of the film's interest: it is about his individual ability to get what he wants without any socially sanctioned authority. Read as allegory, this becomes an interesting statement about the way in which blacks ought to work—not collectively but individually, not actively opposing the police but on the edges of their authority.

Black on White

The implication of a uniform process of change is misleading, as is the failure to acknowledge that the receiving group undergoes change in absorbing the other.[13]

If black comics are coming to wear an invisible whiteface in a kind of minstrelsy-nouveau, white comics, like minstrels of old, occasionally indulge in, if not exactly blackface, then black role-playing. In an attempt at equal opportunity, Hollywood portrays passing on a two-way street: white men can also pass as black. This is another attempt at a configuration in which distinctions between black and white collapse without any real injury to representations of a benign, patriarchal capitalism. There will be fewer films in which whites play blacks, not because no anxiety is involved, but because the historical point being made is in some way more difficult to achieve. Examples include Woody Allen in *Zelig* (1983), Gene Wilder in *Silver Streak* (1976), and Peter Sellers in *Being There* (1979). The very fact that one generally finds this phenomenon in moments of films points to a kind of anxiety about treating the theme of downward mobility, even comically. The great exception is of course

Soul Man (1986), which, because of its status as a minor production with minor casting, will not be discussed herein.

As an example of one moment, in *Back to the Future* (1985), Michael J. Fox finds himself jettisoned back to 1955 and playing in a black rock and roll band. He is trying to get his would-be parents to kiss, or they will not marry, and he will not be born. At some point in his performance he breaks into Van Halen-inspired gyrations during his rendition of "Johnny B. Goode." In fact, Fox's yuppie is *composing* the song, impressing the black band leader, a Mr. Berry, so that he calls his cousin Chuck long distance to hear the new sound.

The chords being struck are extremely different from the theme of, for example, the previous decade's *Watermelon Man* about the torments of a white man who wakes up black. The point of *Back to the Future* is that rock and roll originated not in some arguable combination of black jazz and blues and rockabilly music, but with white, Anglo-Saxon, affluent, suburban, teenagers absorbed with finding an identity outside the moribund culture offered them by their parents. While such an argument has the merit of explaining much about American advertising and marketing trends, it is more interesting than accurate as a part of the historical records already sufficiently obscured in other ways. It accurately reflects a desire on the part of white America to have been less beholden to black culture (among others) for the structure of its own culture, of which rhythm and blues, jazz and rock and roll, are now official components.

This comic obfuscation works by reversing a historical trend— pretending that the causation was the other way around. The wish is presented as comic, but the fact that there is a great deal of audience energy cathected to it is probably significant. The rock and roll scene in *Back to the Future* is one of the more popular for audiences to recapitulate.

Versions of this obscurantism traditionally inform black-white relations in American film and theater. Fred Astaire, in a 1930 recording of "Puttin' on the Ritz," astonishes his black audience ("Boys, look at dat man puttin' on the ritz." "You look at him, I can't") with dance steps, many of which originated in black jazz styles. As late as 1953, Astaire similarly impresses blacks at the beginning of *The Bandwagon*. His stardom cast equally good black dancers—the Nicholas Brothers, for example—in the shade. Even as late as *High Society* (1956) Bing Crosby leads a band for whose style Louis Armstrong is really responsible.

More recently, whites take the position, if not exactly the role, traditionally attributed to blacks in a sly satire of blackness as it is defined by white culture. The most significant versions are some personae of Steve Martin and Dan Aykroyd. Aykroyd is the white investment counselor replaced by Eddie Murphy in *Trading Places*. In that film he makes up for awhile in blackface, imitating a Rastafarian. In *Dr. Detroit* (1983), Aykroyd demonstrates that the best pimp is an Anglo-Saxon pimp. He brings a quixotic, inappropriate nobility to a profession he has entered "accidentally." Aykroyd, in the flamboyant colors and styles the middle class associates with pimps (and that a certain class of intellectuals, best exemplified in Paul Fussell, associates with the middle class), appears ridiculous.[14] The satire is ostensibly directed at a kind of insulated pedantry (Aykroyd is a college professor), but it also works the other way, as a satire of the kind of flamboyant dress associated with urban black street life. In a particularly interesting variation on this strategy of ethnic replacement, *The Karate Kid II* (1986) features an ethnic culture teaching the dominant culture the tools with which to defeat the former group. It is a wonderful allegory about tokenism—the Japanese man teaches the young white boy karate so the boy can use this skill to beat the Asians against whom he competes.

Steve Martin, in *The Jerk*, takes this disguised satire of a version of black culture invented by whites to an extreme when he plays Naven Johnson, a white man raised by black sharecroppers. When he discovers as an adult that he is not black he decides to leave home and make his way in the world. But he behaves in an unacculturated manner: dressing inappropriately, believing everything everyone tells him, and being out of control of his own libido (he calls his penis his "special purpose"). Because he is white he does not behave like the version of the street-smart urban black we have come to accept as more or less politically correct in Eddie Murphy and Whoopi Goldberg. Rather, the Martin role goes back to Zip Coon, the black man trying to imitate the white dandy without understanding the social configurations into which he is trying to place himself. Martin is a version of black passing for white, a man who looks white yet who does not fit into white culture. He even makes the traditional choice of *Pinky* and *Imitation of Life* to return to his people as a prodigal son. As the audience knows he is white, he is as safe to laugh at as were the original white minstrels.

The film's version of the black family that Martin joins at the end of the film is the exemplar of the exotic culture that Said discusses in *Orientalism*, the culture, which exists in some authentic version but which is reinvented by the dominant culture, the spectator culture for psychic purposes of its own. Here it is reinvented as traditionally happy with its lot as a poor Southern farming family. As a film about blacks made by a white industry, Naven's return to his family is a segregationist strategy disguised as a separatist choice, a comic avowal that there is no alternative to passing but a return to the fold.

Black and White in Color

Because of its ambiguous status as allegory, *Who Framed Roger Rabbit?* takes the most fearlessly and extremely racist position on the politics of passing and segregation. Its status as cartoon, and its reliance on our sense of the fluidity of stereotyping, allows for the re-eruption of the most blatant stereotyping.

That *Who Framed Roger Rabbit?* has at its center an anxiety about passing and tokenism is evident in the barest relation of plot: because a new freeway being built will increase the value of Toontown, a ghetto for cartoon characters, a villainous millionaire (Christopher Lloyd) murders one of the more prominent residents in order to gain control of the town. He blames the murders on Roger, a cartoon rabbit. As it turns out, the villain is himself a toon disguised as a human. Further, this passing toon wants to kill all the toons in the ghetto. For attempting this alternative to the ambiguous segregation the film offers as *its* solution to racial tension, this toon is punished with a public unmasking that reveals him as a traitor. He dies at the hands of a white, human detective (Bob Hoskins).

Rabbit director Robert Zemeckis sets most of his work in the past: *I Wanna Hold Your Hand* (1978) and *Back to the Future.* Coming at an extremely late date in the Reagan administration, *Roger Rabbit* takes advantage of the nostalgia that characterized the 1980s; the film is set in the 1940s, a few years after the trauma of war and its attendant racial tensions, a few years before the trauma of the civil rights movement.

The benign nostalgia for a simpler time when toons were toons is a more or less conscious metaphor for a nostalgia over the last moment when coons were coons and ghettos were not front-page news. *Rabbit* is a more or less allegorical treatment of a benevolent relation between two races somewhat tenuously connected by a common need to laugh. The ostensible threats to racial harmony are big business, transportation technology, and a future landscape blighted with shopping centers and overcrowded cities. The vision of our present is offered to us as an insane future. But, because this vision depends completely on a modern technology without which it could not be conceived, such nostalgia deconstructs itself. Disney, one of the makers of this film bashing the freeway, is the proprietor of two of the world's largest parking lots: Disney Land and Disney World. This film about the cretinous destruction of an integrated culture by corporate capitalism is produced by a company that has opened a theme park near Paris.

The film's anti-big business pretense is also undercut by its own paternalistic portrayal of the relation between humans and toons. The toons themselves, except for Roger's girlfriend Jessica, are happy-go-lucky and rather careless of economic and political concerns. Their economic life is guided by human (read white) agents, club owners, and studio bosses. They like to laugh, sing, dance, and make love more than they like to work. Their ideal work is that in which they get to do these things. They are saved in the end from the breaking down to their ghetto by a white detective who does not like them. Compare the behavior of Roger to the behavior of antebellum minstrels:

> Minstrel caricatures mirrored the prevailing belief that slavery was good for the slave since it drew upon his natural inferiority and willingness to serve. Slaves were content. The proof was offered in the image of the happy Sambo. . . .
>
> The old plantation was offered as a kind of paradise. White Americans were constantly being bombarded with the image of happy slaves, is what it amounted to. So slavery must be a good institution if the slave was happy and the masters were kindly. And so that whole cultural image of a benign beneficent institution was projected constantly in the period immediately before the Civil War.[15]

Minstrels portray the Sambo as feebleminded and happy to serve— a description that fits Roger, who asserts that he exists only to make people laugh.

The allegorical quality of the film unintentionally takes off in other directions. The other cartoon romantic lead is Jessica, a pneumatically enlarged adolescent wet-dream placed squarely in the tradition of the tragic mulatto (fig. 7.4), "the part-Black woman—the light-skinned Negress was given a chance at lead parts and was graced with a modicum of sex appeal. . . . The mulatto came closest to the white ideal."[16]

The relation between the voluptuous chanteuse and the rabbit is meant to be merely titillating, but it contains all the undertones and anxieties of an absorption with miscegenation. Further, this repre-

7.4. The relation between the voluptuous mulatto chanteuse and the rabbit contains all the undertones and anxieties of an absorption with miscegenation. The magazine cover depicts the body as a cartoon with the face of a human being, thus exemplifying the mediation of racist stereotypes through animation technology.

sentation carries with it more than a *frisson* of bestiality that the fear of miscegnation always included. ("A man cannot commit so great an offense against his race, against his country, against his God . . . as to give his daughter, in marriage to a negro—*a beast.*")[17] Jessica also implies that Roger is well endowed, or a terrific lover in some unspecified way, playing off the white anxiety about the potency of black men. It is no accident that the character chosen for Roger is a rabbit.

The decision to re-present traditional stereotypes is contingent on their transformation by animation technology. Audiences no longer feel comfortable with unmediated depictions of racist stereotypes, but rather with the encoded message in which cartoon equals black person. But the thematically more significant decision is to depict blacks as cartoons in a film that depicts whites as "real" people. In an allegory about race relations, the opposition "human/cartoon" ("human/non-human," "human/animal") is telling. The historically unproblematic whites (unproblematic at least in this dichotomy) must be given status as real, in time and in history, whereas the toons are by nature fictional and textual. Roger Rabbit's willingness to be beaten and mauled as a part of his job is the visible proof that history as pain is always only text.[18] This text has a primary status as fiction because that part of history which is about segregation, pain, and disenfranchisement is the very stuff of the most blatant fictions. History is recomposed as myth. As Roland Barthes constantly emphasizes, the culture reconstructs the problematic past as a myth whose formulas contain the solution to problems that are historically resistant to solution. Claude Lévi-Strauss, in another context, observes that "a myth always refers to events alleged to have taken place in time: before the world was created, or during its first stages—anyway, long ago. But what gives the myth an operative value is that the specific pattern described is everlasting; it explains the present and the past as well as the future."[19]

The allegory takes place at a more structurally significant level than we, or the filmmakers, had at first thought. The problem stated by the plot and theme—how to create a better working relation between toons and people—is the problem that the technology of the film has already solved. The film leaves us remarking how wonderful it is that toons/coons are able to act so naturalistically, that they can be made to react so well with *real* people. Strides in animation technology enable people to overcome the barrier between the real and the surreal, presenting the animated world as socially presentable. The allegory assumes first that modes of minority representation are important—are a problem—only insofar as they conflict with modes of mainstream representation. The second assumption is of course that such a problem is soluble through the sheer power of technology. The degree of integration achieved is possible only through an extremely expensive technology that can only infrequently be brought into use, because it is cost-effective only as long as it remains sufficiently novel to attract large crowds to offset its own cost. The technology itself suggests a tokenist attitude toward problem-making. Social mobility is available only to those groups that have complete access to the most recent technologies.

As the myth perpetuated by *Roger Rabbit* is structured, the segregation postulated in the plot is necessitated by the technologically visible unfeasibility of portraying the toons and the people as inhabiting the same world. They are composed of different stuff, inhabit a different set of audience expectations. The amazement engendered at seeing the toons react to people in a "lifelike" way is always only possible because of the audience's sense of novelty (fig. 7.5). The film promotes a benign separatism between the races that cannot really be brought together both because they are composed of separate technologies and because the purpose in bringing them together—entertainment—would be defeated by overexposure of one to another. One race is invented and more or less controlled by the other race for the purpose of entertainment by watching it hurt itself or act eccentrically in ways that we cannot allow ourselves. Finally, the technology itself obscures the profundity of the racist message. As mythmakers, Stephen Spielberg and Robert Zemeckis may rank with another pioneer in American film myth and technique: D. W. Griffith.

Passing the Buck

Passing as a strategy of racial compatibility in film allows the cultural hegemony simultaneously to perpetuate the notion that by the 1980s America had solved the "race problem" and to deny the depiction of authentic empowerment. Instead, films create a black population of individuals who are merely unique; they are created in order to devalorize cultural Otherness. Make the black man white and render his power charismatic, not political. Make the white man black and perpetuate all the stereotypes about stupidity and failure to understand the dominant social codes so that whoever behaves in this fashion deserves disempowerment. Subordinate the dialogue about race relations in an allegory dependent on technol-

7.5. *Who Framed Roger Rabbit?* offers viewers a vision of benign separatism between the races that cannot really be brought together because of separate technologies: one race is invented and controlled by the other race.

ogy to furnish a racist utopia in which blacks seek their unempowerment and alienation from the dominant culture. The final scene of *Who Framed Roger Rabbit?* shows the toons traipsing back to their newly reconstituted ghetto—all happy music and Technicolor sunset—content to be severed from the problematics of human empowerment. The vision is best summarized by the tune invented by antebellum whites for a black slave persona:

> Oh hand de banjo down to play
> We'll make it ring both night and day
> We care not what de white folk say
> They can't get us to run away.[20]

NOTES

1. Sigmund Freud, *Jokes and Their Relation to the Unconscious* (London: Hogarth Press, 1960).

2. Marlon Riggs, "Ethnic Notions" (television documentary produced in San Francisco, California by Marlon Riggs and KQED Television,

1986). For this and other assertions about the Reagan era and film culture I am deeply indebted to Richard Onorato of Brandeis University.

3. Leslie Fiedler, *Love and Death in the American Novel* (New York: Criterion Books, 1960).

4. James Monaco, *American Film Now* (New American Library, 1979), p. 212.

5. Marilyn Milloy, "A Schematic in Black and White," *Newsday* (June 1982):123.

6. Donald Bogle, *Toms, Coons, Mulattoes, Mammies, and Bucks: An Interpretive History of Blacks in American Film* (New York: Viking Press, 1973), p. 229.

7. Nola Darling, who, in *She's Gotta Have It*, is even further individuated, is, in her knowledgability of and freedom with her sexuality, characterizable as a variation on the "tragic mulatto." In stereotypical—if comic—fashion, her sexuality becomes problematic for the men surrounding her. Spike Lee's real innovation is in the multiple points of view the film adopts in order to render Nola complex, as if the film is trying to provide in one text the multiple versions of representations that allow us to consider character as more than a stereotype.

8. Edward W. Said, *Orientalism* (New York: Random House, 1979), esp. chapters 1 and 2.

9. Never mind that Spike Lee is as much a persona as Whoopie Goldberg; Goldberg seems less authentic in her films, while Spike Lee or Robert Townsend, both of whom write, direct, and finance their films, seem more authentic.

10. For the sake of making the contrast between the myth of black success and the reality of black male culture more striking, it is worth quoting at length some statistics compiled by Robert Staples in "Black Male Genocide: A Final solution to the Race Problem in America," *Black Scholar* 18 (May-June 1987):3:

> 1. While black men account for only 6 percent of the population in the United States, they make up half of its male prisoners in local, state, and federal jails.
>
> 2. The majority of the 20,000 Americans killed in crime-related incidents each year are black men.
>
> 3. Over 35 percent of all black men in American cities are drug and alcohol abusers.
>
> 4. Eighteen percent of black males drop out of high school.
>
> 5. Twenty-five percent of the victims of AIDS are black men.
>
> 6. Over 50 percent of black men under the age of 21 are unemployed.
>
> 7. Forty-six percent of black men between the ages of 16–62 are not in the labor force.
>
> 8. About 32 percent of black men have incomes below the officially defined poverty level.

11. Freud, *Jokes and Their Relation to the Unconscious*, p. 107.

12. Northrop Frye, *The Anatomy of Criticism* (Princeton: University of Princeton Press, 1957), p. 182.

13. Michael Banton, "The Direction and Speed of Ethnic Change," in *Ethnic Change*, ed. Charles F. Keyes (Seattle: University of Washington Press, 1981), p. 33.

14. In, for example, Fussell's "Notes on Class," in *The Boy Scout Handbook and Other Observations* (New York: Oxford University Press, 1982), pp. 46–60.

15. Riggs, *Ethnic Notions*.

16. Bogle, *Toms, Coons, Mulattoes*, p. 15.

17. Ariel [Buckner H. Payne], *The Negro: What Is His Ethnological Status?* (Cincinnati, 1867), p. 48.

18. For example, in Paul De Man's assertion that all significant historical representations are "masquerade in the guise of wars or revolutions," quoted in *The Nation*, January 9, 1988, p. 22.

19. Claude Lévi-Strauss, "The Structural Study of Myths," *Journal of American Folklore* 78 (October-December 1955):279.

20. Riggs, *Ethnic Notions*.

PART
TWO

Ethnicity: Ideology, Theory,
and Methodology

Ethnicities-in-Relation: Toward a Multicultural Reading of American Cinema

Debates concerning minoritarian and postcolonial discourse, ranging in full force in prestigious literature departments, have as yet had relatively little resonance in cinema studies. Issues of ethnic and racial representation have been marginalized within the field, perhaps on the assumption that such narrowly "sociological" matters are somehow unworthy of the discipline's newly achieved formal sophistication. The debates over ethnicity and race tend to be regarded, furthermore, as having only limited significance, or as being relevant only to a specific corpus of films. But ethnicity and race inhere in virtually all films, not only in those where ethnic issues appear on the "epidermic" surface of the text. I propose that ethnicity is culturally ubiquitous and textually submerged, thus hoping to challenge the widespread approach to ethnicity as limited to "content" analysis, as well as to reconsider the critical approaches toward the (informal) canon on cinema studies from a multiculturalist theoretical frame.

The disciplinary assumption that some films are "ethnic" whereas others are not is ultimately based on the view that certain groups are ethnic whereas others are not. The marginalization of "ethnicity" reflects the imaginary of the dominant group which envisions itself as the "universal" or the "essential" American nation, and thus somehow "beyond" or "above" ethnicity. The very word *ethnic*, then, reflects a peripheralizing strategy premised on an implicit contrast of "norm" and "other," much as the term *minority* often carries with it an implication of minor, lesser, or subaltern. Restricting the quality of "ethnicity" to particular communities, furthermore, is linked to a ghettoizing discourse which considers ethnic and racial groups in isolation. By projecting "minorities" as if they lived apart from the larger cultural-historical dynamics of the United States, this discourse implicitly suggests their "special," allochronic, quasi-anthropological status. (Anthropological texts, as Johannes Fabian argues, have located the "other" in a temporally distinct space, different from that of the speaking subject.)[1] This essentializing and ahistorical discourse masks the fact that no group exists in a vacuum. In a multiethnic society communities are necessarily implicated—economically, historically, politically, and culturally—in one another, subjected to permeable boundaries of identity.

The word *ethnic* in contemporary parlance often evokes little more than sentimental traces of the customs and cuisine of the old country. In this sense the adjective *ethnic* implies a liberal-pluralistic vision which masks contradictions of class, race, and gender, as well as the interdependency of histories and even identities. The hegemonic national imaginary projects (North) America as constituted by an Anglo-American core, subsequently supplemented by ethnic "accretions." Eurocentric historiography posits quasi-magical beginnings with the "discovery" of America, the pilgrims, the puritans, and the pioneers eliding Native-American and African-American perspectives and voices. The liberal concept of a happy plurality of "hyphenated Americans" posits a pseudo-equality in status, as if that which precedes the hyphen—"African," "Greek," "Dutch" (the categories themselves level the continental with the national)—alluded to more-or-less equivalent historical experiences, ultimately subordinated to the amelioristic teleology implied by the post-hyphen "American."

The intersection of ethnicity with race, class, and gender discourses involves a shifting, relational social and discursive positioning, whereby one group can simultaneously constitute "norm" and "periphery." A given community can in a single context exist in a relation of subordination to one group and at the same time in a relation of domination toward another. Flexible contradictory relations, furthermore, can characterize the community itself, suggesting that "ethnicity" is far from being a unitary topos. I use the term *ethnicity,* therefore, to refer to a spectrum of identities and differences, all ultimately involving questions of inequalities of power. Ethnicity does not constitute a fixed entity or category expressing a natural, essential difference, but rather a changing set of historically diverse experiences situated within power relations. Although a poststructuralist formulation of ethnicity carries with it the danger of undermining legitimate struggles for recuperation of cultures which have undergone brutal ruptures and are in a constant process of forging their communal identity, it also has the advantage of transcending essentialist notions of identity. Without falling into essentialist traps and yet without being politically paralyzed by deconstructionist formulations, we may argue for provisional ethnic and racial identities at particular moments of history, articulated in relation to parallel and opposing collectivities. And without positing a hygienic concept of communities, we may speak of *overlapping, de-centered circles of identities*.

Focussing on character stereotypes and social mimesis, studies of images of America's ethnicities have tended to pit an isolated minoritarian group against a fixed, white-American power structure. They have not generally attempted to register the structural analogies underlying Hollywood representation of "subaltern" groups as well as the interplay of social and sexual displacements, projections, and dialogisms among the diverse ethnicities—whether marginalized, hegemonic, or situated between. Even the recounting of the influential role of minoritarian groups on the dominant ethnic culture—for example the striking Africanization or Latization of North American music and dance—tends to ignore the interethnic influences among the diverse of "margins." My interest, however, is not simply to consider the relation between a marginalized group and the "center"—for example its exclusion from representation despite its centrality in social production—but also the relationship among the various groups on the "periphery" and their (potentially) dialogical interlocution with regard to the center(s) of power. The "center," for its part, is also considered as an ambivalence-reflecting category,[2] constantly appropriating the margins, even partially reconstituting itself in terms of its neighboring "others," while yet maintaining what Edward Said has termed its "positional superiority." Positing ethnicities in relational terms can help us envision the possibility of a critical reading which complicates the "center/periphery" dichotomy.

The issue of ethnicities-in-relation is of special importance for the critical and historiographic accounts of American cinema. The United States, as part of the New World, is a society wherein ethnic composition exists at the pulsating heart of its historical and cultural formation. Discussion of ethnicity raises issues, not only of historical-cultural perspective but also of geographical representation. One place to look for a discourse on domestic ethnicity is in films set outside the United States. Since all groups, except for Native Americans, descend from some other part of the globe, Hollywood films' geographical constructs have visceral impact for America's communities. And since immigration is at the core of the American ethos, the sympathetic portrayal of certain lands of ethnic origin—for example European lands—and the caricaturing of others—for example African—indirectly legitimates links to Europe while undermining links to Asia and Africa. The question is complicated, furthermore, by the fact that immigrants themselves played a major role in Hollywood, occupying a contradictory position. Thus the study of American cinema is necessarily as well the study of the projected "American Dream" of these immigrants, their manner of perceiving the image that hegemonic America would desire for itself. Their agility in expressing, and more often repressing and sublimating, America's multiethnic dimension offers a barometer for the sociopolitical context within which these images were produced. As late as the 1950s and 1960s, films shot or set in New York, for example, *On the Town* (1949) or *It's Always Fair Weather* (1955), tended to downplay the ethnic and racial diversity of the metropolis. Despite the role of Jewish immigrants in the industry, Jewishness, for example, was often reduced to the presence of closet Jews. The "problem film" *Gentleman's Agreement* (1947) provides a perfect exemplum of this polite embarassment in the presence of the Jewish "other" (or in this case "self" as "other").[3]

Ethnographic cultural critique has significant implications for film analysis because film narrative entails not only ethos (character) but also ethnos (peoples). The assumption that only certain films are relevant for the discussion of ethnicity is based on a superficially thematic examination of the filmic text, that is, whether or not the film explicitly foregrounds ethnic conflicts or complementarities. But this formulation of the issue ignores such considerations as the body language of the actors or characters and the intonations or accents which define even dominant groups as ethnic in the sense of displaying specific cultural codes. Lily-white films portraying innocuous suburban romances are also ethnic in that they reproduce an ethnically coded language. Cinematic space, far from being ethnically neutral, is the subliminal site of competing ethnic and racial discourses having specific resonances for spectators, themselves constituted by and who constitute these discourses. The orchestration of speech, looks, make-up, costume, decor, music and dance, and locale implies a set of cultural codes whose "white"[4] ethnic composition often remains invisible to those who have power over representation and can formulate the world in their terms. To ignore the issue of ethnicity in dominant films set in hegemonic and homogeneous environments would be as mistaken as to ignore issues of gender and sexuality in films privileging the male presence, for example in war or Western films, in which women and sexuality per se tend to be absent from the narrative but issues of sexual politics and gender roles "haunt" the film.

Filmic images and sounds come inevitably "saturated" with ethnic and racial resonances. The Hollywood linguistic paradigm, for example, is inscribed within the play of artificial hierarchies of languages, dialects, and accents. That Cecil B. DeMille's biblical epics depict both the ancient Egyptians and the Israelites as speaking English, and that the audiovisual presence of God in *The Ten Commandmants* (1956) is conveyed through the voice of male, upper-class North America, has clear racial, national, and theological overtones. The same filmic images or sounds have different reverberations for distinct communities.[5] An iterative[6] shot of a familial Sunday visit to church, a character crossing himself or herself, or the sound of church bells to announce a communal rhythm of birth, marriage and death—to take typical examples—all address themselves to a culturally prepared interlocutor presumed to be, if not Christian, at least familiar with the images and sounds of Christian culture.[7] But while for the implied (white) "Christian" spectator these images and sounds suppose to evoke an extra-cinematic norm, for the non-Christian they might just as easily provoke a sense of exclusion, and in the case of Jewish culture come burdened with overtones of oppression. (In Jewish poetry, for example, church bells often signify danger.)[8] The shots of Mount Rushmore in *North by Northwest* (1959) similarly evoke for the Euro-American patriotic roots and links to the "forefathers," but for the Dakotan Native American, they presumably might elicit a quite different set of feelings having to do with rupture and dispossession. A dialogical structural shift in ethnic perspective would change the emotional and ideological valence of such images. An intercultural reading, thus, would articulate the diegetic ethnic assumptions, problematizing the text's universal norms as exhibited through its formal paradigms.

The view of ethnicity as culturally ubiquitous and textually submerged can hopefully lead to a reconceptualization of the analysis of ethnicity in the cinema, opening its present boundaries. Rather than submit our analysis to the films' discourse of "ethnic" themes, the seemingly nonethnic or ethnically irrelevant text can be regarded as a field for discovery, excavation, and reconstruction of ethnic and racial contradictions. And instead of the traditional "image" analysis applied to an unproblematized notion of "minorities," ethnic representation can be studied in terms of the undertones and overtones which permeate the text. In *Vertigo* (1958), for example, the male and female (white) protagonists are possessed by a traumatic past—Scottie's vertigo, his obsession with "Madeleine's" fixation in Carlotta, and then with Judy's reincarnation of Madeleine. The archeological layers of the psyche, however, can also be read ethnographically, as that hidden strata of the national American psyche. The suppressed Spanish-Mexican history of San Francisco might be analyzed through such inadvertant verbal and visual allusions, for example, the city's Spanish name and architecture, including sites such as Mission Dolores, and more specifically through the haunting iconographic presence of the Hispanic Carlotta Valdez. Her dispossession from wealth and maternity, and her final despairing suicide, allegorize a series of North American and Mexican relations in which her framed muteness in the museum literally conveys her Hispanic voicelessness. A metaphor for her city, Carlotta can be recognized only via the "white" gaze at her— Madeleine/Judy's and Scottie's—as well as Hitchcock's inscription of her (Hispanic) city on the screen, inadvertently defining the history of women as the haunting unconscious of American history.

The concept of submerged ethnicities, in other words, can be highly productive for Hollywood's ethnically embarrassed texts. Even in narratives that explicitly foreground racial and national issues, we may still uncover latent ethnic perspectives. In the *Indiana Jones* series, the third world becomes not only a space wherein first-world interests are played out, but also for submerged ethnic voices even in the *absence* of delegate characters. On one level our analysis can concentrate on the colonial Eurocentric ideology of *Raiders of the Lost Ark* (1981). The full significance of the ancient archeological objects in the film is presumed to be understood only by the Western scientists. The origins of archeology, the search for the "roots of civilization," as a discipline are linked inextricably to imperial expansionism. However, the *Indiana Jones* series reproduces the colonial vision in which Western "knowledge" of ancient civilizations "rescues" the past from oblivion. It is this masculinist rescue in *Raiders of the Lost Ark* that legitimizes denuding the Egyptians of their heritage, confining it within Western metropolitan museums.

On yet another level we might discern a hidden Jewish substratum undergirding the film, despite the absence of such "ethnic" delegates. The American archeologist hero—often cinematically portrayed as a cowboy—implicitly searches for the Eastern roots of

Western civilization. He liberates the ancient Hebrew ark from illegal Egyptian possession while also rescuing it from immoral Nazi control, allegorically reinforcing American and Jewish solidarity with respect to the evil Nazis and their Arab assistants. The geopolitical alignments here are as clear as in the inadvertent allegory of *The Ten Commandments*, in which a WASPish Charlton Heston is made to incarnate Hebrew Moses struggling against the evil Egyptians, thus allegorizing in the context of the 1950s the contemporary struggle of the West, Israel, and the United States against Arab-Egyptians. That at the end of *Raiders of the Lose Ark* it is the American army which is made to be the guardian of the top-secret ark—with the active complicity of the ark—strengthens this evocation of geopolitical alliances. In the ancient past, Egypt dispossessed the Hebrews of their ark, as do the Nazis in the 1930s. In a time tunnel Harrison Ford is sent to fight the Nazis in the name of a Jewish shrine—the word *Jewish* is of course never mentioned—and in the course of events the rescuer is rescued by the rescuee. A fantasy of liberation from a history of victimization is played out by Steven Spielberg, using biblical myths of wonders worked against ancient Egyptians this time redeployed against the Nazis—miracles absent during the Holocaust. The Hebrew ark itself performs miracles and dissolves the Nazis, saving Dr. Jones from the Germans who, unlike the Americans, do not respect the divine law that prohibits looking at the Holy of Holies. The Jewish religious prohibition of looking at God's image and the prohibition of graven images (and from that the cultural deemphasis on visual arts) is triumphant over the Christian prediliction for religious visualization. The film here in the typical paradox of cinematic voyeurism punishes the hubris of the "Christian" who looks at divine beauty while also privileging spectatorial visual pleasure.

Formulating identities in relational terms has the advantage of unbinding our reading from the films' presumed lack of ethnic and racial appearances. A multicultural reading of mass-mediated culture, therefore, will explore the repressed ethnic and racial contradictions, transgressing the segregationist discourse on ethnic representation as limited to either third-world films or to narratives depicting peoples of color. In fact, we may reconsider not only specific texts, but also whole genres according to such theoretical parameters. From *The Jazz Singer* (1927) and *Swing Time* (1936) through *The Gang's All Here* (1943) and *Porgy and Bess* (1959), to *Funny Girl* (1968) and *New York, New York* (1977), the musical genre in particular has articulated ethnic heterogeneity, either explicitly in its themes or, more commonly, implicitly through music and dance. (In the silent era, "exotic" dances, for example in *Fatima's Dance*, already gave indirect expression to white ethnic imaginary.) Carnivalesque parodies of the musical such as *The Producers* (1968) and *The History of the World, Part One* (1981), meanwhile, satirically underline latent ethnic experiences that classical musical comedy usually glosses over. A number of interlinked issues concerning ethnicity and methodology can be discerned in the musical and in carnivalesque parody, emphasizing a relational discourse on ethnicity analyzed through specific cinematic, narrative, generic, and cultural mediations. An analysis of the musical and the parody will serve as a case study from which more general methodological lessons can be extrapolated for ethnicity and representation.

The Dialectics of Presence/Absence

In "Entertainment and Utopia" Richard Dyer analyzes the Hollywood musical as performing an artistic "change of signs" whereby the negatives of social existence are turned into the positives of artistic transmutation.[9] The musical offers a utopian world characterized by abundance, energy, intensity, transparancy, and community instead of the everyday social inadequacies of scarcity, exhaustion, dreariness, manipulation, and fragmentation. The musical's utopia provides the sensation, as Jane Feuer puts it, of what it would "feel like to be free."[10] Fredric Jameson suggests that one must look not only for ideological manipulation but also for the kernal of utopian fantasy whereby entertainment constitutes itself as a projected fulfillment of what is desired and absent within the sociopolitical status quo.[11] It is precisely the musical's intrinsic evocation of social harmony, accentuated in music and dance, that makes the genre appropriate for discussing ethnicities-in-relation. And it is precisely the musical's "management" of harmony that makes Dyer's category of community, of collective activity and communal identity, ethnically problematic. The "imagined community"[12] of the classical musical comedy is often limited to the dominant ethnic group, eliding even a possible "management" of interracial collective harmony. This elision can take various forms, most of which point to the purist exclusionary nature of the musical's communality. Communal harmony, whether set in the Midwest in *Meet Me in St. Louis* (1944) or *Oklahoma!* (1955); in New York in *Dames* (1934) or *Shall We Dance* (1937); or in Hollywood in *Show Girl in Hollywood* (1930) or *Singin' in the Rain* (1952), is a monolithically white harmony which represses, on the levels of narrative, mise-en-scène, and music and dance, America's multicultural and multiracial formation.

Historically, the musical has had a somewhat special relation to marginalized communities since the advent of sound opened the medium to preexisting African and Latin-American expression in music and dance, and subsequently to all forms of performance.[13] With the coming of sound, Euro-American producers and owners of the film industry became the arbiters and filters of black music on the screen, exploiting its popularity at the expense of African-American musicians.[14] The exclusion of African and Latin Americans from access to production, scripting, direction, distribution, and exhibition is therefore especially striking in the production of musicals. The musical genre allows us to illuminate the dialectics of presence or absence of marginalized groups, even in exclusively white-cast films. The occasional allusions to marginalized cultures in all-white-cast films usually occur in the fantasy space of the musical numbers, as in *A Star Is Born* (1954) and *It's Always Fair Weather*, in which Asians, Scots, and Latinos are evoked in bricolage-style song and dance numbers. I am interested, then, in exploring what I would term as the *inferential ethnic presences*, that is, the various ways in which ethnic cultures penetrate the screen without always literally being represented by ethnic and racial themes or even characters.

One of the iconic paradigms of the presence or absence of marginalized ethnic groups is the minstrel figure, constituting a kind of mockery of blackness. The tradition of blackface recital was especially popular in musicals—for example, Al Jolson in *Hi Lo Broadway* (1933), Fred Astaire in *Swing Time*, Micky Rooney and Judy Garland in *Babes in Arms* (1939), and Bing Crosby in *Dixie* (1943), featuring the life of a "pioneer" minstrel Dan Emmett. The presence of "blackness" in the form of a mask, as well as the veiled presence of African-American music and dance in numerous films—"Remember My Forgotten Man" in *Golddiggers of 1933* and "Fascinating Rhythm" in *Girl Crazy* (1943)—only denotes African-American absence from the screen. In fact, historically, minstrel shows evolved largely in the North and were performed on the basis of little significant contact with Southern culture and slavery, or even, for that matter, with African Americans.[15] The African-American intertext is apparent in body movements or gestures appropriated from blacks—for example, "Louisiana Hayride" in *The Band Wagon* (1953) or "Broadway Rhythm" in *Singin' in the Rain*—in which the performers collectively shake their hands, gospel-like, in the air. In musicals, then, African Americans tended to constitute not only a suppressed historical voice but also a literally suppressed ethnic voice because various black musical idioms became associated on the screen with white stars, authorizing a Euro-American signature on basically African-American cultural products.[16]

A similar dialectic of presence or absence operates in relation to other subaltern groups, as in the evocations of Latinas, Africans, and Japanese in the "Les Girls" number in *Les Girls* (1957); of Chinese in "Shanghai Lil" in *Footlight Parade* (1933); or of Native Americans in "Crazy Horse" in *The Girl Most Likely* (1957). The erotic phantasm of the "other" within the musical numbers, seemingly unrelated to the lily-white romances in the films as a whole, manifests tensions between latent interracial desire and monoracial law. The "other" then serves to define diacritically the dominant ethnic self. In *Pal Joey* (1957), as Frank Sinatra sings "Small Hotel," the music suddenly shifts to Latin rhythms, subliminally authorizing Euro-American characters to move their bodies more sensually. The same "sensuality-effect" occurs with the cha-cha in "Too Bad We Can't Go Back to Russia" and in the African-American melody of "Red Blues" in *Silk Stockings* (1957). These brief moments subliminally define essentialist contours of identities as drawn between Euro-America and its "others" while simultaneously functioning as outlets for ephemeral play with ethnic identities.

Within what Rick Altman designates as the musical's "dual-focus narrative,"[17] *Silk Stockings* stages a kind of cold-war romantic imperialism, positing the West as an erotic place of fun and pleasure in contrast to the austerity of the Soviet lifestyle. Latin and African-American rhythms thus come to signify the putative vibrancy of Anglo-American culture through signifiers which, paradoxically, call attention to the absence of the cultural sources of the signifiers, that is, African and Latin American cultures themselves. At the same time, the monological appropriation suggests the North American hegemony representing itself to a competing ideological discourse (Soviet communism) in an ethnically "exotic" spirit. Whereas the Soviets are associated with dull high art—linked to the Old World—North Americans are associated with an exciting popular culture defined, ironically, in Latinized or Africanized terms— precisely that which within the hegemonically imagined American nation is considered as non-(core) American.

Such films as *The King of Jazz* (1930) go even further in their delineation of North American history. By superimposing a series of musical ensembles representing various European ethnicities, *The King of Jazz* (1930) celebrates the origins of jazz, completely eliding the primordial African musical contribution to it. The blending of images and sounds comes to metaphorize the melting pot, vocalizing Euro-American history while silencing the African dimension even where it is most obvious. *Birth of the Blues* (1941) conforms to a similar Eurocentric discourse in its focus on Bing Crosby leading his Basin Street Hot-Shots as they struggle to be heard in New Orleans, with authentic jazz trombonist Jack Teagarden in tow. (The film was loosely based on the formation of Nick LaRocca's Original Dixieland Jazz Band, reportedly the first Euro-American group to play African-American music.) Similarly, in *High Society* (1956), despite the appearance of Louis Armstrong, who plays himself, Crosby enacts a classical musician who turns to jazz, legitimizing the popular music to the East Coast elite. In "Now You Has Jazz" he educates spectators "how Jazz music is made" while introducing the black band and their instruments—the black musicians presumably ignorant of classical music. In such symptomatic instances, the representation of African-American cultural production is mediated through a Euro-American musical authority.

Assuming a quasi-ethnographic role, Hollywood's filmic hegemony undertakes to speak for "marginal" cultures, blocking the possibility of self-representation. Films involving allusions to "subaltern" communities address themselves to a presumably "nonethnic" spectator, claiming to initiate him or her into an "alien" culture. The spectator, along with the textual delegates, comes to master, in a remarkably telescoped period (both in terms of "story" and "discourse" time) the (presumed) codes of a "foreign" culture, shown as simple, stable, unself-conscious, and susceptible to facile apprehension. Such films as *The King of Jazz* and *High Society* thus reproduce colonialist discursive formations by which non-European cultures, rendered as devoid of any active historical or narrative role, become the passive objects of study and spectacle.

In the majority of Hollywood films, Anglo-American protagonists embody what Boris Uspansky terms the "norm of the text."[18] Gérard Genette's notion of "focalization," that is, his reformulation of the classical literary question of point of view in terms of the diegetic level of character perspective as the juncture which links the different narrative roles, can be highly productive here. Genette's recasting has the advantage of pointing to the structuring of information within the story world through the cognitive-perceptual grid of its inhabitants, raising questions of "who sees," "who informs," and thus "who represents" even when a literal point-of-view shot is not deployed.[19] This concept facilitates the analysis of liberal films such as *Gentlemen's Agreement* and *Soldier Blue* (1970), which foster the "positive" images, granting the "other" literal point-of-view shots and dialogues, yet focalized through Anglo-American protagonists who represent hegemonic cultural norms.[20] Reconceptualizing "focalization" in ethnic terms highlights the fact that white characters become radiating "centers of consciousness" or "filters" for information, embodying dominant racial and ethnic discourses. Here it is necessary to expand Genette's term, proposing the notion of "centers of consciousness" as representing less individual characters than a set of specific community discourses mediating the film. Focalization and "norms of the text," however, do not always strictly coincide, and indeed at times cohabit only in tension within the same text. Focalization can be granted to the subaltern, for example to the mulatta in *Pinky* (1947), but the norms of the text are represented by "white" marginal characters, as by the Southern white lady in *Pinky*. In the absence of explicit "white" delegates of such norms, as in the all-black-cast films, for example, *Hallelujah* (1929) and *Cabin in the Sky* (1943), the "white" norms permeate the text through the implicit ethnological examination of the black community as "deviant."

Musicals usually cast minoritarian groups or their presumed representatives only in a few sequences but do not grant them the status even of secondary characters. Generally, the "ethnic" characters lack even the most basic marker of identity—a name. For example, in *The Band Wagon*, Fred Astaire's singing and dancing in "A Shine on Your Shoes" inspires the otherwise nonexistent or dormant dancing talent of the African-American shoeshine (LeRoy Daniels), who is merely used as a kinetic object, a device reminiscent in its objectification of Busby Berkeley's depersonalizing rhetoric of gender (fig. 8.1). Daniels as the shoeshine "boy" (kneeling) literally shines Astaire's shoes and brushes his clothes during the musical number. Just as images of women beautifying themselves in *Dames* yield their quantum of spectacle, the African-American shoeshine servant status in *The Band Wagon* is deployed to form part of the esthetic dynamics of the number. In *High Society*, it is the singing of Bing Crosby that stimulates Louis Armstrong to echo Crosby on the trumpet. *The Bells Are Ringing* (1960) is in this sense an anomaly. Its Hispanic character teaches Judy Holliday the essential steps of the cha-cha, thus connecting the rhythms to a specific ethnos. The Hispanic, furthermore, is conversant with European classical music, in

8.1. Fred Astaire and LeRoy Daniels in *The Band Wagon:* the esthetic dynamics of servitude.

contrast to the ethnic division of prestige in *High Society*, in which the "white" ethnic Crosby remains the center of consciousness who filters "peripheral" culture.

Hollywood's ethnography engendered frequent cultural dislocations. Communitarian representations are often accompanied by the "mark of the plural"—a notion elaborated by Albert Memmi in connection with anti-colonial discourse—the device whereby various ethnic communities and nations are subject to homogenization.[21] Latin American countries are reduced to a stereoptypical cultural emblem, projected as one entity despite their many differences. In *Flying Down to Rio* (1933), Brazilians are made to wear Mexican sombreros, dance the Argentinian tango, and speak with an excessive accent of ambiguous nationality, neither Spanish nor Portuguese (Carmen Miranda, the synecdoche of Latin America in many films, reportedly spoke English fluently and had only a slight accent but was forced by producers into her caricatural speech patterns). In *Kismet* (1955), such diverse nationalities as Arab, Indian, Persian, and Chinese are presented as a single entity; the Orient, as Said puts it, is itself "orientalized."[22] The same mechanism of obscuring the boundries among the "others," while manifesting a distinguished difference of white ethnicity, is seen on a smaller scale in *Gentlemen Prefer Blondes* (1953). In "When Love Goes Wrong," we see, in long shot, children sporting red fezes, which in the French context evokes an Arab cultural presence. But when the camera moves closer, we see black children tap dancing. A process of condensation, then, superimposes on the distant "other"—the Arab—the more familiar "other"—the African American.

The raised ethnic consciousness of the late 1960s brought a resurgence of ethnicity in the cinema, embracing America's diverse ethnic groups via "Roots"-like recuperation of the past. Thus we find narratives set in the Old Country (as in the European shtetl of *Fiddler on the Roof*, 1971), or foregrounding present-day multiethnic America, as in *Nashville* (1975), *Hair* (1979), *Fame* (1980), and *Dirty Dancing* (1987). *West Side Story's* (1961) critically stylized ethnic conflicts ironically conveyed that "everything's right in America/if you're a white in America." (The satire is largely focussed in the such musical sentiments as "I want to be in America.") In early 1960s' musicals, in the wake of rock and roll and the growing popularity of black culture, such films as *Bye Bye Birdie* (1963) deploy Euro-American performers who incorporate, to a certain extent, African-American-style singing and dancing, in contrast to earlier musicals such as *Cabin in the Sky*, which created a segregated "black" filmic zone for such movements. Yet *Bye Bye Birdie's* allusions to Elvis Presley still suppress the African-American sources of white rock and roll. In the wave of musicals of the 1980s about the 1950s and early 1960s—for example, *Dirty Dancing* and *Hair Spray*—black and Latin influence on white popular culture is made explicit and even thematized. The films project moments of desired ethnic communal utopia, heretofore repressed, in which Euro-American characters are viscerally "possessed" by African-American or Latin cultures. *Dirty Dancing*, and even the independent production *Hair Spray*, however, retain the symptomatic hierarchical focalization in which Euro-American (in these cases the marginalized white working-class or Jewish middle-class) perspective is privileged by the narratives even though the music and dance are African and Latin American.

Ethnic Allegories

Although incorporating or alluding to "subaltern" communities through music and dance, the Hollywood musical brought a "well-behaved," domesticated version of jazz to Euro-American audiences within the films' narratives as well as to their counterparts in the movie theaters. In Woody Allen's *Zelig* (1983), the protagonist's transformation into a black trumpeter can be seen, in this sense, as a parody of the musical tradition of Euro-American performers such as Al Jolson, Fred Astaire, and Bing Crosby wearing black masks and capitalizing on African-American culture. Through his physical capacity to enact ethnic and cultural syncretism, Zelig indirectly illuminates Hollywood's penchant for ethnic simulacra. *Zelig*'s narrative underlines its protagonist's blackness as hybridization in contrast with *The Jazz Singer, Swing Time,* and *Dixie,* where blackness is largely a costume worn for show and entertainment.

To fully comprehend the structure of feelings undergirding Al Jolson, Eddie Cantor, or Sophie Tucker's evocation of black America, however, we must take into account not only the racial dimension—their "whiteness"—but also the ethnic one—their Jewishness. In the United States, Jewish entertainers took over the preexisting tradition of blackface, largely from vaudeville, endowing it with their own gesture and intonation. The Jewish minstrel figure is a site of contradictions involving both opportunism and an intuition of deeper affinities.[23] As Jolson's character is told in *The Jazz Singer:* "There are a lot of jazz singers but you have tears in your voice." And as Irving Howe suggests, "Black became a mask for Jewish expressiveness, with one woe speaking through the voice of another."[24] (The "ethnic pastiche," as Ronald Sanders points out, is a propensity of people who live in culturally bilingual situations.)[25] Jews, therefore, thanks to a black "mask," could perform their heritage of emotional expressiveness indirectly, conveniently displacing it onto a group seen as inferior in status. Blackface thus enabled Jewish performers to reach a spontaneity and assertiveness in the declaration of their ethnic selves. First-generation, American-born Jews, eager to assimilate, tended to repress traditional melodramatic sentimentality of theatrical grand gestures, while adopting the relatively more controlled body language of Anglo-American culture, which had stigmatized expressive gestures or bodily undulations as signs of backward and uncultivated societies. In *The Jazz Singer,* the older immigrant generation is associated with melodramatic gesticulation, while the eager-to-assimilate younger generation incarnated by Al Jolson uses more expressive gestures when in blackface, a device employed not only in musical sequences but also in straightforwardly dramatic sequences. Jackie Rabinowitz/Jack Robin's identity crises is articulated in blackface. His mirror reflects not his literal self, but the image of the Jewish community, echoing as

8.2. Al Jolson in blackface: the Jewish minstrel figure as the site of cultural contradictions.

the intertitle suggests, the "call of his race." The ambiguous boundary between Jewish and black identities in this sequence reinforces the question of displacements and dialogisms within the margins, for example "speaking" through a neighboring other.

The American situation in which diverse communities mingled daily in the streets made cultural syncretism virtually inevitable. Films such as *The Jazz Singer* must be considered in this context. Their Oedipal narrative, symptomatic of the melting-pot discourse, reflects at the same time the mutually imbricated dynamics of American culture. At the end of the film the two conflicting worlds, represented by Boradway jazz and Jewish kol nidre music, are reconciled, a reconciliation summed up in Jolson's belting out a "mammy" to his weeping mother (fig. 8.2).[26] In *The Jazz Singer*, Jolson melds Yiddish schmaltz and black-inflected melody with blackface tradition. The black influence on his Yiddish-inflected singing is shown explicitly in the biographical *The Jolson Story* (1946), recounting his fascination with blues musicians in New Orleans. Jolson operated in the same cultural ambiance that allowed Irving Berlin to mingle Yiddishisms with "coon song" conventions (Isaac

Goldberg found a musical kinship between Afro-American "blue notes" and the "blue note" of Hasidic chant)[27] and George Gershwin to blend Yiddish folk tunes with African-American melodies in *Porgy and Bess*.

Along with analyzing the structural analogies in the representation of marginalized communities, for example, the simulacral presence of blacks and Jews in liberal films from the 1940s such as *Pinky* and *Gentleman's Agreement*, we may also examine intertextual dimensions of subaltern cultures and their analogical "structure of feelings." The concept of situated multivalent ethnic relations is well exemplified by *Zelig*, which ultimately concerns a bizarre chameleon man who has an uncanny talent for taking on the accent and ethnicity of his interlocutors. Obviously "white" and Jewish, Zelig chameleonizes at diverse points to become WASP, Native American, African American, Irish, Chinese, and Mexican, thus "condensing" the ambient ethnic and racial plurality.[28] Each particular metamorphosis of the multiethnic protagonist bears its particular burden of historical reverberation, illuminating the latent intercultural "structure of feeling" which undergirds them. Zelig's recurrent chameleonizing to blackness, for example, is deeply rooted in the Jewish experience in Europe. Medieval European iconography contrasted the black image of the synagogue with the white of the church, an iconography which transmuted itself in the nineteenth century into the image of the "black Jew" common in end-of-the-century racist tracts. A Polish noble, Adam G. de Gurowski, reporting on his voyage to the United States in 1857 wrote that "Numbers of Jews have the greatest resemblance to the American mulattoes. Sallow carnation complexion, thick lips, crisped black hair. Of all the Jewish population scattered over the globe one-fourth lives in Poland. I am, therefore, well acquainted with their features. On my arrival to this country [the United States] I took every light mulatto for a Jew."[29] Herman Wegener called Jews "white negroes," and Julius Streicher, one of the most notorious anti-Semites of both Weimar Republic and Third Reich, argued in 1928 for the identity of language between Jew and black: "The swollen lips remind us again of the close relationship between the Jews and the Blacks. Speech takes place with a racially determined intonations."[30] The American heirs of European racism and anti-Semitism, the Ku Klux Klan, have carried on the perception of "colored" people as a threat to white racial purity, constituting a kind of menacing heteroglossia. In Woody Allen's film the K.K.K. views Zelig as a triple threat precisely because of his multiple Otherness as black, Jew, and Native American. The fact that Zelig, in his moments of metamorphosis, is both the ethnic "Other" and recognizably Woody Allen, white, and Jewish, metaphorizes American ethnic interaction and hybridization, personifying the cultural syncretism characteristic of a multiethnic society.

The partial play of identity already in early films such as *The Jazz Singer* inadvertantly touches an intercultural nerve. It implies an affinity—whether past or potential—between African Americans and Jews, between two groups excommunicated by Europe and by WASP-dominated America. In both traditions narratives of slavery and diaspora have played a major role in the collective consciousness. In Jewish religious culture, the yearly Passover recounts the Exodus story, celebrating the liberation of the Israelites from Egyptian enslavement. Bible-based black spirituals, meanwhile, appropriate the Jewish-Hebrew experience, rereading or translating it into their own idiom via such lyrics as "When Israel was in Egypt land. . . . Let my people go." The Jewish conception of exile from the Promised Land and the Nostalgia of Return became significant in the creation of a rebellious black language testifying to the African diaspora experience throughout the Americas. This conception is articulated in the language of the Rastafarian movement and in reggae music with its lyrical leitmotifs of "Babylon," "Jerusalem," and "Lion of Judah," rendered for example in the music of *The Harder They Come* (1973). Much as blacks in America allegorized their collective oppression through the story of the Hebrew-Jewish people, so Jews in America allegorized their historical sorrow via black expressivity; blackface becomes iconic of exclusion.

African-Americans' allegorization, in contrast to the Jewish, however, did not take place in a caricatural show-business context. While searching for multicultural dimensions in American cinema, then, distinct historical situations which determined the access for self-representation in the Hollywood studio system must be taken into account. The marginalization of Jews, Irish, and Italians, as opposed to that of African Americans, was hardly identical, suggesting that ethnicity and race can, at times, form the locus of contradictions on the "periphery." Jews, for example, chose to immigrate to the United States, and their process of assimilation was eased by the facility with which they could pass, their color masking their (ethnic) difference. African Americans, like Asians and Native Americans, meanwhile, could not conveniently mask their features. "White ethnic minorities," furthermore, had much more powerful positions in Hollywood than racially marginalized groups. And although European immigrants, in some ways, had to conform to the institutionalized, establishment-oriented desires for what Americans should see, they still enjoyed enough power to prevent, for example, most anti-Semitic film imagery. Assimilation, the norm of the melting pot, was therefore experienced differently by ethnic and racial groups. If Jewish characters could more easily achieve assimilated status as in *The Jazz Singer*—and if assimilated Jewish actors such as John Garfield and Kirk Douglas could become stars within Anglo-American-oriented institutions—African Americans, due to their undisguisable racial difference, were obliged to perform within the black actantial slot, or within the segregated space of all-black-cast films.

The possibilities of erotic interaction in films before the 1960s were severely limited by apartheid-style ethnic and racial codes. Hollywood could project mixed love stories between Anglo-Americans and Jews or even Hispanics and Arabs—especially if incarnated by white American actors and actresses such as Valentino in *The Sheik* (1921), Dorothy Lamour in *The Road to Morocco* (1942), or Natalie Wood in *West Side Story* (1961)—but was inhibited in relation to African-American or Native-American sexuality. This latent fear of blood-tainting in such melodramas as *Call Her Savage* (1932) and *Pinky* necessitates narratives where the "half breed" (Native American in *Call Her Savage* and black in *Pinky*) female protagonists are prevented at the closure of the films from participating in mixed marriages, ironically despite the roles being played by "pure white" actresses. It is therefore the generic space of melodrama that preoccupies itself with interracial romantic interaction. The trajectory of constituting the couple in the musical comedy could not allow for a racially subaltern protagonist.

The Production Code of the Motion Picture Producers and Directors of America, Inc. (1930–34) explicitly states that "Miscegenation (sex relation between the white and black races) is forbidden."[31] The delegitimizing of the romantic union between "white" and "black" "races" is linked to a broader exclusion of African Americans and Native Americans from participation in social institutions. Translating the obsession with "pure blood" into legal language, Southern miscegnation laws, as pointed out by such African-American feminists as Anna Julia Cooper and Ida B. Wells as early as the end of the last century, were designed to maintain white (male) supremacy and to prevent a possible transfer of property to blacks in the post-abolition era. "Race" as a biological category, as Hazel V. Carby formulates it, was subordinated to race as a political category.[32] It is within this context of exclusionary ideology that we can rethink critically the Production Code's universal censorship of sexual violence and brutality in which the assumption is one of purely individual victimization, delegitimizing a collective notion of victimization. This formulation undermines the racially and sexually based violence toward African Americans, wiping out the memory of the rape, castration, and lynching of slaves. The Production Code eliminates a possible counternarrative by third-world people for whom sexual violence has often been at the kernel of historical experience and identity. Keeping in mind this significant structuring absence, it is ironic to encounter the compensatory "liberal" gesture by which the word *nigger*—hygenically mentioned in the alphabetical list of ethnic slurs defined as "offensive" words to the "patrons of motion pictures"—is proscribed.

An analysis of the history of American cinema in ethnic terms uncovers a tendency toward ethnic "allegories" in Jameson's sense, of texts which, even when narrating apparently private stories, managed to metaphorize the public sphere, where the micro-individual is doubled by the macro-nation and the personal and the political, the private and the historical, are inextricably linked.[33] The ethnic hierarchies of the cinema allegorize extradiscursive social intercourse. The musical's version of ethnic utopia, embodied by such films as *Follow the Fleet*, *Annie Get Your Gun* (1950) and *Oklahoma!*, is often exclusionary; when representatives of marginalized groups do appear, "social order" and the "purity" of ethnic-sexual interaction are still maintained. The overwhelming majority of love stories in musical comedy avoids all hints of miscegenation by focalizing a glamorous hetrosexual white couple, epitomized by Ginger Rogers and Fred Astaire. In *Swing Time*, the narrative role of Rogers's lover, a Latin musician (George Metaxa), is to act as a catalyst for her relationship with Astaire, who wins Rogers from the libidinal Latin— a variation on the romantic plot of *Top Hat* (1935), again with a volatile Latin-lover character (Erik Rhodes). Astaire is foregrounded by the film both as lover and performer. The romantic performance of the Anglo-American entertainers, as the purveyors of the "norms of the text," is narratively and cinematically privileged, while Latin and black entertainers hardly function outside the musical numbers.

Mixed couples are relatively rare in musical comedy, except in times of acute economic lust on the part of North American corporations. In *Flying Down to Rio* (1933), for example, Dolores del Rio discards her Brazilian lover for an American.[34] The film's mythical discourse of love, as Brian Henderson points out, masks the crude promotion of the new airline route of New York-Rio de Janeiro, the merged imperialist interests of PanAm and RCA.[35] In the period of the Good Neighbor Policy, Hollywood attempted to enlist Latin America for hemispheric unity against the Axis. When European film markets reduced their film consumption as the war began, Hollywood, hoping for Latin American markets and pan-American political unity, flooded the screens with films using Latin stars, locales,[36] historical heroes, and particularly Latin American music and dance. (Swing, in this period, was eclipsed by rhumba.) The trope of "good neighbor" very rarely extended to winning family status through interracial or interethnic marriage, however. Latin Americans or African Americans are almost invariably marginalized by the narrative and cinematic codes, and usually limited to roles as entertainers within musical numbers.

The disjunctive structure of the musical, in which a relatively "realistic" mode of narrative representation is foiled by implausible musical numbers which flaunt playfulness and imagination (for example Busby Berkeley's surreal play with abstract esthetic forms), makes possible superficial allusions to the culture of the "Other." The musical often allots its narrative "spaces" in ethnic terms. The presence of marginalized groups is largely felt through music and dance or entertainers, while the "realistic" narrative development becomes largely the space of white action. The disjunctive nature of the musical thus homologizes segregationist attitudes in the larger society. The presumed nonrealistic status of the musical numbers provides a narrative license for displaying "exoticism," while allowing for subliminal eroticism via the safe channel of the "Other." The musical numbers not only provide the spectacle of difference but also function narratively by uniting the North American couple with respect to the "Latins." *Guys and Dolls'* erotic metamorphosis of the Salvation Army worker (Jean Simmons) during her visit in Havana is condensed in the sweeping music and dance, allowing for her romance with Marlon Brando. In this sense, the musical's bifurcated narrative mode enables heightened presence of the subaltern, which otherwise would not merit entering the space of the "real," particularly since "reality" is assumed to be white and Euro-American.

Marginalized within the narrative, the Latin characters in *The Gang's All Here* (1943), *Too Many Girls* (1940), *Pan-Americana* (1945), and *Weekend in Havana* (1941) at the finale tend to be at the exact point from which they began, in contrast with the teleologically evolving status of the North American protagonists. Films such as *The Gang's All Here*, furthermore, demonstrate a generic division of labor, whereby the solid, "serious" or romantic numbers such as "A Journey to a Star" tend to be performed by the North American

8.3. *The Gang's All Here:* sexual metaphors and agricultural reductionism.

protagonists Alice Faye and James Ellison, whereas the Latin American characters perform "unserious," "excessive" numbers involving swaying hips, exaggerated facial expressions, caricaturally sexy
costumes, and "think-big" props embodied by Carmen Miranda.
The bananas in Miranda's number "The Lady with the Tutti-Frutti
Hat" not only enact the agricultural reductionism of Latin America
but also form phallic symbols, here raised by "voluptuous" Latinas
over circular, quasi-vaginal forms (fig. 8.3). This construction of Lat-
inness as the locus of exoticism is not subsumable by North American ethnic codes. The Latin characters therefore do not form part of
any narrative development, and their presence is tolerable on the
folkloric level of music and dance. Character interaction, in this
sense, allegorizes the larger relation between the North and South
and reflects ambivalent feelings of attraction and repulsion toward
the culturally different.

Films which do include a romantic interethnic interaction, such
as *The Jazz Singer, The Jolson Story, La Bamba,* and *Fame,* tend to
project allegories (even quasi-didactic allegories) of ethnic tensions

and reconciliation in which youthful mixed couples microcosmically unite, or attempt to unite, conflicting communities. Thus ethnic and class conflicts are "solved" by "acceptance" or reconciliation and implied harmony. In the process of assimilation, Al Jolson in *The Jazz Singer*, rather like Hollywood's stereotypical tragic mulatto, is torn between two worlds—between the role of a cantor—synecdochic of his Jewish heritage—and the role of a Broadway jazz singer—synecdochic of the contemporary America embodied by his Anglo-American girlfriend. The musical's closure—in contrast to the hesitant integrationist ideology toward "non-white" communities—celebrates the New World as an ultimately utopian place, a perspective underlined by the melting-pot trope. A Jewish cantor is transformed into a jazz singer without completely discarding his heritage. Jewish music is melded with black music, and a mixed Jewish-gentile couple is implied. This implication of an ethnically mixed marriage, however, occurs within the classical narrative largely among white ethnicities, and often presumes the assimilation of the "minority" character.

When assimilationist discourse is no longer politically feasible within the civil rights context, the mixed ethnic love of *West Side Story* is presented as tragic. The love-death nexus, foregrounded by the end of the film, is at the same time accompanied by utopian longing for ethnic and social harmony, the idea that "somehow, somewhere, someday, we'll find a new way of living." The film ends with the implied ethnic peace won by the sacrifice of victims on both sides. Nonassimilationist intercommunal romantic closures, meanwhile, were largely produced since the late 1960s when the pluralist ideology replaced the earlier melting-pot trope. Recent films such as *Breakin'*, *La Bamba*, *Dirty Dancing*, and *Salsa* thematize the subject of "ethnic" music and dance, celebrating its pluralistic integration into mainstream American culture.

If in the past a latent white desire to incorporate the "Other" was reflected in the attempt to absorb jazz, samba, and rhumba rhythms, contemporary Hollywood films center around pronouncedly "ethnic" characters. In *La Bamba*, for example, the class ascendency of the Hispanic character allegorizes the American Dream. In *Dirty Dancing*, the Jewish characters constitute a kind of simulacrum of mainstream Anglo culture, whereas the white working-class male protagonist is associated with Latin and African-American rhythms and dancers. The film ends with integration through Eros. The excluded, even forbidden "dirty" music and dance played only in ghettoized surroundings—and its "ethnic" and lower-class performers—are accepted, and communal harmony is celebrated. Swaying the hips—or "going native"—becomes a collectively desired fantasy of the upper-middle class. The final image of the dancing couple surrounded by a mainstream community that emulates their movements encapsulates a liberal integrationist vision.

Many recent films, in the same vein, give "mythic" expression to the common attitude that cultural differences and class distinctions will be eliminated by the American-born younger generation, especially through love, as in the implied couple of the upper-middle-class Jewish woman and working-class man in *Dirty Dancing*. The differences are "contained" by the over-arching ideology of integration, presumed to solve conflicts, as if mixed marriage were sufficient to eradicate or modify deeply rooted structures of domination. Even when the films are seemingly focalized through "ethnic" protagonists, it is the liberal hegemonic discourse that they represent.

The Carnivalesque Critique

While the canonical musical mythically transcends the oppressive structures of everyday life through stylization and choreography, the carnivalesque parody of the musical at least partially subverts ethnic-racial hierarchies. Parody, which tends to be a marginalized artistic practice, is especially important for the discussion of how marginalized ethnic and racial groups can critique not only explicit racist enunciations, but also what the political theorist Stuart Hall calls "inferential racism," that is, those apparently naturalized representations whose ethnocentric and racist propositions are inscribed in them as a set of unquestioned assumptions.[37] (This approach would question, for example, the invisible racist discourse in films such as *Gentlemen Prefer Blondes*, with its respectful attitude toward white-dominated South Africa and its diamond mines.)

While the musical represents the "management" of an orderly, harmonious, transparent utopia, parody exposes the silences of the American master narrative, and thus can critique inferentially racist discourses. The term *parody* is used here in its contemporary—largely Bakhtinian—sense of a self-reflexive, self-critical, and, frequently satirical mode of discourse which renders explicit the processes of intertextuality through distortion, exaggeration, inversion, or elaboration of a preexisting text.[38] Parody is especially appropriate for the discussion of "center" and "margins" since—due to its historical critical marginalization, as well as its capacity for appropriating and critically transforming existing discourses—parody becomes a means of renewal and demystification, a way of laughing away outmoded forms of thinking. Parody, by exposing the mechanisms of mimesis and the processes of intertextuality, becomes an apt locus for rendering explicit the ethnic "mimesis" of much of American cinema, its representation of the "natural," "American way."

Many of the parodies I discuss are important for their incorporation of the carnivalesque, which Mikhail Bakhtin traces back to Rabelais and to Menippean satire. The carnivalesque, for Bakhtin, represents the transposition into art of the spirit of carnival—popular festivities offering a brief entry into a sphere of utopian freedom in which the conventional world is symbolically turned "upside down."[39] Because both evoke utopias, the carnivalesque parody is a particularly interesting genre to compare with the traditional musical's ethnic discourse. Whereas musicals, even those with "minority" characters, tended historically to offer communal utopia as a cultural monolith, the carnivalesque parodies, even when produced in Hollywood, have to some extent offered a multivoiced ethnic utopia wherein syncretism is privileged. Parody's capacity to appropriate different genres—most associated with hegemonic ethnic discourses—allows for a broad interweaving of different texts, defamiliarized from their original cultural context, especially through associating them with "ethnic" discourses, in order to forge a satiric palimpsest of synchretic identities.

Such films as *Hair Spray* foreground the collectivity of various marginalized groups: the obese, working-class Euro-American female protagonist and her "mother" Divine, as well as the community of African Americans defeat the racists, allegorizing the utopia of a nonracist, communal America. At the film's end, the protagonist dances the black-style "bug" and wins over the "all-American girl" and her racist supporters. In one scene, white paranoid attitudes toward African Americans are satirized by showing blacks playing with the racist expectations of a white matron "stranded" in a ghetto. By focalizing the scene through the traditionally marginalized perspective of the African-American neighborhood, John Waters sutures the spectator into an antracist viewpoint, much as John Sayles, using a similar strategy, represents two terrified midwestern Euro-Americans from the perspective of the patrons of a Harlem bar in *Brother from Another Planet* (1984). In the last scene of *Hair Spray* the triumph of the various "margins" is celebrated, culminating in the police's participation in the collective dance—much as the baton-twirling officer in Lionel Richie's "All Night Long" music video.

If in most films African Americans have been merely the "guests" in the narrative, or the entertainers featured in the musical numbers, and if all-black-cast films partially aimed at the African-American audience consumption reproduced the dominant ideology, in Spike Lee's *School Daze* (1987) issues of race constitute the central focus. Whereas traditionally all-black-cast films were symptomatic of the exclusion and segregation of African Americans from hegemonic culture, *School Daze* subverts this connotation of an all-black space. It represents a conscious choice to foster a provisionally isolated space in which to delve into class and even racial tensions within the African-American community. Exploring ideological conflicts between light- and dark-skinned African Americans, as well as between middle-class and lumpenproletarion blacks, the film subtextually defines black positioning in relation to white centers of power.

One satirical musical number in particular stages the tension between colonized and politically conscious black women. "Straight and Nappy" (fig. 8.4) satirizes not simply the feminine beautification process in general, but also in relation to white (European) versus black (African) models of beauty, a question that also bears obvious relevance to black males—consider Michael Jackson. Set in a stylized decor of a black beauty salon, the jazzy number foregrounds the role within African-American culture of hair in both metonymic and metaphoric terms as an object of praise or blame depending on political outlook.[40] The colonized Wannabees censure the African look—"Don't you wish you had hair like this/then the boys would give you a kiss . . . cain't cha, don't cha hair stand on high/cain't cha comb it and don't you try." Their view is counteracted by the politically conscious Jigaboos—"Don't you know my hair is so strong/it can break the teeth out the comb. . . . I don't mind being BLACK/go on with your mixed-up head/I ain't gonna never be 'fraid."[41] The dancers carry Vivien Leigh and Hattie McDaniel fans, reflexively alluding to the representation of race relations in Hollywood and implicitly to their impact on the African-American self-image. "Straight and Nappy"'s focus on looks and identity must be understood against the backdrop of Malcolm X's suggestion that the white man's worst crime was to make blacks hate themselves. Offering an alternative to the usual tourist status of African Americans within mainstream cinema, a status which

8.4. Spike Lee's *School Daze:* re-invoicing black space.

burdens every black character with the role of representing their community as a whole, *School Daze* literally liberates the narrative space for African-American use to play out the contradictions, complexities, and multiplicities of the African-American community.

Yet another filmmaker who employs ethnic conventions of the classical musical against ethnocentrism is Mel Brooks. His deployment of parody, specifically musical parody as in *The History of the World, Part One* and *The Producers,* allows further exploration of the musical's dissonances concerning ethnicities-in-relation. *The History of the World, Part One* is structured as a series of episodes representing selected moments from history from the Stone Age, through ancient Rome and the Spanish Inquisition, to the French Revolution. Narrated by Orson Welles, the film, much like *Zelig,* plays imaginatively with generic conventions, while also subverting anachronistically time and place as well as the official Western perspective on history. Brooks's parody of historical epic films implicitly conveying the dominant historiography must be appreciated within carnivalesque tradition, with its logic of the turnabout and perpetual decanonizations. *The History of the World, Part One* is told from a marginalized perspective; the periphery moves to the center. The

Rome episode, for example, is focalized not through the emperors and their triumphs and defeats, but rather through the marginalized—the Jewish "fool," schlemiel, and "stand-up philosopher" (Brooks) and the black slave. Brooks's presentation of history recalls that of the *Annales* school of historiography, which shifts the emphasis to peripheralised communities, in contrast to dominant historiographical accounts that focus only on the powerful.

The shift of historical perspective has crucial implications for the issue of ethnic representation, a shift which goes beyond the binaric discourse of negative versus positive images. We tend to associate the musical's esthetic forms with an innocuous, harmonious world, while in the Inquisition episode, much as in "Springtime for Hitler and Germany" from *The Producers*, Brooks employs Busby Berkeleystyle forms, particularly the forms of Esther Williams's musicals, to recount horrifying moments of history. In this sense, it is a film self-declaredly in "bad taste." It neglects the elevated and implicitly offers a critique of the "refined" and rigid conception that serious matters deserve only "serious" genres—and seriousness is artificially contrasted with humor. This separation of styles, as Pierre Bordieu documents, has tended historically to be tied to class—and ethnic—hierarchies.[42] Rather than classical Hollywoodian sublimation, we are given a strategy of reduction and degradation which uses obscenity and caricature. Rather than the musical's idealized, sanitized fetishization of the white female body as a source of pleasure for spectatorial gaze, here we find the crude and satirically cruel fetishization of the "ethnic" male body. The film parodically celebrates sexuality as transcending ethnic and religious differences. Where torture has failed, sex succeeds, that is, in converting Jews. The musical's ethnic purity is also subverted by showing ethnicreligious conflicts transcended through a syncretic ending. The lure of sex is presented reflexively, equated with the lure of Hollywood's entertainment and glamour. The final image associates the Jewish symbol (the menorah) with stereotypically Anglo-American blondes who carry it—all within a mainstream artistic form: the Hollywood musical.

The History of the World, Part One's parody of the musical also incorporates specific languages, dialects, accents, and paralinguistic sounds associated with specific ethnic groups ("Oy!," "Nay, Nay, Nay," "Hey man!") as well as ethnically specific gestures, for example, black-style speech, for purposes of ironic inversion. In the musical show "Springtime for Hitler and Germany," Hitler and Goebbels talk and move in a black-inflected street manner. Brooks thus super-

8.5. Mel Brooks as Torquemada in *History of the World, Part One:* the carnivalesque incarnation of the haunting oppressor.

imposes signs associated with a presumably inferior race precisely on the Nazi ideologues who theorized and tried to enforce that inferiority. By associating traditional musical forms with recognizable marginalized communities, *The History of the World, Part One* and *The Producers* call attention to their traditional exclusion from the musical's communal harmony. The Inquisition musical number, furthermore, imagistically associates the medieval Catholic hierarchy with Busby Berkeley's esthetic order, just as "Springtime for Hitler and Germany" subliminally links fascist esthetics with the Hollywood spectacle.[43] The Inquisition episode satirizes the so-called civilized world celebrated by Hollywood. The episode initially visualizes a Catholic mass as if drawn from a horror film (fig. 8.5). Sounds that the dominant liturgic sensibility associates with purification, spirituality, and holiness are superimposed on the cries of tortured people. In one of the following sequences a tortured Jew asks in Yiddish-accented English: "Is it polite? Is it considerate? To make my privates a public game?"[44] Jews, like other third-world people, were accused of barbarism, savagery, vulgarity; therefore, the projection of bourgeois codes of etiquette of privacy, politeness, and good manners onto an Inquisition context reduces these codes to their hypocritical core. It was in the very name of its civilizing missions that Europe committed its acts of barbarisms against diverse "Others": Jews, Africans, Native Americans, and Asians.

Brooks's *Blazing Saddles* (1974), in which he collaborated on the script with, among others, Richard Pryor, also fosters ethnic syncretisms at once critical of dominant ethnic discourse and pointing to a carnivalesque utopia. The Western, the generic locus of Anglo-American male heroism and the filmic historiographical authority of the American experience, becomes in *Blazing Saddles* the subject of revisionist historical discourse. If the Western embodies the hegemonic ethnic discourse in which the few ethnicities present, except for Anglo-Americans, are "Indians" or Mexicans cast as evil within a Manichean outlook, the parody of the Western brings in these elided subaltern histories and suppressed ethnic and racial voices. The film opens with what is absent from Hollywood historiography, showing forced black and Chinese labor on the railroad, mistreated by the racist and greedy cowboys who also confiscated Native-American lands. Slim Pickens is hijacked from the classical Western to play a satirically revised version of his traditional role. Furthermore, Gene Wilder (the schlemiel rabbi in the West in another ethnic revisionist film *The Frisco Kid*, 1979)[45] is here a gunslinger who joins the black sheriff (Cleavon Little) to rescue the town from an evil judge and cowboys' vandalism. Wilder and Little manage to win over the racist town and give the oppressed blacks, Chinese, and Irish their share of land and equality.[46]

The provocative articulation of previous discursive silence concerning American historiographical representation is also seen in the carnivalesque inversion of an exploited black laborer who is transformed into a sheriff, as well as in the criss-crossing of identifications and displacements among the marginalized. For example, in one scene, the Indians attack a segregated wagon train of which the blacks occupy, as it were, the back seats. The Indians—Brooks plays the chief in dark-face—are not demonic, but sympathetic and release the blacks. Here Brooks merges Native Americans and Jews as well as African Americans, all marginalized groups excluded from the Anglo-American master narrative. The "Indian" chief speaks Yiddish, addressing the blacks as "shvartzes" (*blacks* in Yiddish) and preventing his Indian companion from killing them. When the black family continues to travel, the Indian Mel Brooks says in a Yiddish accent "they are darker than us." On the one hand, his remark is a self-mocking allusion to Jewish racist attitudes toward blacks, while at the same time the remark acknowledges the different colors as nuances on a spectrum, as well as the affinities among all three groups objectified and oppressed on a pseudo-biological basis.

A similar Native American-Jewish affinity is suggested by Zelig in his transformation into a Native-American "Indian." *Zelig* in this sense follows the tradition of such Jewish entertainers as Fanny Brice, who used to sing "I'm an Indian." A whole body of poetry was in fact written by Jewish immigrants alluding to Native Americans, displacing their own sense of marginality onto America's quintessential "other."[47] Jews, as Tzevan Todorov points out in *The Conquest of America*, formed Europe's internal "Other" long before the peoples of Africa, Latin America, and Asia became its external "Other."[48]

The Jewish merging with the Native American, then, forges a link between Europe's external and internal "Other." A Lenny Bruce monologue voiced the bitter irony of Native Americans by having one complain: "Oh Christ! The white people are moving in—you let one white family, and the whole neighborhood will be white."[49] Bruce here calls attention to urban ethnic phobias directed toward marginalized groups, but by placing the sentiment in the mouth of a Native American he also calls attention to white expropriation of the Native-American national land. The concept of the "Indian" is employed as a mode of indirect enunciation, as a political metaphor constructing one's own ethnic subjectivity in terms of another "Other."

Parodies of dominant modes of representation are the products of specific ethnic cultures as well. The Inquisition episode in *The History of the World, Part One*, for example, must also be seen within a specifically Jewish carnivalesque tradition, that of the Purim carnival. The *Purimspiel* tradition celebrates the prevention of genocide through Esther's outwitting of the oppressor. It is the biblical Esther's sexuality—here transformed into the erotic kitsch of Esther Williams—that redeems the Jews. The satirical popular costume in the Jewish carnival, that of Haman, the biblical figure who ordered the genocide of the Jews, marks the rejoicing at the success of Jewish survival. The oppressed who survived, then, wear the self of the oppressor in order to celebrate the continuation of collective history.

Applying the Purim tradition to relatively recent history, in *The History of the World, Part One*, Brooks literally dresses up like the Grand Inquisitor, Torquemada, while in *To Be or Not to Be* (1983) he masquerades as Hitler, and as a Nazi in *The Producers*, much as Woody Allen in *Zelig* transforms himself into a Vatican official and a

Nazi. In *The Producers*, moreover, dozens of saluting Hitlers are revealed to be actors auditioning—a mechanical reproduction which
demystifies the haunting figure of the Fuhrer, as does the ending of
The History of the World, Part One, in which Brooks promises a sequel
which includes "Hitler on Ice" and "Jews in Space."[50] Brooks's
wearing the persona of Torquemada or Hitler can be seen as a form
of metaphorical cannibalism, a symbolic appropriation of the power
of the historical enemy through playfully masquerading as that
enemy.[51] The carnivalesque laughter at power and death through
music and dance also exorcises the community's latent collective
fears. Carnivalesque parody is in some ways the site of a return of
the ethnic repressed. If the musical represented a single American
history and a unified ethnic ideal ego, the carnivalesque parody
presents the multiplicity of histories and conflicting utopian visions.

A discourse of ethnic representation rather than ethnic images involves issues of textual structuring of historical perspective and
power relations. *The History of the World, Part One* implicitly illustrates this point in the ordering of the episodes themselves. The Inquisition number follows the Rome episode whose final sequence
focuses on persecuted Jesus and the Last Supper. The episode of
Christians persecuted by Rome is thus juxtaposed with Christians
as persecutors. Similarly, within the episode itself, the Christian
black is not persecuted by the Romans because of his color but because of his religious persuasion. He even tries to save his life by
insisting that he is not a Christian but a Jew, proving it by tap-
dancing to "Hava Nagila." The following Inquisition episode, in
which Christianity has now become the persecuting norm, fully illuminates ethnic positioning as tied up with the variabilities of
power. Flexible contradictory positionings characterize ethnic and
racial relations. A critical analysis of ethnicity in films, then, also
involves historicizing the question of the specific and evolving articulations of cultural and political power. An awareness of texts as
palimpsests of competing ethnic and racial collective discourses is
thus critical for a multicultural reading which goes beyond any
number of invisible ethnocentricisms.

NOTES

I would like to thank the College of Staten Island-The City University
of New York for providing a Junior Faculty Research Grant (Summer 1989)
that helped support this project.

1. Johannes Fabian, *Time and the Other: How Anthropology Makes Its Object* (New York: Columbia University Press, 1983); for a major critique of Western anthropological representation, see James Clifford, *The Predicament of Culture: Twentieth-Century Ethnography, Literature, and Art* (Cambridge: Harvard University Press, 1988).

2. Richard Dyer has proposed a critical discussion of "whiteness" in cinema, "White," *Screen* 29 (Autumn 1988): 44–64.

3. The reasons for Jewish producers' supression of Jewish presence on the screen, despite their relative power in the industry, are discussed by Patricia Erens, *The Jew in American Cinema* (Bloomington: Indiana University Press, 1984) and Lester Friedman, *The Image of the Jew in Hollywood* (New York: Frederick Ungar Publishing, 1982).

4. In most cases I prefer to use the term *African American* to *black* in order to emphasize not only the racial, but also the historical dimension in the forcing of an African-American critical discourse. For the same reason, I avoid, whenever possible, the problematic term *white*, shifting the focus to Euro-American, or Anglo-American, hegemonic culture as inseparable from the broader history of colonialism and the encounter between the first world and the third world in the United States.

5. For an illuminating discussion of the question of black spectatorship, for example, see Manthia Diawara, "Black Spectatorship—Problems of Identification and Resistance," *Screen* 29 (Autumn 1988): 66–72.

6. On iterative scenes, see Gérard Genette, *Narrative Discourse: An Essay in Method*, trans. Alan Sheridan (Ithaca: Cornell University Press, 1980).

7. Since spectators are ethnically constituted, a marginalized community might be especially alert to certain references on the margins of filmic text. In *Singin' in the Rain*, Gene Kelly and Donald O'Connor, as they sing "Moses," briefly wrap themselves with lined curtains reminiscent of Jewish prayer shawls (*talith*), a visual allusion that Jewish spectators are more likely to catch and appreciate. In *Footlight Parade*, which features a character of a (closet) Jewish producer, a presumably Jewish soldier sings of "Shanghai Lil": "She won't be mine for all of Palestine. . . . Oy!," beating his head with his hand in a Jewish style.

8. See, for example, Shaul Tchernechovsky and Chaim Nachman Bialik's poetic work.

9. Richard Dyer, "Entertainment and Utopia," in *Movies and Methods*, vol. 2, ed. Bill Nichols (Berkeley: University of California Press, 1985).

10. Jane Feuer, *The Hollywood Musical* (Bloomington: Indiana University Press, 1982), p. 84.

11. Fredric Jameson, "Reification and Utopia in Mass Culture," *Social Text* 1 (Winter 1979): 130–48.

12. The phrase is borrowed from Benedict Anderson, *Imagined Communities: Reflexions on the Origins and Spread of Nationalism* (London: Verso, 1983).

13. See, for example, Thomas Cripps, *Slow Fade to Black: The Negro in American Film, 1900–1912* (New York: Oxford University Press 1977), pp. 203–62.

14. This discussion of the problematic nature of the musical's communal interaction concerns only the filmic text. A comprehensive study would have to take into account the context of production—who controls the production, scripting, direction, distribution, and exhibition—as well as the context of reception.

15. For more on the origins of the minstrel show, see Joseph Boskin, *Sambo* (New York: Oxford University Press, 1986).

16. Set during the 1940s, Julie Dash's *Illusions* (1982) foregrounds a black singer who is the singing voice for a white Hollywood star. The "real" presence of the black singer is contrasted with the artificial image of the white star, calling attention to Hollywood's power of representation. The hidden voice of the black singer is privileged over the image of the white star, subverting the racially idealized assumption of the musical and Hollywood.

17. Rick Altman, *The American Film Musical* (Bloomington: Indiana University Press, 1989), pp. 16–58.

18. Boris Uspensky, *A Poetics of Composition* (Berkeley: University of California Press, 1973).

19. Genette, *Narrative Discourse*.

20. This is true as well for films set in "exotic" lands. In *The King and I* (1956), for example, the spectator discovers and is initiated into the Orient quite literally through the point of view of the European cultural missionary, whose initial fears of the mysterious land are summarized as she sings "Whenever I feel afraid . . . . " The spectator is then introduced to Siamese manners and customs through the discourse of the European civilizing mission.

21. Albert Memmi, *Dominated Man* (Boston: Beacon Press, 1968).

22. Edward Said, *Orientalism* (New York: Random House, 1979).

23. Irving Howe, *The World of Our Fathers* (New York: Vintage, 1978).

24. Howe, *World of Our Fathers*, p. 563.

25. Ronald Sanders, cited in ibid., p. 563.

26. Film historiography usually discusses *The Jazz Singer* uniquely in terms of its status as the first sound film and musical, ignoring not only the film's subject of ethnic representation (and its relation to the film's narrative structure and the musical numbers), but also its popular culture intertext. Only few books on ethnicity and cinema, such as Cripps's *Slow Fade to Black* and Daniel J. Leab's *From Sambo to Superspade: The Black Experience in Motion Pictures* (Boston: Houghton Mifflin, 1976), Friedman's *The Image of the Jew*, and Erens's *The Jew in American Cinema*, touch on the question of ethnicity in *The Jazz Singer*. The books largely focus on either the image of the black or the image of the Jew, and there is little discussion of the film's intercultural dimension.

27. Cited in Howe, *World of Our Fathers*.

28. For a full discussion of Woody Allen's *Zelig*, see Robert Stam and Ella Shohat, "*Zelig* and Contemporary Theory: Mediation on the Chameleon Text," *Enclitic* 9 (Summer 1987): 176–94.

29. Adam G. de Gurowski, *America and Europe* (New York: D. Appleton, 1857), p. 177.

30. Sander L. Gilman, *Jewish Self-Hatred: Anti-Semitism and the Hidden Language of Jews* (Baltimore: Johns Hopkins University Press, 1986).

31. Citations from the Production Code of the Motion Picture Producers and Directors of America, Inc. (1930–34) are taken from Garth Jowett, *Film: The Democratic Art* (Boston: Little, Brown, 1976).

32. Hazel V. Carby, "Lynching, Empire, and Sexuality," *Critical Inquiry* 12 (Autumn 1985).

33. Fredric Jameson, "Third World Literature in the Era of Multinational Capitalism," *Social Text* 15 (Fall 1986): 65–88. Although Jameson discusses allegory in a third-world context, I find the category germane for the first world, increasingly characterized by othernesses and differences within itself.

34. In the other exception to mixed ethnic marriage, as in *They Met in Argentina* (1941), the "Latina" Maureen O'Hara is wooed away by James Ellison from her Latin boyfriend, Alberto Vila.

35. On the imperialist interests behind *Flying Down to Rio*, see Brian Henderson, "A Musical Comedy of Empire," *Film Quarterly* 35 (Winter 1981–82): 2–16.

36. Most of the films were shot in studios, often using travelogs. When a film was partially shot on location, the South American population conventionally was part of the decor.

37. Stuart Hall, "The Whites of Their Eyes: Racist Ideologies and the Media," in *Silver Linings*, ed. George Bridges and Rosalind Brunt (London: Laurence and Wishart, 1981), pp. 36–37.

38. Although literary parody was traditionally seen as a dependent, parasitic form, parody has undergone a powerful revalorization in contemporary criticism, largely derived from the modernist privileging reflexivity. For further discussion, see Robert Stam, *Reflexivity in Film and Literature: From Don Quixote to Jean-Luc Godard* (Ann Arbor: UMI Research Press, 1983) and *Subversive Pleasures: Bakhtin, Cultural Criticism and Film* (Baltimore: Johns Hopkins University Press, 1990), and Linda Hutcheon, *A Theory of Parody* (New York: Methuan, 1985).

39. See Mikhail Bakhtin, *Problems of Dostoevsky's Poetics*, trans. P. W. Rotsel (Ann Arbor: Ardis, 1973), *Rabelais and His World*, trans. Helene Iswolsky (Cambridge: MIT Press, 1968), and *The Dialogical Imagination*, ed. Michael Holquist (Austin: University of Texas Press, 1981).

40. Ayoka Chenzira's *Hairpiece: A Film for a Nappy-Headed People* (1985) is a powerful animated satire that examines the self-image of black women who live in a society in which white models of beauty still predominate.

41. Spike Lee with Lisa Jones, *Uplift the Race: The Construction of School Daze* (New York: Simon and Schuster, 1988).

42. Pierre Bordieu, *Distinction: A Social Critique of the Judgement of Taste*, trans. Richard Nice (Cambridge: Harvard University Press, 1984).

43. This imagistic association between Hollywood and Nazi spectacle in Brooks's films evokes Susan Sontag's similar point in "Fascinating Fascism," in *Movies and Methods*, ed. Nichols.

44. Here Mel Brooks ethnocentrically projects an Ashkenazi culture onto a Sephardic history.

45. The attempt to fuse the Jew with the cowboy was depicted previously in the silent dramas *The Yiddisher Cowboy* (1909, 1911).

46. In *Zelig*, similarly, the protagonist admits, under hypnosis to dialogically chameleonizing with a specific group of hyphenated Americans—the Irish. In *The Ordeal of Civility: Freud, Marx, Lévi-Strauss and the Jewish Struggle with Modernity* (Boston: Beacon Press, 1974), John Murray Cuddihy explores the analogies between the Irish and the Jewish immigrant communities as "latecomers to modernity." While the Irish were products of the famines of the 1840s that killed a million Irish and drove their survivors into the world of Anglo-American protestantism, Jews were the products of Russian pogroms that killed thousands of East European Jews and drove them, too, into the world of the New World goyim. Both groups had a precarious grasp on political power, and both had a nostalgia for the Old World convivium. The Irish-Jewish affinity was cinematically engaged by such films as *Ireland and Israel* (1912) and the "Cohen and Kelly" series of the 1920s.

47. David Ignatow and Meyer Shtiker, for example, translated Native-American chants into Yiddish.

48. Tzvetan Todorov, *The Conquest of America*, trans. Richard Howard (New York: Harper and Row, 1984).

49. Lenny Bruce, *The Essential Lenny Bruce*, ed. John Cohen (New York: Ballentine Books, 1967), pp. 27–28.

50. A promise in many ways delivered in *Spaceballs*.

51. One of Purim's rituals involves the eating of special triangular cookies, "the ears of Haman."

Bakhtin, Polyphony, and Ethnic/Racial Representation

My project in this chapter will be to explore the relevance of Mikhail Bakhtin's conceptual categories for the theorization of ethnic representation in the cinema. This project might at first glance seem somewhat "suspect" in the sense that Bakhtin rarely spoke of ethnicity per se, and never, to my knowledge, spoke of the cinema. But perhaps this very "illegitimacy" prolongs the spirit and method of Bakhtin, for whom all texts, including his own, were susceptible to surprising "homecomings," open to reworking by a boundless context. I would like herein to imagine the question of ethnic and racial representation through specific Bakhtinian categories such as "dialogism," "polyphony," and "heteroglossia"—in order to envision the ways in which his thought might contribute to the partial reframing of debates which have often focussed too exclusively on narrowly conceived issues of character stereotypes and sociological accuracy. How might Bakhtinian conceptions, in short, help advance the common goal of formulating a more nuanced, dynamic and multidimensional model for the analysis of ethnic representation?

The Question of Realism

While many of the existing ethnic "image studies" have been productively angry or solidly informative, they have often lacked theoretical and methodological sophistication. While highlighting legitimate issues concerning narrative or characterological plausability, their preoccupation with "realism" has at times implied that the question was simply one of pointing to "errors" and "distortions," as if the truth of an ethnic group were unproblematic, transparent, and easily accessible, and the lies about that group easily unmasked. Much of ethnic image studies has been "corrective," devoted to demonstrating that certain films, in some respect or other, "got something wrong," whether on narrowly historical or biographical grounds, or on grounds of probability and verisimilitude. Debates about ethnic representation often break down on precisely this question of "realism" and "accuracy," at times leading to an impasse in which diverse spectators or critics passionately defend their version of the real.

In such texts as *The Formal Method in Literary Scholarship* and *The Dialogical Imagination*, Bakhtin reformulates the question of artistic representation to avoid this impasse, and in a manner strikingly relevant to issues of ethnic representation. Human consciousness and artistic practice, Bakhtin argues, do not come into contact with the "real" directly, but rather through the medium of the surrounding ideological world. Literature, and by extension cinema, do not so much refer to or call up the world as represent its languages and discourses. Artistic language, for Bakhtin, is not only the instrument and material of representation; it is also the object of representation. Rather than the direct reflection of the real, or even a refraction of the real, artistic discourse constitutes a refraction of a refraction, that is, a mediated version of an already textualized and discursivized socio-ideological world.

By bracketing the question of "the real" and instead emphasizing the artistic representation of languages and discourses, Bakhtin relocates the question to avoid what literary theorists have called the "referential illusion," that is, the notion that films refer back to some preexisting anecdotal nucleus against which a film's "truth" can be checked. Bakhtin's formulation has the advantage of transcending a naive verism without ever falling into a "hermeneutic nihilism" whereby all texts become nothing more than a meaningless play of signification open to an infinity of projections and interpretations. Bakhtin rejects naive formulations of realism while never abandoning the notion that artistic representations are at the same time thoroughly and irrevocably social, precisely because the discourses that art represents are themselves social and historical. An acknowledgment of the constructed, coded nature of artistic discourse does not preclude all reference to social existence. Indeed, for Bakhtin, art is incontrovertibly social, not because it represents the real, but because art constitutes a socially situated "utterance"—that is, a complex of signs addressed by socially constituted subjects to other socially constituted subjects—deeply immersed in historical circumstance.

The issue of realism requires, of course, that the film analyst perform a very delicate balancing act. On the one hand, we want to reserve the right to suggest that certain films are false or pernicious, that *Birth of a Nation* (1915), for example, is an "objectively" racist film. The desire to reserve a right to judgment on questions of realism is especially appropriate in cases in which there are historical antecedents or real-life prototypes for a film. The black musicians who performed at Harlem's Cotton Club have every right to point out that the Coppola film exaggerates both the presence and the violence of the mafiosos who partied there, or that it misleads by suggesting that all Harlem blacks were either criminals or entertainers.[1] Those familiar with Charlie Parker's career have every right to observe that Clint Eastwood's *Bird* (1988), although on one level a sincere homage to Charlie Parker and jazz, on another downplays the role of a supportive minoritarian community composed of such fellow musicians as Thelonius Monk, Miles Davis, Charles Mingus, and Max Roach in favor of the black-white buddy film evoked by the Bird-Rodney relationship. And the veterans of the civil rights struggle in the South in the 1960s have every right to critique *Mississippi Burning* (fig. 9.1) on the grounds that it turns the historical enemy in the 1960s—the racist FBI which devoted most of its energies to harassing and sabotaging the civil rights movement—into the heroes, while turning the historical heroes—the thousands of blacks who marched, suffered, and died—into passive victim-observors waiting for white official "rescue."[2]

But even in such cases a Bakhtinian approach would emphasize the role of choices, of representation, of mediation, defining the issue less as one of fidelity to a preexisting truth or reality than as one of a specific orchestration of discourses in relation to a theme. It makes more sense, within a Bakhtinian perspective, to say of *The Gods Must be Crazy* (1984) not that it is untrue to "reality," but rather that it relays the colonialist discourse of the white South African elite: a discourse which posits a Manichean binarism contrasting noble but impotent Bantustan savages with dangerous but incompetent mulatto-led revolutionaries, a discourse whose racism is hidden behind the facade of a superficial critique of white technological civilization. Such a formulation would see filmic characters, in Bakhtinian terms, not as "real" people, but rather as discursive constructions advanced by one group, in this case white South

9.1. Blacks are passive victims rather than active protestors in *Mississippi Burning*.

Africans, for the consumption of a variety of audiences around the world. A Bakhtinian approach to *Rambo* (1985), similarly, would not argue that it "falsifies" or "distorts" reality, but rather that it "really" represents a rightist and racist discourse designed to flatter and nourish masculine fantasies of omnipotence characteristic of an empire in crisis.

Although it is true that complete realism is an impossibility, it is also true that spectators themselves come equipped with a "sense of the real" rooted in their own social experience, on the basis of which they can accept, question, or even subvert a film's representations. For Bakhtin, all discourse exists in dialogue not only with prior discourses but also with the recipient of the discourse, with an "interlocutor" situated in time and space. Although films are on one level powerful machines which produce an "effet du reel," this effect cannot be separated from the desire, experience, and knowledge of the historically situated spectator. The cultural preparation of a particular audience, in this sense, can generate counterpressure to a racist or prejudicial discourse. Latin American audiences laughed Hollywood's know-nothing portrayals of Argentina and

Brazil off the screen because, for them, it was quite simply impossible to take such misinformed images seriously. Black Americans, similarly, never took Stepin Fetchit as a typical, synecdochic sample of black behavior or attitudes; they knew he was acting and intuitively understood the kinds of circumstances that led him to play subserviant roles. In an excellent article, Manthia Diawara demonstrates why black spectators find it impossible to buy into the racism of *Birth of a Nation*. The black spectator, Diawara argues, disrupts the functioning of Griffith's film, questioning its coherence and rebelling against the order imposed by its narrative. For black spectators, Diawara argues, the character Gus, as a phantasmatic incarnation of a putative black lust and violence, cannot represent blacks but only white prejudice toward blacks.[3] In Bakhtinian terms, Gus does not represent the "real," but only a racist and colonialist discourse generated by fear and prejudice to which the black spectator can respond with a counterdiscourse of liberation.

The Orchestration of Voices

"I hear voices everywhere," Bakhtin was fond of saying, "and the dialogical relations between them." In *Problems of Dostoevsky's Poetics*, Bakhtin argues that Dostoevsky is not to be identified with one or another voice within his novels, but rather with the agency that orchestrates a multiplicity of distinct and even antithetical voices. This view of texts as a polyphonic play of voices is especially appropriate to postmodernist films (Yvonne Rainer's *The Man Who Envied Woman* would be an obvious example) which, rather than represent real humanly purposeful events within an illusionistic esthetic, simply stage the clash of socially generated languages and discourses. But it is also ultimately relevant to all films and artistic representations. A Bakhtinian approach to the issue of ethnic representation, in this sense, would shift attention from the question of realism and positive and negative characters to one of voices and discourses. What are the "accents" and "intonations," to use Bakhtinian language, discernible in a filmic voice? Which of the ambient ethnic voices are "heard" in a film, and which are elided or distorted?

The very term *image studies*, symptomatically, elides the oral and the voiced. Such cultural thinkers as Walter Ong, Johannes Fabian, and Frances Yates have argued, in different ways, that the Western imagination is strongly "visualist," positing cultural facts as things observed or seen rather than heard, transcribed, or invented in dialogue.[4] A "Cartesian perspectivalism," Hal Foster argues, "subtends metaphysical thought, empirical science, and capitalist logic all at once."[5] The Bakhtinian predilection for aural and musical metaphors—voices, intonation, accent, and polyphony—argues an overall shift in priority from the visually predominant logical space of modernity (perspective, evidence in empirical science, domination of the gaze) to a postmodern space of the vocal (oral ethnography, people's history, slave narratives), all as ways of restoring voice to the silenced. The visual organization of space, George Yudice suggests, with its limits and boundaries and border police, is a metaphor of exclusions and hierarchical arrangements, while the concept of voice suggests a metaphor of seepage across boundaries which, as in the cinema, redefines spatiality itself.[6]

A Bakhtinian approach to ethnicity in the cinema, then, would emphasize less a kind of one-to-one mimetic adequacy to sociological or historical truth than the interplay of voices, discourses, and perspectives. Clyde Taylor's work on the defining characteristics of New Black Cinema is in this sense quite compatible with a Bakhtinian approach in that two of the traits he emphasizes are aural in nature; the link to the African-American oral tradition and the strong articulation of black musicality, both of which are indispensible in the effort of black cinema to find what Taylor himself calls "its voice."[7] Less important than a film's "accuracy" is that it relay the voices and the perspectives—I emphasize the plural—of the community or communities in question. If an identification with a community perspective occurs, the question of "positive" images falls back into its rightful place as a subordinate issue. That Spike Lee's *School Daze* (1987) foregrounds tensions within the black community and uses stylization and satire to lampoon the colonized ambitions of the "wannabee whites" at an all-black school whose motto is "Uplift the Race" is ultimately less significant than the fact that an audacious black perspective predominates throughout.

The task of the Bakhtinian critic, then, is to call attention to the voices at play in a text, not only those heard in aural "close-up," but also those voices distorted or drowned out by the text. Formulating the issue as one of voices helps us get beyond the lure of the visual. The question, quite literally, is not of the color of the face in the image, but rather of the literal or figurative voice speaking "through" the image. Television commercials, for example, are often crowded with black faces, but it is white advertisers who have placed the words in their mouths: black soul as white artifact. The work of the analyst, in such instances, would be analogous to that of a mixer in a sound studio, whose responsibility it is to perform a series of compensatory operations, of heightening the treble, deepening the bass, or amplifying the instrumentation, that is, in ethnic terms, of "bringing out" the voices which remain latent or displaced.

It might be objected, of course, that an analysis of textual "voices" would ultimately run into the same theoretical problems as an analysis centered on "images." Why would it be any easier to determine an "authentic voice" than it would be to determine an "authentic image"? The point is to abandon the language of "authenticity," with its implicit standard of appeal to the "real," in favor of a language of "discourses," with its implicit reference to intertextuality. Reformulating the question as one of "voices" and "discourses" has a number of advantages. First, an appeal to voice over image, or better in conjunction with image, disputes the hegemony of the visible and the image-track by calling attention to sound, voice, dialogue, and language. Second, the notion of voice is more likely to allow for plurality. A voice is never merely a voice; it also relays a discourse, because within a Bakhtinian perspective an individual voice is itself a discursive sum, a polyphony of voices. "Heteroglossia," after all, can be seen as another name for the socially generated contradictions that constitute the subject, like the media, as the site of conflicting discourses and competing voices. The same person, within a Bakhtinian perspective, can be traversed by a racist and by an antiracist discourse. The same person can have an antiracist discourse and a racist behavior, or vice versa, be antiracist on a cultural plane but racist on an economic plane, nonracist by day but racist by night. Racism can be visceral, expressed in the semiotics of body language, in open contradiction with verbally professed attitudes. Racial attitudes are multiform, contradictory, even schizophrenic. Ralph Ellison speaks of the white youngster, with transistor radio playing a Stevie Wonder tune, shouting racial epithets at black youngsters trying to swim at a public beach. In *Do the Right Thing*, Spike Lee makes the same point about racial schizophrenia by having the black-hating Pino, whose favorite word is "nigger," have celebrity blacks—Magic Johnson, Eddie Murphy, and Prince—as his "favorite people." In addition, the perpetual discussions between Sal (Danny Aiello) and Mookie (Spike Lee) highlight both interethnic tensions and affinities (fig. 9.2). Third, by highlighting the discursive dimension of artistic texts, a Bakhtinian approach sees characters, for example, not as unitary essences, as actor-character amalgams too easily phantasized as three-dimensional

9.2. Interethnic tensions and affinities in *Do the Right Thing*, as examplified by Sal (Danny Aiello) and Mookie (Spike Lee).

flesh-and-blood entities existing somewhere "behind" the diegesis, but rather as fictive-discursive constructs, thus placing the whole issue on a socio-ideological rather than on an individual-moralistic plane. Fourth, the privileging of the discursive allows comparison of a film's discourses not with an inaccessible "real," but rather with other socially circulated cognate discourses forming part of a discursive continuum such as journalism, novels, network news, television shows, political speeches, scholarly essays, and popular songs.

Ethnic Dialogism

Each cultural voice, for Bakhtin, exists in dialogue with other voices. In a preliminary way, we can define dialogism as the necessary relation of any utterance to other utterances, using "utterance" in Bakhtin's extremely inclusive sense as referring to communicative phenomena as diverse as bodily gestures, spoken phrases, or artistic texts. In "The Problem of Speech Genres," Bakhtin offers a clear formulation of what he calls the inherent dialogism of the utterance: "Utterances are not indifferent to one another, and are not

self-sufficient; they are aware of and mutually reflect one another. . . . Each utterance is filled with echoes and reverberations of
other utterances to which it is related by the communality of the
sphere of speech communication. . . . Each utterance refutes, affirms, supplements, and relies on the others, presupposes them to
be known, and somehow takes them into account."[8]

Social and ethnic diversity is for Bakhtin fundamental to every
utterance, even to that utterance which on the surface ignores or
excludes the groups with which it is in relation. Segregation can be
temporarily imposed as a sociopolitical arrangement, but it cannot
be absolute, especially on the level of culture. Southern whites,
Ralph Ellison observed in the early 1960s, "cannot walk, talk, sing,
conceive of laws or justice, think of sex, love, the family or freedom
without responding to the presence of Negroes."[9] Even the most
devout believer in apartheid, in this perspective, cannot ultimately
separate himself or herself from the black response to white su-
premacism. All utterances inescapably take place against the background of the possible responding utterances of other social and
ethnic points of view. Ethnicity is relational, an inscription of communicative processes within history, between subjects existing in
relations of power.

It is this profoundly relational vision that differentiates Bakhtin's
thought from an innocuous liberal pluralism in several senses. First,
Bakhtin, in counterdistinction to a liberal discourse of tolerance,
sees all utterance and discourse in relation to the deforming effects
of social power. Second, Bakhtin does not preach a pseudo-equality
of viewpoints; his sympathies, rather, go clearly to the nonofficial
viewpoint, to the marginalized, the oppressed, the peripheralized.
Third, whereas pluralism is grudgingly accretive—it benevolently
allows another voice to add itself to the mainstream ("to those who
have yet to share the benefits of the American dream" in the formulaic discourse of the politicians)—Bakhtin's view is polyphonic
and celebratory. A Bakhtinian approach thinks "from the margins,"
seeing Native Americans, African Americans and Hispanics, for
example, not as interest groups to be added on to a preexisting pluralism, but rather as being at the very core of the American experience from the beginning, each offering an invaluable "dialogical
angle" on the national experience. Fourth, a Bakhtinian approach
recognizes an epistemological advantage on the part of those who
are oppressed and therefore bicultural. The oppressed, because they
are obliged by circumstances and the imperatives of survival to
know both the dominant and the marginal culture, are ideally

placed to deconstruct the mystifications of the dominant group. Fifth, Bakhtinian dialogism is reciprocal, not unilateral; any act of verbal or cultural exchange leaves both interlocutors changed.

The tension between an open-ended vision of an America as an ethnic polyphony versus a monological model of America as a unitary culture has always operated at the conflictual core of America's self-conception, its dreams and nightmares; it has been at the very kernel of its vision of itself. The political colloquy in the United States, from the first debates concerning slavery and the treatment of the indigenous peoples to the latest presidential campaigns, with their semi-coded language of patriotism and the fight against crime (read "black crime"), has often been expressed or "allegorized" in ethnic terms. The dream of a fuller democracy in a constitutively plural society has always been indissociable from the struggle for full participation by all of America's races and ethnicities. From the beginning, two discourses have been in conflict: one which saw America as a nation of nations, with all of America's peoples (especially its oppressed peoples) at the epicenter of the American experience, and another which saw one group as primary and central, in a position to show intermittent tolerance to others regarded as peripheral and dispensable.

American popular culture bears constant witness to the dialogue—sometimes violent, often shrill, at times communicative—between Anglo culture and its "Others." In film, this dialogue has often taken the alienated form of hero-and-sidekick (ethnicized latter-day avatars of Don Quixote and Sancho Panza) such as the Lone Ranger and Tonto; or of hero and valet, such as Jack Benny and Rochester; or of hero and entertainer, such as Rick and Sam in *Casablanca* (1942). Sidney Poitier and Tony Curtis in *The Defiant Ones* (1958) offer a chain-heavy allegory of racial interdependency, while the 1970s and 1980s offer more upbeat versions of the biracial buddy film: Richard Pryor and Gene Wilder in *Stir Crazy* (1980) and *See No Evil* (1989), Eddie Murphy and Nick Nolte in *48 Hours* (1982), and Billy Crystal and Gregory Hines in *Running Scared* (1986). The box-office appeal of such films suggests that they touch something within the American Unconscious, a kind of wish for an easy and low-cost racial harmony. And indeed one could easily trace images of ethnic utopia within American culture, from the perennial Thanksgiving celebrations through the latest music videos.

In *Love and Death in the American Novel*, Leslie Fiedler traces the epiphanies of racial harmony—Natty Bumppo and Chingachgook, Ishmael and Queequeg, Huck and Jim—as they affect nineteenth-century American literature, but the same process, at a more advanced stage, also pervades contemporary mass culture. One detects images of ethnic utopia on the "Oprah Winfrey Show," in soft-drink commercials, in public service announcements, and in the happily integrated and multiethnic big-city Eyewitness News shows. The question, however, is not whether Americans enjoy consolatory images of ethnic harmony but rather whether they are willing to participate in the structural changes necessary for making ethnic harmony a living, quotidian reality.

At times, interracial dialogism inflects a film's textual strategies. Think, for example, of the alternating montage in Robert Altman's *Nashville* (1975) between the soporific entoning in one recording studio of Haven Hamilton's country-style bicentennial song "Two Hundred Years," and the rousing chant, in an adjacent studio, of a black handclapping gospel song (led, somewhat improbably, by an out-of-tune Lily Tomlin). Altman suggestively juxtaposes two musical styles, each redolent of what Bakhtin would call the "accents" and "intonations" of a "socio-ideological world." Rather than polyphony, we are given a contrastive diaphony or counterpoint: in one studio, the bland music of jingoistic complacency—"we must be doing something right to last two-hundred years"—presided over by an authoritarian (Hamilton) eager to expel long-hair dissidents from the studio. In the other studio is soulful participatory music forged during the same two hundred years, but in this case from the perspective of those whose historical memory includes slavery and segregation. The gospel scene is observed, furthermore, by an effusive BBC journalist (Geraldine Chaplin) who makes inane and ethnocentric comments about darkest Africa and missionaries converting natives. The revolution celebrated by the bicentennial, Altman reminds us, was fought against her ancestors, the British, who had in common with white North Americans an oppressive relation to black people.[10]

Emilio de Antonio's satirical documentary about Richard Nixon, *Milhouse: A White Comedy* (1971), offers a particularly striking instance of this ethnic counterpoint. One sound-image montage counterposes the voice of Nixon extolling "law and order" against a black voice giving an account of what really transpired in the Miami black community during the Republican convention in 1968. The ensuing images decode Nixon's grand phrases about "order" to reveal their subsurface signification—that is, intention to crush any outbreaks of black rebellion. Another sound-image montage plays off Nixon's innocuous "I See a Day" speech against Martin Luther

King's stirring "I Have a Dream" oration—a speech whose rhetoric and syntax the Nixon speech clearly borrows—showing transparent sympathy for the emotional force and political commitment of the latter while mocking the petit-bourgeois mediocrity of the former. Nixon's voice, promulgating the myth of "equal opportunity," gradually gives way to the resonant authority of the voice of King, who, in the powerful accents of the black Southern preacher, denounces the barriers to equality while articulating a distant yet imaginable promised land of racial harmony. The two voices, in Bakhtinian terminology, have been counterposed at a "dialogical" angle, generating a social message far transcending the individual content of the two discourses.

Polyphony

Another Bakhtinian formulation relevant to the conceptualization of ethnicity is his notion of "polyphony." This music-derived trope, originally formulated in reference to the complex play of ideological voices in the work of Dostoevsky, calls attention to the coexistence, the collaborative antagonism in any textual or extratextual situation: a plurality of voices which do not fuse into a single consciousness, but rather exist on different registers and thus generate dialogical dynamism. Polyphony does not point to mere heterogeneity per se, but rather to the "dialogical angle" at which voices are juxtaposed and counterposed to generate something beyond themselves. What might be termed the ethnic dimension of polyphony is relevant here. Although all cultures are polyphonic and include distinct genders, professions, and age groups, some cultures are striking in being ethnically polyphonic. Bakhtin's multiethnic Russian source culture, existing at the crossroads of Europe and Asia, provided innumerable exemplars of cultural polyphony. New World countries such as the United States, similarly, deploy myriad cultural voices (no matter how oppressed or muffled those voices might be)—that of the indigenous peoples, that of the Afro-American, along with the voices of the Jewish, Italian, Hispanic, Asiatic, and many other communities—each of which condenses, in turn, a multiplicity of social accents having to do with gender, class, and locale.

The potentially idealizing notion of polyphony, with its overtones of harmonious simultaneity, must be completed, then, by the notion of heteroglossia, the shifting stratifications of language into class and ethnic dialects, with its undertones of social conflict rooted not in the random individual dissonances but in the deep structural cleavages of social life. A Bakhtinian analysis would also be aware of the dangers of "pseudo-polyphonic" discourse, one which marginalizes and disempowers certain voices, and then pretends to undertake a dialogue with a puppetlike entity that has already been forced to make crucial compromises. The film or television commercial in which every eighth face is black, for example, has more to do with the demographics of market research or the bad conscience of liberalism than with authentic polyphony, because the black voice, in such instances, is usually shorn of its soul, as well as deprived of its color and intonation. "Market-place heteroglossia," as John Fiske points out, merely exploits subcultural differences as a marketing strategy for incorporating ethnic and minority audiences.[11] Polyphony does not consist in the mere appearance of a representative of a given group but rather in the fostering of a textual setting where that group's voice can be heard with its full force and resonance. The question is not one of pluralism but one of multi-vocality, an approach which would strive to abolish social inequalities while heightening and even cultivating cultural difference.

One form of pseudo-polyphony consists of a superficial integrationism which simply inserts new heroes and heroines, this time drawn from the ranks of the subaltern, into old functional roles which are themselves oppressive, much as colonialism invited a few assimilated "natives" to join the club of the elite. A film like *Shaft* (1971) simply substitutes black heroes into the actantial slot normally filled by white ones, in order to flatter the fantasies of a certain (largely male) sector of the black audience. *Guess Who's Coming to Dinner* (Stanley Kramer, 1967), as its title suggests, invites a superqualified black into the club of the elite, but always on white terms. Indeed, many Kramer-style "liberal" films tried to persuade the white audience not to be racist, and the audience was indeed so persuaded, at least as long as the black person encountered in real life conformed exactly to the superhuman "ebony saint" standards set by the characters played by Sidney Poitier or Harry Belafonte.

Other films, such as *In the Heat of the Night* (1967) and *Pressure Point* (1962), and such television series as "I Spy" or "Miami Vice" project blacks, within the generic framework of the black-white buddy film, into the role of law-enforcers, implying a black link to the power structure quite out of keeping with the actual configuration of social power. Countless films elide important differences by reducing the trajectory of oppressed racial groups to the mere recapitulation of the melting-pot assimilations of European immigrants. *El Norte* (1983) begins by denouncing the oppression of Central Americans by dictatorial governments enjoying United States government support, but ultimately presents the move to Los Angeles as a kind of solution for the problems of immigrants. The television series "Roots," finally, exploited positive images in what was ultimately a cooptive version of African-American history. The series "subtitle" (the "saga of an American family") reflects an emphasis on the European-style nuclear family (retrospectively projected onto Kunta's life in Africa) in a film which casts blacks as just another immigrant group making its way toward freedom and prosperity in democratic America.

Urban Heteroglossia

Many North American cities provide privileged sites of heteroglossia and the ethnic interplay intrinsic to a heteroglot culture. New York, for example, has become a "minority-majority" city without any clear or overwhelming ethnic majority; each apparently unified community itself breaks down into numerous subcultures traversed by class, generation, and the nuances of ethnicity, thus making it a fractured and conflictual paradigm of heteroglossia rich in (often frustrated) polyphonic potential. The cinema has frequently "translated," reflected, refracted, or sublimated the ethnic diversity of New York into filmic sounds and images. Many New York-based films pivot around some sort of ethnic interplay as a key structuring strategy: black and white in *Brother from Another Planet* (1984); Anglo-Latino in *Crossover Dreams* (1985) and *Wild Style* (1984); Jewish, black, and Puerto Rican in *The Pawnbroker* (1965); and bohemian-polyphonic in *Next Stop Greenwich Village* (1976) and *Hair* (1979).

In such films as Alan Parker's *Fame* (1980), Paul Mazursky's *Moscow on the Hudson* (1984), and Woody Allen's *Zelig* (1983) a New York setting helps generate a rich weave of ethnic voices. A Bakhtinian analysis of such films would point both to their polyphonic potential and to the political myopia which undermines that potential. In *Fame*, youthful representatives of diverse communities—black, Puerto Rican, Jewish, and gay—collaborate within a kind of utopia of artistic expression (fig. 9.3). In *Moscow on the Hudson*, the Robin Williams character enters into dialogic interaction with an entire gallery of synecdochic ethnic figures—a black security guard, an

9.3. The artist's ethnic utopia in *Fame*.

Italian sales clerk, a Korean taxi-driver, a Cuban lawyer, and a Chinese anchorwoman. Each dialogue is inflected by the specific accents of a culturally defined interlocutor. And Zelig's capacity to take on the accent and ethnicity of those with whom he interacts turns him into a self-creating one-man polyphony of cultural voices.

At the same time that these films evoke the play of ethnic and cultural polyphony, they fail to reveal the political obstacles to true polyphony and equality, much as political liberalism speaks of dialogue but fails to address the ways in which hegemonic power conditions and limits dialogue. Rather than subvert the existing power relations between the diverse communities, the films tend to orchestrate superficially defined ethnic types. *Fame* ultimately subordinates polyphony to a "making it" ethos less dedicated to transpersonal community than to individual "Fame!" *Moscow on the Hudson* begins as critical both of political repression in the Soviet Union and of laissez-faire cruelty in the United States, but finally degenerates into just another sentimental immigrant saga. And *Zelig* ultimately retreats from the utopian implications of its fable by having its protagonist rediscover his "true self" and acquiesce in suburban middle-class values, while the film offers precious little indication of the limitations of its protagonist's vision. A Bakhtinian approach to such films, in any case, would tease out, in an "anticipatory" reading, the latent multiethnic utopias stirring within such texts, while unmasking the ways in which they repress their utopian potential and fail to signal the real social and political impediments to community.

The self, in a context of polyphony, is necessarily syncretic, especially when that polyphony is amplified by the media. This syncretism is first of all linguistic; in cities like New York the language itself is hybrid, consisting of Yiddishized English, Anglicized Spanish, and so forth. When Rupert Pupkin, in Martin Scorcese's *King of Comedy* (1983), calls Masha "el schmucko supremo," he gives voice to the hybridized language of the city. The United States, speaking more generally, is a country, as Philip Roth puts it in *The Counterlife*, full of "Chicanos who want to look like Texans, and Texans who want to look like New Yorkers, and any number of Middle Western Wasps who, believe it or not, want to act and think like Jews."[12] The process of cultural syncretism began even before the American Revolution, as Euro-Americans appropriated not only the vocabulary but also the military and political wisdom of the indigenous Native American peoples. (I am referring, for example, to the indigenous influence on the Revolutionary Army's way of fighting the British, and to the contribution of the Iroquois Federation to the initial conceptualizations of the American "federal" government.) Cultural syncretism occurs at the margins and between the margins and a changing mainstream, resulting in a creative intermingling of cultures as part of a general movement of American history, by which indigenous, African-American, and local-immigrant experiences flow into a broader "nonfinalized" polyphony.

Countless American films stage the processes of ethnic syncretism, sometimes ponderously, sometimes comically, sometimes poignantly: Whites learning Native American ways in such films as *Hombre* (1967) and *A Man Called Horse* (1970); Eugene Martoni learning to play the blues from Willie Brown in *Crossroads* (1985); Appalachian whites, Italians, and black Americans collaborating musically and politically in *Matewan* (1987); young, white David learning Jamaican patois from Clara (Whoopie Goldberg) in *Clara's Heart* (1988, fig. 9.4); Woody Allen armed with Wonder Bread and a crucifix and ready for conversion in *Hannah and Her Sisters* (1985); and Charlie Parker in a yarmulke jazzing up a Hassidic wedding in *Bird* (1988). Indeed, any binary grid which pits Anglo whiteness

9.4. Ethnic syncretism—whites adopting native ways—in *Clara's Heart,* as Clara (Whoopie Goldberg) teaches her young charge to speak Jamaican patois.

against black, red, or yellow others inevitably fails to catch all the complex contradictions and gradations of the American experience. One of the merits of Spike Lee's *Do the Right Thing* is that it foregrounds both tensions and affinities between Italian Americans and African Americans. The film implicitly calls attention to the ways that some members of immigrant communities have used blacks as a kind of "welcome mat," as a way of affirming, through antiblack hostility, their own insecure sense of American identity. At the same time, the film highlights the more subtle interactions between the two communities by having the Italians act just a little black and the blacks just a little Italian. We learn from the published screenplay that Lee even thought of having Giancarlo Esposito, who is himself half black and half Italian, play a character called "Spaghetti Chitlins." The metaphor drawn from cuisine is highly apposite because American cuisine is now multicultural, having been soul-foodized, taco-ized, felafel-ized, and sushi-ized. A polyphonic historical process has in effect generated the rich peculiarities and syncretisms of North American culture. American music, to take an-

other example, now thoroughly melds European with African traditions. The majority of contemporary white popular singers work
within a black-inflected musical idiom that ultimately traces its roots
to Africa. Virtually all of the participants, black and white, in the
music video "We Are the World" sing in a melismatic, soulful, im-
provisational gospel style which has everything to do with the spirit
of black musicality.

Zelig allegorizes this syncretic process in the most hyperbolic and
paradigmatic fashion, a feat somewhat surprising coming from a director who rarely shows sensitivity to the ethnic diversity of New
York City. *Zelig* illustrates the pragmatic, opportunistic appropria-
tions typical of a mobile, heteroglot culture. Zelig the chameleon
literally becomes his ethnic neighbors. Each of the protagonist's
metamorphoses is informed by a deep social, cultural, and historical
logic; each carries its specific weight of historical association. Not
only does Zelig the Jew chameleonize to other oppressed minorities—Native American, black, Mexican—but he also chameleonizes
to his fellow swimmers in the immigrants' melting pot. Under hypnosis, Zelig admits to dialogically chameleonizing with another
group of hyphenated Americans. Entering a bar on Saint Patrick's
Day, he relates: "I told them I was Irish. My hair turned red. My
nose turned up. I spoke about the great potato famine."

In *The Ordeal of Civility,* John Murray Cuddihy explores the analogies between the Irish and the Jewish immigrant communities as
"latecomers to modernity."[13] While the Irish were the product of
the famines of the 1840s which killed a million Irish and drove them
into the world of Anglo-American protestantism, the Jews were the
product of the Russian pogroms which killed thousands of East European Jews and drove them too into the cultural universe of the
New World goyim. *Zelig* illustrates the process by which the streets
of a city like New York become a kind of medium in which diverse
ethnicities meet, clash, and interact. The dialogical encounter, according to Bakhtin, is never a complete merging, but rather a reciprocal interchange taking place within what he terms the in-between
of two interlocutors. The result of this Creole-like situation is "hybridization" and "assimilation" of the other's word. *Zelig* renders
syncretism visible by offering us a figure who is at once Woody
Allen, and therefore white and Jewish, as well as black, Indian,
Chinese, and Irish. Zelig's metamorphoses, in this sense, simply
render visible and palpable what is usually invisible—the constant
process of synchresis which occurs when ethnicities brush against

and rub off on one another in a context of cultural "many-languagedness."[14]

The Mutual Illumination of Cultures

Within dialogism, entire genres, languages, and cultures are susceptible to what Bakhtin terms "mutual illumination." His insight takes on special relevance in a contemporary world where communication is global, and where cultural circulation, if in many respects assymetrical, is still multi-vocal, and where it is becoming more and more inappropriate to corral human diversity into the confining categories of discrete cultures and independent nations. It is useful, in this respect, to regard the question of ethnic representation in North American culture in relation to the other multiethnic cultures of the Americas. Take, for example, the case of Brazil and the United States, two vast New World countries similar in historical formation and ethnic composition. Both countries began as European colonies, one of Portugal and the other of Great Britain, and in both, colonization was followed by the conquest of vast territories that entailed the near-genocidal subjugation of the indigenous peoples. Both countries massively imported blacks from Africa to form the two largest slave societies of modern times until slavery was abolished with the Emancipation Proclamation of 1863 in the United States and the "Golden Law" of 1888 in Brazil. Both countries received successive waves of immigration, indeed often the same waves of immigration, from all over the world, ultimately forming pluri-ethnic societies with substantial Indian, black, Italian, German, Japanese, Slavic, Arab, and Jewish communities.

A Bakhtinian approach would emphasize mutual illumination both "within" and "between" cultures. A useful comparative analysis would stress the analogies not only within American cultural representations—for example, analogies between the representation of African-Americans and Native Americans—but also the analogies and disanalogies between the representations of both groups in relation to their representation within the other multiethnic cultures of the Americas. Such an analysis would juxtapose whole constellations of representional practices within a larger, cross-cultural, pan-American context. It is revelatory, for example, to compare the cinematic treatment of the indigenous peoples in Brazil as opposed to the United States, and the relation of that treatment to the representation of blacks. In both countries we find scores of films, even in the silent period, devoted to the "Native American" or the "Native Brazilian." Both cinemas feature numerous adaptations of nineteenth-century "Indianist" novels, for example of Jose de Alencar's *Iracema* in Brazil, or of James Fenimore Cooper's *The Last of the Mohicans* in the United States. (In Brazil, there were four filmic adaptations of *O Guarani* and three of *Iracema* in the silent period alone.) In Brazil, however, there is no tradition of denigration of the Indian as a dangerous war-whooping savage, no "imagery of encirclement," as Tom Engelhardt calls it, pitting threatened whites against screaming hordes. Instead, the early Brazilian films recapitulate the values of the romantic Indianist movement whereby the Indian is portrayed as healthy, pure, heroic, and a nostalgic exemplar of a vanished golden age. The myths purveyed in these films and novels, moreover, are myths of racial syncretism, of the fusion of white European and Indian elements into a new entity— "the Brazilian." *O Guarani*, for example, concludes with the symbolic merging of two rivers, a figure for the fusion of the indigenous peoples with those of Europe. North American novelistic and filmic treatments of the Native American, in contrast, tend to emphasize apartness and otherness, and the doomed nature of love between white and Indian. The idea of racial miscegenation, then, is celebrated in Brazilian culture, while it has tended to generate fear and paranoia in North America, a paranoia encapsulated in an intertitle from William S. Hart's 1916 film *The Aryan*: "Oft written in letters of blood, deep carved in the face of destiny, that all men may read, runs the code of the Aryan race: our women shall be guarded."

But this difference in approach between the two cinemas does not, ultimately, indicate that Brazilian cinema is more "progressive" toward the Native Brazilian. Rather, the celebration, in Brazilian films, of the Indian as "brave warrior," the spiritual source and symbol of Brazil's nationhood, the mark of its difference from Europe, involved an element of bad faith toward both Indian and black. Because the behavior of white Europeans, in Brazil as in the United States, was fundamentally murderous, this exaltation of the disappearing Indian, dedicated as it was to the very group being victimized by literal and cultural genocide, involved a strong element of hyprocrisy. The ambiguous "compliment" to the Indians— compliments paid only much later in the history of the American cinema with such countercultural films as *Little Big Man* (1970)—was in Brazil a means of avoiding the vexed question of blacks and slavery. The proud history of black rebellion in Brazil—most dramatically manifested in the *quilombos* or fugitive slave communities—

was ignored; the brave Indian, it was subtly insinuated, resisted slavery, whereas blacks did not. The white literary and filmmaking elite in Brazil, in sum, chose the safely distant and mythically connoted Indian over the more problematically present black, victim of a slavery abolished just a decade before the inauguration of the cinema in Brazil.

A Bakhtinian analysis might then further complicate these multiple comparabilities by introducing a third intermediate group entering into a complex and shifting set of relationships—European immigrants. In both Brazil and the United States much early cinema was the product of immigrants, largely Italian in the case of Brazil, and largely Jewish-European in the case of the United States. In Brazil, this relationship meant that while the immigrant filmmakers bore no direct responsibility for the institution of slavery, and while Italians were often themselves the objects of exploitation by the Portuguese-based elite, collectively they were the winners, and blacks the losers, of this period of Brazilian history. Immigrant filmmakers, as a consequence, were not eager to explore filmically the oppressive situation of the very group that they themselves had economically displaced. (This displacement was quite literal because the Brazilian elite consciously opted to recruit European immigrants as workers rather than employ the newly freed slaves.)

In the case of the United States, the situation was quite different. First, the wave of immigration that contributed to the formation of Hollywood cinema came many decades after the abolition of slavery, not just one decade later as in Brazil. Blacks, furthermore, formed a clear minority in the United States, not the marginalized majority as in Brazil. That the Hollywood immigrants were Jewish, furthermore, a group not only European but also the victim of Europe—its "internal other" in Tzvetan Todorov's apt phrase—meant that a complex play of analogy and identification operated between Jews and blacks. The relationship was seen in the black appropriation of the historical perspective implicit in the images and myths of the Hebrew Bible, and in the Jewish appropriation of black voices and musicality (Gershwin, Jolson)—an intricate dynamic more or less absent from the relation between Italian immigrants and blacks in Brazil.

A comparative study of ethnic representation in the two countries reveals fundamental differences in perception and approach. Much of the literature on blacks in North American cinema revolves around the existence of the specific stereotypes dissected by Donald Bogle in his classic study: lazy Sambos, servile Toms, obese mammies, libidinous bucks, and tragic mulattoes.[15] The temptation, for the North American critic, is to look for these same stereotypes in Brazilian cinema. But the congruencies are only partial. The *mae preta* (black mother) figure does have a good deal to do with the "Mammy," just as Pai Joao (Father John) has much to do with the "Uncle Tom." But the analogy breaks down when we come to the figure of the "Tragic Mulatto." Certain film characters, such as Tonio in *Bahia de Todos os Santos* (1960), would seem to recall the Tragic Mulatto figure common in North American cinema and literature, but the context is radically different. North American society, for historical reasons, has tended to divide along clear racial lines. Its vision inclines toward binarism: white or black.

The Brazilian system is more complex; its spectrum nuances shades from *preto retinto* (dark black) through *mulato escuro* (dark mulatto) and *mulato claro* (light mulatto) to *moreno* and *branco-de-bahia* (Bahia-style white). Brazilian racism consists not in a binary white-over-black but rather in the superimposition of an official integrationist ideology ("racial democracy") on a reality pervaded by assymetrical power relations and a subtle prejudice that "white is better." Brazil has always been a racist but never a segregated society; its racism does not take the form of virulent hatred and lynchings, but rather of quiet paternalism and role stereotyping. The notion of "passing for white," so crucial in films like *Pinky* (1949) and *Imitation of Life* (1934, 1959), has little resonance in Brazil, where it is often said with a laugh that all Brazilian families have "one foot in the kitchen," meaning a partial black ancestry, a point comically demonstrated in the film *Tent of Miracles* (1976) when it is revealed that Nilo Argilo, a rabid partisan of white supremacy and enemy of racial "mongrelization," is himself part black.

Orson Welles and Black Atlantic Civilization

This issue of the mutual illumination of diverse New World cultures, and the issue of racial definition, became live and practical issues in the case of Orson Welles's ill-fated efforts to make the pan-American documentary *It's All True* in Brazil in 1942. Welles filmed two sequences of the film: one highlighting the black contribution to the Rio de Janeiro carnival, the other celebrating four real-life mestizo fishermen who traveled more than a thousand miles by raft to present their social grievances to then President Vargas. When Orson Welles went to Brazil in 1942, it is important to remember, he was already well attuned to the power and intelligence of what Robert Farris Thompson calls "black Atlantic civilization" and therefore well prepared to appreciate the black contribution to Brazilian culture. More than a "tolerant liberal," Welles was a passionate opponent of racism and anti-Semitism. In a period of extreme antiblack racism, of Jim Crow laws and lynchings, of segregation in the South and discrimination in the North, Welles was attracted to black themes and black performers, as exemplified by his "Voodoo" *Macbeth* performed in Harlem with an all-black cast in 1936, by his 1940 theatrical adaptation of Richard Wright's *Native Son*, and by his involvement in the Duke Ellington "Jazz Story" project originally slated to form the fourth episode of *It's All True*. It was only when he realized that samba was the Brazilian counterpart to jazz, that both were expressions of African diaspora culture in the New World, that Welles abandoned the jazz project in favor of the story of carnival and the samba. Welles used his knowledge of pan-American "comparabilities" and "mutual illuminations" to conceptualize his film. Thus New Orleans was replaced as setting by another Africanized New World carnival city—Rio de Janeiro; the African-American music called jazz was substituted by the African-Brazilian music called samba; such songs as "Didn't He Ramble" give way to Brazilian tunes like "Bahia" and "Praca Onze"; and performer-composers like Duke Ellington and Louis Armstrong made way for Pixinguinha and Grande Otelo (fig. 9.5).

Welles's approach in *Its All True* sharply challenged the racial conventions of Hollywood filmmaking. Edgar Morel, hired by Welles to research the raftsmen story, describes Welles as an "antiracist by formation" and attributed much of the hostility directed toward Welles to the fact that he enjoyed the company of blacks and that he was treating carnival as a "black" story. As a result, Welles was hounded by a racism which came both from the Brazilian elite who were not eager to expose the "secret" that Brazil was a very black country, from higher-ups in the RKO production hierarchy, and from the Rockefeller Committee of the Coordinator of Inter-American Affairs. A memorandum from the Rockefeller Committee to RKO recommends that the film "avoid any reference to miscegnation" and suggests that the film should "omit sequences of the film in which mulattos or mesticos appear conspicuously."[16]

There were also complaints from RKO executives, and occasionally from members of the *It's All True* production crew, that Welles was overemphasizing the black element and showing too much "ordinary social intercourse" among blacks and whites in carnival, a feature that might offend some North American viewers. A July

9.5. Grande Otelo performs his Afro-Brazilian music for Orson Welles's cameras in *It's All True*.

1942 letter from William Gordon, of the production team of *It's All True*, to an RKO executive, complains about Welles "indiscriminate intermingling of blacks and whites."[17] Citing Goldwyn's deletion of two close shots of two black members of Gene Krupa's orchestra in *Ball of Fire*, Gordon argues for the deletion of all such shots. An RKO memorandum from studio head Charles Koerner to Gordon, meanwhile, notes that "the heroes on the raft are referred to as Indians," a perspective that "will be impossible to sell to audience, especially south of the Mason-Dixon line." But the democratic, antiracist spirit animating Welles's project was antithetical to such colonizing attitudes. Welles wanted to show Brazilian heroes, not North American stars against Brazilian backdrops. That Welles could see a black *sambista* from the *favelas* and a quartet of mestizo fisherman as authentic popular heroes speaks volumes about the distance that separated Welles from the ambiant racism of his time. By choosing to focalize such a subject, Welles chose the margins over the center, even to the detriment of his own career.[18]

Bakhtinian categories, for their part, tend to reject all binarisms, including racial binarisms, in favor of the in-between, the hybrid, the oxymoronic, and the syncretic. I have not here explored the relevance for ethnic representation of all the Bakhtinian categories. I have downplayed, for example, his concepts of "chronotope" and "parodic carnivalization."[19] But I have tried to suggest that Bakhtinian thought demonstrates a consistent sympathy for all that has been marginalized, an intrinsic identification with difference and alterity that makes it especially suitable as a grid for the analysis of ethnic representation. Although Bakhtin did not address specifically the question of racial oppression, a conceptual space is staked out for it in advance. What is suspended in carnival, Bakhtin writes in *Problems of Dostoevsky's Poetics*, is "hierarchical structure and all the forms of terror, reverence, piety and etiquette connected with it—that is, everything resulting from sociohierarchical inequality or any other form of inequality among people. . . . "[20] Unlike many theoretical grids, Bakhtinian methodology does not have to be "stretched" to make room for the excluded; it is perfectly suited to them. Rather than "tolerate" difference in a condescending spirit, the Bakhtinian approach respects and celebrates difference. Rather than expand the center to include the margins, it interrogates and shifts the center from the margins.

NOTES

1. See Stanley Crouch, "The Rotton Club," *Village Voice*, February 5, 1985.

2. For more on FBI harassment of civil rights activists, see Kenneth O'Reilly, *"Racial Matters": The FBI's Secret File on Black America (1960–1972)* (New York: Free Press, 1989).

3. See Manthia Diawara, "Le spectateur noir face au cinema dominant: tours et detours de l'identification," *CinemAction* no. 46 (1988).

4. Walter Ong, *The Presence of the Word* (New Haven: Yale University Press, 1967) and *Interfaces of the Word* (Ithaca: Cornell University Press, 1977); Frances Yates, *The Art of Memory* (Chicago: University of Chicago Press, 1966); and Johannes Fabian, *Time and the Other: How Anthropology Makes Its Object* (New York: Columbia University Press, 1983).

5. Hal Foster, ed., *Vision and Visuality* (Seattle: Bay Press, 1988).

6. George Yudice, "Bakhtin and the Subject of Postmodernism," in *Bakhtin: Radical Perspectives* (Minneapolis: University of Minnesota Press, in press).

7. Clyde Taylor, "Les grands axes et les sources africaines du nouveau cinéma noir," *CinemAction*, no. 46 (1988):

8. M. M. Bakhtin, "The Problem of Speech Genres," in *Speech Genres and Other Late Essays* (Austin: University of Texas Press, 1986), p. 91.

9. Ralph Ellison, *Shadow and Act* (New York: Vintage, 1973), p. 116.

10. Elsewhere this kind of racial exchange is more positive in nature, evoking a complex play of identifications between ethnicities. For example, in Haskel Wexler's *Medium Cool* (1969) there is a brief sequence in which Eileen, a poor Southern white woman migrated to Chicago, watches a television report concerning the assassination of Martin Luther King. The words and images of King's "I Have a Dream" speech trigger flashback memories of her own Southern Baptist upbringing, thus evoking black and white commonalities rooted in historical experience. For example, blacks historically were not only forced to learn Christianity, but they also "taught" preaching to admiring whites and thus black rhetorical style inflected the white preaching style. See Albert J. Raboteau, *Slave Religion* (New York: Oxford University Press, 1978).

11. John Fiske, *Television Culture* (London: Methuen, 1987).

12. Philip Roth, *The Counterlife* (New York: Farrar, Strauss and Giroux, 1987), p. 166.

13. John Murray Cuddihy, *The Ordeal of Civility: Freud, Marx, Levi-Strauss and the Jewish Struggle with Modernity.* (New York: Basic Books, 1974).

14. For more on *Zelig*, see Robert Stam and Ella Shohat, "*Zelig* and Contemporary Theory: Meditation on the Chameleon Text," *Enclitic* 9 (Summer 1987): 176–94.

15. Donald Bogle, *Toms, Coons, Mulattoes, Mammies and Bucks: An Interpretive History of Blacks in American Film* (New York: Bantam, 1973).

16. Memorandum quoted by Servulo Siqueira in "Tudo e Verdade," *Folha de Sao Paulo*, December 2, 1984.

17. These documents and memoranda are to be found in the Welles collection at Lilly Library, Indiana University, Bloomington.

18. For more on Welles and *It's All True*, see Robert Stam, "Orson Welles, Brazil, and the Power of Blackness," *Persistance of Vision*, no. 7 (1989): 93–112, a special issue devoted to Welles.

19. Paul Willemen explores the relevance of the concept of "chronotope" for "Third Cinema" in "The Third Cinema Question: Notes and Reflections," in *Questions of Third Cinema*, ed. Jim Pines and Paul Willemen (London: BFI, 1989). In terms of ethnic carnivalization, one might examine the ways that Mel Brooks, for example, plays against conventional expectations by having the whites in *Blazing Saddles*, sing "The Camptown Races," while the blacks sing "I get no kick from champagne," or the way that Robert Townsend, in *Hollywood Shuffle*, imagines a black "acting school" where middle-class black actors learn to jive, pimp, and shuffle.

20. M. M. Bakhtin, *Problems of Dostoevsky's Poetics*, trans. Caryl Emerson (Minneapolis: University of Minnesota Press, 1984).

Ethnicity, the Cinema
and Cultural Studies

> This film does not intend to demean or to ignore the many positive features
> of Asian-Americans and specifically Chinese-American communities. Any
> similarity between the depiction in this film and any associations, organiza-
> tions, individuals or Chinatowns that exist in real life is accidental.
>
> —disclaimer added to the beginning of *Year of the Dragon.*

Hollywood generally obscures the peculiar relationship it has
to actual racial and ethnic communities. However, occasionally, ethnic and racial groups bring this very unbalanced relationship into
question. When Michael Cimino's *Year of the Dragon* opened in August 1985, for example, a coalition of Asian-American associations
and media groups picketed theaters and organized other types of
protests against the film. After national media coverage of the protest, MGM-UA responded by tacking the preceding statement onto
the film (ignoring the fact that the film is actually set in New York's
Chinatown) and promising possible better roles for Asian-American
actors in the future.[1]

As this grass-roots protest against *Year of the Dragon* indicates,
ethnic and racial media representations are not simply passively accepted by the audience. Rather, these protests only point to an extreme moment of anger at media racism. Admittedly, vocal reactions
occur relatively infrequently, although well-organized protests
against specific filmic representations of racial and ethnic groups
can be traced back at least to D. W. Griffith's *Birth of a Nation.* However, these visible protests only point to the most extreme form of
what must occur on a quotidian basis, that is, a resistance to the

dominant culture's ability to label, limit, and define the racial and ethnic Other.

Seen in this light, the MGM-UA disclaimer is almost ironic. Positive or negative, intended or accidental, real or imagined, the image Hollywood creates of race and ethnicity points to something far more fundamentally pernicious about the relationship between American society and the mass media. Hollywood has the power to define difference, to reinforce boundaries, to reproduce an ideology which maintains a certain status quo. Although organized protests always exist as a last resort, the means to challenge Hollywood's hegemony over the representation of race and ethnicity remain elusive. Alternative media exist, but appear marginal and far-removed from a popular audience. Access to the industry also exists, but entrance demands a tacit agreement to assimilate, at least to a certain degree, with the dominant culture.

Hollywood loves to see itself as the big "melting pot," assimilating all in its fantasy image of America. However, access to that America has a price: the rejection of any marker of "foreignness"—for example, a language, a religion, or a culture. When an accent or skin color or a desire to maintain a self-identity out of keeping with white, male, Anglo-Saxon America intervenes, Hollywood fiercely maintains boundaries in a ruthless bid to keep its own exclusive identity intact. After all, that identity means power, wealth, the ability to represent and define, to include and exclude, to dominate.

However, this picture of Hollywood has its contradictions. As even the limited lip-serve paid to *Year of the Dragon* indicates, Hollywood fears losing any part of its audience. Although most consumer-oriented capitalist enterprises love to picture their buyers as "typical" Americans (i.e., white, middle-class, Anglo-Saxon, Protestant), any successful business catering to the massive American market (not to mention the international market most corporations must also hope to conquer) must look realistically at the U.S. public as it actually is, that is, working-class, ethnic, nonwhite, often non-English-speaking. A tacit acknowledgment of this extreme heterogeneity must be structured into the product (or at least the advertising campaigns for it) in order for profits to be rung up consistently.

Hollywood, as a dealer in fantasies which must appeal to the widest possible audience in order to make a profit, has always been keenly aware of this contradiction. Although mass-produced for a mass audience, Hollywood texts tend to be extremely complex in their ability to allow for various possible viewer positions. Thus, while certainly privileging the dominant ideology and rewarding viewers who can manage to conform to it with the most comfortable reading of the text, these fantasies also contain enough diverse elements to draw in those outside the mainstream due to race, ethnicity, class, gender, age, and sexual orientation. Moreover, Hollywood films often play these various positions one against the other, so that a text can appear to espouse rather liberal attitudes toward race and also maintain a rigid hierarchy regarding class or gender.

Year of the Dragon provides an excellent example of these textual operations. It features all sorts of stereotypical Asian drug kingpins and exotic "China dolls" that any remotely sensitive viewer would find distasteful on the grounds of both racism and sexism. However, the film also plays with sexual ambiguity, crises of ethnic identity, and class distinctions which work against any reading of the film as unambiguously supportive of the white, male, middle-class establishment.

Year of the Dragon's contradictory textual play, moreover, seems to have done its job even within the Asian-American community. Of those Asian-American viewers with whom I have discussed the film (albeit informally), several counted it among their favorite films because of the action-adventure plot or because of the performances of its Asian leads, John Lone and Ariane. Furthermore, among those who expressed various degrees of concern over the film's racism, the majority in this group still grudgingly admitted finding the film entertaining in some way. Despite organized protests against the film, those who found it completely unappealing were definitely in the minority. Thus, the question must be posed as to how a particular ethnic group can view a Hollywood film as both entertaining and repulsive, exploitive and yet somehow appealing.

A critical methodology developed under the rubric of "cultural studies" can provide one way of examining the relationship between media texts like *Year of the Dragon* and race, class, gender, and ethnicity within contemporary social structures. Although primarily associated with scholars affiliated with Birmingham and Open Universities in Britain, cultural studies has, at various points, included such Marxist theorists as Raymond Williams, and several writers for the film journal *Screen,* as well as many others based in the United States, Australia, and elsewhere. Drawing on an eclectic assortment of critical perspectives incorporating Marxism, semiology, and ethnography, cultural studies takes the operation of ideology within advanced capitalist societies as its main object of exploration and often focuses on the orchestration of representations of race, class, gender, and ethnicity within popular media texts.

After first looking at what cultural studies has to offer in Hollywood films, a close examination of *Year of the Dragon* will illustrate what this approach may reveal about the textual operations of a specific film. Next, the representation of race, ethnicity, and gender in an independently produced documentary, Third World Newsreel's *Mississippi Triangle* (1989), will be discussed as an alternative to Hollywood's depictions of ethnicity. This film's exploration of the complex ethnic and racial relations in the Mississippi Delta shows that commercial texts and their representations of difference cannot be seen in a vacuum. Rather, any possible alternative readings generated within a Hollywood text must be placed within the broader context of alternative representations which may lead viewers to engage actively and critically with other media depictions of ethnicity, class, race, or gender.

Cultural Studies: Subcultures and Polysemic Texts

Although it comes from a mixture of intellectual traditions, cultural studies seems to have its deepest roots in Marxist critical social thought, and it takes the field of ideology as its primary area of interest. In *The German Ideology* (1845–46), Karl Marx and Frederick Engels state:

> The ideas of the ruling class are in every epoch the ruling ideas, i.e. the class which is the ruling *material* force of society, is at the same time its ruling intellectual force. The class which has the means of material production at its disposal, has control at the same time over the means of mental production, so that thereby, generally speaking, the ideas of those who lack the means of mental production are subject to it. The ruling ideas are nothing more than the ideal expression of dominant material relationships, the dominant material relationships grasped as ideas. . . . [2]

Since the time of *The German Ideology*, Marx and Engels' general conception of how ideology operates has been open to extensive and often heated debate. Although most Marxists agree that ideas are materially based and that those in power generate the ideas that dominate any given epoch, the actual operation of ideological domination and the way it is mediated through social institutions, language, and the individual's own subjectivity continue to be hotly contested points. Within British cultural studies, the move has been away from seeing ideology as a "false consciousness" imposed by the dominant class on its subordinates, one easily erased by changing the economic base which gave rise to the false thinking, to a more sophisticated understanding of the operation of ideology as developed by the French structuralist theorist Louis Althusser and the Italian political theorist Antonio Gramsci. Although Althusser's and Gramsci's ideas diverge greatly on several key points, they both agree that any direct equation of the economic base with the actual thinking of any given individual is inadequate to understand how ideology operates and how revolutionary change can possibly occur.

In his highly influential essay, "Ideology and Ideological State Apparatuses (Notes towards an Investigation)," Althusser discusses the importance of ideology in the reproduction of capitalist power relations. While granting that repressive agencies of the State (e.g., the police) do their share in maintaining ruling-class domination, Althusser observes that the ideological agencies of the State play a more varied and compelling role in assuring the continuation of the ruling order. Rather than looking at ideology as a veneer of "false consciousness" uneasily accepted by those enthralled by the ruling class, he sees ideology as the "imaginary relationship of individuals to their real conditions of existence."[3] Just as the structuralist psychologist Jacques Lacan sees language as creating the illusion of subjectivity through its acquisition, Althusser sees ideology as also constituting its own "subject" through the socialization of the individual within a class-stratified society. The dominant ideology creates certain circumscribed ways in which an individual can fit into class, racial, ethnic, or gender categories. Although the subject may see himself or herself as free, in reality, the parameters of that individual's thoughts, beliefs, and identity have been determined by ideological formations.

While recognizing the strengths of Althusser's view of ideology as only partially conscious and concretely absorbed by the individual in the development of identity and the acquisition of language, British cultural studies has also noted the limitations of Althusser's approach. Certainly, this view of ideology is highly deterministic, seeing the individual as interpellated within and essentially created by a preexisting structure. Although Althusser does mention class struggle and the uneasy, contradictory accommodation the subject must make in order to accept these "imaginary relations" which have put him or her at a distinct social disadvantage, he fails to do theoretical justice to the operation of resistance and ideological struggle.

To rectify this lack in Althusser's formulation, cultural studies theorists have turned to the work of Antonio Gramsci. In his prison notebooks, written while in jail during the Mussolini regime, Gramsci formulates a conception of ideology which emphasizes contradiction and the constant struggle for power of the ruling classes.[4] In their exercise of hegemony over the social formation, the ruling classes must solidify power not only through coercion, but also through consensus. To this end, "common sense" plays a role in mystifying relations of power by masquerading them as ahistorical, natural, and unquestionably true. However, common sense is actually historical and subject to constant ideological assault, reformulation, and accommodation to changing economic and political circumstances.

This interplay between the thought of Althusser and Gramsci profoundly affects the ways cultural studies theorists look at the discursive strategies employed by the mass media in their constant attempt to navigate the complex ideological currents of advanced capitalist societies. From Althusser comes an emphasis on structure and on the relationship among the psyche, language, and the social hierarchy, while Gramsci provides a view of ideology as historical, fragmentary, constantly in flux, and subject to the exigencies of the moment.

In order to better appreciate the concrete workings of ideology within the social formation, Dick Hebdige, Simon Frith, Angela McRobbie, and many others associated with cultural studies have turned to the examination of "subcultures." Roughly speaking, a subculture is any coherent group which defines itself as outside the dominant culture due to race, ethnicity, age, gender, sexual orientation, class, or some other factor or combination thereof. Although part of any subculture's identity does come from the negative stigma attached to it by the dominant culture's authority to label it, subcultural identification also has a self-conscious, positive aspect whereby members identify themselves through a distinctive style which is more or less visible through dress, language, gesture, music, or dance. As outsiders, subcultural members exist in a highly contradictory relationship to the dominant culture, that is, drawing on it, transforming it, resisting it, or rejecting it outright.

Any given subculture's relationship to the mass media is also highly contradictory. On the one hand, the media can stigmatize a subculture as deviant, dangerous, and radically foreign to dominant beliefs and values. On the other hand, the media, by exploiting and sensationalizing a subculture's differences, can inadvertantly spread it as a style, and, with that style, the possibility of resistance to the dominant order that alternative world vision may represent. In his essay "Style," John Clarke sees this relationship between the media and subcultures as one of diffusion and defusion.[5] Through their representation of a subcultural group, the media both make that group more diffuse geographically while defusing the ideological challenge the group may pose to the dominant culture by emptying its style of its original subversive significance.

In his essay "Encoding/Decoding," Stuart Hall discusses the ways in which televisual texts create meaning and can be open to alternative or subcultural readings.[6] Instead of looking at signification as wholly determined by the producer and simply accepted by a passive audience, Hall observes that the reception of any text must be a dynamic, dialectical process. Any text, in fact, can be seen as open to dominant/preferred, negotiated, or oppositional decoding, so that the viewer may fit in with the position in which the text puts him or her uneasily, or may consciously oppose this position outright. Given the structural complexity of most texts which allow for variant decodings, coupled with the lived social differences of most in the audience, it is not surprising to find a wide range of possible readings for the most ostensibly unambiguous of texts. In "Television: Polysemy and Popularity," John Fiske describes this as "semiotic excess":

> The theory of semiotic excess proposes that once the ideological, hegemonic work has been performed, there is still excess meaning that escapes the control of the dominant and is thus available for the culturally subordinate to use for their own cultural-political interests . . . the dominant and the oppositional are simultaneously present in both the text and its readings. The dominant is found in the preferred reading, the oppositional in the semiotic excess that the preferred reading attempts to marginalize, but that can never be finally or totally controlled by the dominant.[7]

Thus, cultural studies views media texts as sites of constant ideological struggle. The industry has its own interests in perpetuating the dominant ideology; however, it still must make a profit. To do this, the viewer outside the dominant culture must get pleasure from the text in order to keep the commercial operation running. As a result, these contradictions and possibilities for alternative readings must be structured right into the film text.

Ethnicity has always been a central concern of cultural studies research. Rather than looking at ethnicity as an absolute classifier of difference—as a set, ahistorical category—cultural studies approaches ethnicity as a field of struggle and contestation. Instead of viewing any ethnic group as monolithic, for example, the concept of subculture allows the ethnic community to be seen as criss-crossed by divisions of age, class, and gender. Time of immigration, relative amiability to assimilation, and self-conscious participation in the community also play their roles in dividing an ethnic group into subcultural communities. Looking at the ethnic composition of a viewing group and its reception of a given text, then, can be examined as an aspect of the ethnic subculture. This approach foregrounds the complexity of the interaction between text and culture. No film exists in a vacuum and, for any understanding of a text to take place, a definite audience—gendered and ethnically, racially specific—must be taken into account.

Ethnicity involves labeling and self-identity, represented and lived relations, dominant and minority points of view, so cultural studies also underscores the importance of looking at ethnicity as ideological. As both a structure that molds thought and a field for the orchestration of consensus and the expression of resistance, ethnicity exists as both imprisoning stigma and potentially liberating identify. As Stuart Hall points out:

> As social movements develop a struggle around a particular program, meanings which appear to have been fixed in place forever begin to loose their moorings. In short, the meaning of the concept has shifted as a result of the *struggle* around the chains of connotations and the social practices which made racism possible through the negative constructions of 'blacks.' . . . 'Black,' then, exists ideologically only in relation to the contestation around those chains of meaning, and the social forces involved in that contestation.[8]

Just as the structuralist linguist Ferdinand de Saussure and the structuralist anthropologist Claude Lévi-Strauss see language and myth as creating meaning through relations between terms rather than arising absolutely from any given element in isolation, so too, Stuart Hall and other cultural studies theorists see the categories of race and ethnicity not as absolutes, but subject to constant definition and redefinition by not only the dominant culture, but also by minority cultures.

Cultural studies' added interest in ideology, textuality, and signification makes this approach particularly fruitful for an examination of race, ethnicity, and cinematic representation. Rather than looking at racial and ethnic media images as simply "positive" or "negative," "realistic" or "racist," "progressive" or "reactionary," cultural studies views the ideology of ethnicity and race in film as contradictory, historical, and subject to a variety of changing interpretations.

For film scholars, this constant ideological contestation over racial, ethnic, class, and gender categories necessitates not only careful scrutiny of a single text, its producers and audience, but also attention to quests for self-definition and oppositional practices, to alternative as well as Hollywood film practices. Intertextual relations are extremely important. Part of the way in which oppositional possibilities can be structured into the Hollywood text and deciphered pleasurably by the subcultural viewer involves the existence of alternative media representations. Thus, the Asian-American community can protest *Year of the Dragon* not only because lived experience has highlighted the contradiction between this film and the life experiences of Asians in the United States, but also because other media representations exist, have helped to create the community as it sees itself, and have provided an alternative visual and narrative definition of race and ethnicity.

This particular study of *Year of the Dragon* and *Mississippi Triangle* deals primarily with how these two texts function within the complex ideological sphere of contemporary American attitudes; as such, the emphasis is on textual operations, ideological positionings, and possible readings. Although this analysis is informed by extratextual factors of ethnic and cultural history, production information, and community reception, it does differ from other more sociological, ethnographic, and anthropological studies of media texts associated with British cultural studies. However, despite these differences, this primarily textually based exploration of these films is offered as a starting point. Cultural studies includes a range of methods, and particular research coming out of this eclectic blend does vary. The analysis that follows provides simply one way of opening a discussion of the interrelationship of community, ideology, and cinematic representation.

As difficult as it sometimes might be, cultural studies calls for looking at ideology, media, and society as a complex whole. Analysis depends on an understanding of economic and political power, social hierarchies based on race, class, ethnicity and gender, as well as on the operation of a variety of texts within a complex cultural formation which includes constant ideological struggle. This discussion offers one way of beginning to understand this complicated ideological configuration using the close analysis of *Year of the Dragon* and *Mississippi Triangle* as starting points.

Ethnicity as Spectacle: The Case of *Year of the Dragon*

Ostensibly, *Year of the Dragon* tells a simple story basic to Hollywood cinema. An uncorrupted lawman, Stanley White (Mickey Rourke), is assigned to clean up a corrupt town—in this case, Chinatown. His principal adversary is a young gangster on the way up, Joey Tai (John Lone).

As in many action-adventure narratives, the hero and the villain are quite similar. In this case both men find themselves on the outside—set apart from their colleagues, their families, and their communities. Stanley rails against a police force which refuses to do anything about corruption in Chinatown, and Joey Tai shakes up his sluggish criminal organization by using youth gangs to move in on Italian and Southeast-Asian drug trafficking. Both are identified as flamboyant, violent, impatient with the "older generation," rebellious, and desirous of making good in mainstream American society. In addition, both are ethnic: Stanley White has changed his Polish surname to whitewash his ethnicity, while Tai exploits his Chinese ethnicity to rise within the underworld.

As in most similar sorts of narratives, the main plot line revolves around the hero's attempt to prove himself different from the villain, that is, justified in his violence and supportive of the white, Anglo-Saxon mainstream. He sees himself as having the moral right to eradicate the villain because the foreign represents a threat to the racial and ethnic status quo. A great deal of the ideological tension of this sort of plot revolves around who can and who cannot be assimilated into American society. The hero must prove his ability to "melt" into the mainstream by drawing a line between himself and the villain, thereby coming into grips with his own ethnicity. *Year of the Dragon* begins with a fundamental ideological contradiction revolving around ethnicity and American identity. Melting into America is acceptable only if a white, male, Anglo-Saxon definition of identity is taken as the ideal. White does this, whereas Tai does not.

In addition, similar ethnic and racial tensions are played within a romance between the hero and a Chinese-American woman. Although married, White finds himself attracted to a young Chinese newswoman, Tracy Tzu (Ariane). Their romance parallels both White's unrelenting push to rid Chinatown of gang influence and Tai's bid to become undisputed boss of the underworld. The romance also plays out similar tensions in what can and cannot constitute American identity. Through her involvement with White, Tzu renounces her Chinese ethnicity and subordinates herself to White's championing of mainstream ideals.

Year of the Dragon takes up issues related to race, gender, class, and ethnicity, and then eases any contradictions this may raise by eradicating the villain and allowing romance to triumph. However, no Hollywood narrative, no matter how neat, can tie up all the issues and social problems it invariably brings up (in order to be topical, exciting, controversial, and not so boring that it will alienate viewers). Gaps remain. By analyzing those gaps both within the narrative itself as well as in the more excessive moments of spectacle, the power of the dual pleasure of both resistance and acquiesence to the dominant ideology can begin to be fathomed.

Year of the Dragon begins with a moment of spectacle as Chinese New Year is celebrated in the streets of Chinatown. This sets a pattern which operates throughout the course of the film. The entire text is punctuated by moments of spectacle—displays of violence, sexuality, ritual, or sheer exoticism which have little, if any, narrative import. Instead, spectacle opens up the text to a contradictory play of possible viewer positionings and multiple interpretations.

Although quite a bit of scholarly attention has been paid to the way in which cinematic spectacle displays and deals with sexual difference, critics have written little on the way in which Hollywood represents racial and ethnic differences within moments of spectacle.[9] Just as spectacle often fortifies gender differences, by allowing for the contemplation of the woman as an object contained and domesticated by the male gaze, spectacle can also allow for the similar contemplation of the ethnic and racial Other as an object, separated from and under the visual control of the viewer positioned with the camera, in power, as the eye of the dominant culture.

Year of the Dragon presents Chinatown, as well as its inhabitants, in this way, in terms of spectacle. The film begins with a high-angle shot of a ceremonial lion head and pulls back to show lively, chaotic lion dancing, firecrackers, and drums characteristic of Chinese New Year celebrations. At first, the emphasis is placed on the exotic aspect of Chinatown, on the allure and charm of its foreign rituals. However, quickly, the dancing turns into a riot as rival lions begin to fight, and the young men under them toss their costumes aside and begin to brawl. Although this gang rivalry and the lion brawl is never explained clearly within the narrative, the next scene, depicting the bloody execution of the Chinese gangster Jackie Wong, Tai's father-in-law, clarifies the link between the exotic and the dangerous. Later, during Wong's elaborate funeral, the Chinese youth gangs strike again and kill a Caucasian shopkeeper who refuses to pay protection money. Each moment of spectacle—whether it is a festival, funeral, banquet, or bedroom scene—has a threatening edge. Underneath a picturesque veneer, Chinatown hides its violence and corruption.

Spectacle both attracts and repulses, encourages viewer identification and keeps that involvement at a distance. Moments of spectacle which feature ethnic and racial differences tend to define and reinforce the boundaries the dominant culture encourages between ethnic and racial groups in order to keep its own power intact. However, these moments are also often violent eruptions which challenge the dominant culture's ability to define those differences and boundaries. Violence erupts against the racial and ethnic status quo, and the viewer may identify with this antiestablishment aspect of the spectacle as well as with its ostensible condemnation.

In *Year of the Dragon*, the importance of spectacle is even emphasized in the narrative by making Tracy Tzu, the proganist's love interest, a reporter. Both a creator of spectacle and an object on display herself, Tzu provides the perfect rationalization of the film's voyeuristic treatment of Chinatown. Stanley White, helped by a gangland attack in the restaurant they meet at for dinner, quickly convinces the at first reluctant Tzu to expose Chinatown as decadent, corrupt, and threatening. By using a Chinese character as the point of identification for the contemplation of the spectacle, the text does the same thing the fictitious White does in the narrative. That is, the film hides its own racism by using a nonwhite character to focus attention on the racial and ethnic Other as a threat to the status quo.

Beyond this function, however, Tracy Tzu also operates as a specular object in her own right. When she enters a large, lavishly decorated Chinatown establishment to dine with Stanley White, for example, the camera dollies to follow her as she almost regally ascends a flight of stairs, a Mandarin pop singer providing background music, to join her dinner companion (fig. 10.1). Thin and elegantly dressed, her body always carefully framed and followed by the camera, Tzu provides the white, male viewer with an image of racial, ethnic, and gender difference which may both titillate and disturb. Like all moments of spectacle in *Year of the Dragon*, this moment leads to violence. During an assault on the restaurant, Tracy Tzu's elegance and composure crumble as bullets fly, fishtanks burst, and White saves the hysterical Tzu from harm (fig. 10.2). In fact, all displays of Tzu's body in *Year of the Dragon* are coupled with moments of violence. For example, during their love scenes together, White slaps and verbally assaults Tzu, and in another scene, the camera follows the elegantly dressed Tzu into her apartment where a group of thugs lie in wait to rape her.

Ethnicity is never neuter; rather, images of ethnicity and race always conjure up images of masculinity and femininity. As Eugene

10.1. Surrounded by the kitsch opulence of a Chinatown restaurant, Stanley White (Mickey Rourke) and Tracy Tzu (Ariane) are on display in this scene from *Year of the Dragon*.

Franklin Wong points out in *On Visual Media Racism: Asians in the American Motion Pictures*, images of race and sexuality are always intimately intertwined in the Hollywood cinema.[10] Racial and ethnic hierarchies, for example, are often maintained through fantasies which reinforce those differences through references to gender. Thus, fantasies of threatening Asian men, emasculated eunuchs, alluring Asian "dragon ladies," and submissive female slaves all work to rationalize white, male domination.

In *Year of the Dragon*, the ideological operation of these racist and sexist myths exists beneath a veneer of liberalism which denies the text's own legitimation of white, male privilege and control. For example, the text denies that it looks at ethnic differences as threatening by making a point of Stanley White's own Polish ethnicity. If Chinatown is treated as exotic, then White's working-class Polish neighborhood, filled with Eastern European church domes, Catholic icons, and rituals, can also be seen as exotic from the standpoint of mainstream Anglo-American, Protestant viewers. Likewise, the

10.2. Gangland violence legitimizes White's desire to bring a white, patriarchal sense of "order" to Chinatown by saving Tzu from her own people, winning her confidence as an Asian American and conquering her as a woman.

text complicates its racist image of Chinatown by depicting Little Italy as a definitely Caucasian community also overrun by organized crime and having a similarly alien flavor.

Moreover, the text shows White's ethnic self-identity in crisis (fig. 10.3)—a crisis apparently linked to a similar crisis of sexual identity. The text presents White as having marital problems with his wife, Connie (Caroline Cava) because he seems to be unable to impregnate her for whatever reason—impotence, sterility, or simple lack of interest in sex. Living in a working-class brownstone filled with Polish-Catholic religious icons, Connie represents those ethnic roots Stanley wants to escape and deny.

However, once again the text obscures the issue of ethnicity by linking it intimately with questions of sexuality and sexual identity. Stanley's identity is in doubt both because of his ethnicity and because of his masculinity, hence the text takes on a dual operation of solidifying both ethnic and gender boundaries to assure the hero's ability to maintain white, male domination within the film fantasy. The fact White is a Vietnam veteran, a survivor of a lost war, further questions his identity as a potent hero able to perform this task.

Stanley encounters both Tracy Tzu and Joey Tai for the first time at the funeral of Jackie Wong. The film depicts both characters in remarkably similar ways. If Tzu's body is displayed as spectacle, then Tai also functions as an object of sexual contemplation in the

10.3. Mickey Rourke in *Year of the Dragon*. His name—Stanley White—conjures up questions of ethnic and racial identity, while his foppish attention to dress (indicated by his careful coiffure and stylish combination of suit and tie) signals the possibility of a sexual identity crisis.

text. Both are elegantly dressed in tailored suits and long coats; both are lean and lithe, similarly shaped; both have similar facial features and move in a highly dramatic way that betrays John Lone's Chinese opera training and Ariane's background in modeling. Certainly, these visual parallels coupled with the narrative's insistance that both be conquered by the hero place a further strain on White's identity as a heterosexual male. Moreover, Tzu's career as a newswoman and her single life-style and Tai's nearly absent family and close association with other men in the text (e.g., his black bodyguard) tie the threat of racial and ethnic difference to the threat of homosexuality, loss of male power and privilege, and the weakening of gender boundaries.

In the case of Joey Tai, *Year of the Dragon* merges both the myth of the Asian man as a sexual threat with the image of the eunuch. Feminized, Tai does not safely drop out of sight as a passive buddy figure, the role fulfilled by Herbert Kuang (Dennis Dun) in the text, but instead, becomes more of a threat to Stanley's identity by bringing into play a homosexual subtext.

In the climactic scene in which the beaten Tai lies at White's feet on a railway trestle and Stanley opts to give Tai a pistol to commit suicide rather than face trial (fig. 10.4), an extensive Freudian analysis is certainly unnecessary to understand the scene as sexually charged. White gives Tai the phallic means to his own end, and Tai

10.4. *Year of the Dragon*'s showdown between White and Joey Tai (John Lone), in which Tai submits masochistically to White's offer of an "honorable" suicide, affirming white, male, Anglo-Saxon domination over the ethnic and racial other.

accepts this end, masochistically submits to it and to White's domination. His suicide is the ultimate confirmation of his subordinate, feminized position; Stanley's role in it allows him to do away symbolically with the threat Tai represents to the hero's identity as white, male, and decidedly heterosexual.

This moment of violent spectacle also opens the text to possible alternative readings. The villain accepts his end and dies with grace and a certain panache. Stanley, in allowing this, looks on Tai as an equal. Although punished violently for his hubris, Tai, like the American gangster heroes before him, must also be respected for his ability to climb so far, for the assertion of his individualism despite the pressures to keep it contained. Tai represents the ambivalence at the root of the gangster mythos; he is both condemned and applauded for being a good capitalist.

In fact, class seems to be the last significant way in which issues of ethnic and racial identity are complicated in the film. If *Year of the Dragon* is a male-centered, white fantasy, it is also a working-class fantasy that allows viewers the satisfaction of seeing bourgeois characters controlled by a working-class policeman. Tai falls because he has risen above his station in his desire to fulfill the American Dream illegally through drug running. He represents capitalism out of control, and his death may have a particular appeal to working-class viewers suspicious of the power that wealth brings.

Likewise, part of Stanley's desire to dominate Tracy comes from a voiced class antagonism. At one point, for example, he remarks, "I hated you before I even met you. I hated you on TV. I hated you in Vietnam. . . . Most of all, I hate rich kids. . . . " Thus, Stanley may want to dominate Tracy because she challenges gender roles (i.e., through her profession), or because of her face and ethnicity (i.e., the challenge her exotic allure poses to heterosexual identity and the nuclear family), or because of her class standing (i.e., not only is she successful at her profession, but she also comes from a wealthy family). Because the relationship is ideologically overdetermined, charges of racism or sexism can fall by the wayside as the viewer focuses on the character's class standing and roots for the "rich kid" to get her comeuppance. Therefore, the issue of racial and ethnic difference can be obscured by issues of class, gender, and sexuality.

In fact, the homosexual subtext which put Stanley's identity in doubt in his relationship with Joey Tai also operates in a similar way in Stanley's relationship with Tracy. In this case, Tracy poses a threat to Stanley not only because she represents the nonwhite seductress whose exotic allure draws the white male away from hearth and home, but she also embodies a threat to gender boundaries through her independence, active pursuit of a career, and boyish short hair and slender physique. Throughout *Year of the Dragon*, both plot events and the actions of the hero himself tighten the gender boundaries that this character at first seems to loosen. Not only does Stanley take away Tracy's independence by moving in and telling her how to run her career, but he also abuses her verbally and strikes her. Moreover, plot events like the attack on the Chinatown restaurant and the assault in her apartment force Tracy to depend more and more on Stanley's protection. By taking away her independence, the text domesticates Tracy, places her under male control, and forces her to side with Stanley against the Chinese community. Although she objects to this throughout the text, by the end of the film, she is happily in Stanley's embrace.

But as a woman and as an Asian, Tracy has submitted to Stanley's authority; through their romance, the text legitimizes Stanley's right to dominate her as a woman and as a Chinese American. The consummation of their romance dispells doubts about Stanley's potency and identity; he has affirmed white, male, American dominance over nonwhite, feminized, foreign threats. White transforms Tzu from a seductive dragon lady into a passive, loyal, and subservient China doll. The shift from one to the other marks White's personal conquest and assimilation of the foreign into the domestic mainstream, thereby assuring his own identity, his own right to also be a part of that American melting pot.

However, this romance, like White's relationship with Tai, also has its contradictory aspects. If Stanley has legitimized white, male power over a nonwhite woman, he has also allowed for the fulfillment of the working-class fantasy of possessing wealth magically through romance and dominating it through sexuality. A desire for class equality, thus, obscures the text's otherwise too-obvious racism and sexism. Moreover, the film's concluding romantic embrace can be read symbolically as a liberal call for racial understanding and harmony. Stanley's romance with Tracy can also be seen as the way the character comes to grips with and overcomes his own racism by falling in love. In this case, the myth of romantic love can be seen as not only the cure-all for crises of male identity but also an antidote for the text's rather open racism. According to this reading, the containment of Tracy's possible sexual threat through heterosexual romance can be seen as a function of her gender rather than her race or ethnicity, so the text can use sexism to mask its racism if this interpretation is pursued.

Year of the Dragon's openess to contradictory interpretations can perhaps most clearly be seen in the representation of Stanley White's Chinese "buddy," Herbert Kuang. Kuang acts as a eunuch figure, nonthreatening, sexless, and totally under the domination of the hero who is both boss and "best friend." Taken straight from the police academy to assure his anonymity for his undercover work in Chinatown, Kuang, at first, appears as an innocent dupe who can bearly drive a car, speaks the accented English of a recent immigrant, and whose only concern is to make enough money to send home to China. If Joey Tai and Tracy Tzu, in their own ways, pose a threat to the hero because of their ethnic exoticism, Kuang simply functions as the "good" Asian legitimizing White's mission to clean up Chinatown by agreeing to work with him.

In terms of class, Kuang functions as a "good' working-class Chinese. Like the other working-class Chinese who dot the text to provide atmosphere, Kuang is seen as a victim of capitalism out of control in his own community. Once again, class relations are used to hide what otherwise could only be read as racism in the film. Only the rich are villainous among the Chinese. The Chinese workers may be ignorant, passive, and impotent, but the text can cling to its liberalism by showing them as decidedly not villainous.

Kuang, however, only reluctantly accepts this buddy role. Although Tracy taunts Stanley with his racism as part of their sexual gaming, Kuang accuses White of racism in earnest. At one point he challenges the way Stanley treats him by saying, "You make us all die for you. I'm not going to kill myself for you, Captain White. No more 'Chinaman Joe.' Those days are over." Still, even after Kuang complains that he cannot die for White because his family counts on him for income, he does precisely that, and his death becomes another rationalization of White's right to control Chinatown.

In yet another moment of spectacle, which has an excessive almost operatic quality, Kuang is riddled with bullets as he tries to run to Stanley with information on Tai's drug trafficking. Eventually, Kuang dies, bleeding grotesquely, in White's arms; his last words give Stanley the location of Tai's next drug shipment. Clearly, this moment places Kuang's earlier speech in a new perspective. No longer the unwitting dupe, Kuang here willingly gives his life for Stanley's cause, choosing this white American mission over the well-being of his Chinese family. He has become "Chinaman Joe" again, placing his life and his loyalty firmly within Stanley's camp.

Prefiguring Tai's suicide, Kuang's death functions in a similar way as spectacle. In fact, these moments of violence featuring Asians dying in the arms or at the feet of the white hero stand outside the narrative as images of ethnic and racial relations which seem to go beyond the parameters of the text itself. Outside of the implied history the temporal dimension of narrative must assure at some level, spectacle reifies images and places them beyond history. It also mythologizes social relations and makes concrete the racial and ethnic hierarchies which may have been hidden in other parts of the text. Although still vibrating with the contradictions the text raises and then abandons, spectacle assures that these moments of violent domination of the ethnic Other are somehow justified, correct, proper, and even inevitable. Functioning as spectacle, ethnicity exists as ahistorical, set, preordained, and unchangable. Even after contradictions have been voiced and various viewer positionings established to assure a variety of readings, the text, in these moments, closes itself off to ideological shifts and draws the boundaries between dominant and oppositional readings far more clearly. Spectacle provides those exaggerated moments in which the social boundaries are demarcated most clearly. In these moments of spectacular display, the viewer may refuse to identify with the hero in the bedroom or in a brawl. Then, that viewer may realize that she or he has not been drawn into the ideological workings of the text, and the possibility of resistance can begin to surface.[11]

Ethnographic Alternatives: An Analysis of *Mississippi Triangle*

At first glance, perhaps no film could be less like *Year of the Dragon* than Third World Newsreel's *Mississippi Triangle*. While *Year of the Dragon* is Hollywood fiction, *Mississippi Triangle* is a socially critical, political documentary. *Year of the Dragon* does everything in its power to avoid clearly addressing the ideological issues it raises and cultivates a textual ambiguity to insure viewer pleasure. *Mississippi Triangle*, on the other hand, self-consciously tries to address the ideology of race, ethnicity, class, and gender in operation in contemporary American society. It engages the viewer in a contemplation of these issues rather than disguising social inequality through the operation of spectacle.

Although very different, both texts do, however, address the interrelationship of race, ethnicity, class, and gender. By taking the two together, an understanding of how alternative media representations function within a broader cinema culture can be approached. If *Year of the Dragon* is open to contradictory readings, then those readings are made possible by the existence of real racial and ethnic communities, communities with their own self-representations and their own understanding of their relationship to the dominant culture and its media. *Mississippi Triangle* provides simply one example of this alternative media culture.

If *Year of the Dragon* fits snugly into its place as a Hollywood film text, *Mississippi Triangle* fits less easily into the category in which it ostensibly belongs—that is, the ethnographic film. With claims to scientific "truth" and "objective" accuracy, the ethnographic filmmaker generally looks at a foreign culture from a perspective strikingly similar to his Hollywood filmmaking cousins who only hope to entertain and turn a profit. If Hollywood uses "entertainment" to shield itself from the implications of its ideological operations, then the ethnographic filmmaker uses "science" for similar ends. Under this cloak, the white, male, bourgeois perspective of the text can be universalized as the "truth," that is, verifiable, objective reality. The way in which the camera frames, selects, and presents this reality is never questioned; the process behind the production of the discourse simply falls away as the viewer engages the text as a representation of "real life."

The conventions of ethnography are so strongly a part of our cultural semiotic system that even *Year of the Dragon* pays lip-service to it. The film is careful, for example, to show Stanley White's genuine interest in Chinese culture and the history of the Chinese in America. At one point, he proudly shows Tracy Tzu the books he has been reading on the exploitation of the Chinese in the building of the Trans-Continental railroad. The film never questions White's right to define the Chinese-American experience for Tzu, to tell her about her own ethnic history and identity. Instead, his expertise, although newly acquired, remains unchallenged. This illustrates white America's power to define identity, to set racial and ethnic boundaries, to describe the foreign and, through this monopoly on knowledge, to control it.

This discursive process and the prerogative of the dominant culture to define Asian ethnic and racial "otherness" fits into the category of "Orientalist" scholarship that Edward Said defines in his book *Orientalism*: "Taking the late eighteenth century as a very roughly defined starting point Orientalism can be discussed and analyzed as the corporate institution for dealing with the Orient—dealing with it by making statements about it, authorizing views of it, describing it, by teaching it, settling it, ruling over it: in short, Orientalism as a Western style for dominating, restructuring, and having authority over the Orient."[12]

Although Said limits the scope of his study to representations of North Africa and the Middle East, the concept of Orientalism can be helpful in understanding all sorts of discourses that deal with Asia and Asians in general. In *Year of the Dragon*, for example, Stanley White acts as an Orientalist, and the text tacitly accepts this by allowing the viewer to identify with White as the hero, favoring his perspective, his definition of the "problem" as well as the "cure" for the Chinese community. As the hero, White unifies the text and provides a privileged vantage point from which to judge other characters, and, by extension, other racial, ethnic, and gender positions.

Traditional ethnographic films very often do the same thing by privileging the point of view of the ethnographer as expert, allowing a voice-over narration to situate the object of the study, the ethnic group in question, within the parameters of the dominant culture's views of the foreign and the exotic. Ideologically, the dominant culture's right to define and limit is affirmed; discursively, the singular, univocal perspective of the ethnographer tends to obscure or silence the voice of the group under study.

Working against the Orientalism of mainstream documentaries on Asian Americans, *Mississippi Triangle*, both in the organization of its production as well as its actual operation as a text, tries to open this univocal rendering of ethnic and racial otherness. It constantly makes the viewer aware of its polysemic nature through a dialectic interplay of conflicting discourses. No single, unified point of view dominates; rather, a number of perspectives vie for the viewer's attention and support.

Mississippi Triangle, however, does not provide a model rendering of Mikhail Bakhtin's notion of the "dialogic."[13] Instead of presenting these various voices as socially and textually equal, the film recognizes inequality, unequal power relations, and the way this hierarchy affects representations of people and their communities. Through music, editing, cinematography, and other textual operations, the film both reveals the unequal organization of the Mississippi Delta culture under investigation and tacitly sides with certain groups over others. The dialogic structure comes from the utopian wish for a society in which two voices can have equal force and power; *Mississippi Triangle*'s dialectic organization recognizes the operation of a racial, class, gender, and ethnic hierarchy and uses every cinematic means at its disposal to redress that imbalance.

Perhaps the first thing to point to *Mississippi Triangle*'s difference from other ethnographic documentaries occurs during the opening credits. Unlike most films, *Mississippi Triangle* does not have a single director, but, instead, it has three co-directors, Christine Choy, Worth Long, and Allan Siegel. Each, moreover, had his or her own production crew during filming, and each focused on one ethnic group within the Mississippi Delta region (fig. 10.5).[14] Choy, one of the founding members of the radical filmmaking collective Third World Newsreel and director of several politically committed documentaries including *Who Killed Vincent Chin?* (1988), worked primarily within the Chinese and the black-Chinese communities. Long, a civil rights activist and son of sharecroppers, worked within the black community. Siegel, a long-time activist and member of Third World Newsreel, dealt with the white community.

Each director focuses on issues of personal concern. For example, Choy devotes attention to issues of gender, sexuality, and family relations, whereas Long focuses on the lives of poor blacks in Mississippi—their music, the sharecropping system, and the perpetuation of racism in the area. Siegel's interest is in class divisions within the

10.5. *Mississippi Triangle* features an alternative ethnography of the black, white, and Chinese communities in the Mississippi Delta. Here, a Chinese grocer operates his business in a predominantly black community.

white community in the Delta, and he examines the organization of cotton farming and the area's distribution of wealth.

When finally edited together, the juxtaposition of these three perspectives on the three principal racial and ethnic groups in the Delta area creates a complex picture of the interrelation of class, race, ethnicity, and gender. Unlike the standard ethnographic documentary which privileges the ethnographer's voice over the subject's, *Mississippi Triangle* allows the existence of two levels of discourse which can accommodate a number of different perspectives. On one level, the three filmmakers each look at Delta society from a different point of view. Although all are ostensibly looking for the same thing—the racial dynamics of the Mississippi Delta region—each focuses on that subject in a unique way and adds different information to the project.

On a second level, the interviewees add their voices to the film in a way which differs somewhat from more standard ethnographic treatments. In a sense, each interviewee speaks to a filmmaker who is both an "insider" and an "outsider." The candor of many of the interviewees in the film, therefore, extends beyond the superficial treatment of many similar documentaries. Speaking to a filmmaker who is not immediately perceived as Other due to racial and ethnic difference allows the participants to voice "in group," insiders' views on their lives. The participants, then, seem to go beyond telling the story of their lives the way the filmmaker may want to hear it. Instead, the perceived "sameness" of the interviewer allows for a quite different perspective to be voiced, a point of view very different from the all-knowing, all-seeing, "objective" perspective of many ethnographic filmmakers who have no roots in the community they investigate.

The importance of the ethnic and racial diversity of the filmmakers can be seen clearly in the way in which *Mississippi Triangle* represents the Chinese community. Christine Choy's own ethnicity and her gender place her in a position to look at this community in a way in which Siegel or Long cannot. For example, Choy and her crew film a young Chinese-American bride changing from her wedding gown into the dress for her wedding reception. Because all of Choy's crew were women, she was able to film this moment as well as many other intimate moments with young Chinese women in the community.

Choy's interest in gender, sexuality, and family relations also led her to investigate topics usually considered taboo. For example, at one point, a young, upwardly mobile, Chinese-American man discusses his relationship to his family and also his love life. His parents' marriage had been prearranged by his grandparents, and they had subsequently divorced. Despite their problems, the interviewee still feels pressured to date Chinese women and eventually marry within his own ethnic group: "I dated Chinese girls because I was expected to. Generally Chinese girls are much more conservative and sexually uptight than the other kind—the off-brand." At another point in the film, this same interviewee explains that he would never date a black woman because it would mean loss of social status. Choy insistently explores those topics which the Delta Chinese often most want to hide, for example, divorce, interracial sexuality, racism, and the existence of the black Chinese, who are the result of interracial unions.

Mississippi Triangle's material comes from present and past, from rich and poor, from new immigrant and fourth and fifth generation, from young and old, from Protestant and Catholic, from Asian, white, and African-American, all filtered through the perspectives of three different directors. A variety of issues emerge, ranging from the economy to politics, from interracial marriage to the organization of the school system. Also, the film blends three rather different documentary styles—archival news footage, "talking head" interviews, and cinéma-verité slices of life. A patchwork or kaleidescopic organization of the information might be expected, with equal voice given to each issue, each interviewee, and equal weight given to each image. However, this is really not the case. Rather, *Mississippi Triangle*, despite a surface tendency to ramble, is actually quite focused. The focus comes from two different cinematic strategies—a dialectical organization of the material and a linking of all the different issues addressed to the politics and ideology of race, gender, and sexuality.

Mississippi Triangle organizes itself around several principal dialectical oppositions that give rise to concepts that go beyond the sum of the parts. For example, as already mentioned, a dialectical relationship exists among the various points of view of the filmmakers, between the filmmakers' perspectives and the voices of the interviewees, between whites and blacks, Chinese and whites, and the Chinese and the black communities. These dialectical relations tend to be tied to a series of issues which, in turn, center around the main social institutions in the Delta area, the cotton industry, the small retail economy, the school system, local political organizations, the church, and the family. Each topic is dealt with by juxtaposing interviews with white, black, and Chinese respondants, so that each perspective is not only voiced but also set off against the perspective of a community with which it is in conflict.

The topic of education in the Delta begins with one of the older, black Chinese informants, Arlene Hen, discussing education in the area. Next, the film cuts to a man who discusses the problems of Chinese, who could not attend either the white or the black schools in the segregated South. The film continues its focus on the Chinese community, with photos of Chinese school children and people playing mah-jong. Middle-aged Chinese reminisce about the difficulties they faced going to public school. Berda Lum Chan is then introduced. *George Lum v. Rice*, brought by her father against the public school system, went to the Supreme Court and upheld the school's right to segregate the educational system. The film cuts back to a white woman interviewee, who also remembers the case; she recalls her father mentioning that it had something to do with whether or not Lum had "black blood."

In this case, the issue of education is put in the context of the racial dynamics of the Delta region not only by the information presented, but also by the organization of that information. The segment begins with the testimony of a black Chinese woman, moves to the Chinese community and then the white community, and finally back to the issue of the black Chinese. All three documentary styles are represented, cinéma verité in the mah-jong scene, archival photos, and interviews. The effect is a dynamic, dialectic exchange of different types of information—personal testimony, legal evidence, photos, and snippets of daily life—presented through the different points of view of white, black, and Chinese communities. The result of the conflicting positions of these three communities lies in what cannot be included in any of the three exclusively—the black Chinese.

This structuring device forms the foundation for most of *Mississippi Triangle*, and its effect is compounded by the fact that no point made by the film is brought to a conclusion. Rather, each issue comes up again and again to form further dialectical associations. The issue of education, for example, appears again when the film begins to deal with youth and interracial relationships and examines the differences between the lives of Chinese children who go to the region's predominantly black as opposed to predominantly white schools. Therefore, the viewer constantly must reevaluate information in the light of new associations and must question his or her own perspective on the issues.

The film does not give each perspective equal weight, however. Images and perspectives are presented in conflict, and any understanding of the conflict comes from an appreciation of the situation of the black Chinese in the Mississippi Delta. These informants have the privileged voice in the film. They represent the synthetic moment of understanding created by the film's dialectical representation of race and ethnicity.

In this way, *Mississippi Triangle* not only deals with, but also foregrounds, what *Year of the Dragon* could barely voice, and then in only the most veiled terms. That is, that the issue of racial and ethnic difference may not be resolved socially through assimilation into white society or through the clear separation between ethnic groups, but instead, through the merging of those ethnic and racial groups maligned and marginalized by the white, middle-class mainstream.

In *Year of the Dragon*, the unnamed character called the "Yellow Nigger," Joey Tai's Chinese-speaking, black bodyguard, acts as that text's acknowledgment of the threat African-American and Asian-American relations pose to the mainstream white society. If Tai takes his support from the black community rather than the white, American identity as white and primarily Anglo-Saxon comes sharply into question. However, *Year of the Dragon* sweeps this issue under the rug by making Tai's henchman a marginal figure and using him only to add to Tai's own identity as radically and threateningly outside not only white-American, but also Chinese-American society.

Mississippi Triangle, on the other hand, faces the issue head on. The black Chinese community is not marginalized or hidden in any way, but held up as the real focus of the film, the site in the text in which all dialectical exchanges find their fruition. Like *Year of the Dragon*, however, *Mississippi Triangle* hinges its discussion of race and ethnicity on the related issues of gender and sexuality. Certainly, given the dominant ideology's tendancy to sexualize racial relations in order to legitimize them through reference to the patriarchal order, it comes as no surprise that *Year of the Dragon* should choose to affirm the racial and gender status quo through a narrative about sexuality and that *Mississippi Triangle* should condemn those relations by attacking the partiarchal organization of sexuality.

Who can or cannot be married to whom, who can or cannot have sexual relations with whom, and who can or cannot have children with whom all stand as the key questions at the root of the perpetuation of the racial, ethnic, class, and gender divisions in the Mississippi Delta. Sexuality becomes the key. The young Chinese-American man quoted previously provides a case in point. The reason he gives for not dating black women is fear of ostracism by both the white and the Chinese communities. Any hopes for assimilation or upward mobility would be squelched. Ironically, the promise of acceptance within the white world the civil rights movement gave to many middle-class Chinese in the Delta region has also separated these Chinese Americans more completely from the black communities which agitated for these reforms.

In *Mississippi Triangle*, the life of Arlene Hen becomes the principal conduit for the exploration of the issues of race, ethnicity, class, and sexuality. Her testimony sheds light on each institution examined by the film, and her voice ends it. As the daughter of a Chinese immigrant railway worker and an emancipated slave, she has lived through a great deal of the Delta's history and knows the meaning of being on the edges of both the black and the Chinese communities.

Like the filmmakers, Arlene Hen is both a part of the Delta community and outside it. Because she embodies what the Delta most wants to repress, she can voice a perspective different from any given member of the white, black, or Chinese communities. As a woman, she is a constant reminder of the way women are used to mark the ethnic and racial limits within the region, that is, of the way women can function as "off brands" to insure the perpetuation of the racial, ethnic, and class hierarchy in operation.

Because Arlene Hen is an invalid, the film visually reinforces her isolation by always showing her within the confines of her home, lying on her sofa alone or receiving a priest, a few friends, or family members. Through this isolated individual, the viewer becomes more clearly aware of the real conflicts at the root of Delta life. Thus, *Mississippi Triangle* does not ignore those who are isolated and fall through the cracks of the Delta's main ethnic and racial groups. Rather, Arlene Hen is used to get at the root of their interrelationship, to show how and why the black Chinese do not fit into the picture the Delta people paint of themselves.

At the film's conclusion, Arlene Hen, in a voice over an image of a field, states, "I can't be buried in a Chinese cemetary. I'm mixed with Negro, you see." This reverberates with an earlier remark made by Mississippi's first black female mayor, who stated that she, coming from the black community which paid a lot of attention to funerals, could never remember hearing about a Chinese funeral. She found this odd. As both Chinese and black, Arlene Hen cannot find either a life or a death in either community. Conjuring up this image of funerals, cemetaries, and death at the film's conclusion also brings up the fact that Arlene Hen, the black Chinese, and the issues of racial, ethnic, class, and gender inequalities in the area also remain unresolved. Unlike *Year of the Dragon* which provides narrative closure through death and romance, *Mississippi Triangle* uses sexuality and death to keep the issues raised by the film open, to stimulate rather than close off thought, to provoke the viewer to action rather than the self-satisfaction of a narrative's cathartic pleasure.

Mississippi Triangle represents only one effort within the Asian-American community to define an alternative to Hollywood's dominant image of Asians and Asian Americans. As an independent production coming from Third World Newsreel, an organization committed to social and political change, it is viewed differently from Hollywood texts. Not only does the text itself encourage serious contemplation of ethnic, racial, and gender issues, but the context in which *Mississippi Triangle* and films like it are shown also encourages community involvement and lively discussion. Usually screened in classrooms, at film festivals, or as part of special events designed to showcase alternative media productions, *Mississippi Triangle* and similar films match their discursive organization with a reception environment more personal and active than the typical Hollywood exhibition venue. The film's challenge to the Hollywood mainstream, therefore, extends beyond the parameters of the text to create a different sort of viewing experience and a very different relationship to the ethnic community it examines.

Cultural studies provides one way of looking at the complex relationship among ideology, media texts, and society. It allows film scholars to view ethnicity not as a self-evident and self-contained category, but as subject to the dynamics of class, race, gender, and other cultural variables. Cultural studies always makes the analyst aware of the changing nature of any conception of ethnicity, which is subject to the constant struggle between the dominant culture's definition of a social group and the minority culture's battle to define its own identity and to move for social equality.

To this end, the work of cultural studies theorists on ideology as both established structure and contested field for resistance, as well as their work on subcultures' place within contemporary social formations, become quite important to any understanding of ethnicity and the cinema. By seeing ethnicity as ideological, the power dynamics behind representations of ethnic groups become clearer. Moreover, ethnicity's cultural and historical aspect surfaces, and the contradiction becomes less obscure between the lived experience of any given individual and the way the dominant culture represents that individual's race, class, ethnicity, age, or gender. The notion of subculture adds an even more concrete dimension to this by providing an avenue for the understanding of the relationship between text and viewer, between image and specific social group which goes beyond simply looking at texts as subject to only one reading. This concept also forces researchers to investigate alternative representations which come from the subculture itself and question the dominant media's portrayal of people it marginalizes.

This examination of the Hollywood text *Year of the Dragon* and the alternative documentary *Mississippi Triangle* has illustrated simply one way that cultural studies can provide an inroad to an understanding of ethnicity in the cinema. The analysis has centered on two texts which feature Chinese Americans to unearth the possible ways the texts could be read. Cultural studies also provides for other ways of approaching the interrelationship of text, viewer, and society. However, although the focus may shift, cultural studies always forces researchers to be aware of the historical and cultural specificity of the texts and to constantly be aware of the fact that nothing exists in a vacuum. Even if the main emphasis of a particular study is textual, the cultural framework in which that work exists and functions must also be taken into account for any understanding of the ideological operation of the text to take place.

NOTES

1. Martha Gever, "Dragon Busters," *The Independent* 8 (October 1985): 8–9.

2. Karl Marx and Frederick Engels, *The German Ideology*, ed. C. J. Arthur (New York: International Publishers, 1970), p. 64.

3. Louis Althusser, "Ideology and Ideological State Apparatuses (Notes towards an Investigation)," in *Lenin and Philosophy and Other Essays*, trans. Ben Brewster (New York: Monthly Review Press, 1972), p. 162.

4. Antonio Gramsci, *Selections from the Prison Notebooks*, ed. and trans. Quintin Hoare and Geoffrey Nowell Smith (New York: International Publishers, 1971).

5. John Clarke, "Style," in *Resistance through Rituals: Youth Subcultures in Post-war Britain*, ed. Stuart Hall and Tony Jefferson (London: University of Birmingham, 1976), pp. 175–91. For more information on subcultures and the media, see Dick Hebdige, *Subculture: The Meaning of Style* (London: Methuen, 1979) and Gina Marchetti, "Subcultural Studies and the Film Audience: Rethinking the Film Viewing Context," in *Current Research in Film*, vol. 2, ed. Bruce A. Austin (Norwood: Ablex, 1986), pp. 62–79.

6. Stuart Hall, "Encoding/Decoding," in *Culture, Media, Language*, ed. Stuart Hall et al. (London: University of Birmingham, 1980), pp. 128–38.

7. John Fiske, "Television: Polysemy and Popularity," *Critical Studies in Mass Communication* 3 (December 1986): 403.

8. Stuart Hall, "Signification, Representation, Ideology: Althusser and the Post-Structuralist Debates," *Critical Studies in Mass Communication* 2 (June 1985): 112–13.

9. For example, see Laura Mulvey, "Visual Pleasure and Narrative Cinema," *Screen* 16 (Autumn 1975): 6–18.

10. Eugene Franklin Wong, *On Visual Media Racism: Asians in American Motion Pictures* (New York: Arno Press, 1978).

11. For a different view of *Year of the Dragon*, see Robin Wood, "Hero/Anti-Hero: The Dilemma of *Year of the Dragon*," *CineAction!*, no. 6 (August 1986): 57–61.

12. Edward W. Said, *Orientalism* (New York: Vintage, 1978), p. 3. For work on the relationship between ethnography, ideology, and the academy, see James Clifford and George Marcus, eds., *Writing Culture: The Poetics and Politics of Ethnography* (Berkeley: University of California Press, 1986).

13. See chapter 9 in this volume.

14. For more information on the production of *Mississippi Triangle*, see Erick Dittus, "*Mississippi Triangle*: An Interview with Christine Choy, Worth Long and Allan Siegel," *Cineaste* 14, no. 2 (1985): 38–40. The subject for the film was inspired by James Loewen's sociological-anthropological study of the Chinese in the Delta. After the production of the film, Loewen returned to do additional fieldwork in the Delta, findings included in *The Mississippi Chinese: Between Black and White*, 2d ed. (Prospect Heights: Waveland, 1988). This second addition includes some film stills and further information on many of the interviewees in *Mississippi Triangle*.

Black Bodies/American Commodities: Gender, Race, and the Bourgeois Ideal in Contemporary Film

The representation of women in advertisements for Virginia Slims cigarettes in the 1980s tells an interesting story about black women and white in U.S. culture, a story that reflects on both contemporary cinematic production and feminist debates about gender's relation to race, class, and ethnic differences.[1] While most readers are familiar with the formulaic inset of the browbeaten housewife denied her right to smoke, they might be surprised to consider that the advertisement violates it own format when the central female figure is black.[2] Here, the narrative pictorial of women's past enslavement is deleted even as the modern black woman is applauded, like her white counterpart, for "com[ing] a long way." The erasure of the black woman's historical specificity, her literal and metaphoric enslavement to a patriarchal culture structured by race and class, is produced not simply by the demands of the marketplace—the unsaleability of a humorous reflection on slavery—but also by the advertisement's construction of a bourgeois feminism that equates woman's liberation with equal access to corporate and commodity worlds. In this sense, the blank space of the advertisement is emblematic of U.S. culture's appropriation of a feminism where race, class, and ethnic differences among women have been negated and white middle-class women elevated as the source and symbol of the feminist critiques of patriarchal relations.

In foregrounding the "modern" white woman against a pictorial of her past patriarchal enslavement, the Virginia Slims advertisement works by selling women the masculine power supposedly won through the transition from housewife to independent spirit, a representation that displaces the economic changes shaping American society since the early nineteenth century. Through the simple equation of work with domesticity and domesticity with oppression, the advertisement can celebrate white woman's entrance into a market economy, where she supposedly can own her own labor—no patriarch presides over her—and where labor itself is no longer the center of her life. By linking commodities (cigarettes) to this tableau of women's place in patriarchal culture, the advertisement negotiates women's relation to capitalism through the discourse of gender, displacing not only the economic relations underlying the image of female emancipation, but also the feminist quest for equal rights into a triumph of equal access to the commodity world. In this process, woman is herself commodified, her body so layered with products—hose, clothes, makeup, jewelry, cigarette—that the social relations constructing her position have faded into abstraction. This presentation of women's escape from domesticity as the ultimate liberation simultaneously casts high-commodity capitalism as the site for individual emancipation, while ensnaring the female body as the representational playground for capitalism's enactment.

While the advertisement's ideological workings are thus articulated at the intersection of class and gender, this construction has specific force for the white female figure whose economic emancipation from the kitchen can be revised as emblem of feminist progress. For the black woman, whose positioning via race, gender, and class creates a historical narrative of slavery and domestic service less easily cast as amusing, the pictorial inset of patriarchal enslavement must be deleted and her commodified body alone left to signify her "progress" in American culture. Only through this deletion can the black woman be positioned as the central player, for the advertisement's very construction of "woman" is historically at odds with the material existences of black women. Consider, for instance, who would be cast as her oppressor: the white master, his culturally enshrined wife, or his black male slave? From whose kitchen would the black woman be liberated? And what story would this speak about the "feminist" narrative that gives the advertisement its cultural marketability? Actual differences among black women and white become unrepresentable within the advertisement's ideological construction because the advertisement claims a changed patriarchal economy for all women—a change brought on by a feminism that, in reality, can hardly be credited with the (albeit limited) emancipation of black women in American culture.

This representation of the white middle-class woman as synonymous with "women" and with "feminism" has been a primary way that American culture throughout the nineteenth and twentieth centuries has contained the most radical challenges to white masculine hegemony. Through the image of the white, heterosexual, middle-class woman, for whom gender is the *only* means of cultural disempowerment, other categories of oppression are rendered invisible while sexual difference is reinscribed as a seemingly universal, natural distinction.[3] During the first wave of the women's movement, for example, a rejuvenation of the "feminine sphere"—of the duties of wife and mother—helped to divert attention from calls for overt political action by offering women images of fulfillment and subjectivity within the already established cultural space of gender. But for working-class white women who were entering the labor market in large numbers and black women who were still enslaved, the ideology of a womanhood based on the bourgeois ideal was an exclusionary rhetoric which only helped strengthen race and class hierarchies. Through the alignment of the bourgeois white woman with feminism, potential bondings among all women can be disrupted, thereby dispersing the broad potential for feminism to articulate a revolutionary ideology that can challenge the various structures of oppression that constrict women's lives, including but not limited to gender.

Most problematically, feminist theory has itself duplicated the homogenizing practices of American culture by adopting a theoretical paradigm that asserts transculturally and transhistorically the primacy of gender, thereby rendering race, class, sexuality, and ethnicity as secondary inscriptions of difference and not as structures integrally linked to one another. But, as Bell Hooks writes, "[f]eminist theory would have much to offer if it showed women ways in which racism and sexism are immutably connected rather than pitting one struggle against the other or blatantly dismissing racism."[4] For black women in particular, the feminist mandate for gender solidarity has proved most untenable, as bonding between black women and black men has been necessary to the struggle against racial oppression—a struggle significantly posited against white women as well as white men. For these reasons, the circulation of the image of the white middle-class woman as signifier for the category "woman"—the use of her political and economic positioning as indexes of gender disparity—can only prohibit the very aims of feminism to end the oppression and exploitation of women.

The demand for feminist theory in the closing decade of the twentieth century is precisely the articulation of how various structures of difference reinforce one another, for it is the complicity among categories of oppression that enables U.S. culture to enhance hegemonic power even in the process of negotiating with "marginalized" groups and discourses. In this sense, race as a category of difference is not a structure that parallels gender relations, but one that intersects and confirms them—a structure intrinsic to the patriarchal economy of U.S. culture. This notion of patriarchy as constitutive of more than gender difference is crucial not only to an understanding of cultural relations but also to the future of feminism; indeed, the intersecting, contradictory, and cross-category functioning of U.S. culture necessitates a theoretical framework that can account not only for hierarchies between men and women, but also those among women *and* those among men as well. But although this last suggestion—that power differentials among men are centrally important to feminist critique—seems to contradict the epistemological foundations of feminist thought (which seeks to make *women's* exploitation and oppression visible), the charting of differences among women requires the recognition that some women hold cultural power over certain groups of men, that feminist politics based simply on notions of shared gender oppression misconstrue the complicated nature of cultural hierarchies.[5]

As the Virginia Slims advertisement itself demonstrates, black women's simulation of a white bourgeois womanhood—wrought through the erasure of historical material conditions—simultaneously renders invisible black male disempowerment via patriarchal relations. The image repressed in the advertisement's deletion of the pictorial inset, then, is not only that of black women's enslavement, but also that of black males, a repression indicative of the historical difficulty of equating black men with the white patriarch as the primary oppressor of black women. To read such concern with the displacement of black men in cultural ideology as a reinscription of patriarchal logic (through its attention to men) dangerously limits feminism's ability to intervene in the multiple structures of women's oppression. As I will later demonstrate, readings of the exploitation of black men and their positioning in ideology can reveal further the mechanisms by which racial difference disempowers black women. A fuller understanding of the cultural terrain of race as it intersects with gender is made possible by viewing, at the broadest level, the implications of a social formation constructed along multiple lines of difference and disempowerment.

Such a rethinking of feminism's ideological and theoretical basis is particularly important in the early moments of the 1990s when the broad conservative retrenchment instigated by the Reagan administration and legally secured under George Bush makes it imperative that feminism confront its own complicity with dominant power structures. This is most urgent in the arena of racial relations where, as civil rights advancements of the 1960s have been steadily eroded, dominant cultural discourses can proclaim the victimization and discrimination of white men and, as restrictions on reproductive freedom are enacted, a poor female population disproportionately composed of women of color is positioned for its most devastating impact. Given the recuperatory nature of such shifts in ideological and material practices, it is hardly coincidental that representation—U.S. cinema in particular—finds itself marked by the contradictory conditions of cultural racial ideology in this era: on one hand, the rhetorical dream of a post-1960s egalitarianism manifested in greater visibility for black actors while, on the other, the containment of this visibility by narrative scenarios that reaffirm white masculine power and its bourgeois basis of dominance. These scenarios, like the narrative played out in the Virginia Slims advertisement, displace the specificity of African-American tradition and culture while foregrounding racial difference as a component of the democratizing practices of commodity culture itself.

In order to explore these issues as they relate to the ideological investments of U.S. film, this chapter traces the historical development of black female representation—beginning only briefly with *Gone With the Wind* (1939) and *Imitation of Life* (1934, 1959), and exploring in more depth *Mahogany* (1975) and *Lethal Weapon* (1987)—arguing that the contemporary images of the black woman as model, entrepreneur, and housewife that replace classic cinematic stereotypes of mammy or whore are themselves complicit with broader strategies of negotiation in the (post)-Reagan era. While the movement away from demeaning stereotypes into a larger field of cultural representation has the potential for counterhegemonic effects, mainstream cinema reveals, for the most part, a disturbing reliance on narrative structures that foreground the bourgeois ideal as symbol of racial egalitarianism.[6] In this sense, such representations transform historical demands for civil rights into images of class homogeneity—an ideological response to radical discourses of the 1960s that reiterates what Houston Baker calls, in another context, "AMERICA as immanent idea of boundless, classless, raceless possibility."[7] Such "positive" images of black women are thus mediations for a reconstruction of hegemonic power, offering—through the very visibility of black female inclusion—a seemingly nonhierarchical culture in which all political and social interventions can be contained through a discursive nod to "you've come a long way."

Although black women have been featured in U.S. cinema since the early days of silent films—in *The Wooing and Wedding of a Coon* (1905) and *The Masher* (1907), for example—the basic representational paradigm governing their image has changed little until recently. Cast as mammy in *Gone With the Wind* (1939), *Pinky* (1949), and *Such Good Friends* (1971); seductress in *Hallelujah* (1929), *Porgy and Bess* (1959), and *Carmen Jones* (1954); matriarch in *A Raisin in the Sun* (1961); or whore in *Anna Lucasta* (1959), *Take a Giant Step* (1961), *The Pawnbroker* (1965), or *The Hit Man* (1972), black women have served primarily as white women's Other, a dark continent of difference whose various lacks—of beauty, morality, and intelligence—subtend the cultural elevation and adornment of white womanhood.[8] These stereotypes, drawn and nourished in the slave era, effectively exclude black women from cultural notions of the feminine—an exclusion that ironically provides the structural basis for such cultural articulations. As Hazel V. Carby writes of nineteenth-century ideologies of womanhood, "exist[ing] in an antithetical relationship with the values embodied in the cult of true womanhood. . . . [b]lack womanhood was polarized against white womanhood in the structure of the metaphoric system of female sexuality."[9] While this dichotomous structure functions as the primary mechanism for the representation of black women throughout the twentieth century, the shifts in configuration that occur in the post-civil rights era provide an important context for exploring some of feminist theory's most pressing concerns.

Second only to *Gone With the Wind* (fig. 11.1)—with its intense and violently racist opposition between Scarlet and Mammy—*Imitation of Life* is the classic construction of the racial dichotomy governing the representation of black and white women in American culture, a film so popular it was made twice. Centered on the struggles of two widowed women, the original casts Louise Beavers as Aunt Delilah, the good-natured, robust black maid to Claudette Colbert's sophisticated Miss Bea. By tracing their "common" problems as single mothers, the film establishes a rare vision of interracial female bonding only to betray it by failing to question the political and economic structures underlying the bond's construction. For it is Aunt Delilah's pancake recipe, passed down through various generations of black women, that provides the means for both women's financial success. In a telling scene, Miss Bea, whose idea it was to

11.1. *Gone With the Wind*'s Scarlett O'Hara (Vivien Leigh) and Mammy (Hattie McDaniel) in a scene graphically demonstrating cinema's classic representation of the "differences" between black and white female bodies in U.S. culture.

market the recipe, offers Aunt Delilah 20 percent of the profits—to which Delilah responds in typical mammy fashion: "You kin have it. I makes you a present of it." This scenario as well as the physical contrasts drawn between the two women—Bea fair-haired and sexual, Delilah big-boned and maternal—reiterate the traditional dichotomies governing black women and white in dominant U.S. film.

This reiteration of racial ideologies is compounded in the 1959 remake of *Imitation of Life*, featuring Juanita Moore and Lana Turner. Unlike the original, with its emphasis on the combined efforts of black and white women for economic survival, the remake deletes the recipe scenario and casts Turner as Lora Meredith, a model and actress pampered and nurtured into stardom by her black maid, Annie Johnson, who remains financially dependent throughout her life on Lora's generosity (fig. 11.2). In focusing more fully on Johnson's mulatto daughter, Sarah Jane (Susan Kohner) this later version heightens the melodramatic depiction of the light-skinned black woman caught between worlds by portraying her not only as

11.2. While this still from the 1959 *Imitation of Life* features Annie (Juanita Moore) and Miss Lora (Lana Turner) exchanging looks, the mirror's reframing of the scene focuses the spectator's gaze on cinema's traditional spectacle: the white woman. At the same time, the black woman's desexualization as a "modern" mammy is marked by the children flanking her, Susie (Terry Burnham) in front and her own daughter Sarah Jane (Susan Kohner) in the rear.

an exploited chorus girl but also as the victim of her white boy-friend's physical abuse. (In an interesting confusion of cultural signifiers, the scene of the beating is accompanied by loud jazz music.)[10] Through these seemingly minor plot shifts, the later film simultaneously foregrounds the problem of dichotomized womanhood while reinscribing the traditional roles assigned to black and white women. As Sarah Jane's tragic plight reveals, any deviation from ascribed racial roles results in social alienation and personal destruction.

In the decades following the civil rights movement, when Hollywood's portrayal of blacks was most vociferously challenged, representations of the tragic mulatto and her caring mammy decreased in frequency, to be replaced by shifting configurations of the white woman-black woman dichotomy. *Mahogany* is particularly interesting in this regard, for here the traditional contrast between black woman and white has been replaced by a narrative scenario that collapses the dichotomous structure, allowing a black woman to embody the dual representations that had previously been articulated along racially determined lines. Torn between the twin demands of career and family, Tracy Chambers (Diana Ross) is a woman whose lifelong ambition is to escape the poverty of Chicago's South Side by becoming an international fashion designer. In the process of rising to the top, Tracy is transformed by the effete white photographer Sean McEvoy (Anthony Perkins) into "Mahogany," a high-powered model whose face eventually graces Europe's most fashionable magazines (fig. 11.3). Mahogany's quasi-affair with the sadomasochistic Sean ends with her involvement with a wealthy Italian who, in exchange for sexual commitment, finances her long-desired design business. But in the film's final scene, Mahogany renounces this commodification by white culture and turns instead to the domain of black middle-class familial life. Returning to America to mend her failing relationship with Brian Walker (Billy Dee Williams), a grass-roots Chicago politician, she seemingly overcomes her alienation as the camera lingers over the embracing figures of the reunited couple.

While Jane Gaines has argued that the final "reconciliation of the black heterosexual couple is thwarted by the commercial appropriation of [Mahogany's] image,"[11] it is significant that the film's resolution not only reunites Mahogany with Brian—and by entension, the black community—but more important, extradites her from the sexual economy of white masculine desire that characterizes her European life-style. In the last scene, Brian delivers a campaign speech to a crowd of predominately black onlookers as Mahogany enters and, in the rhetorical style of call and response, begins a dialogue with Brian. When he finally sights her in the crowd, they move from seemingly opposite sides of the frame toward one another, and the music crescendoes above the approving applause of the spectators. But while the black woman has thus escaped the suffocating and exploitative realm of white masculine desire—a role almost exclusively reserved for white women in American cinema—her "return" guarantees that her image remains within a circuit of masculine exchange. Moving from black man to white and back again, Mahogany mediates between them, her image providing the means for a negotiation of power among black and white men.

The film's most revealing expression of the phallic power at stake in Mahogany's image occurs during Brian's visit to Rome, where the disjuncture between his communal politics and Mahogany's

11.3. In Diana Ross's 1975 vehicle *Mahogany*, the dichotomy between black and white womanhood governing earlier cinematic production is collapsed. Here, as the black woman "enjoys" the role of female spectacle, her commodified image functions as sign for the democratizing potential of bourgeois culture.

commercial exploitation by Sean are brought into stark opposition. At a party Sean gives for Europe's fashion elite, Mahogany plays the role of centerpiece while Sean coaxes Brian upstairs to a room decorated with photos of Mahogany. There, the two men engage in an evasive but gradually threatening rivalry that reaches its peak when Sean draws a gun. Seemingly intent on shooting Brian, Sean is quickly wrestled to the floor where, in an amazingly sexual configuration of bodies—the black man on top of the white—Brian inserts the gun into Sean's mouth and pulls the trigger. The gun/phallus empty, Brian is at least momentarily consigned to impotency in his quest to counter the sadomasochistic white male world that has enveloped Mahogany. By setting their struggle within a narrative context literally framed by Mahogany's sexualized image, the scene overtly inscribes the black woman as mediation in a racially contested economy of masculine desire—an economy invested in and constructed by the phallus itself.

But while the scene ends in the symbolic castration of the black man, it is significant that the ensuing narrative recuperates this moment of white masculine supremacy not only by depicting Sean as sexually impotent, but also by ultimately aligning Mahogany with Brian as the mechanism for the film's closure. Such narrative turns produce an important ideological counter to the historical legacy of white male appropriation of the black female body in U.S. culture even as we must question the patriarchal basis of such a strategy. What does it mean, in other words, that the black woman's escape from the circuit of white masculine desire can be envisioned only as her return to the black man? Is this not an ideological move that posits the black woman's dual oppression—as both black and female—against one another, circulating her image as signifier of the racial power imbalance between black and white men? Indeed, *Mahogany* fails to escape the very structure of cultural relations it purportedly critiques, veiling the black woman's complex positioning by casting her oppression solely within the symbolic register of white masculine desire. As such, it can only envision her liberation from the constraints of both race and gender structures along a singular trajectory, positing her escape from the destruction of white male culture as a return "home."

The two worlds dichotomized in *Imitation of Life* are thus embodied in *Mahogany* in a single figure, Tracy Chambers, whose eventual commitment to the black family is a radical departure from Annie Johnson's earlier role as servile helpmate to the beautiful Lora and her equally golden child. Significantly, Tracy's role as fashion model closely resembles the career goals of Lora, where feminine beauty and the ability to act as specular image for white masculine desire are the ingredients necessary for economic achievement. In *Mahogany*'s many photographic montages, as Gaines notes, Tracy's color "is washed out in bright light or powdered over, and as her long-haired wigs blow around her face, she becomes suddenly 'white.' "[12] As such, the competing demands in Tracy's life—the film's positing of a fashion career in opposition to home and family—can be read within this historical narrative of black female representation as evocations of racial ideologies of womanhood. The black woman's return home, the withdrawal of her image from the white masculine economy, and the establishment of her own business are purposely constructed to deny her stereotypic status as the white woman's Other in U.S. culture.

But although the film rightly reveals these positions as constructions, as opposed to natural inscriptions, it fails to challenge the binary structure on which they are based. Instead, it remains content to envision the black woman's liberation as the ability to *choose* her position within the unchallenged realm of capitalist and patriarchal structures. In particular, class values—the Horatio Alger image of ascent from poverty and disenfranchisement into democratic fulfillment as well as the affirmation of black entrepreneurship[13]—act as the positive counters to Mahogany's ensnarement in and exploitation as cultural commodity. The disparity between the economic conditions of U.S. blacks and the ethic of free enterprise goes unquestioned, enabling the film to forego a critique of the larger system of complicit structures that compel Mahogany's choice—a choice that ultimately poses no release from the representational confines of U.S. cultural production.

Mahogany's construction of a "choice" in the black woman's negotiation of dichotomized womanhood—even as that choice is revealed as ideologically limited—becomes reframed in the conservative retrenchment of the 1980s to produce a vision of cultural relations seemingly unaffected by difference. This is particularly true of the 1987 box-office hit *Lethal Weapon*. Cast no longer in the traditional stereotypes of mammy or whore, here, in a film featuring the black man as both father and police officer, the black woman is offered roles—of housewife and virginal daughter—that had been previously reserved for white women. As the wife Trish Murtaugh (Darlene Love), whose "bad cooking" becomes a joke between men and as the virginal daughter Rianne Murtaugh (Traci

Wolfe), who must be saved by them, the black woman's homogenization into categories traditionally occupied by the white woman is part of a broader program of hegemonic recuperation, a program that has as its main focus the reconstruction of white masculine power in the face of feminist and civil rights discourses of the 1960s. So strong was this recuperation in the Reagan era that even affirmative action programs were challenged for "depriving" white men of their civil rights. By seeking to evoke a social order in which minority status no longer inculcates one into oppressive structures, contemporary cultural production dismisses as impertinent continued challenges to hegemonic power.

As part of the process of returning America, in the Reaganesque language of the 1980s, to its "traditional values and past glory," *Lethal Weapon* manipulates the imagery of the black woman by denying her historical and material differences as wrought by white patriarchy. While for some the representation of black women in the more traditional images of wife, mother, and virginal daughter signals a "progressive" narrative, offering as it does black access to the realm of bourgeois culture widely denied until the civil rights era, it would be a mistake to view such representation as evidence of black women's real advancement in the struggle for race and gender equality. Indeed, as Robert Stam and Louise Spence write, "[t]he insistence on 'positive images' . . . obscures the fact that 'nice' images might at times be as pernicious as overtly degrading ones, providing a bourgeois facade for paternalism, a more pervasive racism."[14] The bourgeois facade of *Lethal Weapon* operates, in fact, to tie the black woman to a heterosexual economy where her body functions not only in the role of wife, as the plot space for the establishment of a normative heterosexuality, but also in the role of virginal daughter, as the landscape across which interracial masculine bonds can be maintained.

Most specifically, by focusing its action on the interracial relation of Roger Murtaugh (Danny Glover) and Martin Riggs (Mel Gibson), *Lethal Weapon* seeks to override the potential disruption caused by race by establishing bourgeois culture as the signifier of racial indifference while constructing gender as the only significant—and seemingly natural—category of differentiation. All notions of historically constructed differences among black and white are thus recast as capitalist attainment, the spectacle of middle-class life providing the representation of America as embodiment of its own democratic ideals. While the alignment of black females with the representational space most often reserved for white women ini-

11.4. The box office hit of 1987, *Lethal Weapon* revamps race and gender relations in the contemporary moment by figuring the white man as both
victim of the social order and its rejuvenated hero. In this climatic fight
scene, Martin Riggs (Mel Gibson) and Roger Murtaugh (Danny Glover)
demonstrate the highly masculinized realm of interracial male bonding configurations.

tiates this democratic ethos, it is the relationship between black and
white men that is the film's pivotal site for democratic wholeness—
the black woman achieving her status only through the black man's
connection to, and reaffirmation of, hegemonic power itself. A more
refined and less ideologically resistant film than *Mahogany*, *Lethal
Weapon* thus circulates the black woman in an economy of masculine power where racial differences among men are seemingly erad-
icated as the means for the reinscription of patriarchal power.

Like other interracial cop scenarios, *Lethal Weapon* is constructed
on a basic pattern. By initially depicting the contrary lives of Murtaugh and Riggs, who are thrown together as partners against their
wishes, the film charts their growing respect and affection for one
another as they face death together (fig. 11.4). Displacing racial difference into less volatile forms such as age, life-style and mental
health, *Lethal Weapon* begins in contrast: while Murtaugh enjoys a

bath in his well-decorated home with his wife and three children singing happy birthday to him, Riggs is shown lying in bed smoking a cigarette, his mobile home strewn with debris. A man on the edge of breakdown, suicidal because of the recent death of his wife, Riggs is lost, the squalor of his environment indicative of his alienation from the commodified heterosexual norm that the black family represents. Here, in a reversal of paternalistic ideology, it is the white man who, debilitated by grief, can be restored to life only through the aid of the black "father"—the figure responsible, in the film's resolution, for drawing the alienated white man back into the folds of sanity and the bourgeois family. In this way, the black family acts as the great cultural equalizer, diffusing potential challenge to hegemonic inscriptions by flattening out racial difference in middle-class achievement.

The black family thus functions as the site for the rejuvenation of the white male character who, as the social outsider denied the traditional benefits of U.S. familial life, can eventually rejoin society, cleansed of his angst, his anger, and his isolation. Such a narrative design in the late 1980s is no accident, for its rearrangement of the racial positioning of marginality—its construction of the white male as alienated and victimized—embodies a major strategy for the reconstruction of hegemonic power. In this way, *Lethal Weapon* can simultaneously posit a fully egalitarian society—blacks signifying the idealized middle-class scenario—while depicting that scenario as necessary to the recuperation of the white man who is now in need of cultural healing. Earlier cinematic versions of blacks as alienated outsiders are displaced in the narrative economy of *Lethal Weapon*, providing a representation that shifts the terms of U.S. racial structures through which the white man is both victimized—by fate (his wife's death), by his peers (who think he's crazy), and by himself (his suicidal tendencies)—and rehabilitated from such victimization.[15] At its deepest level, then, *Lethal Weapon*'s evocation of a world beyond race enables the white man to regain identity and power across a seemingly egalitarian representation of the black bourgeoisie.

Cast against the domesticated figure of the black man, the representation of Riggs, whose body is itself the "lethal weapon," clarifies the phallic power at stake in the film's depiction of post-1960s' cultural egalitarianism. In the initial meeting between the male players, it is Murtaugh who mistakenly reads the white man's possession of a gun as evidence of criminality and attacks; swiftly, with the aid of his martial arts training from Special Forces in Vietnam,

Riggs nails Murtaugh to the floor, his foot on the black man's chest. Although the issue of race is carefully avoided throughout the film, the image of Riggs, pistol drawn, above Murtaugh evokes a more traditional ideological configuration where the white man achieves physical and, significantly, phallic superiority in the clash of masculine forces. In the process of unraveling a young white woman's supposed suicide, Riggs's marksmanship and martial arts ability become increasingly important as the men confront a gang of heroin smuggling, ex-mercenary veterans, men who can only be stopped by someone "like them." When this gang abducts Rianne, Riggs's role is crucial to the ultimate restoration of the black family. The film thus allows the white figure to be culturally healed by the same familial unit that he himself is responsible for preserving.

This reconstruction of U.S. cultural relations depends, for its full articulation, not only on the film's discourse of gender—through which the masculine can be elevated as source of democratic preservation—but also on that discourse's depiction of the differences among black and white women. Much like the reversals at work in the representation of black men and white, here it is the black woman who occupies the role of mother and of virginal daughter, while the stereotypically negative connotations often consigned to black women are shifted to the white female figure, Amanda Hunsaker (Jackie Swanson), who now becomes the whore. Where *Mahogany* embodied the dual positions of dichotomized womanhood, *Lethal Weapon* simply reverses these paradigmatic relations; in this way, the film's seemingly progressive representation of the black woman is still tied to a cultural economy that constructs the feminine within the domain of racial difference. The most empowered position that emerges is consequently that of the white masculine itself, which draws its power from the discourses of difference constructing the film's dichotomized representation of women.

In the film's opening sequence, sexual difference, in particular the voyeuristic gaze at the white female body, is established as the primary discourse across which the film's negotiation of interracial relations will be formed. From an aerial view of downtown San Francisco, the camera slowly focuses in on Amanda Hunsaker who, clad in lace stockings, lingerie, and high heels, seductively runs her finger along her ruby lips in a clear suggestion of auto-eroticism. As the camera gazes upon her partially nude body, Amanda moves to the balcony, teters briefly on the railing, and then jumps. Here, the voyeuristic gaze is so insistent that even as her body crashes on top of a parked car, we look at her body exposed, spread out *facing* the camera, her femaleness forever open to view. Such a representation of the white female body stands in stark contrast to images of black women in the following scene where, as mother and daughter, they gather around Murtaugh, happily celebrating his fiftieth birthday. The differences between these women's bodies—as mother (Trish), as virgin (Rianne) and, as we find out later, as whore (Amanda)—evoke the classic construction of female sexuality in patriarchal culture.

To complete the emphasis on normative sexuality, Amanda is revealed not only as whore but as lesbian, a revelation that displaces all homosexual tension in the film between the closely bonded men onto white female sexuality. Significantly, the assertion of Amanda's lesbianism is made during a conversation between Riggs and Murtaugh at the police firing range—the woman's lesbianism being framed by images of the men firing their weapons. In this overdetermined phallic setting, Amanda's sexuality reaffirms the masculine as itself the site of heterosexual wholeness; in this way, white female sexuality, while initially charting a heterosexual space, is fully negated as the masculine comes to stand for all culturally accepted sexuality. The narrative of Amanda's sexuality and the images of her body thus function in two ways and, importantly, in this order: first to assert heterosexuality at the film's beginning so that the ensuing scenes of Riggs and Murtaugh naked are read as heterosexual and not homosexual, and second, to assume the sexual tensions between the men entirely to herself, to the white female and not the male or black female body. In her dual function, the representational paradigm governing the white female is resexualised as mother/virgin–lesbian/whore, a reconstruction most significantly based on racial difference.

In establishing this racially dichotomized paradigm of sexual difference as the frame of the film, masculine sexuality can appear to be constructed rather homogeneously, with no internal hierarchies or imbalances of power. This illusion is provided by the text of sexual difference which diffuses and renders secondary the bond's reconstruction of racial difference; through the discourse of gender, the interracial male bond can seal over the frisson of its own construction, enabling all differences among men to be subsumed in the seemingly natural discourse of gender. In addition, differences among black women and white can be strengthened, as it is the white woman's death—and her sexually illicit life-style—that initiates the narrative drama that threatens the sanctity as well as the individual lives of the black family. The white woman's uncontainability within the bourgeois family, contrasting as it does with the black woman's happy domesticity, thus signifies a further threat to cultural stability. In the film's system of reversals, the white woman ironically emerges as the primary locus of race and gender disruption.

By foregrounding middle-class achievement as signifier of racial indifference, *Lethal Weapon* reconstructs the image of the white man by casting him first as alien outsider and then as the source necessary for the reconstitution of black family life. In this sense, the representation of blacks in a mode that denies race as a significant category of difference enables the white male figure to move rather easily between the status of victim to that of hero, from outsider to insider, from suicidal maniac to cultural preserver. The film's conclusion, with Riggs joining the Murtaughs for Christmas dinner, evinces this movement as the now healthy Riggs gives his partner the special gold bullet that he had been reserving for his own death; "I won't be needing it anymore," he says. In this way, *Lethal Weapon* makes explicit the economy of masculine power relations within which the black woman's image is circulated, depicting her representation in nonstereotypical roles not as an empowerment of her own cultural position but as the means by which race and gender structures can be more firmly entrenched.[16] Like the Virginia Slims advertisement, this representation of the black woman as stand-in for a white bourgeois womanhood denies her own historical specificity, exchanging the racial context of U.S. cultural production for the safe realm of the commodified bourgeois ideal.

By tracing the representation of black women in mainstream U.S. cinema by foregrounding the various configurations that structure her image in cultural ideology, I have tried to demonstrate how the traditional dichotomy between black women and white has shifted in the contemporary era toward conflations and reversals, and how both of these strategies depend, for their fullest articulation, on the diffusion of race and gender through class. In such a diffusion, the black woman's access to commodity culture—and her ability to serve as its specular embodiment—are the mechanisms for envisioning a reconstruction of U.S. cultural relations in the era that followed the 1960s. The black body, in this sense, becomes a commodity, a representational sign for the democratizing process of U.S. culture itself. What may have begun as cultural responses to the demands posed by civil rights, black power and (to a lesser extent) feminism—for greater representational terrain—have thus become strategies for recuperation, mystifying narrative scenarios that negotiate race and gender disempowerment through the symbol systems of bourgeois culture.

For feminism, which has its historical and at times theoretical roots in the domain of middle-class ascendency, these contemporary strategies disturbingly replicate our tendency to circulate "racial difference"[17] as a commodity in our own discourse, pasting over the white bourgeois woman who occupies the center of our theoretical paradigm with images of black women whose historical and material specificity we thereby render indecipherable. Like other feminist theorists who explore this problem, Elizabeth Spelman describes the phrase " 'as a woman' as the Trojan Horse of feminist ethnocentrism,"[18] suggesting that the very epistemological center of our discursive heritage must be excavated for its hegemonic complicities, making it clear that the future of feminism depends on revealing the inadequacies of its most privileged theoretical category. In the process, it becomes necessary to view masculine relations as crucial sites for the articulation and maintenance of power structures and to forge readings of culture that can account for the intersections of multiple hierarchical constructions. Most disturbingly for the white middle-class feminist, this means jettisoning some of our favorite claims to counterhegemonic power, including the call for a shared gender oppression. In a historical moment violently marked by the recuperation of white masculine power, such a loss is barely a beginning.

NOTES

1. I think that it is important to maintain race and ethnicity as separate although at times overlapping categories of difference. This distinction is particularly crucial in considering contemporary cultural production's use of the visibility of difference—the inclusion of black characters, for instance—as the means for representing a social order supposedly healed of its violent racial past.

2. The advertisements are routinely featured in such magazines as *Cosmopolitan* and *Essence*.

3. For further discussion of this problem in feminist theorizing, see Angela Y. Davis, *Women, Race and Class* (New York: Random House, 1981); Bell Hooks, *Feminist Theory: From Margin to Center* (Boston: South End Press, 1984); Audre Lorde, *Sister Outsider* (Trumansburg: Crossing Press, 1984); Hazel V. Carby, *Reconstructing Womanhood: The Emergence of the Afro-American Woman Writer* (New York: Oxford University Press, 1987); and Elizabeth V.

Spelman, *Inessential Woman: Problems of Exclusion in Feminist Thought* (Boston: Beacon Press, 1988).

4. Hooks, *Feminist Theory*, p. 52.

5. Eve Kosofsky Sedgwick's *Between Men: English Literature and Male Homosocial Desire* (New York: Columbia University Press, 1985) is perhaps the most significant feminist contribution to date that demonstrates how relations among men are constructed through gender and why they must therefore be viewed as a crucial site for feminism's political intervention into patriarchal structures of domination and exploitation.

6. By "mainstream" I mean films that have received wide commercial release.

7. Houston Baker, *Blues, Ideology, and Afro-American Literature: A Vernacular Theory* (Chicago: University Press of Chicago, 1984), p. 65.

8. For discussions of these films, see Donald Bogle, *Toms, Coons, Mulattos, Mammies and Bucks: An Interpretive History of Blacks in American Films* (New York: Viking Press, 1973), Thomas Cripps, *Slow Fade to Black: The Negro in American Film 1900–1942* (New York: Oxford University Press, 1977), and Daniel Leab, *From Sambo to Superspade: The Black Experience in Motion Pictures* (Boston: Houghton Mifflin, 1975).

9. Carby, *Reconstructing Womanhood*, p. 32; see also Davis, *Women, Race and Class* and Hooks, *Feminist Theory*.

10. Leab, *From Sambo to Superspade*, p. 213.

11. Jane Gaines, "White Privilege and Looking Relations: Race and Gender in Feminist Film Theory," *Cultural Critique* 4 (1986): 75.

12. Gaines, "White Privilege," p. 71.

13. Given the film's clear support of black enterprise, it is perhaps significant that Berry Gordy, head of Motown Industries, produced and directed *Mahogany*. As Gaines writes, "[w]ith *Mahogany*, Motown president and founder Berry Gordy . . . helps Diana Ross make something of herself again (on a larger scale) just as he helped so many aspiring recording artists by coaching them in money management and social decorum in his talent school" (ibid., p. 73).

14. Robert Stam and Louise Spence, "Colonialism, Racism and Representation," *Screen* 24, no. 2 (1983): 3.

15. Susan Jeffords's discussion of the representation of white men as cultural victims in *The Remasculinization of America: Gender and the Vietnam War* (Bloomington: Indiana University Press, 1989) has been instrumental in my analysis of *Lethal Weapon*.

16. The sequel, *Lethal Weapon II* (1989), almost completely omits Murtaugh's wife and daughter in its narrative while still articulating the white male figure as the central player in a drama that is significantly about the evilness of the South African Aparthied regime. By thus foregrounding race as a difference that matters only *elsewhere* and never here in the United States, the sequel nonetheless continues to construct the black male as the castrated figure, as evinced by in his inability to control his daughter's sex-

uality—she poses as a model for a condom commercial—and in the scene in which Riggs must rescue Murtaugh from a toilet wired with explosives. In this way, the second film similarly prepares the way for the white male figure to once again play the role of cultural hero and even more gratuitously lingers over the masochistic spectacle of the white male body in pain.

17. I use quotations around "racial difference" to indicate the problematical construction of such a notion, for its operation in feminist theory—like U.S. culture at large—is to designate and mark an "Other" body, for example, black, Hispanic, or Asian, but never to interrogate the racial difference that is whiteness.

18. Spelman, *Inessential Woman*, p. x.

Postmodern Modes
of Ethnicity

I want to begin this exploration of the representation and cultural meanings of *ethnicity* in contemporary American cinema with a scenario set in the early 1920s. Imagine, if you will, a giant black pot has been built outside the gates of a large automobile factory in preparation for a festival sponsored by its owner, Henry Ford. The day of celebration arrives. Into the pot go "groups of gaily dressed immigrants dancing and singing their native songs." And out of the pot emerges "a single stream of Americans dressed alike in the contemporary standard dress and singing the national anthem."[1] Eventually the music of tarantellas and polkas and other ethnic dances fades away, and the rising sound of the "Star Spangled Banner" is heard as the last of the immigrants is absorbed into an intensely patriotic, identically dressed, and utterly homogeneous American chorus.

This highly cinematic scenario seems as if it might have come from some forthcoming Monty Python or Robert Townsend film, or from a projected companion piece to Milos Forman's *Ragtime* (1981) or David Byrne's *True Stories* (1986). That is, we would be hard-pressed to take its representation as a serious or sincere and moving commentary on ethnic experience in America. Rather, its blatant lack of subtlety, its dramatic literalism in regard to the metaphor of the "melting pot," and its vision of a wholly assimilated, self-identical and identified American culture seems at once outrageously simple, crudely funny, and reflexively ironic. Nonetheless, it is more than likely that in the early 1920s when it was staged, this melting-pot scenario did touch the hearts of the spectators who watched it—not on a movie screen, but as the culmination of an actual public festival. At a time when a massive influx of diverse European immigrants challenged the dominant myth of American national community, main-line Henry Ford's ritual of "forced conversion,"[2] and its celebration of total ethnic transformation and assimilation, must not only have been utterly sincere in the demands it made of its participants, but also patriotically stirring and deeply reassuring to its spectators.

Today, however, it is nearly impossible to imagine that spectators might be brought to tears by such a scene unless they were tears of laughter—for even as we live and go about our business as members of what we think of as contemporary "American culture," most of us are fully aware that, insofar as the term signifies a clearly bounded and unified category of social being, *there is no such thing*. The closest counterparts we can find to Ford's scenario of total conversion and assimilation occur in the fantastic and patently simulated "small" worlds of Disneyland and other American theme parks—or in such parodic and ironic films as Woody Allen's *Zelig* (1983), Paul Mazursky's *Moscow on the Hudson* (1984), or John Sayles's *The Brother from Another Planet* (1984). All three take Ford's utopian vision of complete assimilation to a similar extreme, and yet each, in its own way, also wryly turns that vision back on itself. *Zelig*, for example, gives us a Human Chameleon as the central figure of a "mock documentary," someone so desirous of fitting in that he literally—and, of necessity, continually—assumes the ethnic, linguistic, and even occupational characteristics of those around him. New York, to the Russian defector in *Moscow on the Hudson*, is *all* ethnic, so assimilation ironically means *not* fitting in—just like everyone else. And in *The Brother From Another Planet*, total assimilation is viewed totally ironically as a black alien from outer space is easily absorbed into the marginalized black culture of that "outer" (if still terrestrial) space alien-ated as Harlem. In highly conscious ways, these films foreground Werner Sollors's suggestion in *Beyond Ethnicity* that "In America, casting oneself as an outsider may in fact be considered a dominant cultural trait. . . . Every American is now considered a potential ethnic."[3] Yet, if every American is literally and narratively "cast" as an "outsider" or ethnic "other" (as they are in these films), then the meaning of "American-ness" as it is constituted through assimilation—described as an inclusionary and culturally dominant "sameness,"—and composed of "insiders" loses its conceptual and experiential validity.

Zelig, Moscow on the Hudson, and *The Brother from Another Planet* are both symptomatic and explicitly aware of our contemporary confusion and ironic doubt about what, in earlier moments of our public history, seemed much more clear-cut. Today the distinctions and boundary conditions implicit in the terms *American* and *ethnic* and the concept of a unified and singular *culture* are widely and commonly experienced as problematic, if not indeed paradoxical. Likewise, the experiential ground upon which notions of "ethnic difference" or "assimilation" were based is no longer the same terrain traversed by the participants and spectators of Henry Ford's "melting-pot" pageant. We now live in an age when electronic interfaces and instant communication have nearly erased the boundaries and distances of national geography. A pervasive and dispersed global network of commercial franchise has sent Kentucky Fried Chicken to Beijing and Holiday Inns everywhere—and pizza has become America's "national" food supplanting the "all-American" frankfurter. Multinational corporations and international co-production challenge the "Buy American" legacy of Henry Ford to market nationally ambiguous automobiles—and movies.[4] In effect, we are hard-pressed to locate where, what, and who is either "all-American" or "ethnic."

Indeed, the very idea of making such a clear-cut distinction, of being sure of what kind of difference constitutes a radical or meaningful difference in a culture both over(and under)whelmed by distinctions and differences, has been transformed in contemporary experience. A *TV Guide* article sharply foregrounds the paradoxical way in which our shopping-mall and television culture has both magnified and trivialized the value of distinction and difference. "It's a world in which Revlon now makes 158 shades of lipstick, in which there are 36 sizes and flavors of Crest toothpaste, and in which, in about half of all American homes, there are more than 20 TV channels to choose from. . . . We can choose from 33 flavors of a single brand of cat food . . . , at least 227 different types and sizes of shampoo, and 481 models of new cars."[5] Horrific a thought as it may be to those of us who abhor the temptations of consumer culture and are loathe to praise it, it just may be Revlon, Clairol, and contact lens manufacturers that ultimately trivialize the significance of the visible markers that permit racial discrimination—by selling us a leveling and meaningless range of *too many* skin, lip, hair, and eye colors with which we may construct and represent ourselves. On the one hand, all this choice seems to foreground the heterogeneous quality of our "culture"—that is, the latter's constitution as a seeming multiplicity of singular individuals, ethnic cultures, and idiosyncratic subcultures upon which we can borrow. On the other hand, however, the leveling of differences through their trivialized assertion and proliferation points simultaneously (and paradoxically) to the homogeneous quality of "mass culture"—that is, to both the common social experiences and generic representations we share of this artfully and artificially constructed heterogeneity, and to the peculiar and dulled lack of discrimination that seems to emerge as an effect of too much diversity, of having too many choices among too many differences. If, in this culture of advanced capitalism, we all cast ourselves as outsiders, as Sollors suggests we do, then we are all also insiders—and the distinction between cultural outsider and insider becomes meaninglessly reversible, or is self-consciously experienced as an "acute sense of doubleness."[6]

In an earlier time, being ethnic meant being part of a marginalized, yet coherent and relatively stable social group—one both perceived and represented by the dominant (and unethnic or assimilated) culture and by its own members as exclusively different and other from that dominant culture by virtue of its maintenance of specific codes of language, dress, manner, kinship, social and religious structure, and of its particular history and mythology. Thus, being ethnic meant having a cultural identity structured and regulated by the constraints of *descent*—whereas being American (unethnic, assimilated) meant having a cultural identity structured and transformed by the freedoms of *consent*. As Sollors elaborates: "Descent language emphasizes our positions as heirs, our hereditary qualities, liabilities, and entitlements; consent language stresses our abilities as mature free agents and 'architects of our fates' to choose our spouses, our destinies, and our political systems."[7] Regarded from another perspective, we can suggest that descent—with its stress on maintaining connections with cultural origins and roots— also emphasizes a "natural" and/or "authentic" mode of cultural identity, whereas consent—with its stress on the conscious choice and construction of social being—emphasizes the "assumption" of cultural identity, and the latter's ultimately theatrical and "inauthentic" nature as always a "re-presentation" of self.

We live in what seems to be the advanced stages of an age of representation, and thus we are perhaps more aware of the inauthenticity and theatricality of "being American" than were either Ford's pageant participants or its spectators. We have been marked indelibly and made unprecedentedly self-conscious by television and its entailment of consumer culture. We exist at a moment when identity, memory, and history are re-cognized as mediated and media productions—constructed and consumable images available for countless acts of recombination, revision, and recycling. We are also part of a society which experiences the particularity of celebrity more intimately than it does the coherence of community. In this context, nearly all those visible markers that once separated the cultures of "ethnic" descent from the "American" culture of consent, that signaled the boundaries of otherness and gave it ethnic identity, integrity, and authenticity, are detached from their original historical roots and have become "floating signifiers" available for purchase by anyone. Ethnicity, too, seems based on consent. We can put ourselves together in almost any fashion we like—and our self-consciousness about so inventing ourselves tends to be reflected in the fact that the fashion we like asserts this "right of representation" through pastiche or parody, through a scavenging or playful ironizing of those costumes, speech, and manners that once were held separate and discrete and that conferred upon a portion of the culture's members their particular identity, history, and sense of community.

In such a contemporary context as ours, then, the allegorical drama of Henry Ford's melting-pot scenario is more than likely to be interpreted ironically—as a denial or interrogation of that which it also asserts. This is because the normative standard (being "uniformly American") the scenario provided against which that value called "ethnicity" could be clearly and simply identified is no longer perceived as having much experiential or symbolic validity. If the norm of a uniform, stable, and single notion of what it is to be American no longer holds, then a stable or sure notion of what it is to be ethnic also weakens.

The sense we make of both American-ness and ethnicity is highly dependent upon the coexistence of and negotiation between cultures of descent and consent, upon the construction of such conceptual boundaries and their trespass. However, given our current self-inventiveness, our reflexivity about who and what we are and what we look like, our ability to assume a cultural identity not originally our own or to make one up from scavenging bits and pieces of the cultural identity of others, these once discrete categories have become so contaminated and their boundaries so trespassed that their outline and content are no longer visible. Rather, the constructed and provisional nature of *all* identity is what we see, and this vision of social being radically calls into question the oppositional terms and relations which, for Sollors, bound American culture as such. The notion of an "ethnic," "American," "authentic," or "invented" self conflate as *all* selves are perceived as chosen and constructed by consent—even ethnic ones.

Within the context of this theatrical and "play-full" reflexivity we have about our own personae, it is hardly surprising that a film such as Norman Jewison's *Moonstruck* (1987), for example, makes ironic its own nostalgia for the "authenticity" of Italian-American "experience."[8] On the one hand, the comedy's charm emerges from its sentimental romanticism and loving celebration of a discrete ethnic community based on descent, but, on the other, its parodic bite comes from a self-mocking use of grand opera as ironic commentary on the theatrical excesses of its Italian characters and, indeed, as a gloss on the consensual construction of "Italian-ness" itself.

It is clear, then, that since the historical occurrence of Ford's pageant in the early 1920s, various events of a social, economic, and technological kind have moved us (indeed, forced us) toward our contemporary acknowledgement of "the mixed, plural and contradictory nature" of the age in which we live, an age "caught between 'myths of totality' and 'ideologies of fracture',"[9] an age whose historically unique characteristics, cultural values, and representations have been described, theorized, and debated as *postmodern.* These descriptions, theories, and debates have implications for our understanding of the way we newly perceive and value ethnicity and for the way these new perceptions and values find representation in contemporary American cinema.

For cultural critics such as Fredric Jameson, postmodernism is virtually a global term that describes a new and unprecedented "cultural logic"[10]—a logic that emerges from and informs all aspects of those cultures based on and homogenized by multinational capitalism and its new technologies of production, consumption, and communication. While coextensive with other and earlier logics of structuring and representing social experience (for example, realism and modernism), the new logic of postmodernism has become culturally dominant—altering the previous sense we lived and made of time, space, the world, and ourselves, and both consciously and unconsciously transforming *all* our cultural productions, whether radical and progressive or traditional and conservative. This totalized cultual transformation of sense, meaning, and value is revealed in certain novel esthetic values and features seen as characteristic of postmodern representation—among them, "a new depthlessness, which finds its prolongation . . . in a whole new culture of the image or the simulacrum," and "a consequent weakening of historicity, both in our relationship to public History and in the new forms of our private temporality. . . . "[11] We are seen as living on the surface—the screen—of things, engaged with the play of display. We are seen as subjectively decentered and dislocated in space and time. Our individual identities and memories and particular histories have been objectified and circulated as images and supplanted by the simulated and extroverted memories and history given us by the visual media.

Correlatively, our social and ethnic affinities have been supplanted by affinities of consumption and cosmetic display. What once was an emotional investment in and subjective connection to a specific community and its historical past has been objectified, dispersed, and transformed into free-floating stimulation and consumer desire. This general and detached rather than specific and grounded interest in community and history leads to the practice of what Jameson describes as "aesthetic populism"—a kind of wonderment at and valuation of everything ordinary and banal, an embrace and incorporation of the "whole 'degraded' landscape of schlock and kitsch, of TV series and *Readers' Digest* culture, of advertising and motels, of the late show and the grade-B Hollywood film, of so-called paraliterature with its airport paperback categories. . . . "[12] Lacking a sense of our roots, distanced from the gravitational pull of community and history, we have become strangers to our own lives—transients, tourists, cultural anthropologists who estheticize the everyday and wonder indiscriminately at everything.

The leveling of value described in this ultimately negative version of postmodernism is a consequence of living in a capitalist, high-tech, media culture. While in some ways liberating us from a stuffy and arbitrary allegiance to old traditions and canons, such a free-floating and indiscriminate interest in cultural flotsam and jetsam also suggests the end of old forms of human connection and cohesion, and seems to offer little hope for the kind of historical consciousness that would be responsible to either a past or a future. Bits and pieces of identities and artifacts once historically and personally located now primarily cohere in the *simulated* history and memory of the media—generally sensed as subjectively "ours," but given to us by others as objective images, rather like the photographs given to *Blade Runner's* replicant Rachael as testament to a memory not really her own. Increasingly estranged from a personal connection to memory and history by this pervasive awareness of mediation and its objectifications, we now nostalgically collect or schizophrenically combine the fragmented remains of history into an ahistorical pastiche put together somewhat like Madonna's costumes. Indeed, in the age of such supremely self-conscious, self-constructed, and invented presences as Madonna and Prince, it would seem that the previous historicity, specificity, and force of ethnic identification have re-solved themselves into a more general and provisional identification with individual fashion and generic subcultures.

Thus, many of the more cultish films of the 1980s seem to subsume questions of ethnicity under broader questions about the specificity, nature, and location of human identity, memory, and history in an age of media, microchips, and multinationals. We can see such inquiry going on not only in Ridley Scott's *Blade Runner* (1982) with its "more human than human" replicants and "less human than human" human beings, but also in Aaron Lipstadt's comic *Android* (1982). Max—the title figure and protagonist—not only contemplates the difference between humans and their simulations, but also is completely "image conscious"; "aware of his own existential status as an imitation," he "still strives to further model himself after images of images: the personae of Jimmy Stewart and Humphrey Bogart he has seen in old movies."[13] Susan Seidelman's *Making Mr. Right* (1987) has a heroine who is an "image consultant" and falls in love with a "perfect man" of an android, while Paul Verhoeven's *RoboCop* (1987) gives us the cyborg Murphy, half man, half robot, who fights crime in an America ruled by corporations and pervaded by mindless television game shows and an endless stream of commercials. In an age of electronic reproduction and replication, these films and others are compelled less by the specific otherness of *ethnic* being than by the technological challenge made to the generic status and sameness of *human* being.

Other contemporary films level ethnicity rather than hierarchically subsume it under a more general problem. That is, they dramatize its *lack* of meaningful difference from any other difference. For example, by using one performer for the two major roles in *Liquid Sky* (1983), it might be argued that Russian emigré director Slava Tsukerman was filming an allegory of that "acute sense of doubleness" Werner Sollors identifies as marking ethnic consciousness. Yet the film's exploration of cultural identity and alienation is so diffused and dispersed that it tends to refuse such a reading. Instead, the performer's "split subjectivity" as Margaret/Jimmy *erases* the differences between human and alien other, between gender and sexual preference, and disperses itself across the overdetermined differences within a punk-rock, new-wave, Soho, drug subculture that is fatally preyed upon by extraterrestrials who (like the subculture's own "members") feed off its orgasmic and heroin highs. Similarly, Alex Cox's *Repo Man* (1984) may evoke traces of ethnic and racial cultures (and their stereotyping by dominant culture) in the persons of two notorious Hispanic car thieves and a number of broadly drawn black characters. Nonetheless, their cultural "otherness" or "difference" is made narratively meaningless in a world in which everyone is equivalently other and different and wired into their own version of reality. What we get in this bizarre and episodic comedy is a leveling of difference that generates *sameness* across an endless series of small differences among small differences which ultimately do not make enough of a difference to matter. In these films and others like them cultural identity, indeed personal identity, is always provisional and always representational.

Thus ethnic consciousness is flattened into a more culturally pervasive self-consciousness. On the one hand, it is telling that it is a character named Roberta Glass who is *Desperately Seeking Susan* in Seidelman's 1985 postmodern comic pastiche about amnesia and switched identities. The suggestion of Jewishness about the name (and Roberta's circumstances as a bored, suburban New Jersey housewife) should give one pause, as should the fact that the Susan who arouses Roberta's curiosity in a personals column, the Susan she longs to be, is hardly coded as Jewish—played (and costumed) as she is by Madonna. On the other hand, the cultural and personal identities at stake in this film have little to do with Jewishness or WASPishness, so Roberta's name does not give pause. Instead, the film celebrates the picaresque possibilities of inventing and changing identities, of being different from oneself, of assuming other people's lives and living them as theatrical experience.

Most of the aforementioned films and others like them describe and dramatize the liberating possibilities of this more generalized and provisional kind of cultural identity and identification. Only a relative few suggest that self-invention and the ability to choose and construct identity might be seriously problematic. Thus, it is not surprising that many of these films are *comedies* of errors, of mistaken identities. It is also not surprising that a great many also borrow upon the science fiction film—given the genre's aliens, androids, travel across time and space, and its imagination of transformation.[14] As Werner Sollors points out, noting that Mario Puzo, who is Italian, wrote its screenplay, *Superman—The Movie* (1978) is "the ultimate immigrant saga."[15]

However, such a remark should not lead us to the immediate conclusion that these films are *repressing* their ethnic consciousness and concerns by disguising and hiding them. Rather, it might suggest that within the context of postmodern culture, those once highly charged affects generated by the representation of ethnicity in its relations to dominant culture have lost most of their emotional force. They are now weakened—more diffuse and free-floating than they are unconsciously condensed and displaced in the metaphoric representations of a "dream work" which, of necessity, dramatizes its repressed problematic in more psychically bearable form.[16] That is, ethnicity does not seem to be so much repressed and disguised in such films as *Blade Runner* or Jim Jarmusch's *Stranger than Paradise* (1984) as it is dispersed and defused—explicitly part of the mise-en-scène, yet subordinate to what seem to be the more pressing problems, pleasures, dislocations, and curiosities of constructing identity in postmodern culture. It seems hardly accidental that despite the pointed punning of its title, Graham Baker's *Alien Nation* (1988), although seeming to address allegorically ethnic difference and cultural discrimination in a science fiction framework, actually diffuses these concerns with a lack of specificity and a comic tone. The immigrant, alien "slags" are seen as having a few ethnocentric idiosyncracies and encountering a generalized and Archie Bunker-ish bigotry—but both idiosyncracy and bigotry are overcome through the generic diffusions and resolutions of the conventional "buddy cop" narrative.

Blade Runner provides a related example. Its confusion and conflation of human and technological (or "replicated") being transforms the problem of ethnic assimilation into the problem of human simulation (fig. 12.1). The narrative fact that the film's Los Angeles of 2019 is a polyglot megalopolis apparently dominated by signs of Japanese culture from SONY to sushi seems less a comment on ethnicity as a mode of being than on the objective conditions of international economics. Issues of racial discrimination, the nature of cultural and personal memory and history, issues of identity and its markers, or otherness and the kind of difference that makes a difference—these are dramatized through the confrontation and confusion between human and replicant, not between American and Japanese. Indeed, the Oriental domination of Los Angeles in *Blade Runner* is effectively defused and diffused by the impression the mise-en-scène gives us of a cultural crazy quilt, of an ethnic pas-

12.1. The replicants (Rutger Hauer and Daryl Hannah) in *Blade Runner*, a film in which the problem of ethnic assimilation is transformed into the problem of human simulation.

tiche. As Jameson suggests, "advanced capitalist countries today are now a field of stylistic and discursive heterogeneity without a norm."[17] That is, there is a neutral mimicry of forms of ethnic specificity in *Blade Runner*, but the forms have lost their distinctive meaning, their affective content, and become blanks. Indeed, Deckard remarks upon the hybrid, pidgin language of the city—narratively commenting upon (as does the mise-en-scène's flashing signs and advertisements) what Jameson sees as "a linguistic fragmentation of social life . . . to the point where the norm itself is eclipsed: reduced to a neutral and reified media speech (far enough from the Utopian aspirations of the inventors of Esperanto or Basic English), which . . . becomes one more idiolect among many."[18] Thus, "Japanese-ness" in *Blade Runner* is not represented as a rich form of social being which generates the effects of ethnic identification. Rather, its representation constitutes part of a much cooler and more global economic code.

This dispersal, diffusion, and devaluation of ethnic specificity and identification in the cultural pastiche that marks Jameson's version of postmodernism is perhaps most blatantly articulated by the hybrid hero of W. D. Richter's *The Adventures of Buckaroo Banzai: Across the Eighth Dimension* (1984). Born of an American mother and Japanese father, Buckaroo is a race-car driver, neurosurgeon, physicist, rock star, and adventurer in time and space who lacks personhood in any psychological or historical sense. All "image and action," Buckaroo Banzai (much like his name) is hybrid: "made up of pieces of the pop cultural landscape, and . . . defined moment by moment—each one erasing any smudges of history from the last— by aggressive actions."[19] Suffering no angst about his mixed ethnic origins, no dis-ease with his lack of rootedness in time or space, Buckaroo's philosophy could stand as the celebratory slogan of those living in the ahistoricist present tense of postmodern culture: "Remember," he says, "wherever you go, there you are."

Indeed, this philosophy seems to inform the entire narrative and esthetic structure of *Stranger than Paradise* and Jarmusch's second film, *Down by Law*. Here, too, we see the vestiges of ethnic identity, traces of something which has lost nearly all its meaning—as has the specificity and distinctiveness of time and space. In *Stranger than Paradise*, sixteen-year-old Eva has come from her native Hungary to visit her cousin Willie and his friend Eddie in New York City before going to live with her aunt in Cleveland; after being bored in both New York and Cleveland, the three drive off to be bored in Florida. The cultural and geographical specificity here is hilarious by virtue of its meaningless differentiation and the characters' general indifference to it—and to everything else. Eva's "Hungarian-ness" is barely marked and she expresses only a minimal and short-lived curiosity about things American. Wherever they go, there they are—the characters' spontaneity about going on the road and their adventures comically fragmented and minimalized both by their passivity and lack of discrimination and the filmmaker's (who uses the same long takes, fades, and static set-ups to record everything and every place with an equivalent lack or plenitude of emphasis). In sum, although the cultural logic of postmodernism is liberating in its capacity for self-invention, its embrace and leveling of difference, and its effacement of discrimination, it achieves this liberation through a correlative flattening and dulling of his historical and political consciousness.

There are cultural critics, however, who offer a less global and more positive version of postmodernism. Linda Hutcheon, for example, is more sanguine than Jameson about the possibilities for responsible social and historical existence in the high-tech and consumer culture of representation, and she offers another conceptual framework within which to think about contemporary changes in the meaning and value of ethnicity. This version of postmodernism operates not within the deep structure of an informative and pervasive cultural logic, but rather as a highly explicit and reflexive "cultural activity that can be discerned in most art forms and many currents of thought today." For Hutcheon, "postmodernism is a . . . phenomenon that uses and abuses, installs and then subverts, the very concepts it challenges." It is "fundamentally contradictory, resolutely historical and inescapably political."[20] Rather than a weakening of historicity that leads to the nostalgic scavenging of bits and pieces of the past in which Jameson sees as "the well-nigh universal practice today of . . . pastiche," Hutcheon sees postmodernist representation as a culturally limited phenomenon that institutes a very specific "critical revisiting, an ironic dialogue with the past of both art and society, a recalling of a critically shared vocabulary of . . . forms."[21] This dialogue is not merely comic—nor is it a pastiche cannibalized, as Jameson would have it, from random bits and pieces of the past in an "imitation of dead styles," and in a "speech through all the masks and voices stored up in the imaginary museum of now global culture."[22]

Not denying many of the features Jameson describes as unique to the consumer and media culture of multinational capitalism, Hutcheon nonetheless suggests that "contemporaneity need not signify wholesale implication without critical consciousness." For Hutcheon, such critical consciousness is constituted in postmodern representation through parody and it is governed by irony. Neither a random cannibalization or "ridiculing" imitation of past forms, parodic representation uses "historical memory" and "aesthetic introversion" systematically to initiate a "kind of self-reflexive discourse" that "is always inextricably bound to social discourse"[23] in its conscious recontextualization of past historical and esthetic elements in relation to a present which will change their meaning. Parody, then, is a "repetition with critical distance that allows ironic signaling of difference at the very heart of similarity." This repetition or formal doubling offers "a perspective on the present and the past which allows an artist to speak TO a discourse from WITHIN it, but without being totally recuperated by it."[24]

Here, for illustrative purposes, consider again *Moonstruck*'s reflexive use of grand opera and how, by doubling and thus drawing emphatic attention to the characters' grand—and Italian—passions, the music paradoxically both asserts and undermines their authenticity and makes us conscious of romance and specific ethnic enactments of it—as social and historical constructs. Our laughter at and affection for the characters emerge from the critical distance at which the film's parodic form positions us—and from which we can see romance and "Italian-ness" as fictions. As Hutcheon suggests, this exposure of the fictional and ideological premises upon which specific historical and social forms of heterosexual relations and ethnicity are based, "does not necessarily destroy their 'truth' value, but it does define the conditions of that 'truth'. Such a process reveals rather than conceals the tracks of the signifying systems that constitute our world—that is, systems constructed by us in answer to our needs. However important these systems are, they are not natural, given or universal."[25]

Postmodern parody with its doubling of forms, and irony with its contradictory structure of assertion and denial, constitute texts that consciously make us aware of being both cultural insiders and outsiders, of being always provisionally positioned in a plurality of histories and societies. Thus, postmodern texts create that "acute sense of doubleness" which Sollors identifies with "ethnic consciousness" and Hutcheon with "critical consciousness"—both engaged in an ongoing dialogue with the premises of their culture. This is a far cry from that more systemic than systematic version of postmodernism whose pervasive cultural logic levels and flattens value, views the proliferation of distinctions and differences as finally not making much of a difference, and—by virtue of its consciousness of mediation and representation—nostalgically mourns or celebrates the end of history. This postmodernism, according to Hutcheon, is both dystopic and naive in its "reductive belief that any recall of the past must, by definition, be sentimental nostalgia or antiquarianism." Indeed, the formal and thematic contradictions of postmodern representation "confront and contest any . . . discarding or recuperating of the past in the name of the future." Parody and irony function "to call attention both to what is being contested and what is being offered as a critical response to that, and . . . do so in a self-aware way that admits its own provisionality."[26]

This is, in fact, precisely what certain films do in relation to the contemporary value or meaning of ethnicity: parodically and ironically contest it, and critically engage it in a dialogue with its own past meanings so as to explicitly foreground both its current value and that value's historical and cultural provisionality. These are films which do not disperse and diffuse ethnicity across other kinds of difference or subsume it under more general explorations of cultural identity. Rather, they address ethnic consciousness and its

12.2. Leonard Zelig (Woody Allen), the "meta-person" who both affirms and denies the possibility of total ethnic transformation in *Zelig*.

changing context directly—foregrounding it as a contradictory, paradoxical, and multivalent experience. Thus we return to those films mentioned at the beginning of this chapter which parody and ironize Henry Ford's melting-pot scenario by recontextualizing it in the present, doubling and exaggerating its formal structure, and simultaneously affirming and denying its cultural values: *Zelig, Moscow on the Hudson,* and *The Brother from Another Planet.*

Zelig institutes a critical dialogue with Henry Ford's celebratory notion of total ethnic conversion and assimilation (as well as the naive literalization of the melting pot) by taking it to its parodic limits. By descent, the "originally" Jewish protagonist, Leonard Zelig, is conceived as a single "meta-person" whose parodically continual representation both generalizes and makes literal the very structure and function of ethnic conversion and assimilation in a way that *affirms* the fact and possible value of total ethnic transformation (fig. 12.2). Assuming a multitude of body types and occupations to become "perfectly" black, Italian, Chinese, French, Irish, Catholic, and Greek, Leonard Zelig has so deep a need to fit in with those in his immediate vicinity that he is the Human Chameleon. "It's safe to be like the others," he tells his psychiatrist. "I want to be liked." At the same time, however, his parodic and literally repetitious representation of this assimilative process denies both its successful achievement and its value. Caught up in a dynamic of continual transformation and always provisional assimilation, "Zelig's own existence," as the voice-over narrator tells us, "is a non-existence"; he is "a cipher, a non-person" rather than "the useful *self-possessed* citizen" his psychiatrist sees as the model of civic and psychic health.

Zelig calls explicit attention to the fictional status of ethnic identity, interrogates the problematic nature of its specificity, and emphasizes its very existence as always provisional. On the one hand, Zelig's ability to assume the physical, linguistic, and occupational characteristics of those who surround him ironically literalizes the ethnic "dis-ease" of the cultural Other, the desire to fit in—and, on the other hand, paradoxically points to everyone's very normal and continuous construction and revision of him or herself as always different. The newspaper headline that announces "Human Who Transforms Self Discovered" ironically refers to us all—and denies while it affirms traditional notions of both ethnic identity and cultural assimilation.

Finally, *Zelig* is supremely reflexive and historical, its parodic documentary form both allowing Zelig's capacity for transformation and assimilation to enter into dialogue with, among other historical phenomena, Hitler's fascism and accommodating a range of voice-over commentaries and analyses from fictional documentary narrators and real cultural critics. At the film's beginning, for example, Irving Howe tells us that Zelig's "story reflected the nature of our civilization, the character of our times, yet it was also one man's story, and all the themes of our culture were there: heroism, will, things like that." But later he tells us that Zelig's case "reflected the Jewish story in America—he wanted to assimilate like crazy." The polyphony of voices and opinions and the mixture of fictional characters and real people create continual debate about the on-going and provisional nature of the construction and meaning of ethnic and American experience.

Both *Moscow on the Hudson* and *The Brother from Another Planet* also parodically repeat Ford's scenario of the assimilation of ethnic difference from a critical distance. They too insist upon and make explicit the "ironic discontinuity . . . at the heart of continuity," the "difference at the heart of similarity"[27] as well as paradoxically revealing the reverse: the ironic continuity of discontinuity and the

12.3. Robin Williams and Cleavant Derricks in *Moscow on the Hudson*, a film suggesting that all Americans are ultimately ethnics.

homogeneously similar experience we all have of difference. One of the characteristics of advanced capitalist society is the "increasing tendency towards uniformity in mass culture," a uniformity which Hutcheon sees postmodern representation as challenging, but also not denying. Postmodern representation "does seek to assert difference, not homogeneous identity, but the very concept of difference could be said to entail a typically postmodernist contradiction: 'difference,' unlike 'otherness,' has no exact opposite against which to define itself."[28] This is precisely the theme whose contradictions are put into play in the ethnic explorations of both *Moscow on the Hudson* and *The Brother from Another Planet*.

In *Moscow on the Hudson* (fig. 12.3), an illuminating moment occurs that parallels Ford's conversion scenario in which ethnic otherness is transformed into its opposite: American sameness. The scene is at once sentimental and ironic. Lucia, the Italian heroine, joins a virtual United Nations of other former immigrants to become a citizen of the United States. The unity of the disparate congregation pledging its allegiance to America affirms and revisits Ford's melting-pot conversion. Yet it does so critically and paradoxically and the possibility of the total conversion and assimilation of ethnic Others is denied as well as affirmed. It is denied and affirmed by the black woman judge who administers the oath of citizenship, her presence a simultaneous, contradictory, and visible marker both of ultimate assimilation and social ascension, and of racial and gender otherness not all that easily assimilated or socially transcended.[29]

Moscow on the Hudson also tests Ford's traditional concept of otherness (which has an opposite) against the postmodern concept of "difference" or "differences." The film's representation of New York suggests that *all* Americans are ethnics—whether national, racial, or religious. And it is hardly Ford's melting pot. The film's primary and running joke is that no one in the melting pot has exactly "melted"—possibly because there is virtually no one in the entire city who can serve as the "standard American" upon whom assimilation might be modeled and against whom it might be judged. Indeed, the film begins on a bus as a Frenchman asks Vladimir, the Russian protagonist, directions while we see out the bus's window a delicatessen sign advertising "Italian-Heroes" and a Hassidic Jew in traditional dress walks by. Thus, in context, the plot complication later initiated by Lucia's romantic rejection of Vladimir when she becomes a citizen because he's still an ethnic Other and not merely a "different" American like she is functions parodically as well as sentimentally.

Indeed, throughout the film Mazursky destroys the neat binary *opposition* of Ford's vision of ethnic otherness and American sameness ironically suggesting that in postmodern America such a system of definition has collapsed because its oppositional terms have become *reversible*. Ultimately the film posits American-ness as constituted from postmodernist difference, or as Hutcheon corrects this formulation, from postmodernist "differences, in the plural— always multiple and provisional."[30] As well, Mazursky suggests that the vicissitudes and freedoms of capitalism are the only homogenizing characteristics of American-ness. Not only does Vladimir defect in Bloomingdales, but his assimilation into American culture is also marked primarily by his economic movement up the lowest rungs of the occupational ladder—from kitchen dishwasher to selling novelties on the street to working at McDonalds to running his own hot dog stand to cab driver to limo driver to paid musician.

The Brother from Another Planet also simultaneously asserts and subverts the concept of ethnicity as otherness. It is a literal—and thus parodic—black comedy that plays out another highly ironic

12.4. Joe Morton in *The Brother from Another Planet*, a postmodern play of paradox and contradiction, here a doubly negative form of alienation.

version of Ford's vision of total assimilation, but in such a manner and context that traditional ethnic otherness and postmodernist difference are paradoxically conflated as sameness, and yet also foregrounded and maintained as two separate systems of conceiving ethnicity. Like *Moscow on the Hudson*, the film complicates the binary neatness of the opposition between Ford's vision of ethnic otherness and American sameness, but unlike that film, *The Brother from Another Planet* does not suggest that those oppositional terms have lost their cultural value. Instead, it parodies this opposition by narratively *repeating* it. If, as Hutcheon suggests, that parody functions as "a critical revisiting,"[31] then the film both explicitly performs and literalizes this function with its narrative of emigration, space travel, and assimilation explicitly and critically repeating and commenting upon an earlier historical narrative which did not resolve itself in happy assimilation.

Representing ethnic and immigrant otherness, a black alien from outer space lands significantly first on Ellis Island (fig. 12.4) and then in Harlem—where black American Others live out their idiosyncratic differences in the homogeneous and ghettoized sameness of a terrestrial and marginalized "outer" space. Parodying American history, the black alien is a runaway slave being tracked by two white aliens (who, along with two other white men inadvertently lost in Harlem, stand out as alien in context). Yet the otherness of the alien to his hunters is apparently not his blackness at all—but, instead, the physical characteristic of only having three toes on each foot instead of five. Foregrounded here (however cheap the joke) are both the arbitrariness and the power of the particular difference that makes a difference and thereby constitutes otherness.

In sum, Sayles wickedly presents us with a double negative of otherness and difference, effectively both erasing and foregrounding racial ethnicity as at once a double segregation of otherness and a positive assimilation to difference. In its postmodern play of paradox and contradiction, *The Brother from Another Planet* parodically revisits racial inequality and finds the mathematics yield ironic results: ethnic differences are collapsed by blackness into a homogeneous and oppositional otherness which still stands against the whiteness (and five toe-dness) of standard Americans.

These films and quite a number of others directly address the reformulation of ethnicity and ethnic consciousness in postmodern culture. This ethnic consciousness is no longer experienced as something natural based on tradition and descent or as something to be assimilated to and converted in the melting pot. Rather, it is experienced as something cultural which must be constantly invented, consented to, and negotiated with other social beings. Caught up in a dialogue with a past in which it *was* always different than it *is*, ethnicity is presently perceived as provisional, historical, and in continual transformation. It is experienced as a parodic process of self-revision through representations that are ironically aware of and explicit about the social—and symbolic—construction of reality. Contemporary ethnic differences make a different kind of difference than when Henry Ford built his melting pot. Indeed, the paradoxical and contradictory experiences of contemporary ethnic consciousness as they are parodically and ironically made explicit in postmodernist films may be seen as a positive response to the more homogenizing aspects of life in shopping-mall and television culture. "Americans," writes Herbert Gans, "increasingly perceive themselves as undergoing cultural homogenization, and whether or not this perception is justified, they are constantly looking for new ways to establish their differences from each other."[32] In the worst instance, that new way to establish our differences from each other will be the creation of another one hundred fifty-eight shades of

Revlon lipstick. In the best instance, it will be the creation of a substantial, valuable, and polyvocal dialogue with our different pasts and our shared futures.

Postmodernism rejects the totalizing force of master narratives that would homogenize the diversity of cultural experiences into a single and generalized myth such as American-ness. Instead, it opts for the limited and local story that derives its primary value from a specificity that makes no general claims—or it deconstructs the master narratives and myths to expose and parody their contradictions. That is perhaps why the only films that deal explicitly with ethnic experience and that do not necessarily undermine their representations with parody or irony are biographies. Luis Valdez's *La Bamba* (1987) and *Stand and Deliver* (1988), for example, both make limited claims and do not generalize ethnic experience; both are also firmly (and by today's standards somewhat clearly) grounded in a finite historical moment. Such films as Wayne Wang's *Chan Is Missing* (1982) and *Dim Sum* (1985), Peter Wang's *A Great Wall* (1986), Spike Lee's *She's Gotta Have It* (1986) and *School Daze* (1988), and Robert Townsend's *Hollywood Shuffle* (1987) are localized films which play out the construction of American ethnic consciousness as a set of ironically small negotiations with both specific cultural traditions and dominant media represenations. Extremely self-aware of their own historical vision and cultural doubleness, the larger the claims these films make about ethnic experience, the more parodic and ironic become their form and content.

In line with the contradictions of postmodernist thought, Werner Sollors writes that

> Not only the assault on ethnic boundaries but also ethnic boundary construction itself may generate innovation and modernization. As Americans of different backgrounds share larger and larger areas of an overlapping culture, they keep insisting on symbolic distinctions (often not those of "ancient origin" but freshly invented ones), the process known as "ethnicization." Instead of looking at various ethnic traditions as merely growing from very parochial beginnings to modernist assimilation, we may also see ethnic identification itself as a modern phenomenon.[33]

However, also in the spirit of postmodernism, I will conclude with two contradictions which do not deny the preceding, but do make it more provisional. First, I want both to affirm and contradict Sollors by suggesting that the widespread culture awareness of the modern process of "ethnicization" as a symbolic project makes "ethnic identification itself " no longer a modern, but a postmodern phenomenon. And second, I want to affirm and contradict the symbolic nature of this process of "ethnicization" by pointing to the very real effects and limitations of this symbolization and our awareness of it.

In the middle of writing this chapter, on a Sunday evening heading elsewhere, I drove through what was for me a truly foreign and clearly hostile country—a poor Mexican-American neighborhood in Watsonville, California at that moment teeming with street life, most of it male. It struck me in a way that was not at all ironic that I, a white Jewish-American woman of middle-class means, would have been afraid to get out of the car there—and rightfully so given my femaleness and their maleness, my affluence and their poverty, my whiteness and their color. It also struck me—and this *was* an ironic recognition—that I had personally and historically hierarchized the importance of the differences that made a difference in a way hardly consonant with traditions in Ford's America. Now, at least at that moment, gender and class mattered much more than racial or cultural ethnicity.

As I left those streets behind me, I realized I could not tell if their ghettoized boundaries were imposed from without or chosen from within, and it did not matter if it was a little of both. What did matter was that I had the economic and racial privilege of a "critical distance" from which to contemplate the structure of my life-world and theirs. If parody is a critical revisiting of the "old ethnic neighborhood" and its self-representations, before that revisiting is possible one must first have the opportunity to leave it. In sum, the one big problem with the critical distance of postmodern parody, with reflexive and self-conscious irony, with the celebration of differences and their boundaries, is that *both* parties in a cultural negotiation need to recognize and share in them if we are to talk significantly about new forms of ethnic consciousness.

NOTES

1. Robert Bellah, "Evil and the American Ethos," in *Sanctions for Evil*, ed. Nevitt Sanford, Craig Comstock, et al. (San Francisco: Jossey-Bass, 1971), p. 181.

2. Bellah, "Evil and the American Ethos."

3. Werner Sollors, *Beyond Ethnicity: Consent and Descent in American Culture* (New York: Oxford University Press, 1986), pp. 31, 33.

4. In this context it is wonderfully ironic that recently the Ford Motor Company has joined with a certain Japanese automotive corporation to produce "all-American" vans.

5. Joanmarie Kalter, "Television as Value-Setter: Family," *TV Guide,* July 23, 1988, pp. 5, 11.

6. Sollors, *Beyond Ethnicity,* p. 249.

7. Ibid., p. 6.

8. The cast did, indeed, have a Brooklyn-Italian dialect coach to ensure ethnic specificity and authenticity—Julie Bovasso, who also played Aunt Rita.

9. Linda Hutcheon, "Beginning to Theorize Postmodernism," *Textual Practice* 1 (1987): 25.

10. See, for example, Fredric Jameson, "Postmodernism, or The Cultural Logic of Late Capitalism," *New Left Review* 146 (July-August 1984): 53–94.

11. Ibid., p. 58.

12. Ibid., pp. 54–55.

13. Vivian Sobchack, *Screening Space: The American Science Fiction Film* 2d ed. (New York: Ungar, 1987), p. 239. The last chapter, "Postfuturism," deals at length not only with the contemporary SF film's latent and manifest representation of the cultural logic of postmodernism, but also with the new cultural functions of the "alien other" in these films (pp. 223–305).

14. The imaginative possibilities for positive and liberating self-invention and transformation that science fiction encourages have drawn feminists to the genre. See Donna Haraway, "A Manifesto for Cyborgs," *Socialist Review* 80 (1985): 65–107.

15. Sollors, *Beyond Ethnicity,* p. 12.

16. "Affect," "condensation," "displacement," "dream work," and "repression" have specific meaning within the discourse of psychoanalysis and have informed much contemporary literary and film theory and analysis. For a brief elaboration of these specific meanings, see the following psychoanalytic "dictionary": J. Laplanche and J.-B. Pontalis, *The Language of Psycho-Analysis,* trans. Donald Nicholson-Smith (New York: W. W. Norton, 1973).

17. Jameson, "Postmodernism," p. 65.

18. Ibid.

19. Pat Aufderheide, "Sci-fi Discovers New Enemies," *In These Times,* November 21 - December 4, 1984, p. 30.

20. Hutcheon, "Beginning to Theorize Postmodernism," pp. 11, 10.

21. Jameson, "Postmodernism," p. 64; Hutcheon, "Beginning to Theorize Postmodernism," p. 11.

22. Jameson, "Postmodernism," p. 65.

23. Linda Hutcheon, "The Politics of Postmodernism: Parody and History," *Cultural Critique* 5 (1987): 185, n. 18; 204.

24. Hutcheon, "The Politics," pp. 185, 206.

25. Hutcheon, "Beginning to Theorize Postmodernism," p. 19.

26. Ibid., pp. 25, 19.

27. Ibid., p. 17.

28. Ibid., p. 13.

29. In "How American Are You If Your Grandparents Came from Serbia in 1888?" in *The Rediscovery of Ethnicity,* ed. Sallie TeSelle (New York:

Harper and Row, 1973), Michael Novak reminds us that "in the last decade, the word 'ethnic' came to be used not so much for white ethnic groups from Europe, which were presumed to be rapidly 'melting,' but as a synonym for 'minorities,' especially those of color: the Blacks, the Latinos, the Indians; i.e., those who visibly were *not* melting" (p. 6).

30. Hutcheon, "Beginning to Theorize Postmodernism," p. 13.

31. Ibid., p. 11.

32. Herbert Gans, *On the Making of Americans: Essays in Honor of David Riesman* (Philadelphia: University of Pennsylvania Press, 1979), p. 215.

33. Sollars, *Beyond Ethnicity*, pp. 244–45.

Paul S. Cowen

A Social-Cognitive Approach to Ethnicity in Films

Films, whether viewed as art or mass communication, are an enormous repository of explicit and implicit information about the projected and perceived racial, ethnic, and cultural identities of individuals and groups. Social psychology has always been concerned with the way people perceive and understand others, particularly with regard to prejudice and stereotyping based on a group membership of any type. Social psychology has also been concerned with the effects different media have in forming or changing our attitudes. Although any medium can promote or oppose stereotypes, prejudice, and discrimination, film and television are potentially the most powerful because they most closely approximate the array of directly accessible visual and verbal information found in face-to-face interaction.[1]

Social cognition, that is, the way we think about, process, interpret, and retain social information, is considered a crucial component in the study of media influences[2] and can likewise contribute to the study of ethnicity in films, especially if one is concerned with its psychological and social effects. The social-cognitive approach in psychology assumes that film spectators, as much as any observers of social behavior, actively select, organize, transform, and interpret film information, at times in a biased or distorted way, guided by their needs, values and beliefs, especially those concerning "self" and "others."

People's assimilation and interpretation of social information always involves inferences and generalizations which ultimately affect what is retained and learned on a long-term basis. This would apply to spectators' viewing films in which ethnicity is evident (due to characters, actors, action, location, and dialogue) or more implicit (due to the influence of writers and production personnel).

Aside from making inferences, people also quite naturally categorize, stereotype, and conventionalize their experiences because it makes their perceived world more stable, consistent, and organized.[3] Furthermore, categories and rules for their construction are confirmed by others, while exceptions to norms may seem at best to be curiosities if not disturbances to one's social reality and well-being. The cost of such pragmatics and efficiency in thought is bias, prejudice, and errors in our perception of self and others.

Biases and Errors in Social Perception

Numerous studies have shown that people make a "fundamental attribution error"[4] by tending to ignore situational, social, and environmental factors when explaining another person's behavior while overemphasizing the importance of what are perceived to be the other's more enduring characteristics and traits. This tendency increases when explaining others' failures, whereas their successes are explained in terms of external influences or luck rather than in terms of their abilities.

A film portrayal would, therefore, have to present sufficient information about external influences and a character's motives and abilities to counteract these biases. Otherwise, a spectator might satisfactorily explain the behavior of a protagonist from another racial, ethnic, or cultural group on the basis of stereotypes, that is, characteristics assumed to be inherent to all members of the group. Even in the absence of prejudice, if the spectator focuses on the differences between his or her group and the other's, negative attitudes toward the other may emerge simply by virtue of making a comparison.[5]

In a similar vein, research has shown that a person whose ethnic membership is novel and distinct in a particular context, for example the only black person in an office, is perceived as being more influential than he or she actually is as well as strongly possessing traits that conform to a racial stereotype.[6] This suggests a reconsideration of, for example, Sidney Poitier as the only black (and male worker) among nuns in *Lillies of the Field*, or Tina Turner as the only black (and female leader) in *Mad Max, Beyond Thunderdome*, or Eddie Murphy as a black policeman uncovering white crime in the upscale white world of *Beverly Hills Cop*.

The Importance of Visual Information

As much as we might not like to admit it, our first impressions of others are strongly influenced by our stereotypes concerning both natural physical features such as gender, skin color, and body type, as well as acquired features such as hair style, gait, gestures, and accents in speech.[7]

Films by their very nature present these physical features directly, at times emphasizing them or even exploiting their immediate impact on our perception and the stereotypes they evoke. This may be seen in type-casting, whereby immediately identifiable features trigger recognition of a personality type with expectations that certain motives, actions, situations, and stories are more likely to occur. Consider, for example, how Hollywood has exploited whole races and cultures by creating prototypes for the Latin Lover, the Happy Slave, the Wise Old Jew, the Suave Sophisticated Frenchman, the Inscrutable Oriental, the Primitive/Savage Indian, the Stuffy Englishman, or the Lazy Mexican.

Furthermore, there is a large component of visual imagery to our thoughts, memories, and impressions of others, whereas our self-concepts are more abstract and verbal.[8] This makes sense because access to information about others is most often via interpersonal contact where the visual channel is primary, whereas we cannot perceive ourselves directly (except via mirrors or video feedback) and depend instead on verbal feedback from others or our own internal verbal dialogues about ourselves. Because of this distinction, a film presenting people from a visibly different group is even more likely to lead spectators to interpret and permanently store information on the basis of visible characteristics or appearances rather than in terms of abstract concepts or underlying traits. As a consequence, in the naive viewer this could unintentionally promote stereotyping rather than reflection and self-questioning about the validity of one's assumptions, attributions, and interpretations.

Psychological Representation of Groups

Spectators' perceptions of ethnic groups and their members do not simply depend on stereotypical labels, images, and attitudes. Interpretations also depend upon larger and more dynamic cognitive processes which psychologists have called *scripts* and *story schemas*. These processes permit integration of information about actions, roles, conflicts, and goals in our processing of narratives. Unfortunately, there are biases here as well. People tend to misinterpret, invent, delete, and rearrange information when they are unfamiliar with either the content or structure of a story.[9] Younger children seem especially prone to these types of errors. Even if the film's content and style are familiar, they have difficulty distinguishing between relevant and irrelevant information and often make inferences about motives, goals, and causal relations that are based on stereotypes or personal wishes as much as on the information actually presented in the film.[10] Adults also rely on stereotypes based on immediately visible characteristics when a protagonists' motives, goals, and behavior are ambiguous or ambivalent.[11]

A spectator's interpretation of a film also depends on his or her involvement and the way the film gratifies different needs, for example, to be entertained, to become acquainted with a particular group or culture, or to identify films which are implicitly racist.[12] With regard to *Beverly Hills Cop, 48 Hours*, or *Lethal Weapon*, for example, spectators seeking diversion or entertainment might focus on the melodramatic elements of a film while paying little attention to a subtext about racial relations or prejudice. Other spectators, however, might see conflict or cooperation between characters as an expression of race relations. Yet others might feel conflict resulted from a personality clash and cooperation resulted from comraderie.

Furthermore, attitudes toward film characters depend strongly upon whether the spectator feels mutuality, difference, or opposition when comparing his or her group to the protagonist's.[13] Mutuality is more easily evoked by a film in which protagonists from the viewer's own ethnic group predominate. Watching a film made by and targeted for one's own group tends to evoke positive albeit ethnocentric feelings as a member of an "in-group." A notable exception to this rule occurs when members of a discriminated group adopt the prejudicial attitudes of the dominant group.[14] A film portrayal of this may be seen in the self-denial of the anti-Semitic Jew played by June Havoc in *Gentleman's Agreement*. At the core, however, identification with such negative self-images is symptomatic of a larger conflict among ethnic or racial groups.

Interethnic Conflict and Communication

Different ethnic groups neither value the same personal characteristics nor structure social information, even when based on shared experiences, in the same way. This can lead to misunderstandings and the exacerbation of conflicts between groups. When there are class or status differences between cohabitating ethnic groups, members of the less powerful group are often more adept at changing their roles and communication so as to suit the nature of the situation. As a result, they will not necessarily behave the same way nor pay attention to the same things when interacting with members of their own group as when interacting with members of the dominant group.[15] To spectators from the dominant group, however, such adaptability by the weaker group could be perceived as hypocrisy or trickery, and perhaps in an effort to avoid this, even Hollywood films which are ostensibly for the right cause do not often portray this aspect of social survival.

Of course, an unbiased spectator can identify with a character from any cultural or ethnic group, that is, empathically feel as the character does or sympathize with the character's position. Nevertheless, research suggests that people use different criteria when judging members of their own group as opposed to those of another group.[16] Thus, a white spectator viewing *Platoon* might judge white soldiers as being trustworthy or dishonest while judging black soldiers as being lazy or ambitious, regardless of their honesty and reliability. Although this type of discrimination is more subtle than outright prejudice, it still represents a bias associated with perceived group differences.

Reduction of Prejudice and Discrimination

As the preceding survey of social-cognitive factors suggests, even a well-intended, honest portrayal of members from a given ethnic group must overcome obstacles to avoid stereotyping and prejudice. Commercial films and television programs have a powerful, and at times unrecognized, impact on beliefs and values.[17] Learning may be even stronger if a film does not appear to be didactic, and attitude change may be greater if a film does not appear to be persuasive because this reduces resistance to influence.[18]

Empirical research on direct contact between members of different ethnic groups has shown that certain characteristics of communication promote a reduction in stereotyping and prejudice.[19] More frequent contact with members of an out-group decreases stereotyping because it permits exposure to a wider variety of personalities and types. This permits greater differentiation and an increased likelihood that the viewer will find similarities between themselves and some members of the other group. Unfortunately, however, the advantages of increased contact that film and television can offer have often been compromised by commercial interests which thrive on regularity and standardization of roles, actors, and behaviors as token representations of whole races, religions or cultures.

Reduction of prejudice is also more likely in direct encounter when both parties perceive the person from the out-group or minority to be at least equal in status to the person from the in-group or majority.[20] This suggests that roles which have recognizably high status and high self-esteem, for example Bill Cosby as a physician on "The Cosby Show" and Sidney Poitier as a teacher in *To Sir with Love*, might reduce traditional prejudices (despite what we may think of their performances or their films) more than portrayals of ethnic or racial minorities with low status and low self-esteem, even if due to unjust social conditions, for example Whoopie Goldberg in *The Color Purple*, Ernest Borgnine as the Italian butcher from the Bronx in *Marty*, or John Travolta as the Italian disco dancer from Brooklyn in *Saturday Night Fever*. It is much harder to find examples of the first type of film than of the second type. Even if this reflects Hollywood's desire to represent social reality, which is highly unlikely as a general rule, the effects might not match such good intentions.

When an actor is credible or attractive, he or she is more persuasive.[21] These two factors do not operate in the same way, however. If this influence is due to the actor's perceived credibility, it tends to be more profound and permanent. When persuasion occurs primarily because the actor is attractive, it can dissipate if the actor changes roles or is no longer popular. This type of influence depends more on identifications with the actor as a role model, and rewards for such identification are not that one is right, but rather than one is liked, as is the model. This suggests, unfortunately, that Sylvester Stallone's influence as a role model might remain quite high when switching from *Rocky* to *Rambo* (a character who is part American Indian and part German), given his enormous popularity as a star and his credibility in those incredible roles. More significantly, the influence of those films on original audiences might persist despite his performance in a less popular film such as *F.I.S.T.*

Finally, and quite importantly, prejudice can be reduced if authority figures support minority protagonists (without being patronizing), or if there is evidence of cooperation rather than hostility between in-group and out-group members.

A Taxonomy of Films in which Ethnicity Plays a Role

The factors in social cognition outlined previously can serve as a heuristic in developing a framework for the study of ethnicity in films, particularly with respect to the spectator's abilities, limits, inclinations, and biases as a social cognizer. Such a framework might sensitize the researcher or critic to different types and degrees of influence when analyzing the way specific ethnic groups have been portrayed in American films.

Prominent among these variables are the extent to which a particular group or context is visibly foreign as opposed to familiar to a spectator (this familiarity could be exclusively the result of media experiences), whether the spectator perceives himself or herself to be a member of the same group or a different group, and the extent to which conflict, peace, resolution of conflict, or active cooperation involve characters from different groups.

The following taxonomy is not neat and tidy, because many factors vary simultaneously, and any film can be viewed from several perspectives. The taxonomy was not constructed to support social values because any of its categories can include films that promote prejudice as well as films that do quite the opposite. Instead, category distinctions reflect variations in perceptible characteristics of actors, characters, social contexts, and their interrelations, which the spectator interprets from his or her implied position of a "self" viewing "others" who are seen as being similar to, different from, or opposed to the viewer's own group affiliations and social identities.

Category 1. Films with Americans in a Foreign Place

This category includes films which depict an ethnic group and a context that are foreign to spectators and to American protagonists in the film as well. In addition, the stories of these films tend to explore and develop relationships between protagonists of the same ethnic group while interethnic communication is sometimes minimal and rudimentary. Although this may lead to conflicts between racial, ethnic, or cultural groups, it differs greatly from interethnic conflict within a shared geographical or political unity, as discussed in the fourth category that follows.

The label *foreign* here does not simply refer to what are commonly called "foreign films." American films which take place in a foreign country and depict both Americans and local inhabitants are even more important to consider for present purposes, particularly when the customs, expectations, motivations, behaviors, and settings are less familiar to American audiences. Examples of this type of film would include *Salvador, Midnight Express, The Mosquito Coast, The Year of Living Dangerously, Missing, The Deer Hunter* (with regard to Vietnamese, but not with regard to Ukranian Americans), *The Ugly*

American, Under Fire, The Man Who Knew too Much (in Morocco more than London), and *Frantic* among others. Many war films, for example, *The Deer Hunter* and *Platoon*, despite the clear indication of contact and conflict between different ethnic groups, should be considered in this category because their stories ultimately focus on the bewilderment, frustration, and frenzy of Americans, especially white Americans, rather than more deeply examining the racial antagonisms and prejudice underlying and supporting the war.

The overall narrative thrust of *Under Fire*, in fact, concerns the gradual awakening of American journalists abroad to the reality of Nicaraguans who are ethnically, racially, culturally, linguistically, and geographically foreign and who at first are merely objects for the journalists' cameras, tape recorders, and news reports. Despite the film's intelligence and often brilliant style and execution, its portraits of Nicaraguans are at best two-dimensional, whether they support Somosa or the Sandanistas. Rebels and peasants fare somewhat better because the film is sympathetic to their cause. However, the viewer never has access to the thoughts, feelings, hopes, and fears of the Nicaraguans at a level of depth or complexity comparable to that of the three American journalists, or even to the duplicitous Frenchman (Jean-Louis Trintignant). It is through these outsiders that the film's moral and political issues are played out, perhaps mirroring the likelihood that an audience would more easily understand, identify with, and care about protagonists whom they resemble than foreigners who look, speak, and act differently.

In this sense, Nick Nolte is fooled for part of the film (as some viewers may be), thinking there is a substantial difference between the coarse, pragmatic American mercenary (Ed Harris) and his stylistically antithetical but politically analogous French counterpart (Trintignant), who appears sophisticated and even philosophical. In contrast, Nolte honestly insists for the first half of the film that he is not taking sides, perhaps because there are no clear verbal and visual clues for him to distinguish between government and rebel supporters, despite the canyon dividing them morally and politically.

Nolte's growing concern for the ordinary Nicaraguan's plight parallels his awareness that the relationship between appearances, labels, and inner character is not unequivocal. Shortly after he naively allows his compatriot (Harris) to hide from rebels, Nolte witnesses Harris's assassination of a rebel leader whom Nolte had begun to admire. Much later, Nolte is facing near death at the hands of the army, much as Harris was at the hands of the rebels, and successfully convinces the "enemy" to collude and protect him. The soldier acts without prejudice on the basis of his intuitive judgment of Nolte's nonverbal behavior, even though he is an American plea bargaining in English. In contrast, Nolte's equally intuitive response to Harris's need for hiding is based on a stereotyped, habitual, and incorrect perception that someone from one's own cultural, racial, and linguistic group can be trusted in a foreign context.

The film's power, however, also lies in its self-awareness of its treatment of ethnic differences. A Nicaraguan rebel woman offers no sympathy to the American heroine (Joanna Cassidy), as they watch a television report about the army's assassination of her husband (Gene Hackman). The Nicaraguan punctuates her lack of sympathy by adding that fifty thousand of her countrymen have died without any American noticing, and maybe now, when one of their own has been killed, Americans will pay attention.

Actors and locale are not the only variables which can affect the familiarity or foreignness of a film. Foreign producers, directors, cinematographers, screenwriters, and editors can also potentially influence the surface level of a film. In this sense, one might consider the Canadian production of French director Louis Malle's *Atlantic City*, or Malle's *Alamo Bay*, concerning conflict between Vietnamese immigrants and racist Texans over fishing privileges on the Gulf Coast. A variant of this type of film is *Good Morning Babylon*, which depicts the trials and tribulations of two Italian immigrant brothers whose magnificent art work is ignored until they are discovered by D. W. Griffith.

However, aside from the last film, which is clearly Italian despite taking place in California, it is hard to see what is "foreign" about the others mentioned. In a similar vein, how can we determine what is Dutch about Paul Verhoeven's *RoboCop*, Brazilian about Hector Babenco's *Ironweed*, or Australian about Peter Weir's *Witness*? If such influences could be discerned, they would not trigger stereotypes about the director's cultural or ethnic membership as might actors or other physical features of the film. Even in a clear case of a misfire, such as Michelangelo Antonioni's *Zabriskie Point*, inauthenticity appears in the depiction of problems, relations, dialogue, and behavior that are familiar to Americans. Unfortunately, when the inauthenticity concerns foreign or unfamiliar people, it may be less apparent and can produce quite different effects, as described in category 2.

Category 2. Films with Simulations of Ethnicity

The second group of films includes those which might be characterized by a certain inauthenticity (but not necessarily insincerity) in depicting a member of a particular ethnic group or the group per se. This is usually due to casting an actor whose physical features significantly resemble the stereotype of another ethnic or cultural group, but may also result from translating a foreign genre and foreign cultural values into a standard American melodrama depicting American values, as in Sydney Pollack's *The Yakuza*.

Pretending is inherent to fiction, to acting, and to film art. Inauthentic locales, actors, or directors are neither a clear index of a film's esthetics nor its power to convince an audience of its authenticity. However, if a film's artifice becomes obvious, it has more difficulty creating traditional pleasures of film viewing, unless the film acknowledges its artifice or its awareness of the pleasure expected. In particular, if a familiar actor plays a protagonist from another ethnic group (often requiring a fake accent and other disguises), the audience may be as much involved in judging the success of the performance as in the character being portrayed. Examples would include Meryl Streep in *Sophie's Choice* or William Hurt in *Kiss of the Spider Woman*, both of which are arguably performances of merit.

In certain contexts, however, inauthenticity in depicting members of ethnic groups or foreigners can lead to erroneous interpretations of their beliefs and values as well as the scenarios in which they are playing. In John Milius's film *The Wind and the Lion*, Americans in Tangiers at the turn of the century are attacked by hordes of seemingly merciless Arabs from which one protagonist clearly emerges as distinct and distinguished compared to the others. Sean Connery may be an unlikely choice to play an Arab leader, but he is unquestionably well cast as a romantic hero (fig. 13.1). This does not, however, help the uninformed non-Muslim American viewer to understand Arabs. If anything, it hinders any understanding because the one character from this group of outsiders who contradicts our stereotyped expectations for the group as a whole is in fact played by an actor who has nothing in common with that ethnic, cultural, or religious group except for his dark hair, dark eyes, and a beard.

Despite the film's intention to depict at least one Arab as more honorable and courageous than an American president, the spectator in fact sees and hears a Scotsman (with an accent that is both distinct and atypical of English-speaking Arabs) persuade Candice Bergen to love and admire him despite her strong initial impulses to

13.1. *The Wind and the Lion* with Sean Connery, Candice Bergen, and members of the cast. Simulated ethnicity marked by a smiling Scotsman in a white turban arriving to assuage fears of Arab terrorism.

the contrary. With all the other Arabs on murderous rampages, this inauthenticity cannot alter stereotypes of Muslim fundamentalism as "crazy," a meaningless label that nevertheless serves the important social function of separating "them" from "us." Had a real Arab played the role of this historical figure whose status was so great that Teddy Roosevelt felt threatened, spectators might not only have a different impression of the character, and of Candice Bergen's change in heart, but also of the values of the ethnic group being represented, although this would still require drastic changes in the dialogue.

In this second category, Anthony Quinn would probably win the award for the greatest variety of ethnic groups played in a lifetime, including an Eskimo in *The Savage Innocents* and a Roumanian in *The Twenty-fifth Hour*, as well as the leads in *Zorba the Greek* and *The Greek Tycoon*. This category also includes Sal Mineo's portrayal of a Jew in *Exodus*, Marlon Brando as a Mexican in *Viva Zapata!*, Rudolf Nureyev as the Italian matinee idol *Valentino*, Rosalind Russell as a Jew and Alec Guinness as a Japanese in *A Majority of One*, Robert de

Niro and Elizabeth McGovern as Jews in *Once upon a Time in Amer-ica*, and, most incredibly, Spencer Tracy and Hedy Lamarr as Mexi-can Americans in *Tortilla Flats*.

Category 3. Ethnic Films: Foreigners and Ethnic Minorities in America

A third category of films includes those which deal with ethnic groups who share a common boundary with another group which is more dominant (historically, politically, or economically) in their shared context. The ethnic group in question may be seeking to es-tablish itself, be recently settled, or have long-established roots as an out-group in their own land. The action of films in this category takes place within the shared boundaries of an in-group and out-group, rather than in some place foreign to either or both. The lon-gevity of the group's presence as "outsiders" is important because this would increase the chances that any spectator, regardless of group affiliation, would be familiar with the shared history between the group in question and other racial or ethnic groups, even if this familiarity is stereotyped and prejudiced. Obviously, the effects of any film in this category depend strongly on whether spectators are from the minority group depicted in the film or from another group having shared experiences in a common environment, or from the group considered dominant in their shared sociocultural context.

Films in this category include *Car Wash, Saturday Night Fever, Hester Street, El Norte, Crossing Delancey, Chan Is Missing, La Bamba, Flower Drum Song, The Godfather, Mean Streets,* and *Once upon a Time in America*. As these films indicate, inclusion in this category does not depend upon explicit acknowledgement of conflicts (or har-mony) between the dominant and minority groups. Some of these films focus almost exclusively on the interactions between members of their own group. This is one of the distinctive criteria of films in this category. In extreme cases, however, there may ironically be a fuzzy border between this category and the first category (Ameri-cans in a foreign place) because the depiction of certain groups and conditions in America may be so removed from the average specta-tor's experience that they are perceived as unknown, different that is, foreign. This is emphasized when the film's surface information (characters, places, or historical period) suggests that the viewer has little in common, either historically or currently, with the film's pro-tagonists despite a common culture or nationality. In that sense, it is as if the story were happening in a place that seems foreign but which also seems familiar. Despite this ambivalence, films in this

13.2. *Sounder* with Paul Winfield, Cicely Tyson, Taj Mahal, and members of the cast. As foreigners in their own land, the black family and community survive racism during the depression.

category, in sharp contrast to those in the first and fifth categories, tend to present richer and more detailed portraits of individuals and subcultures within an ethnic group.

This type of film can have an extremely significant impact on viewers from outside the group portrayed because it gives them a privileged and perhaps rare opportunity to witness social interaction among members of another in-group, without their perceptions being excessively biased as can occur when conflict and confrontation between groups are a film's major theme.

Martin Ritt's *Sounder*, for example, presents an episode of black American history in the segregated South of the depression era (fig. 13.2). Many viewers might have some knowledge about blacks in that locale in those times, obtained indirectly through the media, but not many members of other racial groups would have experienced that situation first-hand, and if they did it would most likely be from the perspective of segregation and discrimination.

The film's strength lies in its simple, quiet, but unswerving dedication to painting a portrait of a courageous black family living in poverty, enduring hardship and abuse in the most difficult of circumstances. As with other films in this category, there is clearly a potential to expand the audience's awareness of another culture from its point of view. In *Sounder*, much more time and attention is dedicated to blacks interacting among themselves and to their various points of view than is accorded to whites. As in better portraits, the film also pays attention to distinguishing features of expression, personality, and style among the various black protagonists, qualities that would probably be more difficult to develop if the film's primary focus were on intergroup relations.

Nevertheless, the story is repeatedly punctuated by white southerners' hostility and prejudice toward blacks. Their hostility, however, is usually either camouflaged, passively aggressive (exacerbating difficulties by being unaccommodating or by "just following the law"), or hidden to themselves. Even the well-intentioned Mrs. Boderight tells David Lee (Kevin Hooks), the black family's eldest son, "there ain't a Chinaman in all the world who can beat your mother's ironing," without any apparent awareness of the racist implications of her compliment. Fortunately, Mrs. Boderight has enough social conscience and courage to defy unjust rules and secretly helps David Lee find out where his father was sent to do hard labor.

Although the film unavoidably refers to intergroup conflict, much greater time and emphasis is placed on the relations between blacks. Ultimately, Miss Johnson (Janet MacLachlan), the black teacher and school supervisor whom David Lee meets by accident while searching for his father, proves to have the most significant influence on this intelligent, inquisitive, and impressionable young scholar. She clearly has greater insight and stronger rapport with David Lee than either Mrs. Boderight or David Lee's white teacher back home. The film clearly associates the rapport between Miss Johnson and the boy as crucial to black identity; she becomes the model for his awakening awareness and pride in their shared racial heritage.

This is one of several exchanges in the film which would typically be accessible only to members of the in-group in daily life, but which non-blacks have the privilege of witnessing by viewing this film. It is through this privileged access to the other group's perceptions, beliefs, and values as shared by them, not only as viewed by us, that films in this category attain their distinctive power.

Films in this category, however, also risk being inauthentic. However, this is not due to simulating the stereotyped surface characteristics of an ethnic group, as was found in films from category 2.

Instead, inauthenticity in category 3 results from perpetuating stereotyped traits, behaviors, and roles that have perhaps been accepted by the minority group as much as by the group in power, although this is less prevalent among black Americans in recent years. It is interesting to note that *The Color Purple, Flower Drum Song, Saturday Night Fever, Marty, Car Wash,* and *Sounder,* among others, depict a minority ethnic or racial group but were written, directed, and produced by people who are not members of that group. Rare exceptions to this rule are *Do the Right Thing* and *Chan Is Missing.*

At the opposite extreme, films in this category also risk being so authentic in their portrait of a particular group and environment that they create an aura of "foreignness" to a domestic American market. This is used to advantage in *El Norte* because Spanish with English subtitles creates greater authenticity in the story, which concerns the plight of newly arrived non-English-speaking immigrants. However, a film such as *Sounder* concerns an ethnic group that has witnessed its own American history for hundreds of years. By setting the story in the depression-era South, non-blacks can more easily distance themselves from an appreciation of contemporary black suffering. For example, a white viewer, who at least acknowledges the injustices to which blacks have been subjected in the past, could still rationalize current prejudicial attitudes by arguing that the depression was hard for everyone or that segregation was a violation of civil rights but the constitution has since been amended to protect civil rights. In this way, despite its historical validity and emotional appeal, it can be viewed by non-blacks without any particular significance for themselves today.

In addition, by today's standards, the family in the film has very low social status; they are uneducated, in poverty, and the equivalent of indentured slaves. Although such a portrait may be faithful to reality, it does not tend to change negative attitudes or promote behavior aimed at helping those in need. In *Sounder,* the black schoolteacher and black priest can potentially transcend this stigma, but only the teacher succeeds in consciously raising the status of her group. Finally, the film's slow pace and undramatic treatment of events, although eloquent at moments, hardly counter the possibility that viewers will distance themselves from the film.

In contrast to *Sounder,* a film may emphasize contact between ethnic groups, whether based on mutuality, indifference, or conflict. If the film focuses on interethnic contact it will tend to activate the viewer's memories of past experiences or imagined future interactions with members of the other group. As a consequence, the viewer's involvement in the film is heightened because his or her thoughts and feelings about members of the other group have real consequences for his or her own self-concept and social well-being. The next category includes films which deal more specifically with contact and shared experiences between the protagonists of different racial, ethnic, or cultural groups.

Category 4. Films Highlighting Interethnic Conflict or Cooperation

Films in this category have a predominant theme of interethnic contact within a common culture. The drama, suspense, narrative complication, or resolution of these films pivot around relations between protagonists from different ethnic or racial groups. A distinction should be made, however, between films which clearly depict interethnic problems, for example, *Living on Tokyo Time*, *Summertime*, *The King and I*, or *The Landlord*, and films directly concerned with prejudice and discrimination, for example, *Gentleman's Agreement*, *West Side Story*, *Tell Them Willie Boy Was Here*, *Heaven's Gate*, or *Alamo Bay*.

One film from this category is Arthur Penn's *Little Big Man*, which depicts the racial conflict between white Americans and Native Americans during the last half of the nineteenth century. Its atypical comic tone, which softens its theme of genocide, was at least partly responsible for its wide popularity (fig. 13.3). Despite the seriousness of its thesis, its tone is diametrically opposed, for example, to that of *Judgment at Nuremberg*, which is humorless, glum, even ponderous in its indictment of Nazi genocide. Perhaps Americans find it easier to be humorous, albeit satirical, when treating their own attempt to exterminate another race. Penn's comic treatment may also be acceptable because it refers to a much more distant past than the Holocaust or the Cambodian genocide depicted in *The Killing Fields*.

The film's humor also derives from its joke on the "I passed for White" theme as we watch Dustin Hoffman's dismay at not "passing for Indian" at several points during the film. The twist on the theme of racial masquerade is underscored with even greater irony when a Pawnee incorrectly assumes that because Jack Crabbe (Hoffman) is white, he is a friend, when in fact he is fighting with the Cheyenne, the Pawnees' enemy. This error based on surface information costs the Pawnee his life and makes Hoffman a hero for saving the life of his Cheyenne rival, who is insulted that he

13.3. *Little Big Man* with members of the cast: interracial conflict depicting the genocide of Native Americans amid the ironies of an American comedy.

owes his life to a white man's inadvertant bravery. Instead of playing with words, the film plays with the equivocality of visual information about racial and ethnic affiliation while showing that equivocal signs are always misinterpreted to favor a prejudicial basis for power.

Through Hoffman's dual citizenship and split personality, a non-Indian viewer can become acquainted with the extreme contrast between our own beliefs and values and those of another culture, as well as the way in which these differences render foreigners vulnerable to misunderstanding, exploitation, and ultimately destruction. In fact, Hoffman's conflict of roles and racial identity personifies the larger social and political conflict in which he must finally choose sides. A white spectator's appreciation of Native-American civilization is made easier by placing Hoffman, with whom the spectator can more easily share thoughts and feelings, inside their culture. When Hoffman chooses to return to live with the Indians, it breaks down our tendency to merely see them as "others." In addition, his voice-over narration and direct interaction with them often clarify statements, customs, and behavior which might otherwise appear peculiar or foreign and therefore might be misinterpreted or forgotten by viewers who are not Native Americans. Thus, through the film's depiction of Hoffman's personal conflict, the spectator gains access to another culture's perception of the larger racial conflict in which they are both engulfed.

The film's popularity, however, is also ensured by its romanticized if not idealized portrait of Native Americans, who seem closer to a white stereotype of the Noble Savage (intended to contradict the more popular stereotype of the Primitive Uncivilized Savage) than to any reality of demise and ruin as a race. For example, when Hoffman feels that he is unworthy of his (adopted) heritage, he becomes an alcoholic, but only temporarily. Although this suggests the humility Hoffman suffered, it in no way indicates the extent to which alcoholism became Indians' suicidal approach to the whites' successful but incomplete attempt at their destruction.

Little Big Man is to be recommended for its deliberate attempt to show many different personalities and cultures among Indians rather than treating them as one large, undifferentiated mass of people. Unfortunately, certain characterizations in the film seem to be unintentionally false, reducing to some extent the power of the film's premise. The depiction of the gay tribesman and Hoffman's squaw are especially striking in this respect because their voices, gestures, and behavioral style are characteristic of, if not exaggerations of, contemporary America circa 1970. However, the story suggests that unlike some other characters, they should be taken seriously rather than seen as parodies.

There is, however, no question of authenticity regarding the most important Indian role in the film, the chief of the Cheyenne and Hoffman's adopted grandfather (Dan George). Nevertheless, the film is ambivalent even in its treatment of his sincere expression of religious beliefs and faith. For example, he miraculously escapes injury when running through the mayhem of a cavalry attack because Hoffman has convinced him that he is invisible, but Hoffman's voice-over narration leads us to believe that the chief survived because of pluck and luck. At the very end of the film, the chief gives an eloquent soliloquy about the end of his race, "The Human Beings," while waiting to die as he believed the gods had instructed him to do in a dream. Yet when it is clear he is still very much alive, he says "I was afraid of that," followed by a string of nearly illogical non-sequitors as he talks about his new wife, whom he is sure copulates with horses! An outsider witnessing these events and statements might interpret the chief's behavior (here and throughout the film) as consistent with his values and beliefs, but nevertheless categorize them as the expression of a superstitious, primitive man. One wonders to what extent a religious Christian protagonist's unanswered prayers would be similarly presented or would lead to similar attributions.

Finally, as in many other films depicting minority groups, there is emphasis on the Native American's unfavorable, downtrodden, miserable existence. Although this may intuitively seem adequate as a plea for greater understanding of their plight, people do not necessarily respond favorably to another group just because they are faithfully presented in their misfortune.[22] In that sense, falsifying, simplifying, and romanticizing the image of the Indian may unwittingly succeed in making the overall message more appealing and more palatable to white audiences.

Within the larger context of conflict, *Little Big Man* also depicts interracial harmony, especially in the relation between Hoffman and the chief. In general, films which emphasize interethnic cooperation, mutuality, or sharing need not differ in structure or content from films showing interethnic conflict, because it is usually through the perception of common goals or a struggle against a common enemy that such cooperation emerges. Films in this subcategory would include *Sammy and Rosie Get Laid*, *My Beautiful Launderette*, and *Chariots of Fire* (none of which are American films) and *Lillies of the Field*, *Fame*, and *Guess Who's Coming to Dinner* (which are, perhaps, quintessentially American films).

John Landis's *Trading Places* may be analyzed along these lines because its successful resolution of potential racial and class conflict depends upon Dan Aykroyd and Eddie Murphy (fig. 13.4) joining forces to retaliate against their common enemy, the Duke brothers (Don Ameche and Ralph Bellamy), wealthy elders who have smugly manipulated their lives for a $1 bet on the outcome of a nature versus nurture experiment. *Trading Places* is also interesting because its subtext confirms Ralph Bellamy's hypothesis that class and racial differences are due to environmental rather than hereditary factors. This is made obvious through concrete auditory and visual information, rather than abstract conceptual information, throughout the entire film (Murphy's action, dress, and speech become serious, hard-working, and "classy," whereas Aykroyd becomes frenetic, unscrupulous, and "vulgar").

Furthermore, the film suggests at least indirectly that animosities based on the perception of racial or class differences are perpetuated by the abuses of those in power who treat other people as mere pawns in a game. Although the film could hardly be cited as a call

13.4. *Trading Places* with Dan Aykroyd and Eddie Murphy; interethnic cooperation in which enemies join forces and beat the bosses at their own game.

for social or economic reform, it nevertheless manages to make a
rather intricate joke out of significant themes. As the pun of the
film's title subtly suggests, its multiple meanings only make full
sense in a capitalist, materialist (i.e., American) milieu.

The theme of changing one's identity by changing one's surface
traits is played with several variations in the film's denouement,
where Winthorpe's (Aykroyd's) butler is disguised as a priest; Jamie
Lee Curtis, Aykroyd's new girlfriend, is disguised as a Swede; Murphy is charading as a foreigner from Cameroun; and Aykroyd himself, in a gesture of comraderie with Murphy, pretends to be a
Rastafarian with his face painted black. The foursome successfully
steals secret information from Beaks, the Duke brothers' spy, while
he is inadvertently forced to wear a gorilla's costume, much as our
heroes were originally stuck in their reversed roles due to the Duke
brothers' manipulations. After it is clear that the good guys have
won, the film's final shots show a real gorilla satisfied from having
subdued and seduced his newfound mate (Beaks in costume) and
also an accompanying ironic commentary on stereotypes and biases
based on surface appearances, as baggage attendants watching the
pair incorrectly assume that Beaks "must be the female"!

With regard to stereotypes, rather than make a joke of Murphy in the role of lawyer and businessman, his character emerges with at least as much status as Aykroyd began with. He not only changes his manners, dress, and taste, but also becomes at least as astute and accurate as Aykroyd was in predicting market changes while lacking Aykroyd's conceit and snobbery. Aykroyd's character, on the other hand, develops skills that are appropriate for his new circumstances but which accordingly have much lower status. This can only help perceiving Murphy more positively because his transformation is a result of his own efforts and abilities once the trade has been implemented. Although this film might be classified as light entertainment, some of its effects could be greater (and hopefully more positive) than those of more dramatic works. Its greatest risk, as is true of any comedy, is that people will not take it seriously.

Other films which show some form of cooperation between members of different groups are more ambivalent and ambiguous in their message about interethnic relations and prejudice. These may be considered in category 5, along with films in which the role of ethnicity is unclear with regard to the story or to interpersonal relations.

Category 5. Films with Ambivalence/Ambiguity about Ethnicity

A sub-genre that has become increasingly popular is the interracial "buddy" film, typically an action-adventure yarn or police story (e.g., *Lethal Weapon, Off Limits, Shoot to Kill*). Walter Hill's *48 Hours* is notable among these films because it was the first and was very popular. It is also full of contradictions in its depiction of the relationship between a white police officer (Nick Nolte) and a black thief and convict (Eddie Murphy) teamed to capture an escaped convict and killer (fig. 13.5). There are contradictions between words and deeds on the part of each protagonist in relation to the other, and there are contradictions between expressed feelings toward each other at different times during the film. Both of these levels of inconsistency create the image of an ambivalent and uneasy relationship, the type that in real life would tend to promote negative feelings about self and other if permitted to continue beyond two days, which in any event would be unlikely. In Hollywood, however, such conflict is often presented as harmless, natural, and acceptable, especially if it concerns the relationship between two men.

If one cuts through the genre machinations typical of action-adventure police films involving buddies, the interracial portrait

13.5. *48 Hours* with Nick Nolte and Eddie Murphy. Ambivalent and ambiguous interracial relations that feature interlocking dominance and submission while confounding conflict and cooperation.

depicts comaraderie-cooperation simultaneously with conflict-discrimination throughout much of the film. However, the film is neither clear about the racist overtones in Nolte's behavior toward Murphy, nor those in Murphy's attitude either toward himself or toward his companion. Shortly after Murphy genuinely takes risks and helps Nolte, he is refused the reward he was promised and is further bullied by Nolte into one of the longest, most violent fist fights in screen history, with an abundance of racial slurs before and during the encounter. Later in the film, however, Nolte is in a more civilized mood and seems genuine in his apology for his earlier prejudicial comments (calling Murphy "nigger" and "watermelon"), claiming he did not really mean them.

How are we supposed to interpret this confession? Nolte's earlier behavior seemed authentic and filled with emotion, with no clue that he was merely trying to assert his authority. Any fascist could rationalize the same behavior in the same way. Furthermore, even though Murphy's reply to Nolte's apology hints at this, his subsequent supportive behavior and friendship suggest that either expressions of prejudice and discrimination do not matter much, or that he is resigned to except such indignities, or that he believes they were not really intended to be insults, or that racial insults are legitimate or comprehensible forms of asserting power when one is insecure, or any or all of the above, none of which are particularly good foundations for interracial or interpersonal relations.

The film's ambivalence is not assuaged by the attitudes of the black police chief, when toward the end of the film he yells at Nolte for protecting "a nigger convict." This kind of projected self-hatred counteracts any benefits associated with his higher status. One positive element in this scene, however, is its play on the classic image of Sidney Poitier handcuffed to Tony Curtis as two escaped convicts in *The Defiant Ones*. Whereas Poitier and Curtis treated their bond as a constraint, Nolte willfully handcuffs himself to Murphy at the police station in a symbolic gesture of his loyalty to his teammate.

In the end, the moral is that despite Murphy's honesty in trying to help Nolte, he is a crook and therefore must return to prison. Even more, he owes his life to Nolte, who rescues him at the end by killing the gang leader just as he is about to shoot Murphy. Thus, in the end Nolte is the "good" guy and hero, saving his partner but effacing the fact that he expressed more prejudice than any other character during the entire film and that his apparent comraderie with Murphy was actually full of violence, hostility, and mistrust supported by racial differences. In essence, he took Murphy as his slave and treated him as such, despite any misgivings to the contrary.

Although some films are not ambivalent in their portrayal of ethnicity, they remain unclear about its role and importance. For example, what if any influence did ethnic differences (Jewish versus gentile) have in causing the couple's break-up in *Annie Hall*? In a funny scene at Annie's family's house, Woody Allen assumes that her grandmother is an anti-Semite and that everyone at the dinner table is scrutinizing him because he is Jewish (the visual gag shows Allen in the stereotypical dress of an orthodox Hassidic Jew). A cursory reading suggests that this scene is more of a stylistic element than a necessary component of the story, but that may be due to Allen's masquerade and the tendency not to take him seriously. However, even if this scene is treated only in terms of a visual gag, one cannot ignore the fact that the relationship between the principal characters (Allen and Diane Keaton) begins to deteriorate shortly after this episode, although the seeds may have been sown beforehand.

Social Cognition, Spectatorship and Phenomenology

When a film is ambiguous and ambivalent in its story, structure, or formal characteristics, the spectator's conscious or unconscious motives, biases, and attitudes can potentially have a greater influence in reading the text. The fifth category, perhaps more than any other of the present taxonomy, highlights the delicate interaction between the film's positioning of the spectator and the spectator's processing of film narration through use of story schemas, scripts, and the perception of spatial and visual relationships. Because people generally do not like ambivalence, ambiguity, or uncertainty, films in the last category may invite spectators to rely more heavily upon stereotypes, norms, and personal experiences while processing information, that is, reading the text. This influence is not simply at the level of post hoc interpretations, but at the more crucial stage of encoding, defining, and retaining film information and one's experience as spectator.

Interaction between the text and the spectator is common to each of the proposed categories. Each has been implicitly defined in terms of a particular combination of film characteristics and cognitive orientations. Concretely, this is most apparent in my discussion of prototypical films. More generally, this indicates that the social-cognitive approach has links with certain more orthodox trends in film theory. On one hand, this chapter is concerned with the ways in which a particular film, or film type, imposes limits on the spectator's identification with the absent narrator, a process analyzed by Nick Browne in far greater detail than is possible here.[23] In a similar vein, the theoretical orientation of the present essay is consistent with suggestions that there might be collusion between the filmmaker and audience such that particular readings, usually culturally defined, are more likely.[24]

On the other hand, the social-cognitive approach posits an active role for the spectator, a theoretical position that derives principally from its historical roots in phenomenology. Although phenomenology has traditionally been neglected in film theory, as Dudley Andrew indicates, it has received greater attention in the context of reader-response criticism.[25] For example, Wolfgang Iser's phenomenology of the reader presents an essentially interactionist position, whereas Norman N. Holland argues that readers approach texts as they approach social reality.[26] Both of these notions are implicit herein. Distinguishing between "empirical spectators," that is, real persons who interpret and respond to a film, and abstract "subject positions," that is, the ways in which an analysis of the film text reveals its constraints on any spectator, can be constructive in developing film theory.[27] This is particularly true for the study of ethnicity in films and its psychological or social effects. Audiences can surely differ as a function of ethnic, cultural, or racial affiliations, but are not free to project any interpretation on film data, as they might with a Rorschach card.

The eternal debate over which set of variables (external versus internal; physical versus psychological) is more influential in human behavior—of which film spectatorship is but one example—has been as prevalent in the history of psychology as it has been in the evolution of film theory, most likely because of common philosophical and cultural underpinnings. This discussion has attempted to show that both sets of variables must be considered. Moreover, it suggests that both theoretical and empirical studies can and should contribute to our understanding of the roles, functions, and effects of film ethnicity in its diverse forms.

NOTES

1. K. J. Gergen and M. M. Gergen, *Social Psychology* (New York: Harcourt Brace Jovanovich, 1981).

2. B. Reeves, S. Chaffee, and A. Tims, "Social Cognition and Mass Communication Research," pp. 287–326 in *Social Cognition and Communication*, ed. M. E. Roloff and C. R. Berger (Beverly Hills: Sage, 1982).

3. S. T. Fiske and S. E. Taylor, *Social Cognition* (New York: Random House, 1984).

4. F. Heider, *The Psychology of Interpersonal Relations* (New York: Wiley, 1958).

5. H. Tajfel and J. Turner, "An Integrative Theory of Intergroup Conflict," pp. 33–47 in *The Social Psychology of Intergroup Relations*, ed. W. G. Austin and S. Worchel (Monterrey: Brooks-Cole, 1979).

6. P. W. Linville and E. E. Jones, "Polarized Appraisals of Outgroup Members," *Journal of Personality and Social Psychology* 38 (1980): 689–703.

7. D. J. Schneider, A. H. Hastorf, and P. C. Ellsworth, *Person Perception*, 2d ed. (Reading: Addison-Wesley, 1979).

8. W. B. Swann and L. C. Miller, "Why Never Forgetting a Face Matters: Visual Imagery and Social Memory," *Journal of Personality and Social Psychology* 43 (1982): 475–80.

9. F. C. Bartlett, *Remembering: A Study in Experimental and Social Psychology* (London: Cambridge University Press, 1932).

10. A. Collins, "Children's Comprehension of Television Content" pp. 179–201 in *Children Communicating: Media and Development of Thought, Speech and Understanding*, ed. E. Wartella (Beverly Hills: Sage, 1979).

11. P. S. Cowen, "Manipulating Montage: Effects on Film Comprehension, Recall, Person Perception, and Aesthetic Responses," *Empirical Studies of the Arts* 6 (1988): 97–115.

12. E. Katz, J. G. Blumler, and M. Gurevitch, "Uses of Mass Communication by the Individual," pp. 11–35 in *Mass Communication Research*, ed. W. P. Davison and F. T. C. Yu (New York: Praeger, 1974).

13. L. Festinger, "A Theory of Social Comparison Processes," *Human Relations* 7 (1954): 117–40; M. Sherif and C. Hovland, *Social Judgment* (New Haven: Yale University Press, 1961).

14. H. Tajfel, "Social Psychology in Intergroup Relations," *Annual Review of Psychology* 33 (1982): 1–39.

15. S. L. McNabb, "Stereotypes and Interaction Conventions of Eskimos and Non-Eskimos," pp. 21–41 in *Interethnic Communication*, ed. Y. Y. Kim (Beverly Hills: Sage, 1986).

16. W. B. Gudykunst, "Ethnicity, Types of Relationship, and Intraethnic and Interethnic Uncertainty Reduction," pp. 201–24 in *Interethnic Communication*, ed. Kim.

17. G. Comstock et al., *Television and Human Behavior* (New York: Columbia University Press, 1978).

18. R. E. Petty and J. T. Cacioppo, "Forewarning, Cognitive Responding, and Resistance to Persuasion," *Journal of Personality and Social Psychology* 35 (1977): 645–55.

19. J. E. Alcock, D. W. Carment, and S. W. Sadava, *A Textbook of Social Psychology* (Scarborough, Ont.: Prentice-Hall, 1988).

20. E. G. Cohen and S. S. Roper, "Modification of Interracial Disability: An Application of Status Characteristic Theory," *American Sociological Review* 37 (1972): 643–57.

21. D. J. Schneider, *Social Psychology* (New York: Harcourt Brace Jovanovich, 1988).

22. M. J. Lerner, "The Desire for Justice and the Reaction to Victims," in *Altruism and Helping Behavior*, ed. J. R. Macaulay and L. Berkowitz (New York: Academic Press, 1970).

23. N. Browne, "The Spectator-in-the-Text: The Rhetoric of 'Stagecoach,' " pp. 458–75 in *Movies and Methods*, vol. 2, ed. Bill Nichols (Berkley: University of California Press, 1985).

24. C. Saxton, "The Collective Voice as Cultural Voice," *Cinema Journal* 26 (Fall 1986): 19–30.

25. D. Andrew, "The Neglected Tradition of Phenomenology in Film Theory," pp. 625–31 in *Movies and Methods*, ed. Nichols.

26. W. Iser, "The Reading Process: A Phenomenological Approach," and N. H. Holland, "Unity Identity Text Self," pp. 50–69 and 118–33 in *Reader-Response Criticism*, ed. J. P. Tompkins (Baltimore: Johns Hopkins University Press, 1980).

27. S. Johnston, "Film Narrative and the Structuralist Controversy," pp. 222–50 in *The Cinema Book*, ed. P. Cook (New York: Pantheon, 1985).

The Cinematic Melting Pot:
Ethnicity, Jews, and Psychoanalysis

To say that psychoanalysis has provided film theory and film studies with a number of crucial methodologies and metaphors would not only be an understatement, it would be nearly tautologous, for contemporary film theory is intimately and definitively linked with psychoanalysis (variously conceived to be sure). Having stated what is perhaps obvious, it is especially important to particularize what kind of psychoanalysis one has in mind, and how one is using psychoanalytic terms and concepts—as methodology or as metaphor. Thus as this discussion uses terminology and methodology drawn from Freudian dream interpretation as it has permeated various later methodologies, including myth criticism and structuralism, it proceeds from the basis of a metaphor: Film is like a dream.

The relationship between film and dream has a lengthy pedigree in both film theory and practice. In fact, film practice precedes film theory in this instance, from the "trick" films of Georges Méliès, to the use of overt dream states in American silent comedy (*The Gold Rush* [1925], *Sherlock Junior* [1924]), to the expressionistic fantasies of the golden age of German cinema. This tradition, inaugurated by Méliès, functioned as a justification for various cinematic tricks. To motivate the appearances, disappearances, and transformations of characters and things within the mise-en-scène, Méliès would overtly set up an altered state. These states might variously be a magician's act, a fantasy world (science fiction included, as in *A Trip to the Moon*, 1902), a drunken stupor, or a dream. We may detect a *photographic* assumption, derived from the Lumières, behind this altered-state tradition—that film is somehow tied to the real in its content, but contains infinite unreal possibilities as a form. To justify patently unreal occurrences that are nevertheless quite easily accommodated by the filmic medium, Mélìes, Edwin Porter (*The Dream of a Rarebit Fiend*, 1903), Charles Chaplin, Buster Keaton, Robert Wiene, and others motivated them by a common appeal to literary, or life-derived, altered states, most significantly, dreams.

The theoretical relationship between film and dream appears most prominently in the writings of the surrealists in the 1920s. They were primarily concerned with dream content as it expressed the unconscious, drawing directly from Freud's ongoing attempts to come to terms with the nocturnal narratives of his patients and himself. Of course, the theoretical writings of the surrealists about both literature and film led directly to literary and filmic production.[1] The works of René Clair are exemplary of this trend: *Paris qui dort* (1923), *Entr'acte* (1924), and *Le Voyage imaginaire* (1925). The writings and films of Jean Epstein, such as *La chute de la maison Usher* (1928), and *Gold of the Sea* (1931), also overtly reveal Freudian dream theory.[2]

What was it about dreams that led filmmakers to compare the two forms? The use of the term *narrative* hints at the beginning of this answer. For while the Lumière brothers might have begun with a photographic model in mind for this movie camera, even these exemplars of the documentary-realistic tradition of the cinema quickly experimented with narratives, or proto-narratives at least, such as *L'Arroseur arrose*. The narrative potential of film distinguished it from photography, while the theatrical presentation of it helped push film closer to the theater and, with D. W. Griffith's fundamental help, to the novel. And while the surrealists did indeed link photography, novels, and other artistic and literary forms (painting and poetry particularly) to dream, the relationship between film and dream predominated, and still does.[3]

Narrative alone, obviously, cannot explain the continued invocation of links between film and dream. Theater and novels both involve narrative, theater sharing with film a reliance upon the human form (and dialogue since the late 1920s), and novels sharing with film the flexibility of (implied) space and time. But as Petric points out, it is "[t]he similarity between the psycho-physiological processes occurring in the film viewer and the dreamer [which] is the central issue in discussions concerned with the relationship between cinema and dreams."[4] Such similar processes include the hypnagogic effect created by certain kinds of camera movement through space, illogical juxtapositions of characters, objects, and settings, immediate shifts in temporal and spatial transitions, and the "ontological authenticity" of filmic images which makes us accept them as "real" just as we do during the time we are dreaming.[5] These similar processes are aided by the essentially similar surroundings involved with film viewing and dreaming: the darkened room and our sense of isolation.

Some go even further, making a claim that the film-viewing experience is pleasurable precisely because of film's similarity to dream:

> Our relationship to the physical screen in the theater as we watch *any* film owes much to our experience as nurtured infants and to our earliest dreams. Films in general seem both real and dreamlike because they appear to us in a way that activates the regressive experience of watching dreams on our psychic dream screens. The actual screen in the theater functions as a psychic prosthesis of our dream screen, a structure constituted by the mother's breast, or a surrogate for it, and by our own ego.[6]

However, these similarities enable one to compare films with dreams in only a general way (film is "like" dream) and to enable filmmakers deliberately to use dreams, dream imagery, or dream analogies. Thus it is no surprise that the most careful attention to the relationship between film and dream has been undertaken when discussing filmmakers who overtly use dreams within their narratives: Keaton, the surrealists, Bunuel, Fellini, and Bergman especially.[7] Ultimately, film may be like a dream, but a film is not a dream. Freudian dream interpretation is not suitable, not appropriate, for analyzing a film; the interpretation of a dream is not solely a function of the manifest content of a dream, nor an analysis of its latent content. Rather, the thoughts of the analysand in talking about the dream to the analyst are of equal importance. At heart, of course, is the fact that the dream was experienced by *someone*, a function of an individual's repressed infantile fantasies, the residue of one's day and other recent events and the like, sifted through the dreamwork to emerge as a disguised wish-fulfillment. To the extent that one applies Freudian dream theory to the analysis of individual films, one tends toward biographical criticism of the filmmaker, to the analysis of the dreams of characters within a film, or most problematically, to an appeal to some form of universalist interpretation of dream imagery.

Without ignoring these significant caveats, consider another situation in which one has a group of dreams but no dreamers. That is, one has texts (called films or dreams) but no access to those who created or dreamed them. Should all analysis of such texts be abandoned because the analytical situation is impossible, or could we use a methodology and work backward to a text-producer, a dreamer? This chapter will use a group of films from the American silent cinema and let the films guide us to the tensions, residues, wish-fulfillments, and erotic components which produced them. If we allow that films are like dreams, then we postulate that cultures (which produce films and other culturally shared and shaped products) are like individuals; that in the production of films, the contents are sifted through a censor (as once they were literally) which mangles troublesome issues leading to a manifest content produced by the linked dream work processes of displacement and condensation.[8]

Charles Eckert, who intelligently combines Marxism, Freudianism, and structuralism to offer a fascinating reading of a single film, *Marked Woman* (1937), defines displacement as "the substitution of an acceptable object of love, hate, etc., for a forbidden one."[9] For Robert Eberwein, displacement is "the shifting of psychic attention from important to apparently irrelevant or minor details."[10] For Freud himself, the power of displacement in the dream work was of crucial importance: "It could be seen that the elements which stand out as the principal components of the manifest content of the dream are far from playing the same part in the dream-thoughts. And, as a corollary, the converse of this assertion can be affirmed: what is clearly the essence of the dream-thoughts need not be represented at all." Condensation was less fundamental for Freud: "The first thing that becomes clear to anyone who compares the dream-content with the dream-thoughts is that a work of *condensation* on a large scale has been carried out."[11] For Eckert, condensation is defined as "a process whereby a number of discrete traits or ideas are fused in a single symbol."[12] While other factors account for the odd look of dreams, and the need therefore, of analysis, such as overdetermination—being "represented in the dream-thoughts many times over"—Freud maintains that "Dream-displacement and dream-condensation are the two governing factors to whose activity we may in essence ascribe the form assumed by dreams."[13]

In adapting theoretical formulations from structuralism in the following analysis, I do not claim an easy fit between diverse methodologies, save to note that structuralism certainly owes much to the Freudian formulations. And I note, along with Eckert (among others), that a mixture of methodologies like structuralism and Freudianism "is not heretically eclectic: structures and their permutations are central to each form of analysis. . . . "[14] An examination of American silent films points out the particular ways in which an ongoing cultural dynamic was handled in the early years of the cinema—chosen precisely because the censoring agency of the Production Code allowed more overt expressions of certain themes, allowing that other form of censorship, the dream work, to predominate.

As American commercial film solidified its base as a popular form of entertainment produced within an industrial context in the middle 1910s, it also took on an overtly propagandistic character. Whether it did so out of fear of outside censorship or control, or out of an inchoate sense of gratitude on the part of the major emerging film producers to their new American home, American moviemakers worked toward envisioning a unified society of white, middle-class citizens. One of the problems of this society, one of its contradictions, was between a vision of unified culture and the facts of difference, primarily ethnic difference. Ethnicity was a fact of American life, as was racism, sexism, and other forms of bigotry and discrimination. The question of unifying these cultural variations, of erasing differences, constituted a "cinematic dream," one obviously aligned to the American Dream, the American mythos of the melting pot, but like Freudian dreams, a work subject to displacements, condensations, and overdeterminations. It can be argued that this cinematic dream during the silent era provides a privileged site of analysis for understanding how the discourse of the melting pot was structured into the American psyche, and how the contradictions and repressions of the myth can similarly be isolated.

A little less than half way through Buster Keaton's *Seven Chances* (1925), Jimmie (Keaton) comes upon a woman reading a newspaper at a bus stop (fig. 14.1). Desperate at this point to get a woman to agree to marry him—any woman—he asks this young, relatively attractive female. Without intertitles (for we know by now what he is asking), we watch Keaton's character meet with a distinct lack of response. The woman does not say no; in fact, she says nothing and simply shrugs a little after he has finished. She then opens her paper, which we and Jimmie see is in Yiddish. Sighing a little, Jimmie exits the frame, leaving the woman alone with her paper. Before we can further puzzle over or analyze the gag, Keaton's character is already pursuing the next possible female subject. As he walks away from the camera, we see a woman enter from the lower corner, frame right, and pass Keaton, who is looking forlornly down-ward. He catches a glimpse of her from the rear, that is, of her rear, which he tilts his head to admire as she sashays up the street (fig. 14.2). Jimmie runs to catch up to her, beginning to pop the question. The camera angle changes to a front view, and we see momentarily—before he does—that the woman is black. Jimmie shuts his mouth in abject embarrassment. The "joke" is clearly a racist one, the implication being that no white man would ask a black woman to marry him, even, as in this case, for a quite temporary marriage of convenience.

Relieved at having nearly popped the question to an inappropriate object of desire, Jimmie sees a woman sitting in a barber's chair having her hair styled. As he begins to approach the woman, the barber suddenly removes the woman's head. Jimmie's investigation reveals that it was a modeling dummy, and that the barber was shaping a wig. Jimmie, dismayed but undaunted, then comes upon the stage entrance to a theater, next to which is a poster of an attractive chanteuse (fig. 14.3). A trunk blocks the bottom of the poster. Jimmie bribes the stage manager to enter so that he may ask the songstress to marry him. The camera remains outside as a stage-hand appears to remove the trunk. We see the name "Julian Eltinge" written on the bottom of the poster; a close-up of the name follows, so that we see it clearly. The "chanteuse" is a man, according to Daniel Moews, in fact, a then-famous female impersonator.[15] Jimmie soon comes staggering out of the theater, with a blackened eye and his boater crushed around his shoulders (fig. 14.4).

This gag sequence has introduced a new rhetorical dimension to the humor of the film. In Jimmie's previous attempts to find a bride, he asked women who rejected him (save for one woman who said yes, but turned out to be a young girl). To put it plainly, previously the women said no. In this sequence, we find a significant change: women do not really *say* anything. From a woman who is unable to speak his language and thus is unable to speak to him; to a woman to whom he may not speak; to a woman who is unable to speak at all (because the dummy is not a woman and is not alive); to a woman who is not a woman—there is a certain similarity. An equation is made: All these "women" are unable to speak *as women*. Their inability to speak in some sense makes them not women, or less than women, and in any case, therefore, none could marry him.

The dummy aside (a Keaton gag involving miscognition and mis-taken perception), an equation is made between Jew, black, and gay

14.1. and 14.2. Scenes from *Seven Chances:* Buster Keaton attempts to find a bride among various ethnic choices, an early example of how the discourse of the melting pot was structured into the American psyche.

14.3. and 14.4. Scenes from *Seven Chances*: Keaton and his encounter with a female impersonator, another of the film's women who are unable to speak as women.

(an obvious implication of the female impersonator). Whereas it is a given in the context of the film's diegesis (and the world view of American culture at the time) that marriage to a black woman is inconceivable for a white man (Jimmie does not even talk to her) and that "marriage" to a female impersonator is literally laughable, there seems to be nothing wrong with the first, Jewish, woman. Save perhaps for a slightly "Semitic" straight nose and a definitely conservative coiffure, the woman is conventionally attractive. We may take it that had she known the English word *yes* she might have become Jimmie's (temporary) bride. But it is precisely within the context of the gag, within the rhetorical significance of the sequence, that she becomes inappropriate, inferior, linked to the black woman and the non-woman, the "gay" (linked for that matter to the literally non-woman, non-person dummy). The Jew is a woman whom he may not marry, for all intents and purposes a non-woman, like the black and the homosexual.[16]

It is during the second half, the second act, of the stage-derived farce that is *Seven Chances*, that the film achieves its brilliance as Keaton runs for his life from a deadly mob of women. Here male fears of women are unleashed; that is, male fears of woman unleashed. As Moews notes: whereas in the first act of the film, the women whom Keaton pursues are all constrained spatially—the garden of his girlfriend's home, the space of the country club where he asks seven women to marry him—in the second half, Keaton is pursued by women who are unconstrained. Filling a church where an advertisement of marriage has brought them, the women literally burst their bonds, their boundaries, and—once unconstrained—unleash their hellish fury on Keaton, chasing him with murderous intent.[17] It is clear that the women's unconstrained rage has a sexual basis. But there was, in fact, a *transition* from constraint to openness, from the place where women were contained to the place where their very uncontainedness became a frightening spectacle—during Jimmie's confrontation with ethnicity.

Preceding Jimmie's encounter with the Jewess, he asks one more appropriate object, an attractive white woman driving a car. She is thus spatially constrained in a way in which the Jewish woman, sitting on a bench at a bus stop, or the black woman walking down a city street, are not.[18] It is entirely appropriate that the women to whom he spoke, and who spoke to him, were to be found in a country club, that iconic bastion of WASPishness. Keaton's rejection by these women is humorous but safe. But his confrontation with ethnicity was in the open, *out there*, and preceded the horrific vision of women unconstrained.

There is a paradox to this constraint-openness dichotomy involving the issue of speech and silence. The constrained women in the
country club possess the power of speech—they may reject *him*.
The women in the open do not speak—he may reject *them*. But Jimmie desires the country club women only for a marriage of convenience; the sexual content of such marriage does not exist, these
constrained women have no desire (for Jimmie). Yet even without
this sexual dimension to such a marriage, the Jew, black, and gay
may not be considered. But it is precisely during the confrontation
out there, with the ethnics who may not speak as women, that the
repressed sexual dimension is literally unleashed.

It is not the intention of this chapter to castigate Keaton for his
sexism. Rather, as it happens, in this two-minute sequence in a relatively minor (but fascinating) Keaton film, we see commonly held
images of male fears of women and a commonly, less well understood image of the sexual dimension to ethnicity. We might understand this sequence as being paradigmatic of the white male
American's encounter with ethnicity.[19] Deep in the substructures of
American history, literature, and mythology, we find the problem at
the heart of the American experiment—the European white man's
encounter with the dark Other.[20] From the Indian, already here
when the whites arrived, to the black, imported by the whites, to
the varieties of other ethnics (ethnic Others) who immigrated to
American shores in the nineteenth century (Italians, Irish—
England's Other—Chinese, and the Jews of Eastern Europe), the
American experiment in building a culture has been a multiracial,
multiethnic experiment unique in the annals of modern societies.[21]

The solution to the problem of race and ethnicity in American
society exists in competing images. There is the image of the
"multi-racial, multi-ethnic society," the implication of which is the
"separate but equal" credo that once obtained with regard to school
segregation in the South. This credo holds no mythic appeal, for it
clearly implies the *failure* of a multiracial, multiethnic society. That
this model is perhaps closer to the reality of postwar American life
is literally beside the point, for it is the myths, the unconscious of
the American psyche, which concern us.

On the other hand, another, albeit ambiguous, model remains
mythically potent, present in a variety of discourses throughout the
twentieth century—the melting pot. The reality of a multiracial,
multiethnic society has given rise to a myth of national identity torn
between the forces of sameness and difference. As Mary Dearborn
has it: "the central feature of American identity is the experience of

migration, that Americans are in fact all descended from immigrants and that American selfhood is based on a seemingly paradoxical sense of shared difference. As Americans we partake of a national identity, a communally determined and accepted sense of self; at the same time, as Americans and ethnics all, we define ourselves ancestrally."[22]

The melting-pot model contains within it the fundamental concept of assimilation. Initially, the model itself existed in two competing images: that there is a culture into which newcomers may assimilate; or that the culture itself is the pot into which the ethnic stew is placed. Philip Gleason defines the first mode, assimilation, as the "purging away [of] cultural impurities of immigrant groups and transforming them into 100% Americans according to the Anglo-Saxon model." The second ideal conceives of "the whole society as in the melting pot" leading to "a new culture, blended from the elements of all," this blending defining "a new national character."[23] But as the twentieth century progressed, the myth of the melting pot became more of a unitary process, more in tune with only the first, the assimilatationist, model—the new must disappear into an already existing structure, which remains essentially the same.

The repressed dimension of the assimilationist model, the darkness at the heart of the myth of the melting pot, has, unsurprisingly, been the sexual one. And most repressed of all has been the relationship, the relations, between black and white. Ideally, in the melting-pot model, white and dark must merge. Yet in such mythic merging the fearsome spector of desire and sexuality looms large, for melting, merging, and assimilation can occur only through sexual interrelations—intermarriage. If the American experiment is to succeed in this model, the races must have relations. In the confrontation with the racial Other, the new American psyche was immediately confronted with the sexual dimension of Otherness. Dearborn recognizes that "it is hardly surprising that the 'first' American woman in our national cultural imagination is also the first American ethnic woman: Pocahontas. . . . " The Pocahontas legend has crucial implications for the myth of the melting pot and for an understanding of the relationship between ethnicity, gender, and the emerging American identity, for "the legend [of Pocahontas] is about love and marriage between an ethnic woman and a white man [but] it is also about sexuality."[24] Yet we note that in generalized mythic discourse such as political campaigns or educational forums, and in popular cultural forms, that rarely, if ever, has white-black intermarriage been put forth as a positive value, this in comparison to quite common images of white-Indian and white-Asian intermarriage, of which the Pocahontas tale is a paradigm. Indeed, white-black intermarriage was so heinous to the American imago that it was illegal in the many states in the American South for many years, and the horror of miscegenation underlies the image of both the male and female villains in *Birth of a Nation*. The villainy of Silas Lynch is frequently noted on this level; less often noted is the female housekeeper who "reeks" of sexuality and blood lust in an almost hysterical characterization. The half-breed is a common villain or figure of fright in the image of the white-Native-American intermarriage as well, but white-Indian relations never had the horror of white-black. One can find as many heroic half-breed offspring of white-Indian marriage as villainous descendents.

Even more revealing than the horror of white-black relations, however, is the realization of the *site* of such relations as it is expressed in popular cultural discourses: most often it is the "dark" woman who merges with (marries) the white male. The fear of dark sexuality, on the one hand, of the dark male's sexual desires for white women (seen in racist and anti-Semitic imagery), and the ethnic woman's rapacious desires (for example, *Seven Chances*), cannot, on the other hand, repress the white male's attraction to the dark woman. In the melting-pot myth, as seen especially in popular culture, it is a white male prerogative to have relations with the dark female, who may be fearsome or villainous but who is nevertheless in many instances a potential object of desire so long as she marries the white male and lives in his white society. Dearborn sees this specific white male-ethnic female structure as "one of America's most ideologically potent myths."[25] But as in many—indeed, any—myths, a contradiction can be found at its heart, the contradiction between the mythwork and the social reality which the mythwork tries to overcome. In this specific instance, attraction to the dark woman, and the eventual marriage to her or the rejection of such a marriage in favor of one's own race, is problematized because of the questions of race and gender. A kind of intermediary is therefore needed, a gender and racial ambiguity needs arise—one found in that conflated, mythic Other known as the Jews.

This sequence from Keaton's film, in addition to revealing the generalized ambivalence about ethnic sexuality, the simultaneous attraction-repulsion, demonstrates a highly common conflation of ethnic, racial, and gender imagery. In Christian, white, patriarchal societies in which heterosexuality is the explicit norm, Jew, black, and gay are linked in a triumvirate of the Other. In fact, if we allow woman into this group, we are presented with a fearsome foursome of Otherness to male identity as it is ideally constructed in Euro-American culture. By the process of linkage in Keaton's film, the Jewish woman becomes an inappropriate mate, literally a laughable choice. Some sort of equation was made between Jew, black, and gay by virtue of a lack, the lack of speech as a woman. And we claim that this linkage among Jew, black, and gay, especially as it relates to gender issues (to *the* gender issue) is a commonality in the discourse about the Other. In thinking about this highly complicated issue which made its appearance innocently enough in a slapstick farce of the 1920s, we see how the Jew may be understood as a kind of "free floating ethnic signifier," a signifier of Otherness across a wide spectrum of discourses. In fact, equations have been made among Jews, women, blacks, and gays.

Sander Gilman, in his provocative work *Difference and Pathology*, discusses Otherness as seen by dominant society, in specific, European culture of the Victorian era. Otherness is postulated on difference—sexual, racial, even medical (madness and pathology). There were (are) many Others for Victorian males: women, blacks, Jews, and gays primarily. Similarities of difference exist among all these groups; they are all Other, all inferior to the dominant, healthy, whole, and wholly male group. Yet only the Jews manage to be equated with the others, to be consistently Other. Gilman notes that "the two major examples for theories of race in the nineteenth century were the blacks and the Jews."[26] It was the sexuality of blacks with which white European men of science were concerned, especially that of black women. This was a carry over of the general discourse about female sexuality, and it was to women that Jews (Jewish men, obviously) were habitually compared. The Jew was also linked to the homosexual by the homosexual's (alleged) link to women. For example, Walter Rathenau's monograph "Hear, O Israel" (1897), included the "description of the male Jew as possessing all of the qualities usually ascribed to the woman (or indeed the homosexual). . . ."[27]

Some ingenious comparisons were put forth in the name of science and objectivity, comparisons which would become part of the foundation of "racial science" and eugenics which the Nazis used to give some legitimacy to their nightmare of torture and murder. For example, the work of Otto Weininger was widely read and influential. He posited a linguistic base for the inherent "insanity" of women: "Women are predisposed to illness, to hysteria, by the very nature of their biology, not because of their womb . . . but because of their language. For their language reflects the manner of seeing the word, a manner that is inherently flawed." For Weininger, both Jew and women have no sense of humor, stemming, somehow, from the fact that both lack ego, or lack a "center" to their ego. For Weininger, real "humor is rooted in the ability to transcend the material, a gift possessed by Aryan males but not by Jews and women. Humor is thus a central marker of the difference between the self and the Other. It is a mode of truthful discourse which Jews and women cannot possess." Even later, in America, a doctor writing in 1920 could claim that "Jews, like women, possessed a basic biological predisposition to specific forms of mental illness."[28]

We might even note an equation between Jew and Oriental in the white European mind. Eastern-European Jews were commonly called Orientals, while it is in fact the Middle East, cradle of Judaism, which Edward Said has in mind when he writes of "Orientalism." And why should the term *mogul*, which typically refers to Middle-Eastern or Oriental potentates, be applied and commonly used to refer to the primarily Jewish heads of American motion picture studios? In addition, racist imagery directed at Asians in America was similar both to anti-black bigotry and anti-Semitism.[29] Richard Oehling writes of a "dual focus of anti-Asian prejudice [in the period before 1924]: economic competition for jobs and the threat of 'racial mongrelization,' of corruption of white women and miscegenation. Of the many ethnic groups victimized, only blacks were feared so passionately on the sexual issue, which traditionally arouses the most violent and persistent hostility of all the various forms of prejudice."[30] And there is this all too clear recollection of anti-Semitic imagery: "the . . . *diabolical* Asians [who] continually plotted and connived the destruction of America in general and white women in particular. Asians were never what they seemed to be. Ruthless and clever . . . they serve with great subtlety and infinite patience the goal of the eventual mastery of the world by the 'yellow' race."[31]

A study of the portrayal of Jews in the cinema marks a privileged site of analysis for an understanding of how ethnic issues in American society have been "treated" by and in American films. Jewish characters have appeared in numerous films; figures who are recognizably Jewish appear as frequently as any other ethnic or racial group. More significantly, the idea that Jews are a "free-floating ethnic signifier" has allowed Jews to stand in for questions of race and ethnicity across the spectrum. From the other side of the coin, the Jewish presence behind the camera—as directors, writers, and, even more significantly, as production executives—allows isolation of some of the tensions involved when one ethnic group seems to be able to control its own images. Portrayals of Jews in cinema, and the absence (the "structuring absence") of such portrayals at different times in film history, in this respect allow us to see the tensions, displacements, condensations, and overdeterminations, as one ethnic group attempts to negotiate the conflicting images of the American dream and the myth of the melting pot.

If intermarriage between the white male and the ethnic female is the primary mythic mode of ethnic harmony and the erasure of difference, then one would expect to find films in which Jewish women marry non-Jewish men. Yet unquestionably the image of intermarriage between Jew and gentile that most Americans hold is the image of the Jewish man who marries a gentile woman—the shiksa. Such an image, such an automatic response to the Jew-gentile marriage, that it is a Jewish man and a gentile woman, is due to two factors. First, a greater portion of Jewish men indeed married outside the faith than did Jewish women. Yet, as Charles Silberman has pointed out, "among first- and second-generation Eastern European Jews, intermarriage was a rare event; between 1900 and 1940 . . . no more than 2 to 3 percent of American Jews married people who had been Gentile at birth." Silberman points out further that although the percentage of intermarriage increased in the 1940s and 1950s, its level was no more than 5 or 6 percent.[32] Therefore, we may conclude that while the shiksa image has a basis in reality on a comparative level of intermarriages between Jew and gentile, given the relative lack of such marriages in the first place, the image is owed to a second factor. It has been the creation of a number of highly visible *male* Jewish artists, primarily filmmakers and novelists, working through their own private demons, rebeling against their own traditions, reveling in their own exposure to a wider world, unconsciously reproducing the phenomenon of Jewish self-hatred, or taunting gentiles with their own secret fears of ethnic sexuality and prejudice. And it may be that if mainstream American male ideology finds interethnic, interracial marriage acceptable only when it is the white male and the ethnic female, it may be that Jewish male ideology finds that the non-Jewish woman is his ethnic Other.

Given that intermarriage was relatively rare for Jewish Americans (immigrants or their offspring), and that whatever small reality such marriage did possess was primarily Jewish man to shiksa, what about the cinema produced during this period of immigration and acculturation? That many films made about Jews were comedies is the province of another study. That, however, a number of films with Jewish characters focused on intermarriage is significant; that the majority of these films featured a Jewish woman loved by and in love with a non-Jewish male is critical.

A survey of films made in the pre-feature film era (1908–15) reveals an astonishing overdetermination of films which focus on intermarriage between a non-Jewish man and a Jewish woman. Fully 90 percent of such films feature Jewish women involved with a gentile man.[33] Typical would be *Becky Gets a Husband* (1912), which focuses on the intermarriage of a Jewish girl and an Irish boy. Variations include a film like *A Daughter of Israel* (1914), in which a Jewish antique dealer's foster child, initially rejected by an aristocratic young man, is found acceptable when it is revealed that she is not Jewish. There is the occasional film in which such relationships do not work out, in which social, cultural, and familial pressures break up the relationship. Perhaps the most interesting and revealing is *Faith of Her Fathers* (1915), in which a young woman who does not marry her gentile boyfriend at her family's insistence soon dies thereafter of a broken heart. On the other hand, in *The Faith of Her Fathers* (1914), a girl is courted by a gentile boy but decides to stick with her own kind after having been ashamed of her father's profession (and by extension, of course, ashamed of her father's Jewishness).[34]

In most of the films in which the relationships do work out (that is, in most of these films), the initial resentment to such a marriage comes on the part of the Jewish family, especially the Jewish father. *The Jew's Christmas* (1913), for example, thus does double duty—assimilating the Jewish female offspring into the American male mainstream and overcoming old-fashioned attitudes on the part of mostly immigrant ethnics. Occasionally gentile anti-Semitism is held up for blame, such as in *The Pawnbroker's Daughter* (1913), but that is quite rare compared to the majority of films in which the Jewish father opposes his daughter's relationship to someone outside the faith.

The "double duty" of a film like *The Jew's Christmas* may be related to the appeal of intermarriage stories to women writers and readers. As Dearborn states, on one level, "intermarriage between white men and ethnic women becomes a symbolic literalization of the American dream, both in terms of success and of love: variously, it suggests an assertion of melting-pot idealism, of the forging of a 'new man,' of Cinderella success, of love 'regardless of race, creed, or color,' of the promise of America itself."[35] A significant handful of films, in fact, specifically juxtapose the prejudice of the Old World against the promise of America. Such films as *Threads of Destiny* (1914) and *Escape from Siberia* (1914) focus on the reality of Russian anti-Semitism and the promise of freedom from prejudice in America in these tales of Russian noblemen and their Jewish fiancees.

While it may be assumed as natural that women writers and readers, especially of the mid-nineteenth through the mid-twentieth century, would find such tales intriguing (ethnic women dreaming of worldly rewards and escape from their ethnic confines, non-ethnic women identifying with the powerlessness and subjugation of their ethnic sisters), it cannot account for a cinema primarily produced by men in which the pattern of "white man-ethnic woman" is reproduced. One's first instinct might be to find such roots in the fact that the cinema of the pre-feature period was not yet solidified under the major studio system in which Jewish production executives had a dominant role; or that the pre-Hays Code system allowed greater freedom of social and sexual mobility. As it happens, however, these factors cannot account for this extraordinary variance from reality in the earlier films, for it is the case that this same overdetermination of Jewish women-non-Jewish men is reproduced in the feature period. While films like *Abie's Irish Rose* (1930, from the successful Broadway play) and *The Jazz Singer* (1927) might immediately leap to mind, they are two of the most notable exceptions to this pattern as *The Melting Pot* (1915, based on Israel Zangwill's famous play) is the exception in the pre-feature period. In fact, the reverse pattern of *Abie's Irish Rose* predominates: *Clancy's Kosher Wedding* (1927), the "Cohens and Kelly" series; *Shamrock and the Rose* (1927) among others focus on an Irish boy marrying a Jewish girl. While there seems to be a kind of lull between 1918 and 1923 in the production of interethnic romances and comedies, when such films reappear, often produced or directed by Jewish men, the pattern of white man-ethnic woman (non-Jewish boy and Jewish girl) appears.

One might point to Edward Sloman's *We Americans* (1928) as a paradigm, for not only does a WASP boy marry a Jewish girl, but this boy marries the sister of a Jewish boy who saved his life in combat during World War I. The manifest content deals with the Jew as all-American, and the film may be seen as a precursor of a similarly overdetermined motif in World War II films in which the Jewish member of the combat platoon always overtly fights for

America and typically dies for the cause. Covertly, latently, the Jewish boy gives up his sister to the non-Jew, as ethnic women are ceded to the white, all-American man in the dominant paradigm of the myth of the melting pot. A Jewish male presence behind the camera does not stop the union of the white male to the ethnic woman, even—especially—when that ethnic woman is Jewish.

The claim that the large percentage of intermarriage stories which have a Jewish woman at their center is a kind of displacement of sexual anxiety about ethnicity on the part of mainstream (white male) America, an anxiety which must be alleviated by sexual conquest and ethnic denial (removal), goes hand in hand with an overdetermination of the gender issue. On this score, one can point to another kind of overdetermination involving gender and ethnicity: A large number of films in which the recalcitrant father (it is most often the father who is recalcitrant) is not simply Jewish, but a rabbi. The majority of these films have a European setting, as if to emphasize the relationship between ethnicity and the Old World. Films such as *In the Czar's Name* (1910), *Bleeding Hearts (or) Jewish Freedom under King Casimir of Poland* (1913), and *Surrender* (1927, directed by Edward Sloman) find rabbis' daughters desired by Russian or Polish noblemen; and in two of the films, the couple escapes to America to find romantic freedom and happiness. Again, while the overt or manifest content prizes the promise of the New World and suggests to immigrants that the old (ethnic) ways are no longer applicable, the latent content suggests the repression of ethnicity and the denial of difference.

While films with Jewish characters may be taken as paradigmatic, the way in which Jews may be seen as paradigms of the ethnic struggle in the American psyche, the pattern of white male-ethnic female may also be seen in stories with an Asian or Asian-American setting. While these films are much less frequent than tales of Jewish-gentile intermarriage, although more frequent in the silent period than films focusing on a white man-Indian woman relationship, they are equally revealing. One takes it as highly significant that the majority of films which focus positively on Caucasian-Asian marriage (all of which, of course, have a white male at their center) take place in Asia. The implications of this are twofold. First, the unavailability of white women presumably excuses the white man's attraction to the dark woman. Second, the dark races can be civilized by the white race—at the expense of the dark race's identity and culture. Thus we see films such as *Without Benefit of Clergy* (1921), in which an Englishman marries a native girl, who dies by film's end shortly after their child dies (a possible reading indicating that such marriages cannot work); or *Lotus Lady* (1930), with its setting in Indochina, perhaps the first film of the Vietnam War. And then there is *The Wrath of the Gods* (1914), in which a stranded U.S. sailor falls in love with a native girl, much to the chagrin of her family and community.

Richard Oehling has it that this film is paradigmatic of the whole issue of interethnic romance and marriage: "Of the few films of the 1920's that dealt with Asians or the Asian world, the most prevalent theme was race relations between Asians and Caucasians. These films suggest that interracial love affairs and marriages cannot work. . . . There are no happy endings, except where whites and Asian rejoin their own."[36] Even at home, in America's Chinatowns, it was only the Asian girl who could escape the ghetto via the white boy, as in *Wing Toy* (1921), in which a mixed-heritage girl (Asian father and white mother) marries a white reporter investigating Chinatown gangsterism.

The attraction-repulsion complex of white, male America toward ethnic sexuality saw the dark side in the dramas in which dark men pursued white women. Although a cliche from *Birth of a Nation* onward, it had enough force into the 1960s to drive many a plot. So, for example, John Ford's condemnation of Ethan Edwards's (John Wayne), racism in *The Searchers* (1956), as in Ethan's crazed look when he shouts that Debbie "has married a buck," or Ford's condemnation of the good white citizens at the fort who reject Elena (Linda Cristal) who had been "Stone Calf's Woman" in *Two Rode Together* (1962). On the other hand, Ford is not above using the horror of the sexual desire of Asian men for white women to drive the plot of *Seven Woman* (1966)—and neither actor who portrays the Asian warlords is Asian. Mike Mazurki is white, and Woody Strode (who had also played the Indian Stone Calf) is black.[37]

Again, however, it may be that the situation of Jews—Jews in reality and Jews on film—can reveal the tensions of white male ideology. For there are a handful of films in which the Jewish man loves and weds the non-Jewish girl. But there is still a kind of strange modulation, a hesitation, on the part of these films. In most cases, the films are based on successful stage shows—*The Melting Pot*, *Abie's Irish Rose*, even *The Jazz Singer*; thus there was an acceptance of the basic plot, a pre-testing of the potential controversy. Both *The Jazz Singer* and *Private Izzy Murphy* (1926) featured big stars, Al Jolson (fig. 14.5) and George Jessel respectively (Jessel, in fact, originated the leading role of *The Jazz Singer* on Broadway), and,

14.5. Al Jolson in *The Jazz Singer:* Jackie Rabinowitz, son of a cantor, finds success in America as Jack Robin, the singer of jazz songs, in a film that highlights the struggle between Old World Jewish and New World American ways.

as in the case of Sessue Hayakawa, major stardom overcomes, in some fashion, the ethnic factor. Finally, the only other major instances of Jewish boy-shiksa romance emerged from the struggle with Americanism and ethnicity on the part of the British-born, Jewish filmmaker Edward Sloman: *The Woman He Loved* (1922) and *His People* (1925).

We also see a repression of the intermarriage idea, a softening of the dark man-white woman fear. *Abie's Irish Rose* is basically a comedy, in contrast to so many of the melodramas of Jewish women's interethnic romances which meet with paternal resistance, and focuses on Jewish-Irish intermarriage, the most common interethnic pairing. In *The Jazz Singer*, the fact that May McAvoy's character is a shiksa is hardly even alluded to, the famous "struggle" in this film is between retention of the Old World Jewish ways and the New World success as a jazz singer. Once again it is a father who stands in the way, who represents an inappropriate clinging to the past, and in this instance a love of American popular culture and an over-determined form of mother love represses the intermarriage component. Success in the American mainstream, a breakthrough into stardom, a breakout of the ghetto, "naturally" brings with it the WASP woman. Intermarriage becomes secondary to assimilation. The Jewish man is de-Semiticized—Jakie Rabinowitz becomes Jack Robin, after all.[38]

There is yet another kind of modulation of Jewishness in Sloman's *The Woman He Loved*. A Jewish boy, given up for adoption in childhood to a rural WASP couple, falls in love with the girl next door (or down the road in this case) whose parents do not approve of him; their disapproval is not a function of his Jewishness, for he recalls nothing of his parents and background. Repression is clearly the operative word. Late in the film he discovers his true origins, rediscovers his Jewishness, and finally does marry the non-Jewish girl. Jewishness has in some sense been put on hold, abandoned in favor of rural America, seat of the traditional American myth, returned to only after total assimilation has been achieved.

His People is one of Sloman's most important films. Here we find another Jewish household with a recalcitrant immigrant father and a sympathetic, loving mother. Again the Jewish hero is in love with a non-Jewish girl, another Irish girl, in fact. What modulates the Jewish element is a surprisingly common recurrence of Jewish male activity in films up through the late 1940s: the Jewish boxer. One might attribute this to another kind of overdetermination, in which the implicitly anti-Semitic association of the Jew with women is denied explicitly in the image of the Jewish man as sportsman, as fighter, man-to-man in the ring. In fact, however, the image of the Jewish boxer was not an overdetermined one, for it is the case that by the end of the 1920s, Jewish fighters were the dominant ethnic group in boxing, and almost 20 percent of champions across weight classes were Jewish.[39] And there might be something to the Jewish-Irish intermarriage films, given that the second most dominant ethnic group in the prewar fight game was the Irish, and that Irish-Jewish rivalry in the ring was anything but the comedy of the Cohens and the Kellys. Moreover, and more importantly, *His People* condemns the father for his attitude toward his boxing son, while his other son, the father's favorite, is a social climber who moves in higher-class German-Jewish circles. This son goes so far as to deny his family's background, claiming to be an orphan to his fiancée's family. For the Jewish Sloman, this is clearly condemnatory behavior, and he plays upon the deep ethnicity in all Americans when this other son (who has shown to be physically weak and cowardly previously) denies his heritage entirely. On the other hand, to be a real American, the good son has to be a fighter and has to be willing to marry outside the faith of his fathers.

Such ambivalence and modulation on the part of a Jewish filmmaker shows the struggle at and in the heart of ethnic America. The cinematic dream of the American dream, a product of Jews as much as any group, is a nightmare of contradictions, confusions, and ambivalences which, however, can never hide the deep wish-fulfillment to become a part of a dominant culture which at once promises and denies assimilation to the ethnic Others who have come to its shores.

NOTES

1. Much of the following discussion is drawn from *Film and Dreams: An Approach to Bergman,* ed. Vlada Petric (South Salem: Redgrave, 1981), pp. 2–48.

2. Petric, *Film and Dreams,* p. 26.

3. That is to say, that while there is no necessary relationship between film and dream (i.e., one does not have to invoke dream theory to explain narrative cinema), the relationship between film and dream has dominated all attempts to relate dreams to something else. Even the significant uses of dreams, dream states, and stream-of-consciousness in literature have been theorized as owing as much to film as to dream.

4. Petric, *Film and Dreams,* p. 6.

5. Ibid., pp. 23–24.

6. Robert T. Eberwein, *Film and the Dream Screen: A Sleep and a Forgetting* (Princeton: Princeton University Press, 1984), p. 192, emphases added. Of course, adding the concept of "nurturing" to the dream analogy expands the implications of Eberwein's remarks to encompass, variously, the works of Laura Mulvey and Christian Metz among others working in the mainstream of psychoanalytically derived film theory and criticism.

7. Petric's anthology devoted to Bergman demonstrates this, as does Eberwein's *Film and the Dream Screen,* despite the broad implications of the remark quoted previously. To this short list of filmmakers must be added Robert Altman, especially *Three Women,* and the works of Woody Allen, whose admiration for the works of Bergman borders on the parodic. Altman and Allen are analyzed in Krin Gabbard and Glen O. Gabbard, *Psychiatry and the Cinema* (Chicago: University of Chicago Press, 1987).

8. I am here invoking the same principle used to underwrite some of the theoretical and analytical strategies used in Gaylyn Studlar and David Desser, "Never Having to Say You're Sorry: *Rambo's* Rewriting of the

Vietnam War," *Film Quarterly* 42 (Fall 1988): 9–16, in which the concept of "cultural trauma" is invoked and linked to psychic trauma experienced by an individual in the face of overwhelming guilt.

9. Charles W. Eckert, "The Anatomy of a Proletarian Film: Warner's *Marked Woman*," *Film Quarterly* 27 (Winter 1973–74): 10–24.

10. Eberwein, *Film and the Dream Screen*, p. 12.

11. Sigmund Freud, *The Interpretation of Dreams*, trans. and ed. James Strachey (New York: Avon, 1965), pp. 340, 312–13.

12. Eckert, "The Anatomy of a Proletarian Film," p. 21.

13. Freud, "Interpretation of Dreams," pp. 318, 343.

14. Eckert, "The Anatomy of a Proletarian Film," p. 23. Eckert includes Marxism, as noted previously, in his claim that structures are central to the methodologies he employs. Eckert is invoked as a model as well by Gabbard and Gabbard, who similarly employ psychoanalytic, structural, and ideological methodologies to their interpretations of the image of the psychiatrist in cinema and to readings of selected films. Robert Ray performs a similar methodological move in *A Certain Tendency of the Hollywood Cinema, 1930–1980* (Princeton: Princeton University Press, 1985). Ray primarily uses the idea of structural displacement and ideological overdetermination, although after invoking these terms early in the work, he allows his penetrating insights into a diverse group of films to carry the argument.

15. Daniel Moews, *Keaton: The Silent Features Close Up* (Berkeley: University of California Press, 1976), p. 138.

16. This is not to say that the female impersonator is a homosexual. In fact, according to the violence with which Jimmie's question was received, Julian Eltinge was obviously highly insulted. Rather, that in any case Jimmie would have found himself with an inappropriate bride, and that the humor stems from a clear homosexual undercurrent.

17. Moews, *Keaton*, pp. 136, 153–54.

18. The barber's dummy is constrained, framed by the window of the barber shop—had she, in fact, been a woman, she would have been appropriate, and would have been able to say no. We do not even see the woman who is not a woman.

19. Although ethnicity and race are not typically taken as identical in meaning, there is ample precedent for equating the two terms. In Randall Miller's *Ethnic Images in American Film and Television* (Philadelphia: Balch Institute, 1978), along with chapters on images of Jews, Italians, Germans, and Poles, there are essays on blacks and Asian Americans. Equating race and ethnicity seems increasingly common in social science discourse in general.

20. See Leslie A. Fiedler, *Love and Death in the American Novel*, rev. ed. (New York: Stein and Day, 1975), especially pp. 366–90.

21. Perhaps only Australia has any similarities with the United States in this respect, especially the encounter of the white with the aboriginal, which might in part account for the spectacular success of Australian films in the United States since the late 1970s. However, the Australian experi-

ence with immigration and racial restriction is fundamentally different; Glen Lewis, *Australian Movies and the American Dream* (New York: Praeger, 1987), pp. 15, 19–21. Since World War II, Great Britain has also participated in multiculturalism.

22. Mary V. Dearborn, *Pocahontas's Daughters: Gender and Ethnicity in American Culture* (New York: Oxford University Press, 1986), p. 3.

23. Philip Gleason, "Confusion Compounded: The Melting Pot in the 1960s and 1970s," *Ethnicity* 6 (March 1979): 10–20.

24. Dearborn, *Pocahontas's Daughters*, pp. 5, 97.

25. Ibid., p. 10.

26. Sander Gilman, *Difference and Pathology: Stereotypes of Sexuality* (Ithaca: Cornell University Press, 1985), p. 119.

27. Gilman, *Difference and Pathology*.

28. Sander Gilman, *Jewish Self-Hatred: Anti-Semitism and the Hidden Language of the Jews* (Baltimore: Johns Hopkins University Press, 1986), pp. 245, 188, 162. The seeming oddity that both Weininger and Myerson, the author of the final quote, were Jewish is the subject of Gilman's *Jewish Self-Hatred*.

29. Of course, similarities of rhetoric directed against certain groups demonstrates only that the Other can take the form of any particular group as an expression of fear and resentment, that Others are there to be filled in with such expressions.

30. Richard A. Oehling, "The Yellow Menace: Asian Images in American Film" in *The Kaleidoscopic Lens: How Hollywood Views Ethnic Groups*, ed. Randall M. Miller, (n.p.: Jerome S. Ozer, 1980), p. 183.

31. Oehling, "The Yellow Menace," p. 183.

32. Charles Silberman, *A Certain People: American Jews and Their Lives Today* (New York: Summit Books, 1985), p. 287.

33. Titles of films, plots, and other characteristics have been culled from the following sources, checked against each other for accuracy and consistency: *AFI Catalog of Feature Motion Pictures Produced in the U.S. 1921–30* (New York: R. R. Bowker, 1971); Patricia Erens, *The Jew in American Cinema* (Bloomington: Indiana University Press, 1984); Lester Friedman, *Hollywood's Image of the Jew* (New York: Frederick Ungar, 1982); and Stuart Fox, comp., *Jewish Films in the United States: A Comprehensive Survey and Descriptive Filmography* (Boston: G. K. Hall, 1976).

34. John Murray Cuddihy terms this phenomenon "the guilt of shame" in *The Ordeal of Civility: Freud, Marx, Levi-Strauss and the Jewish Struggle with Modernity* (New York: Basic Books, 1974), pp. 58–63.

35. Dearborn, *Pocahontas's Daughters*, p. 103.

36. Oehling, in *Kaleidoscopic Lens*, ed. Miller, p. 187.

37. In fairness to Ford, a horror of sexuality pervades all of the characters in the film, save for Anne Bancroft's character, and Ford ambiguously condemns these missionaries for their racism, ethnocentrism, and feelings of cultural superiority, which may be read as a function of their sexual dysfunction.

38. The use of blackface performance in this film is of course yet another link between Jew and black—a link not only forged by European anti-Semitism, but also by Jewish, and later black filmmakers. See David Desser and Lester Friedman, *In Search of a Tradition* (Urbana: University of Illinois Press, in press).

39. See, for example, Steven Riess, "A Fighting Chance: The Jewish-American Boxing Experience, 1890–1940," *American Jewish History* 74 (March 1985): 223–53.

Are All Latins from Manhattan?
Hollywood, Ethnography, and
Cultural Colonialism

She's a Latin from Manhattan
I can tell by her mañana
She's a Latin from Manhattan
And not Havana.
                    —Al Jolson in
              Go Into Your Dance (1935)

The commonplace of ethnic studies of the Hollywood cinema is to begin with the obvious: the classic Hollywood cinema was never kind to ethnic or minority groups. The standard claim is that, be they Indian, black, Hispanic, or Jewish, Hollywood represented ethnics and minorities as stereotypes that circulated easily and repeatedly from film to film. More significantly, minorities and ethnics were most noticeable by their absence in classic Hollywood films. Rarely protagonists, ethnics merely provided local color, comic relief, or easily recognizable villains and dramatic foils. When coupled with the pervasiveness of stereotypes, this marginalization or negation completes the usual "pattern" of Hollywood's ethnic representation and its standard assessment as damaging, insulting, and negative.

But Hollywood's relationship to each ethnic and minority group is far more nuanced than this simple narrative at first seems to allow. And, in fact, each of these relationships is unique; each has its own complex history with a specificity derived from Hollywood's position as a socioculturally bound ethnographer.

What does it mean to say that Hollywood has served as an ethnographer of American culture? First, it means to conceive of ethnography not as a scientific methodology that through detailed description and analysis unearths holistic truths about "other" cultures,[1] but as a historically determined practice of cultural interpretation and representation from the standpoint of participant observation.[2] And it also means to think of Hollywood not as a simple reproducer of fixed and homogenous cultures or ideologies, but as a producer of some of the multiple discourses that intervene in, affirm, and contest the socioideological struggles of a given moment. To think of a classic Hollywood film as ethnographic discourse is to affirm its status as an authored, yet collaborative, enterprise, akin in practice to the way contemporary ethnographers have redefined their discipline. James Clifford, for example, has analyzed the discursive nature of ethnography "not as the experience and interpretation of a circumscribed 'other' reality, but rather as a constructive negotiation involving . . . conscious politically significant subjects."[3]

When ethnographers posit their work as "the mutual, dialogical production of a discourse" about culture that "in its ideal form would result in a polyphonic text," we also approach a description of the operations of an ideal, albeit not of Hollywood's cinema.[4] The difference lies in the deployment of power relations, what Edward Said calls the "effect of domination," or the ethnographic, cinematic, and colonial process of designing an identity for the other and, for the observer, a standpoint from which to see without being seen.[5] Obviously, neither ethnography nor the cinema have achieved that ideal state of perfect polyphony or perspectival relativity where the observer-observed dichotomy can be transcended and no participant has "the final word in the form of a framing story or encompassing synthesis."[6] Power relations always interfere. However, both ethnographic and cinematic texts, as discourses, carry the traces of this dialogic-polyphonic process and of the power relations that structure it.

Thinking of Hollywood as ethnographer—as co-producer in power of cultural texts—allows us to reformulate its relationship to ethnicity. Hollywood does not represent ethnics and minorities; it creates them and provides its audience with an experience of them. It evokes them, as the postmodern ethnographer Stephen Tyler might say. Rather than an investigation of mimetic relationships, then, what a critical reading of Hollywood's ethnographic discourse (a meta-ethnography) requires is the analysis of the historical-political construction of self-other relations—the articulation of forms of difference—sexual and ethnic—as an inscription of, among other factors, Hollywood's power as ethnographer, as creator, and translator of otherness.

One characteristic of standard "Hollywood's image of ——— " studies is that, no matter how bleakly the overall mimetic accuracy of Hollywood's representations of a particular group is evaluated, the analyst always manages to pinpoint a golden, or near-golden, moment when Hollywood, for complex conjunctural reasons, sees the light and becomes temporarily more sensitive to an ethnic or minority group. In the history of Hollywood's treatment of the American Indian, for example, that moment arrives in the 1960s and 1970s. For other ethnic and minority groups—Jews and Latin Americans, for example—usually there is a significant improvement noticed in the post-World War II period of "social consciousness."[7] What interests me are not the historical specifics of each of these moments, but the fact that such moments of the "discovery" and inscription of ethnic otherness play a critical role in the structure of texts about Hollywood and ethnicity, serving as the linchpin of te-leological historical arguments decrying Hollywood's stereotypical, unrealistic, and biased representations of ethnics.

My project is to question precisely this historical-narrative *topos* in the history of Hollywood's representation of Latin Americans. I will focus upon what is perceived as the "golden moment" or "break" in that history—the Good Neighbor Policy years (roughly 1939–47)—in order to analyze the moment's historical coherence and its function for Hollywood as an ethnographic institution, that is as creator, integrator, and translator of otherness. What happens when Hollywood self-consciously and intentionally assumes the role of cultural ethnographer?

My emphasis is on three stars whose ethnic otherness was artic-ulated according to parameters that shifted as Hollywood's ethno-graphic imperative became clear: Dolores del Rio, Lupe Vélez, and Carmen Miranda. That these three figures are Latin American and female is much more than a simple coincidence, for the Latin Amer-ican woman poses a double threat—sexual and racial—to Holly-wood's ethnographic and colonial authority.

The Good Neighbor Policy: Hollywood Zeroes in on Latin America

After decades of portraying Latin Americans lackadaisically and sporadically as lazy peasants and wily señoritas who inhabited an undifferentiated backward land, Hollywood films between 1939 and 1947, featuring Latin American stars, music, locations, and stories flooded U.S. and international markets. By February 1943, for example, thirty films with Latin American themes or locales had been released and twenty-five more were in the works. By April 1945, eighty-four films dealing with Latin American themes had been produced.[8] These films seemed to evidence a newfound sensibility, most notably, a sudden respect for national and geographical boundaries. At the simplest level, for example, it seemed that Hollywood was exercising some care to differentiate between the cultural and geographic characteristics of different Latin American countries by incorporating general location shots, specific citations of iconographic sites (for example, Rio de Janeiro's Corcovado Mountain), and some explanations of the cultural characteristics of the inhabitants.

Why did Hollywood suddenly become interested in Latin America? In economic terms, Latin America was the only foreign market available for exploitation during World War II. Before the war, the industry had derived a large percentage of its gross revenues from foreign markets, and upon the closing of the European and Japanese markets, it set out, in Bosley Crowther's words, on "a campaign to woo Latin America" with films of "Pan-American" interest.[9]

Pan-Americanism was also, however, an important key word for the Roosevelt administration, the Rockefeller Foundation, and the newly created (1940) State Department Office of the Coordinator for Inter-American Affairs (CIAA) headed by Nelson Rockefeller. Concerns about our Southern neighbors' dubious political allegiances and the safety of U.S. investments in Latin America led to the resurrection of the long-dormant Good Neighbor Policy and to the official promotion of hemispheric unity, cooperation, and nonaggression (in part, to erase the memories of the not-so-distant military interventions in Cuba and Nicaragua). Charged with the responsibility of coordinating all efforts to promote inter-American understanding, the CIAA set up a Motion Picture Section and appointed John Hay Whitney, vice president and director of the film library of the Museum of Modern Art (MOMA) in New York, as its director.[10]

The CIAA sponsored the production of newsreels and documentaries for Latin American distribution that showed "the truth about the American way," contracted with Walt Disney in 1941 to produce a series of twenty-four shorts with Latin American themes that would "carry the message of democracy and friendship below the

Rio Grande," sponsored screenings of films that celebrated the "democratic way" in what became known as the South American embassy circuit, and, together with the Hays Office's newly appointed Latin American expert, began to pressure the studios to become more sensitive to Latin issues and portrayals.[11] This impetus, when coupled with the incentive of Latin America's imminently exploitable 4,240 movie theaters, was sufficient to stimulate Hollywood to take on the project of educating Latin America about the democratic way of life and its North American audience about its Latin American neighbors.

This self-appointed mission, however, needs to be questioned more closely. How does Hollywood position itself *and* North Americans in relation to the Southern "neighbors"? How is its friendliness constituted? How does it differ from Hollywood's prior circulation of so-called stereotypes and its negligent undifferentiation of the continent?

From an industrial perspective, Hollywood's policies in the Good Neighbor period were directed by the assumption that Latin Americans would flock to see themselves created by Hollywood in glorious TechniColor and with an unexpected linguistic fluency. The pre-Good Neighbor films of the 1930s dealing with Latin Americans (primarily dramatic stories) were notorious for linguistic blunders and regional undifferentiation. They also directly promoted the development of proto-industrial filmmaking in Argentina, Mexico, and Brazil which had already begun to compete for the Latin American market. Furthermore, several Latin American nations had regularly begun to ban or censor Hollywood films deemed offensive to the national character, most notoriously, RKO's *Girl of the Rio* (1932), a film banned by a number of Latin American countries because its lecherous and treacherous central character, Sr. Tostado (Mr. "Toast," "Toasted," or "Crazed"), was considered "the most vile Mexican" ever to appear on the screen.[12] To forestall censorship and protests and to decrease the competitive edge of national productions, Hollywood began to feature more Latin American actors, songs and dances, and to differentiate among different cultures.

Three basic kinds of Good Neighbor Policy films were produced. First, there were a number of standard, classic Hollywood genre films, with North American protagonists, set in Latin America and with some location shooting, for example, Irving Rapper's *Now Voyager* (1942), with extensive footage shot in Rio de Janeiro; Edward Dmytryk's *Cornered* (1945), shot totally on location in Buenos Aires; and Alfred Hitchcock's *Notorious* (1946), with second-unit location shots of Rio de Janeiro. Then there were B— productions set and often shot in Latin America and that featured mediocre U.S. actors and Latin entertainers in either musicals or pseudo-musical formats, for example, *Mexicana* (1945) starring Tito Guizar, Mexico's version of Frank Sinatra, and the sixteen-year-old Cuban torch singer Estelita; Gregory Ratoff's *Carnival in Costa Rica* (1947) starring Dick Haymes, Vera Ellen, and Cesar Romero; and Edgar G. Ulmer's remake of *Grand Hotel*, *Club Havana* (1945), starring the starlet Isabelita, Tom Neil, and Margaret Lindsay. Finally, the most successful and most self-consciously "good-neighborly" films were the mid-to-big budget musical comedies set either in Latin America or in the U.S. but featuring, in addition to recognizable U.S. stars, fairly well-known Latin American actors and entertainers.

Almost every studio produced its share of these films between 1939 and 1947, but Twentieth Century-Fox, RKO, and Republic specialized in "good neighborliness" of the musical variety. Fox had Carmen Miranda under contract and produced films that featured her between 1940 and 1946; RKO followed the Rockefeller interest in Latin America by sending Orson Welles on a Good Neighbor tour of Brazil to make a film about Carnival,[13] and with films such as *Panamericana* (1945); Republic exploited contract players Tito Guizar and Estelita in a number of low-budget musicals such as *The Thrill of Brazil* (1946).

Notwithstanding the number of films produced, and the number of Latin American actors contracted by the studios in this period, it is difficult to describe Hollywood's position with regard to these suddenly welcomed "others" as respectful or reverent.[14] Hollywood (and the United States) needed to posit a complex otherness as the flip side of wartime patriotism and nationalism and in order to assert and protect its colonial-imperialist economic interests. A special kind of other was needed to reinforce the wartime national self, one that—unlike the German or Japanese other—was nonthreatening, potentially but not practically assimilable (that is, nonpolluting to the purity of the race), friendly, fun-loving, and not deemed insulting to Latin American eyes and ears. Ultimately, Hollywood succeeded in all except, perhaps, the last category.

The Transition: From Indifference to "Difference" Across the Bodies of Women

Before the Good Neighbor Policy period, few Latin Americans had achieved star status in Hollywood. In fact, most of the "vile"

Latin Americans of the early Hollywood cinema were played by U.S. actors. In the silent period, the Mexican actor Ramón Novarro, one of the few Latin American men to have had a consistent career in Hollywood, succeeded as a sensual yet feminized "Latin Lover" modeled on the Valentino icon,[15] but the appellation "Latin" always connoted Mediterranean rather than Latin American. Ostensibly less threatening than men, Latin American women fared differently, particularly Dolores del Rio and Lupe Vélez.

Del Rio's Hollywood career spanned the silent and early sound eras. Although considered exotic, del Rio appeared in a variety of films, working with directors as diverse as Raoul Walsh, King Vidor, and Orson Welles.[16] After a successful transition to talkies in Edwin Carewe's *Evangeline* (1929), her place in the Hollywood system was unquestionable and further legitimized by her marriage to the respected MGM art director Cedric Gibbons. Undeniably Latin American, del Rio was not, however, identified exclusively with Latin roles. Hers was a vague upper-class exoticism articulated within a general category of "foreign/other" tragic sensuality. This sensual other, an object of sexual fascination, transgression, fear, and capitulation not unlike Garbo or Dietrich, did not have a specific national or ethnic provenance, simply an aura of foreignness that accommodated her disruptive potential. Her otherness was located and defined on a sexual rather than an ethnic register, and she portrayed, above all, ethnically vague characters with a weakness for North American "white/blond" men: Indian maidens, South Seas princesses, Latin American señoritas, and other aristocratic beauties. Although she often functioned as a repeatable stereotype (in her role in *Girl of the Rio*, for example), her undifferentiated sexuality was not easily tamed by the proto-colonial ethnographic imperatives of Hollywood's Good Neighbor period. In a precursor of the Good Neighbor films like *Flying Down to Rio* (1933), the explicit and irresistible sensuality of her aristocratic Carioca character (all she has to do is look at a man across a crowded nightclub and he is smitten forever) could be articulated because it would be tamed by marriage to the North American hero. However in the films of the Good Neighbor cycle, that resolution/partial appeasement of the ethnically undifferentiated sexual threat of otherness she unleashed was no longer available. Likewise, in another pre-Good Neighbor policy film in which she portrays a Latin American, Lloyd Bacon's *In Caliente* (1935, fig. 15.1), del Rio is not identified as a *Mexican* beauty, but as the *world's* greatest dancer. As Carlos Fuentes has remarked, del Rio was "a goddess threatening to become

15.1. As "the world's greatest dancer," Dolores del Rio was paired with Leo Carrillo in Lloyd Bacon's *In Caliente* (1935), where she personifies the perfect cinematic example of the "colonial hybrid."

woman,"[17] and neither category—goddess or woman—was appropriate to Hollywood's self-appointed mission as goodwill imperialist ethnographer of the Americas. Del Rio's persona and her articulation in Hollywood films, in fact, comprise a perfect cinematic example of what Homi K. Bhabba has described as the phenomenon of the colonial hybrid, a disavowed cultural differentiation necessary for the existence of colonial-imperialist authority, where "what is disavowed [difference] is not repressed but repeated as something different—a mutation, a hybrid."[18]

Del Rio chose to return to Mexico in 1943 and dedicated herself—with a few "returns" to Hollywood, most notably to appear in John Ford's *The Fugitive* (1947) and *Cheyenne Autumn* (1964)—to the Mexican cinema and stage, where she assumed a legendary fame inconceivable in Hollywood. The impossibility of her status for Hollywood in 1939–47 was, however, literally worked through the body of another Mexican actress, Lupe Vélez.

Like del Rio's, Vélez's career began in the silent period, where she showed promise working with D. W. Griffith in *Lady of the Pavements* (1929) and other directors. But Vélez's position in Hollywood was defined not by her acting versatility, but by her smoldering ethnic identifiability. Although as striking as del Rio's, Vélez's beauty and sexual appeal were aggressive, flamboyant, and stridently ethnic (fig. 15.2). Throughout the 1930s, she personified the hot-blooded, thickly accented, Latin temptress with insatiable sexual appetites, on screen—in films such as *Hot Pepper* (1933), *Strictly Dynamite* (1934), and *La Zandunga* (1938)—and with her star persona—by engaging in much-publicized simultaneous affairs with Gary Cooper, Ronald Colman, and Ricardo Cortez, and marrying Johnny Weismuller in 1933.[19] (Impossible to imagine a better match between screen and star biographies: Tarzan meets the beast of the Tropics.) Vélez was, in other words, outrageous, but her sexual excessiveness, although clearly identified as specifically ethnic, was articulated as potentially subsumable. On and off screen, she, like del Rio, was mated with and married North American men.

The dangers of such explicit on-screen ethnic miscegenation became apparent in RKO's *Mexican Spitfire* six-film series (1939–43), simultaneously Vélez's most successful films and an index of the inevitability of her failure. Vélez portrayed a Mexican entertainer, Carmelita, who falls in love and marries—after seducing him away from his legitimate Anglo fiancee—Dennis Lindsay, a nice New England man. Much to the dismay of his proper Puritan family, Dennis chooses to remain with Carmelita against all obstacles, in-

15.2. Echoes of Lupe Vélez's smoldering sexuality resonate in this publicity shot. Unlike the bearskin upon which she lies, Velez epitomized the dangerous and potentially untameable aspects of Latin American female sexuality.

cluding, as the series progressed, specific references to Carmelita's mixed blood, lack of breeding and social unacceptability, her refusal to put the entertainment business completely behind her to become a proper wife, her inability to promote his (floundering) advertising career, and her apparent lack of desire for offspring. Although the first couple of installments were very successful, the series was described as increasingly redundant, contrived, and patently "absurd" by the press and was cancelled in 1943. Not only had it begun to lose money for RKO, but it also connoted a kind of Latin American otherness anathema to the Good Neighbor mission. Summarily stated, the questions posed by the series could no longer be tolerated because there were no "good neighborly" answers. The ethnic problematic of the series—intermarriage, miscegenation, and integration—could not be explicitly addressed within the new, friendly climate. Ironically highlighting this fictional and ideological question, Vélez, unmarried and five months pregnant, committed suicide in 1944.

Neither del Rio nor Vélez could be re-created as Good Neighbor ethnics, for their ethnic and sexual power and danger were not assimilable within Hollywood's new, ostensibly friendly, and temperate regime. Del Rio was not ethnic enough and too much of an actress; Vélez was too "Latin" and untamable. Hollywood's new position was defined by its double-imperative as "ethnographer" of the Americas; that is, by its self-appointed mission as translator of the ethnic and sexual threat of Latin American otherness into peaceful good neighborliness *and* by its desire to use that translation to attempt to make further inroads into the resistant Latin American movie market without damaging its national box office. It, therefore, could not advantageously promote either a mythic, goddess-like actress with considerable institutional clout (del Rio) or an ethnic volcano (Vélez) that was not even subdued by that most sacred of institutions, marriage to a North American. What Hollywood's Good Neighbor regime demanded was the articulation of a different female star persona that could be readily identifiable as Latin American (with the sexual suggestiveness necessary to fit the prevailing stereotype) but whose sexuality was neither too attractive (to dispel the fear-attraction of miscegenation) nor so powerful as to demand its submission to a conquering North American male.

The Perfect "Good Neighbor": Fetishism, Self, and Others

Hollywood's lust for Latin America as ally and market—and its self-conscious attempt to translate and tame the potentially disturbing radical (sexual and ethnic) otherness that the recognition of difference (or lack) entails—are clearest within the constraints of the musical comedy genre. Incorporated into the genre as exotic entertainers, Latin Americans were simultaneously marginalized and privileged. Although they were denied valid narrative functions, entertainment, rather than narrative coherence or complexity, is the locus of pleasure of the genre. Mapped onto the musical comedy form in both deprivative (the denial of a valid narrative function) and supplemental (the location of an excess pleasure) terms, this Hollywood version of "Latin American-ness" participates in the operations of fetishism and disavowal typical of the stereotype in colonial-imperialist discourses.[20] This exercise of colonial-imperialist authority would peak, with a significant twist, in the Carmen Miranda films at Twentieth Century-Fox, a cycle which produced a public figure, Miranda (fig. 15.3), that lays bare, with surreal clarity,

15.3. Attired in a hyper-version of the traditional *baianas* of Brazilian carnival, Carmen Miranda was the best known Latin American of the 1940s.

the scenario of Hollywood's own colonial fantasy and the problematics of ethnic representation in a colonial-imperialist context.[21]

In these films, Carmen Miranda functions, above all, as a fantastic or uncanny fetish. Everything about her is surreal, off-center, displaced onto a different regime: from her extravagant hats, midriff-baring multicolored costumes, and five-inch platform shoes to her linguistic malapropisms, farcical sexuality, and high-pitched voice, she is an other, everyone's other. Although not even Brazilian-born (she was born in Portugal to parents who immigrated to Brazil and named her Maria do Carmo Miranda da Cunha), she became synonymous with cinematic "Latin American-ness," with an essence, defined and mobilized by herself and Hollywood throughout the continent. As the emcee announces at the end of her first number in Busby Berkeley's *The Gang's All Here*, "Well, there's your Good Neighbor Policy. Come on honey, let's Good Neighbor it."

Miranda was "discovered" by Hollywood "as is," that is, after her status as a top entertainer in Brazil (with more than three hundred records, five films—including the first Brazilian sound feature—and nine Latin American tours) brought her to the New York stage, where her six-minute performance in *The Streets of Paris* (1939) transformed her into "an overnight sensation."[22] Her explicit Brazilian-ness—samba song and dance repertoire, Carnival-type costumes—was transformed into the epitome of *latinidad* by a series of films that "placed" her in locales as varied as Lake Louise in the Canadian Rockies, Havana, or Buenos Aires.

Her validity as "Latin American" was based on a rhetoric of visual excess—of costume, performance, sexuality, and musicality—that carried over into the mode of address of the films themselves. Of course, since they were produced at Fox, a studio that depended on its superior TechniColor process to differentiate its product in the marketplace,[23] these films are also almost painfully colorful, exploiting the technology to further inscribe Latin Americanness as tropicality. For example, although none of the Fox films was shot on location, all include markedly luscious "travelogue-like" sections justifying the authenticity of their locales. Even more significantly, they also include the visual representation of travel, whether to the country in question or "inland," as further proof of the validity of their ethno-presentation within a regime that privileges the visual as the only possible site of knowledge.

Weekend in Havana is a prototypical example. The film begins by introducing the lure of the exotic in a post-credit, narrative-establishment montage sequence that situates travel to Latin America as a desirable sight-seeing adventure: snow on the Brooklyn bridge dissolves to a brochure of leisure cruises to Havana, to a tourist guide to "Cuba: The Holiday Isle of the Tropics," to a window display promoting "Sail to Romance" cruises featuring life-size cardboard cutouts of Carmen Miranda and a Latin band that come to life and sing the title song (which begins, "How would you like to spend the weekend in Havana. . . . "). Immediately after, the romantic plot of the musical is set up: Alice Faye plays a Macy's salesgirl whose much-scrimped-for Caribbean cruise is ruined when her ship runs aground. She refuses to sign the shipping company's release and is appeased only with the promise of "romance" in an all-expenses-paid tour of Havana with shipping-company executive John Payne.

The trip from the marooned cruise ship to Havana is again represented by an exuberantly colorful montage of the typical tourist sights of Havana—el Morro Castle, the Malecon, the Hotel Nacional, Sloppy Joe's Bar—with a voice-over medley of "Weekend in Havana" and typical Cuban songs. Finally, once ensconced in the most luxurious hotel in the city, Faye is taken to see the sights by Payne. They travel by taxi to a sugar plantation, where Payne's lecture from a tourist book, although it bores Faye to yawns, does serve as a voice-over narration for the visual presentation of "Cubans at work": "Hundreds of thousands of Cubans are involved with the production of this important commodity. . . . " These three sequences serve both important narrative and legitimizing functions, testifying to the authenticity of the film's ethnographic and documentary work and eliding the fact that the featured native entertainer, Rosita Rivas (Miranda), is neither Cuban nor speaks Spanish.

More complexly, all the Fox films depend upon Miranda's performative excess to validate their authority as "good neighborly" ethnographic discourses. The films' simple plots—often remakes of prior musical successes and most commonly involving some kind of mistaken identity or similar snafu—further highlight the importance of the Miranda-identified visual and musical regime rather than the legitimizing narrative order. The beginning of *The Gang's All Here*, for example, clearly underlines this operation by presenting a narrativized re-presentation of travel, commerce, and ethnic identity. After the credits, a half-lit floating head singing Ary Barroso's "Brasil" in Portuguese suddenly shifts (in a classic Busby Berkeley syntactical move) to the hull of a ship emblazoned with the name *SS Brazil*, docking in New York and unloading typical Brazilian products: sugar, coffee, bananas, strawberries, and Carmen Miranda. Wearing a hat featuring her native fruits, Miranda finishes the song, triumphantly strides into New York, switches to an English tune, and is handed the keys to the city by the mayor as the camera tracks back to reveal the stage of a nightclub, an Anglo audience to whom she is introduced *as* the Good Neighbor Policy and whom she instructs to dance the "Uncle Sam-ba."

The Fox films' most amazing characteristic is Miranda's immutability and the substitutability of the narratives. Miranda travels and is inserted into different landscapes, but she remains the same from film to film, purely Latin American. Whether the action of the film is set in Buenos Aires, Havana, the Canadian Rockies, Manhattan, or a Connecticut mansion, the on-screen Miranda character—most often named Carmen or Rosita—is remarkably coherent: above all, and against all odds, an entertainer and the most entertaining element in all the films.[24] While the North American characters work out the inevitable romance plot of the musical comedy, Miranda—always a thorn to the budding romance—puts on a show and dallies outrageously with the leading men. Normally not permanently mated with a North American protagonist (with the notable exception of *That Night in Rio,* where she gets to keep Don Ameche, but only because his identical double gets the white girl played by Alice Faye), Miranda, nevertheless, gets to have her fun along the way and always entices and almost seduces with aggressive kisses and embraces at least one, but most often several, of the North American men.

Miranda's sexuality is so aggressive, however, that it is diffused, spent in gesture, innuendo, and salacious commentary. Unlike Vélez, who can seduce and marry a nice WASP man, Miranda remains either contentedly single, attached to a Latin American Lothario (for example, the womanizing manager-cum-gigolo played by Cesar Romero in *Weekend in Havana*), or in the permanent never-never land of prolonged and unconsummated engagements to unlikely North American types. For example, in *Copacabana* she has been engaged for ten years to Groucho Marx and, at the end of the film, they still have separate hotel rooms and no shared marriage vows.

Miranda, not unlike other on-screen female performers (Dietrich in the Von Sternberg films, for example), functions narratively and discursively as a sexual fetish, freezing the narrative and the pleasures of the voyeuristic gaze and provoking a regime of spectacle and specularity. She acknowledges and openly participates in her fetishization, staring back at the camera, implicating the audience in her sexual display. But she is also an ethnic fetish. The look she returns is also that of the ethnographer and its colonial spectator stand-in. Her Latin Americanness is displaced in all its visual splendor for simultaneous colonial appropriation and denial.

Although Miranda is visually fetishized within filmic systems that locate her metaphorically as the emblem of knowledge of Latin American-ness, Miranda's voice, rife with cultural impurities and disturbing syncretisms, slips through the webs of Hollywood's colonial and ethnographic authority over the constitution and definition of otherness. It is in fact within the aural register, constantly set against the legitimacy of the visual, that Hollywood's ethnographic good neighborliness breaks down in the Fox-Miranda films. In addition to the psychosexual impact of her voice, Miranda's excessive manipulation of accents—the obviously shifting registers of tone and pitch between her spoken and sung English and between her English and Portuguese—inflates the fetish, cracking its surface while simultaneously aggrandizing it. Most obvious in the films where she sings consecutive numbers in each language (*Weekend in Havana* and *The Gang's All Here* are two examples), the tonal differences between her sung and spoken Portuguese and her English indicate that her excessive accent and her linguistic malapropisms are no more than a pretense, a nod to the requirements of a conception of foreignness and otherness necessary to maintain the validity of the text in question as well as her persona as an ethnographic good neighborly gesture. That the press and studio machinery constantly remarked upon her accent and problems with English further highlight their ambiguous status.[25] At once a sign of her otherness as well as of the artificiality of all otherness, her accent ultimately became an efficient marketing device, exploited in advertisements and publicity campaigns: "I tell everyone I know to DREENK Piel's."[26]

Throughout the Good Neighbor films, Miranda remains a fetish, but a surreal one, a fetish that self-consciously underlines the difficult balance between knowledge and belief that sustains it and that lets us hear the edges of an unclassifiable otherness, product of an almost undescribable bricolage, that rejects the totalizing search for truth of the good neighborly Hollywood ethnographer while simultaneously submitting to its designs.

"Are All Latins from Manhattan?"

Miranda's Hollywood career was cut short both by the demise of Hollywood's good neighborliness in the postwar era as well as by her untimely death in 1955.[27] However, Hollywood's circulation and use of her persona as the emblem of the Good Neighbor clearly demonstrates the fissures of Hollywood's work as Latin American ethnographer in this period. With Miranda's acquiescence and active participation, Hollywood ensconced her as the essence of Latin American otherness in terms that, on the surface, were both nonderogatory and simultaneously nonthreatening. First, as a female emblem, her position was always already that of a less-threatening other. In this context, the potential threat of her sexuality—that which was troubling in Vélez, for example—was dissipated by its sheer visual and narrative excess. Furthermore, her legitimizing ethnicity, exacerbated by an aura of the carnivalesque and the absurd, could be narratively relegated to the stage, to the illusory (and tameable) world of performance, theater, and movies. This is perhaps most conclusively illustrated by the frequency with which her persona is used as the emblem of Latin American otherness and exoticism in Hollywood films of the period: in *House Across the Bay* (Archie Mayo, 1940) Joan Bennett appears in a Miranda-inspired *baiana* costume; in *Babes on Broadway* (Busby Berkeley, 1941) Mickey Rooney does a number while dressed like her. *In This Our Life* (John Huston, 1942) Bette Davis plays a Miranda record and hums along to "Chica Chica Boom Chic," and in *Mildred Pierce* (Michael Curtiz, 1945) Jo Ann Marlow does a fully costumed Miranda imitation.

At the same time, however, Miranda's textual persona escapes the narrow parameters of the Good Neighbor. As a willing participant in the production of these self-conscious ethnographic texts, Miranda literally asserted her own voice in the textual operations that defined her as *the* other. Transforming, mixing, ridiculing, and redefining her own difference against the expected standards, Miranda's speaking voice, songs, and accents create an other text that is in counterpoint to the principal textual operations. She does not burst the illusory bubble of the Good Neighbor, but by inflating it beyond recognition, she highlights its status as a discursive construct—as myth.

When we recognize that Hollywood's relationship to ethnic and minority groups is primarily ethnographic—that is, one that involves the co-production in power of cultural texts—rather than merely mimetic, it becomes possible to understand the supposed break in Hollywood's misrepresentation of Latin Americans during the Good Neighbor Policy years textually as well as in instrumental and ideological terms. It is particularly important to recognize that Hollywood (and, by extension, television) fulfills this ethnographic function, because we are in an era that, not unlike the Good Neighbor years, is praised for its "Hispanization." While the media crows about the 1987–88 successes of *La Bamba* and *Salsa: The Motion Picture* and a special issue of *Time* proclaims "Magnifico! Hispanic Culture Breaks Out of the Barrio,"[28] it might prove enlightening to look at this particular translation, presentation, and assimilation of Latin American otherness as yet another ethnographic textual creation that must be analyzed as a political co-production of representations of difference and not as a mimetic narrative challenge.

NOTES

1. This is, for example, how Karl G. Heider describes it in *Ethnographic Film* (Austin: University of Texas Press, 1976), one of the few texts to express the relationship between ethnography and the cinema directly (see, especially, pp. 5–12).

2. James Clifford, *The Predicament of Culture: Twentieth-Century Ethnography, Literature, and Art* (Cambridge: Harvard University Press, 1988).

3. James Clifford, "On Ethnographic Authority," in *The Predicament of Culture*, p. 41.

4. Stephen A. Tyler, "Post-Modern Ethnography: From Document of the Occult to Occult Document," in *Writing Culture: The Poetics and Politics of Ethnography*, ed. James Clifford and George Marcus (Berkeley: University of California Press, 1986), p. 126.

5. Edward Said, *Orientalism* (New York: Random House, 1979).

6. Tyler, "Post-Modern Ethnography," p. 126.

7. For an interesting and useful survey of the literature on the cinematic representation of ethnics and minorities, see Allen L. Woll and Randall M. Miller, eds., *Ethnic and Racial Images in American Film and Television: Historical Essays and Bibliography* (New York: Garland, 1987).

8. Donald W. Rowland, *History of the Office of the Coordinator of Inter-American Affairs* (Washington: Government Printing Office, 1947), pp. 74, 68.

9. Bosley Crowther, "*That Night in Rio*," *New York Times*, March 10, 1949, p. 21.

10. For a popular assessment of the power of the cinema as democratic propaganda for the American way of life in South America, see, from the many possible examples, Florence Horn, "*Formidavel, Fabulosissimo*," *Harper's Magazine*, no. 184 (December 1941): 59–64. Horn glowingly describes how well a young Brazilian and her housewife "friends" under-

stand and recognize "America" because of their constant exposure to U.S. films. After reading the following sentence, one wonders whether Orson Welles might have also read this piece before setting off on his CIAA-sponsored Brazilian project in 1942: "He [the Brazilian boy] returns home, almost without exception, to tell his friends that it's all true—and even more so" (p. 60). For self-assessments of the power and efficacy of the Good Neighbor Policy, see, in particular, Nelson Rockefeller, "Fruits of the Good Neighbor Policy," *New York Times Magazine*, May 14, 1944, p. 15, and "Will We Remain Good Neighbors After the War? Are We Killing Our Own Markets by Promoting Industrialization in Latin America?" *Saturday Evening Post*, November 6, 1943, pp. 16–17.

11. See Allen L. Woll, *The Latin Image in American Film* (Los Angeles: UCLA Latin American Center Publication, 1977) and Gaizka S. de Usabel, *The High Noon of American Films in Latin America* (Ann Arbor: UMI Research Press, 1982).

12. Woll, *The Latin Image in American Film*, p. 33.

13. See chapter 9 in this volume.

14. As does Allen Woll's analysis of this period in *The Latin Image in American Film* (and a number of other texts). In particular, Woll praises the "unheard" of cultural sensitivity of RKO's *Flying Down to Rio* (1933), a film that featured Dolores del Rio as a Carioca enchantress and Rio de Janeiro as a city defined by its infinite romantic possibilities and as the South American meeting place of new U.S. communication technologies and capital: airplanes for Southern travel, telegraphs for speedy communication, records and movies for music and romance. See Sergio Augusto, "Hollywood Looks at Brazil: From Carmen Miranda to *Moonraker*," in *Brazilian Cinema*, ed. Randall Johnson and Robert Stam (Austin: University of Texas Press, 1988), pp. 352–61.

15. See Miriam Hansen on the Valentino legend in "Pleasure, Ambivalence, Identification: Valentino and Female Spectatorship," *Cinema Journal* 25 (Summer 1986): 6–32.

16. Del Rio's Hollywood filmography includes, among other titles, *What Price Glory?* (1926, d. Walsh); *The Loves of Carmen* (1927, d. Walsh); *Ramona* (1928, d. Carewe); *The Red Dance* (1928, d. Walsh); *The Trail of '98* (1929, d. Brown); *Evangeline* (1929, d. Carewe); *The Bird of Paradise* (1932, d. Vidor), *Flying Down to Rio* (1933, d. Freeland); *Wonder Bar* (1934, d. Bacon); *Madame DuBarry* (1934, D. Dieterle); *In Caliente* (1935, d. Bacon); *The Lancer Spy* (1937, d. Ratoff); and *Journey into Fear* (1941, d. Foster). In *Journey into Fear*, del Rio worked closely with Orson Welles (the first director of the film), with whom she had previously collaborated in the Mercury Theater production *Father Hidalgo* (1940) and during the production of *Citizen Kane* (1941).

17. Carlos Fuentes, "El Rostro de la Escondida," in *Dolores del Rio*, ed. Luis Gasca (San Sebastian, Spain: 24th Festival Internacional de Cine, 1976), p. 10; my translation.

18. Homi K. Bhabba, "Signs Taken for Wonders: Questions of Ambivalence and Authority under a Tree Outside Delhi, May 1917," in *Race, Writing, and Difference,* ed. Henry Louis Gates, Jr. (Chicago: University of Chicago Press, 1986), p. 172.

19. For the best summary/analysis of Vélez's career, see Gabriel Ramírez, *Lupe Vélez: la mexicana gue escupía fuego* (Mexico City: Cineteca Nacional, 1986).

20. See Homi K. Bhabba's discussion of this process in "The Other Question . . . ," *Screen* 24, no. 6 (1983): 18–36.

21. Between 1940 and her death in 1955, Miranda made fourteen films: ten for Twentieth Century-Fox, one for United Artists, two for MGM, and one for Paramount. The Fox "cycle," between 1940–46, consisted of *Down Argentine Way* (1940, d. Cummings); *That Night in Rio* (1941, d. Cummings); *Weekend in Havana* (1941, d. Lang); *Springtime in the Rockies* (1942, d. Cummings); *The Gang's All Here* (1943, d. Berkeley); *Four Jills in a Jeep* (1944, d. Seiter); *Greenwich Village* (1944, d. Lang); *Something for the Boys* (1944, d. Seiler); *Doll Face* (1946, d. Seiler); and *If I'm Lucky* (1946, d. Seiler).

22. See, Rodolfo Konder, "The Carmen Miranda Museum: The Brazilian Bombshell Is Still Box Office in Rio," *Americas* 34, no. 5 (1982): 17–21. In a review of *The Streets of Paris,* Harry C. Pringle wrote in 1939 that "[the opening] was a pleasant but not an exciting evening until, at approximately 10 o'clock, six young men appeared on the stage and were followed by a vibrant young woman wearing an exotic dress and a turban hat with bananas, peaches, pears and other fruitstand wares on it. . . . But the magic of her appeal lay in the degree to which she seemed to be having an enormously good time: that, and in the implication that she loved everybody in general and all men in particular"; cited by Cassio Emmanuel Barsante, *Carmen Miranda* (Rio de Janeiro: Ed. Europa, 1985), p. 12.

23. See Douglas Gomery, *The Hollywood Studio System* (New York: St. Martin's Press, 1986), pp. 76–100.

24. Among others, see, for example, the *Variety* reviews of her Fox films—especially of *Down Argentine Way* (October 9, 1940), *Springtime in the Rockies* (November 24, 1937), and *That Night in Rio* (March 12, 1941)—which specifically comment upon the weakness of the romance narratives and the strength of her musical comedic performances.

25. See the New York *Post,* November 30, 1955; cited by Allen L. Woll, *The Hollywood Musical Goes to War* (Chicago: Nelson Hall, 1983), pp. 114–15. According to Woll, Fox encouraged Miranda to learn English on a "fiscal" basis: a 50 cent raise for each word she added to her vocabulary. Miranda's quoted response again subverts the intended effect of Fox's integrationist efforts: "I know p'raps one hondred words—preety good for Sous American girl, no? Best I know ten English words: men, men, men, men, and monee, monee, monee, monee, monee, monee." According to Cassio Emmanuel Barsante, one of Miranda's most assiduous biographers and fans, "after living less than a year in the United States, Carmen had

learned to speak English correctly, but started to take advantage of her accent for comic effect," *Carmen Miranda*, p. 188.

26. Full-page advertisement for Piel's Light Beer in the New York *Daily Mirror*, July 25, 1947: "A lighting flash along Broadway means Carmen Miranda! That Luscious, well-peppered dish! She glitters like a sequin, with her droll accent and spirited dances. And Carmen goes for Piel's—with all its sparkle and tang! 'I tell everyone I know to DREENK Piel's' she exclaims."

27. Miranda died at the age of forty-four, of a heart attack, on August 5, 1955, after taping a television program with Jimmy Durante. By this time—after a series of less than memorable screen appearances, alcohol and drug abuse, and a nervous breakdown in 1954—Miranda's presence had waned considerably. Although she was still a recognizable star, she had begun to work far more for television than for the cinema.

28. Special issue of *Time*, July 11, 1988.

References

Abrams, Richard M. *The Burdens of Progress 1900–1929*. Glenview: Scott, Foresman, 1978.

Alcock, J. E., D. W. Carment, and S. W. Sadava. *A Textbook of Social Psychology*. Scarborough, Ontario: Prentice-Hall, 1988.

Allen, Robert C. "Motion Picture Exhibition in Manhattan: Beyond the Nickelodeon." *Cinema Journal* 18 (Spring 1979):2–15.

Allen, Robert C., and Douglas Gomery. *Film History: Theory and Practice*. New York: Alfred A. Knopf, 1985.

Althusser, Louis. "Ideology and Ideological State Apparatuses (Notes towards an Investigation)." In *Lenin and Philosophy and Other Essays*. Translated by Ben Brewster. New York: Monthly Review Press, 1972.

Altman, Charles. "Psychoanalysis and Cinema: The Imaginary Discourse." *Quarterly Review of Film Studies* 2 (August 1977):257–72.

Altman, Rick. *The American Film Musical*. Bloomington: Indiana University Press, 1989.

Anderson, Benedict. *Imagined Communities: Reflections on the Origins and Spread of Nationalism*. London: Verso, 1983.

Andrew, Dudley. *Concepts in Film Theory*. New York: Oxford University Press, 1983.

———. "The Neglected Tradition of Phenomenology in Film Theory." In *Movies and Methods*, vol. 2. Edited by Bill Nichols. Berkeley: University of California Press, 1985.

———. "An Open Approach to Film Study and the Situation at Iowa." In *Film Study in the Undergraduate Curriculum*. Edited by Barry K. Grant. New York: Modern Language Association of America, 1983.

Aufderheide, Pat. "Sci-fi Discovers New Enemies." *In These Times*, November 21-December 4, 1984, p. 30.

Augusto, Sergio. "Hollywood Looks at Brazil: From Carmen Miranda to *Moonraker.*" In *Brazilian Cinema.* Edited by Randall Johnson and Robert Stam. Austin: University of Texas Press, 1988.

Baker, Houston. *Blues, Ideology, and Afro-American Literature: A Vernacular Theory.* Chicago: University of Chicago Press, 1984.

Bakhtin, Mikhail. *Problems of Dostoevsky's Poetics.* Translated by P. W. Rotsel. Ann Arbor: Ardis, 1973.

————. *Rabelais and His World.* Translated by Helene Iswolsky. Cambridge: M.I.T. Press, 1968.

————. *Speech, Genres and Other Late Essays.* Austin: University of Texas Press, 1986.

Banton, Michael. "The Direction and Speed of Ethnic Change." In *Ethnic Change.* Edited by Charles F. Keyes. Seattle: University of Washington Press, 1981.

Barsante, Cassio Emmuel. *Carmen Miranda.* Rio de Janiero: Europa, 1985.

Barth, Fredrik. *Ethnic Groups and Boundaries: The Social Organization of Cultural Differences.* London: George Allen and Unwin, 1969.

Bartlett, F. C. *Remembering: A Study in Experimental and Social Psychology.* London: Cambridge University Press, 1932.

Belasco, David. "The Girl of the Golden West." In *American Melodrama.* Edited by Daniel C. Gerould. New York: Performing Arts Journal Publications, 1983.

Bergson, Henri. "Laughter." In *Comedy.* Edited by Wylie Sypher. Baltimore: Johns Hopkins University Press, 1956.

Bhabba, Homi K. "The Other Question . . . ," *Screen* 24, no. 6 (1983):18–36.

————. "Signs Taken for Wonders: Questions of Ambivalence and Authority under a Tree Outside Delhi, May 1917." In *Race, Writing, and Difference.* Edited by Henry Louis Gates, Jr. Chicago: University of Chicago Press, 1986.

Bodner, John. *The Transplanted.* Bloomington: Indiana University Press, 1985.

Boelhower, William. *Through a Glass Darkly: Ethnic Semiosis in American Literature.* New York: Oxford University Press, 1987.

Bogdanovich, Peter. *John Ford.* London: Studio Vista, 1968.

Bogle, Donald. *Toms, Coons, Mulattoes, Mammies and Bucks: An Interpretive History of Blacks in American Film.* New York: Viking Press, 1973.

Bordieu, Pierre. *Distinction: A Social Critique of the Judgement of Taste.* Translated by Richard Nice. Cambridge: Harvard University Press, 1984.

Bordwell, David, and Kristen Thompson. *Film Art: An Introduction.* 2d ed. New York: Alfred A. Knopf, 1986.

Bordwell, David, Janet Staiger, and Kristin Thompson. *The Classical Hollywood Cinema: Film Style and Mode of Production.* New York: Columbia University Press, 1986.

Boskin, Joseph. *Sambo.* New York: Oxford University Press, 1986.

Browne, N. "The Spectator-in-the-Text: The Rhetoric of 'Stagecoach'." In *Movies and Methods,* vol. 2. Edited by Bill Nichols. Berkeley: University of California Press, 1985.

Burch, Noel. "Porter or Ambivalence." *Screen* 19 (Winter 1978–79):91–105.
———. *Theory of Film Practice*. London: Secker and Warburg, 1973.
Callenbach, Ernest. "Phallic Nightmares." *Film Quarterly* (Summer 1979):18–22.
Carby, Hazel V. "Lynching, Empire, and Sexuality." *Critical Inquiry* 12 (Autumn 1985).
———. "On the Threshold of Woman's Era: Lynching, Empire and Sexuality in Black Feminist Theory." *Critical Inquiry* 12 (Autumn 1985):262–77.
———. *Reconstructing Womanhood: The Emergence of the Afro-American Woman Novelist*. New York: Oxford University Press, 1987.
Cavell, Stanley. *The World Viewed*. New York: Viking Press, 1971.
Clarke, John. "Style." In *Resistance through Rituals: Youth Subcultures in Postwar Britain*. Edited by Stuart Hall and Tony Jefferson. London: University of Birmingham, 1976.
Clifford, James. "On Ethnographic Authority." In *The Predicament of Culture: Twentieth-Century Ethnography, Literature, and Art*. Cambridge: Harvard University Press, 1988.
Clifford, James, and George Marcus, eds. *Writing Culture: The Poetics and Politics of Ethnography*. Berkeley: University of California Press, 1986.
Cobbs, Prince. "Ethnotherapy in Groups." In *New Perspectives on Encounter Groups*. San Francisco: Jossey-Bass, 1972.
Cohen, Sarah Blacher, ed. *From Hester Street to Hollywood: The Jewish-American Stage and Screen*. Bloomington: Indiana University Press, 1986.
Cohen, E. G., and S. S. Roper. "Modification of Interracial Disability: An Application of Status Characteristic Theory." *American Sociological Review* 37 (1972):643–57.
Collins, A. "Children's Comprehension of Television Content." In *Children Communicating: Media and Development of Thought, Speech and Understanding*. Edited by E. Wartella. Beverly Hills: Sage, 1979.
Comstock, G. *Television and Human Behavior*. New York: Columbia University Press, 1978.
Cook, David A. *A History of Narrative Film*. New York: W. W. Norton, 1981.
Cooper, James Fenimore. *The Leatherstocking Tales I*. New York: Library of America, 1985.
Cowen, P. S. "Manipulating Montage: Effects on Film Comprehension, Recall, Person Perception, and Aesthetic Responses." *Empirical Studies of the Arts* 6 (1988):91–115.
Cripps, Thomas. *Black Film as Genre*. Bloomington: Indiana University Press, 1978.
———. *Slow Fade to Black: The Negro in American Film, 1900–1942*. New York: Oxford University Press, 1977.
Crouch, Stanley. "The Rotton Club," *The Village Voice*, February 5, 1985.
Crowther, Bosley. "*That Night in Rio*." *New York Times*, March 10, 1949, p. 21.

Cuddihy, John Murray. *The Ordeal of Civility: Freud, Marx, Lévi-Strauss and the Jewish Struggle with Modernity*. Boston: Beacon Press, 1974.

Davis, Angela Y. *Women, Culture, and Politics*. New York: Random House, 1989.

―――. *Women, Race and Class*. New York: Random House, 1981.

Dearborn, Mary V. *Pocahontas's Daughters: Gender and Ethnicity in American Culture*. New York: Oxford University Press, 1986.

de Beauvoir, Simone. *The Second Sex*. Translated and edited by H. M. Parshley. New York: Alfred A. Knopf, 1952.

DeFleur, Raymond, and Everette Dennis. *Understanding Mass Communication*. Boston: Houghton Mifflin, 1981.

de Gurowski, Adam G. *America and Europe*. New York: D. Appleton, 1875.

deLauretis, Teresa. "Aesthetic and Feminist Theory: Rethinking Women's Cinema." *New German Critique* 34 (Winter 1985):154–75.

―――. *Alice Doesn't: Feminism, Semiotics, Cinema*. Bloomington: Indiana University Press, 1984.

―――. *Feminist Studies/Critical Studies*. Bloomington: Indiana University Press, 1986.

DeMille, William. *Hollywood Saga*. New York: E. P. Dutton, 1939.

DeTocqueville, Alexis. *Democracy in America*. Edited by Phillips Bradley. 1835. Reprint. New York: Alfred A. Knopf, 1945.

DeUsabel, Gaizka S. *The High Noon of American Films in Latin America*. Ann Arbor: UMI Research Press, 1982.

Derrida, Jacques. "Structure, Sign, and Play in the Discourse of the Human Sciences." In *The Language of Criticism and the Science of Man: The Structuralist Controversy*. Edited by Richard Macksey and Eugenio Donato. Baltimore: Johns Hopkins University Press, 1970.

Desnoes, Edmundo. "The Death System." In *On Signs*. Edited by Marshall Blonsky. Baltimore: Johns Hopkins University Press, 1985.

―――. "The Photographic Image of Underdevelopment." Translated by Julia LeSage. Reprinted in *Jump Cut* 33 (February 1988):69–82.

Diawara, Manthia. "Black Spectatorship Problems of Identification and Resistance." *Screen* 29 (Autumn 1988):66–72.

"A Difference of Degree: State Initiatives to Improve Minority Student Achievement." Albany: New York State Higher Education Department, 1987.

Dittus, Erick. "*Mississippi Triangle:* An Interview with Christine Choy, Worth Long and Allan Siegel." *Cineaste* 14, no. 2 (1985):38–40.

Doane, Mary Ann, Patricia Mellencamp, and Linda Williams, eds. *Revision: Essays in Feminist Criticism*. Los Angeles: American Film Institute, 1984.

Dowling, William C. *Jameson, Althusser, Marx*. Ithaca: Cornell University Press, 1984.

Durham, Carolyn A. "*The Year of Living Dangerously:* Can Vision Be a Model for Knowledge." *Jump Cut* 30 (March 1985):6–8.

Dyer, Richard. "White." *Screen* 29 (Autumn 1988):44–64.

Eberwein, Robert T. *Film and the Dream Screen: A Sleep and a Forgetting*. Princeton: Princeton University Press, 1984.

Eckert, Charles W. "The Anatomy of a Proletarian Film: Warner's *Marked Woman*." *Film Quarterly* 27 (Winter 1973–74):10–24.

Eckhardt, Joseph P., and Linda Kowall. *Peddler of Dreams: Siegmund Lubin and the Creation of the Motion Picture Industry, 1896–1916*. Philadelphia: National Museum of American Jewish History, 1984.

Ellis, John Tracy. *American Catholicism*. 2d ed. Chicago: University of Chicago Press, 1969.

Ellison, Mary. "Blacks in American Film." In *Cinema, Politics and Society in America*. Edited by Philip Davies and Brian Neve. Manchester: Manchester University Press, 1981.

Ellison, Ralph. *Shadow and Act*. New York: Vintage, 1973.

Erens, Patricia. *The Jew in American Cinema*. Bloomington: Indiana University Press, 1984.

———. *Sexual Stratagems: The World of Women in Film*. New York: Horizon Press, 1979.

Erikson, Erik. "The Problem of Ego Identity." *Journal of the American Psychoanalytic Association* 4 (1956):56–121.

Fabian, Johannes. *Time and the Other: How Anthropology Makes Its Object*. New York: Columbia University Press, 1983.

Fell, John. *Film Before Griffith*. Berkeley: University of California Press, 1983.

Festinger, L. "A Theory of Social Comparison Processes." *Human Relations* 7 (1954):117–40.

Feuer, Jane. *The Hollywood Musical*. Bloomington: Indiana University Press, 1982.

Fiedler, Leslie A. *Love and Death in the American Novel*. New York: Criterion Books, 1960.

Finch, Christopher, and Linda Rosenkrantz. *Gone Hollywood: The Movie Colony in the Golden Age*. New York: Doubleday, 1979.

Fischer, Michael. "Ethnicity and the Post-Modern Arts of Memory." In *Writing Culture: The Poetics and Politics of Ethnography*. Edited by James Clifford and George E. Marcus. Berkeley: University of California Press, 1986.

Fisher, Seymour, and Rhoda Fisher. "A Projective Test Analysis for Ethnic Subculture Themes in Families." *Journal of Projective Technique* 24 (1960):366–69.

Fiske, John. *Television Culture*. London: Methuen, 1987.

———. "Television: Polysemy and Popularity." *Critical Studies in Mass Communication* 3 (December 1986):391–408.

Fiske, S. T., and S. E. Taylor. *Social Cognition*. New York: Random House, 1984.

Foucault, Michel. *The History of Sexuality*. New York: Pantheon, 1972.

Freud, Sigmund. "Ansprache an die Mitglieder des Vereins B'nai B'rith (1926)." In *Gesammelte Werke*, vol. 16. London: Imago Publishing, 1941.

———. *The Interpretation of Dreams*. Translated and edited by James Strachey, New York: Avon, 1965.

———. *Jokes and Their Relation to the Unconscious*. London: Hogarth Press, 1960.

————. *An Outline of Psychoanalysis*. New York: W. W. Norton, 1949.

Freund, Elizabeth. *The Return of the Reader: Reader-Response Criticism*. London: Methuen, 1987.

Friedman, Lester. *Hollywood's Image of the Jew*. New York: Frederick Ungar, 1982.

Frye, Northrop. *The Anatomy of Criticism*. Princeton: Princeton University Press, 1957.

Fuentes, Carlos. "El Rostro de la Escondida." In *Dolores del Rio*. Edited by Luis Gasca. San Sebastian, Spain: 24th Festival Internacional de Cine, 1976.

Fussell, Paul. *The Boy Scout Handbook and Other Observations*. New York: Oxford University Press, 1982.

Gabbard, Krin, and Glen O. Gabbard. *Psychiatry and the Cinema*. Chicago: University of Chicago Press, 1987.

Gabler, Neal. *An Empire of Their Own: How the Jews Invented Hollywood*. New York: Crown Publishers, 1988.

Gaines, Jane. "Women and Representation." *Jump Cut* 29 (February 1984):25–27.

————. "White Privilege and Looking Relations: Race and Gender in Feminist Film Theory." *Cultural Critique* 4 (1986):59–81.

Gallagher, Tag. *John Ford: The Man and His Films*. Berkeley: University of California Press, 1986.

Gans, Herbert. *On the Making of Americans: Essays in Honor of David Riesman*. Philadelphia: University of Pennsylvania Press, 1979.

Geduld, Harry M., ed. *Authors on Film*. Bloomington: Indiana University Press, 1972.

Geertz, Clifford. "The Integrative Revolution: Primordial Sentiments and Civil Rights in the New States." In *Old Societies and New States*. Edited by Clifford Geertz. Glencoe: Free Press, 1963.

————. "Religion as a Cultural System." In *Anthropological Approaches to the Study of Religion*. Edited by Michael Banton. New York: Praeger, 1966.

Gehring, Wes D. *The Marx Brothers: A Bio-Bibliography*. New York: Greenwood Press, 1987.

Genette, Gérard. *Narrative Discourse: An Essay in Method*. Translated by Alan Sheridan. Ithaca: Cornell University Press, 1980.

Gergen, K. J., and M. M. Gergen. *Social Psychology*. New York: Harcourt Brace Jovanovich, 1981.

Gerould, Daniel C., ed. *American Melodrama*. New York: Performing Arts Journal Publications, 1983.

Gever, Martha. "Dragon Busters." *The Independent* 8 (October 1985):8–9.

Gilman, Sander L. *Difference and Pathology: Stereotypes of Sexuality*. Ithaca: Cornell University Press, 1985.

————. *Jewish Self-Hatred: Anti-Semitism and the Hidden Language of the Jews*. Baltimore: Johns Hopkins University Press, 1986.

Giordano, Joseph. *Ethnicity and Mental Health*. New York: Institute on Pluralism and Group Identity, 1980.

Glazer, Nathan and Daniel Patrick Moynihan. *Beyond the Melting Pot: The Negroes, Puerto Ricans, Jews, Italians, and Irish of New York City.* Cambridge: MIT Press, 1963.

Gleason, Philip. "Confusion Compounded: The Melting Pot in the 1960s and 1970s." *Ethnicity* 6 (March 1979):10–20.

Gledhill, Christine. *Home is Where the Heart Is.* London: British Film Institute, 1987.

————. "Recent Developments in Feminist Criticism." In *Film Theory and Criticism.* Edited by Gerald Mast. New York: Oxford University Press, 1985.

Goldwyn, Sam. *Behind the Screen.* New York: George H. Doran, 1939.

Gomery, Douglas. *The Hollywood Studio System.* New York: St. Martin's Press, 1986.

Gordon, Milton. *Assimilation in American Life: The Role of Race, Religion, and National Origin.* New York: Oxford University Press, 1964.

Graff, Gerald. *Literature Against Itself.* Chicago: University of Chicago Press, 1979.

Gramsci, Antonio. *Selections from the Prison Notebooks.* Edited and translated by Quinton Hoare and Geoffrey Nowell Smith. New York: International Publishers, 1971.

Grazzini, Giovanni. *Frederico Fellini: Comments on Film.* Fresno: The Press at California State, 1988.

Greenfield, Meg. "The Immigrant Mystique." *Newsweek,* August 8, 1988, p. 76.

Gudykunst, W. B. "Ethnicity, Types of Relationship, and Intraethnic and Interethnic Uncertainty Reduction." In *Interethnic Communication.* Edited by Y. Y. Kim. Beverly Hills: Sage, 1986.

Gunning, Tom. *D. W. Griffith and the Origins of American Narrative Film.* Urbana: University of Illinois Press, 1991.

————. *Outsiders as Insiders.* Waltham: National Center for Jewish Film, n.d.

————. "Weaving a Narrative: Style and Economic Background in Griffith's Biograph Films." *Quarterly Review of Film Studies* (Winter 1981):11–25.

Hall, Stuart. "Encoding/Decoding." In *Culture, Media, Language.* Edited by Stuart Hall, Dorothy Hobson, Andrew Loew, and Paul Willis. London: University of Birmingham, 1980.

————. "Recent Developments in Theories of Language and Ideology: A Critical Note." In *Culture, Media, Language.* Edited by Stuart Hall, Dorothy Hobson, Andrew Lowe, and Paul Willis. London: Hutchinson, 1980.

————. "The Whites of Their Eyes: Racist Ideologies and the Media." In *Silver Linings.* Edited by George Bridges and Rosalind Brunt. London: Laurence and Wishart, 1981.

————. "Signification, Representation, Ideology: Althusser and the Post-Structuralist Debates." *Critical Studies in Mass Communication* 2 (June 1985):91–114.

Handlin, Oscar. *The Uprooted: The Epic Story of the Great Migrations that Made the American People.* Boston: Little, Brown, 1951.

Hansen, Miriam. "Early Silent Cinema: Whose Public Sphere?" *New German Critique* 29 (Winter 1983):147–84.

———. *From Babel to Babylon.* Cambridge: Harvard University Press, 1991.

———. "Pleasure Ambivalence, Identification: Valentino and Female Spectatorship." *Cinema Journal* 25 (Summer 1986):6–32.

Haraway, Donna. "A Manifesto for Cyborgs." *Socialist Review* 80 (1985):65–107.

Hebdige, Dick. *Subculture: The Meaning of Style.* London: Methuen, 1979.

Heider, F. *The Psychology of Interpersonal Relations.* New York: Wiley, 1958.

Heider, Karl G. *Ethnographic Film.* Austin: University of Texas Press, 1976.

Henderson, Brian. "A Musical Comedy of Empire." *Film Quarterly* 35 (Winter 1981–82):2–16.

Hennessey, James. *American Catholics: A History of the Roman Catholic Community in the United States.* New York: Oxford University Press, 1981.

Higham, John. *Send These to Me: Immigrants in Urban America.* 2d ed. Baltimore: Johns Hopkins University Press, 1984.

———. *Strangers in the Land: Patterns of American Nativism 1860–1925.* New Brunswick: Rutgers University Press, 1988.

Hoberman, James. *Between Two Worlds.* New York: Schocken, in press.

Hofstadter, Richard. *Social Darwinism in American Thought.* 2d ed. Philadelphia: University of Pennsylvania Press, 1955.

Holland, N. H. "Unity Identity Text Self." In *Reader-Response Criticism.* Edited by J. P. Tompkins. Baltimore: Johns Hopkins University Press, 1980.

Holman, Roger. ed. *Cinema 1900–1906.* 2 vols. Brussels: Federation Internationale des Archives du Film, 1982.

Holquist, Michael, ed. *The Dialogical Imagination.* Austin: University of Texas Press, 1981.

Hooks, Bell. *Feminist Theory: From Margin to Center.* Boston: South End Press, 1984.

Horn, Florence. "Formidavel, Fabulosissimo." *Harper's Magazine* 184 (December 1941):59–64.

Horton, Donald, and R. R. Wohl. "Mass Communication and Para-Social Interaction." *Psychiatry* 19 (1956):215–29.

Hotcher, A. E. *Doris Day: Her Own Story.* New York: William Morrow, 1975.

Hough, Richard. *The Potemkin Mutiny.* Englewood Cliffs: Prentice-Hall, 1960.

Howe, Irving. *World of Our Fathers.* New York: Harcourt Brace Jovanovich, 1976.

Hutcheon, Linda. "Beginning to Theorize Postmodernism." *Textual Practice* 1 (1987):10.

———. "The Politics of Postmodernism: Parody and History." *Cultural Critique* 5, no. 18 (1987):179–207.

———. *A Theory of Parody.* New York: Methuen, 1985.

Huyssen, Andreas. "Mapping the Postmodern." *New German Critique* 33 (1984):5–52.

Isajiw, Wsevold W. "Definitions of Ethnicity." *Ethnicity* 1 (July 1974):111–24.

Iser, Wolfgang. *The Act of Reading: A Theory of Aesthetic Response*. Baltimore: Johns Hopkins University Press, 1978.

————. "The Reading Process: A Phenomenological Approach." In *Reader-Response Criticism*. Edited by J. P. Tompkins. Baltimore: Johns Hopkins University Press, 1980.

Issacs, Harold R. "Basic Group Identity: The Idols of the Tribe." *Ethnicity* 1 (April 1974):15–41.

Jacobs, Lewis. *The Rise of the American Film*. New York: Harcourt, Brace, 1939.

————. "Third World Literature in the Era of Multinational Capitalism." *Social Text* 15 (Fall 1986):65–88.

————. "Reification and Utopia in Mass Culture." *Social Text* 1 (Winter 1979):130–48.

Jameson, Fredric. *The Political Unconscious: Narrative as a Socially Symbolic Act*. Ithaca: Cornell University Press, 1981.

————. "Postmodernism, or the Cultural Logic of Late Capitalism." *New Left Review* 146 (July-August 1984):53–92.

Jarvie, I. C. "Explorations in the Social Career of Movies: Business and Religion." In *Thinking about Society: Theory and Practice*. Edited by Ian C. Jarvie. Dordrecht: Reidel, 1986.

Jefford, Susan. *The Remasculinization of America: Gender and the Vietnam War*. Bloomington: Indiana University Press, 1989.

Jenkins, Henry, III. " 'Shall We Make It for New York or for Distribution?': Eddie Cantor, *Whoopee*, and Regional Resistance to the Talkies," *Cinema Journal* 29 (Spring 1990):32–52.

Johnson, Richard et al. *Making Histories*. Minneapolis: University of Minnesota Press, 1983.

Johnston. S. "Film Narrative and the Structuralist Controversy." In *The Cinema Book*. Edited by P. Cook. New York: Pantheon, 1985.

Jowett, Garth. *Film: The Democratic Art*. Boston: Little, Brown, 1976.

Juteau-Lee, Danielle, and Barbara Roberts. "Ethnicity and Feminity: (d') apres nos experiences." *Canadian Ethnic Studies* 13, no. 1 (1981):1–23.

Kael, Pauline. *Reeling*. Boston: Little, Brown, 1976.

Kalter, Joanmarie. "Television as Value Setter: Family." *TV Guide*, July 23, 1988 pp. 5, 11.

Kaminsky, Stuart. *American Film Genres*. New York: Pflaum, 1974.

Kaplan, E. Ann, ed. *Women in Film Noir*. London: British Film Institute, 1978.

Karp, Alan. *The Films of Robert Altman*. Metuchen: Scarecrow, 1981.

Kass, Judith M. *Robert Altman: American Innovator*. New York: CBS-Popular Library, 1978.

Katz, E., J. G. Blumler, and M. Gurevitch. "Uses of Mass Communication by the Individual." In *Mass Communication Research*. Edited by W. P. Davison and F. T. C. Yu. New York: Praeger, 1974.

Keyser, Les, and Barbara Keyser. *Hollywood and the Catholic Church: The Image of Roman Catholicism in American Movies*. Chicago: Loyola University Press, 1984.

Kibbey, Ann. *The Interpretation of Material Shapes in Puritanism: A Study of Rhetoric, Prejudice and Violence* Cambridge: Cambridge University Press, 1986.

Klein, Judith Weinstein. *Jewish Identity and Self-Esteem: Healing Wounds through Ethnotherapy.* New York: Institute on Pluralism and Group Identity, 1980.

Kolker, Robert Phillip. "On Certain Tendencies in American Film Criticism." *American Quarterly* 38 (1986):327–32.

———. *A Cinema of Loneliness: Penn, Kubrick, Coppola, Scorsese, Altman.* New York: Oxford University Press, 1980.

Konder, Rodolfo. "The Carmen Miranda Museum: The Brazilian Bombshell Is Still Box Office in Rio." *Americas* 34, no. 5 (1982):17–21.

Langer, Susanne. *Feeling and Form: A Theory of Art.* New York: Charles Scribner's Sons, 1953.

Laplanche, J., and J. B. Pontalis. *The Language of Psycho-Analysis.* Translated by Donald Nicholson-Smith. New York: W. W. Norton, 1973.

Leab, Daniel J. *From Sambo to Superspade: The Black Experience in Motion Pictures.* Boston: Houghton Mifflin, 1975.

Lears, T. J. Jackson. *No Place of Grace: Antimodernism and the Transformation of American Culture 1880–1920.* New York: Pantheon, 1981.

Lee, Spike (with Lisa Jones). *Uplift the Race: The Construction of School Daze.* New York: Simon and Schuster, 1988.

Lenihan, John H. *Showdown: Confronting Modern America in the Western Film.* Urbana: University of Illinois Press, 1980.

Lerner, M. J. "The Desire for Justice and the Reaction of Victims." In *Altruism and Helping Behavior.* Edited by J. R. Macaulay and L. Berkowitz. New York: Academic Press, 1970.

Lesage, Julia. "Artful Racism, Artful Rape: Griffith's *Broken Blossoms.*" *Jump Cut,* no. 26 (1981):51–55. Reprinted in *Jump Cut: Hollywood, Politics and Counter Cinema.* Edited by Peter Steven. Toronto: Between the Lines, 1985.

———. "The Human Subject—You, He, or Me? (or, the Case of the Missing Penis)." *Jump Cut* 4 (November-December 1974):26–27.

Lévi-Strauss, Claude. "The Structural Study of Myths." *Journal of American Folklore* 78 (October-December 1955).

Lewis, Glen. *Australian Movies and the American Dream.* New York: Praeger, 1987.

Linville, P. W., and E. E. Jones. "Polarized Appraisals of Outgroup Members." *Journal of Personality and Social Psychology* 38 (1980):689–703.

Loewen, James, W. *The Mississippi Chinese: Between Black and White.* 2d ed. Prospect Heights: Waveland, 1988.

Lorde, Audre. *Sister Outsider.* Trumansburg: Crossing Press, 1984.

Lynch, William F. *Christ and Apollo: The Dimensions of the Literary Imagination.* New York: Sheed and Ward, 1960.

Lyotard, Jean-Francois. *The Postmodern Condition: A Report on Knowledge 1979.* Translated by Geoff Bennington, Brian Massumi, and Regis Durand. Manchester: Manchester University Press, 1986.

McBride, Joseph, and Michael Wilmington. *John Ford*. New York: DaCapo Press, 1975.

McLean, Albert F., Jr. *American Vaudeville as Ritual*. University of Kentucky Press, 1965.

McLennan, Gregor. "Philosophy and History: Some Issues in Recent Marxist Theory." In *Making Histories*. Edited by Richard Johnson et al. Minneapolis: University of Minnesota Press, 1984.

McNabb, S. L. "Stereotypes and Interaction Conventions of Eskimos and non-Eskimos." In *Interethnic Communication*. Edited by Y. Y. Kim. Beverly Hills: Sage, 1986.

Mailer, Norman. *Cannibals and Christians*. New York: Dell, 1966.

Marchetti, Gina. "Subcultural Studies and the Film Audience: Rethinking the Film Viewing Context." In *Current Research in Film*. 2 vols. Edited by Bruce A. Austin. Norwood: Ablex, 1986.

Maritain, Jacques. *Creative Intuition in Art and Poetry*. New York: Pantheon-Bollingen Foundation, 1953.

Marx, Harpo (with Rowland Barber). *Harpo Speaks*. New York: Limelight Editions, 1985.

Marx, Karl, and Frederick Engles. *The German Ideology*. Edited by C. J. Arthur. New York: International Publishers, 1970.

Mast, Gerald, and Marshall Cohn, eds. *Film Theory and Criticism*, 3d ed. New York: Oxford University Press, 1985.

May, Lary. *Screening out the Past: The Birth of Mass Culture and the Motion Picture Industry*. New York: Oxford University Press, 1980.

Mayne, Judith. "Immigrants and Spectators." *Wide Angle* 5, no. 3 (1982):32–40.

———. "The Limits of Spectacle." Wide Angle 6, no. 3 (1983):6–9.

———. "Uncovering the Female Body." In *Before Hollywood: Turn of the Century Films from American Archives*. Edited by Jay Leyda and Charles Musser. New York: American Federation for the Arts, 1986.

Meisel, Martin. *Realizations: Narrative, Pictorial, and Theatrical Art in Nineteenth-Century England*. Princeton: Princeton University Press, 1983.

Mellencamp, Patricia. "Jokes and Their Relation to the Marx Brothers." In *Cinema and Language*. Edited by Stephen Heath and Patricia Mellencamp. New York: American Film Institute, 1983.

Memmi, Albert. *Dominated Man*. Boston: Beacon Press, 1968.

Merritt, Russell. "Nickelodeon Theaters, 1905–1914: Building an Audience for the Movies." In *The American Film Industry*. Edited by Tino Balio. Madison: University of Wisconsin Press, 1985.

Miller, Randall M., ed. *Ethnic Images in American Film and Television*. Philadelphia: Balch Institute, 1978.

———. *The Kaleidoscopic Lens: How Hollywood Views Ethnic Groups*. Englewood: Jerome S. Ozer, 1980.

Milloy, Marilyn. "A Schematic in Black and White." *Newsday*, June 1982.

Moews, Daniel. *Keaton: The Silent Features Close Up*. Berkeley: University of California Press, 1976.

Monaco, James. *American Film Now*. New York: Plume-New American Library, 1979.

Morley, Dave. "Texts, Readers, Subjects." In *Culture, Media, Language*. Edited by Stuart Hall, Dorothy Hobson, Andrew Lowe, and Paul Willis. London: Hutchinson, 1980.

Mukherjee, Bharati. "Immigrant Writing: Give Us Your Maximalists!" *New York Times Book Review*, August 1, 1988, p. 1.

Mull, Martin and Allen Rucker. *The History of White People in America*. New York: Putnam, 1985.

Mulvey, Laura. "Visual Pleasure and Narrative Cinema." In *Movies and Methods vol. 2*. Edited by Bill Nichols. Los Angeles: University of California Press, 1985. Also in *Screen* 16 (Autumn 1975):6–18.

Murray, James. *To Find an Image: Black Films from Uncle Tom to Super Fly*. Indianapolis: Bobbs-Merrill, 1973.

Musser, Charles. *The Emergence of Cinema: The American Screen to 1907*. New York: Scribners, 1990.

Naroll, Raoul. "Ethnic Unit Classification." *Current Anthropology* 5, no. 4 (1964):283–312.

Nichols, Bill. *Ideology and the Image: Social Representation in the Cinema and Other Media*. Bloomington: Indiana University Press, 1981.

———, ed. *Movies and Methods*. 2 vols. Berkeley: University of California Press, 1976.

Novak, Michael. "How American Are You if Your Grandparents Came from Serbia in 1888?" In *The Rediscovery of Ethnicity*. Edited by Sallie TeSelle. New York: Harper and Row, 1973.

O'Connor, John. *The Hollywood Indian: Stereotypes of Native Americans in Film*. Trenton: New Jersey State Museum, 1980.

Ong, Walter J. *Interfaces of the Word*. Ithaca: Cornell University Press, 1977.

———. *The Presence of the Word*. New Haven: Yale University Press, 1967.

O'Reilly, Kenneth. *Racial Matters: The FBI's Secret File on Black America (1960–1972)*. New York: Free Press, 1989.

Peiss, Kathy. *Cheap Amusements: Working Women and Leisure in Turn-of-the-Century New York*. Philadelphia: Temple University Press, 1986.

Peterson, William. "Concepts of Ethnicity." In *Harvard Encyclopedia of American Ethnic Groups*. Edited by Stephan Thernstrom. Cambridge: Harvard University Press, 1980.

Petric, Vlada., ed. *Film and Dreams: An Approach to Bergman*. South Salem: Redgrave, 1981.

Petty, R. E., and J. T. Cacioppo. "Forewarning, Cognitive Responding, and Resistance to Persuasion." *Journal of Personality and Social Psychology* 35 (1977):645–55.

Plecki, Gerald. *Robert Altman*. Boston: Twayne, 1985.

Quart, Leonard. "On Altman: Image as Essence." *Marxist Perspectives* 1 (Spring 1978):121–22.

Raboteau, Albert J. *Slave Religion*. New York: Oxford University Press, 1978.

Ramirez, Gabriel. *Lupe Velez: la mexicana que escupia fuego.* Mexico City: Cineteca Nacional, 1986.

Ray, Robert. *A Certain Tendency of the Hollywood Cinema, 1930–1980.* Princeton: Princeton University Press, 1985.

Reeves, B., S. Chaffee, and A. Tims. "Social Cognition and Mass Communication Research." In *Social Cognition and Communication.* Edited by M. E. Roloff and C. R. Berger. Beverly Hills: Sage, 1982.

Reising, Russell. *The Unusable Past: Theory and the Study of American Literature.* New York: Methuen, 1986.

Reisz, Karel. "Hollywood's Anti-Red Boomerang." *Sight and Sound* 22 (January-February 1953):132–37 +.

Reminick, Ronald. *Theory of Ethnicity: An Anthropologist's Perspective.* Lanham: University Press of America, 1983.

Rich, B. Ruby. "Cinefeminism and Its Discontents." *American Film* 9 (December 1983):68–71.

Riess, Steven. "A Fighting Chance: The Jewish-American Boxing Experience, 1890–1940." *American Jewish History* 74 (March 1985):2–11.

Riesman, David. *The Lonely Crowd.* New Haven: Yale University Press, 1950.

Rockefeller, Nelson. "Fruits of the Good Neighbor Policy," *New York Times Magazine,* May 14, 1944, p. 15.

Rogin, Michael. "The Sword Becomes a Flashing Vision." *Representations* 9 (Winter 1985):150–95.

Rosen, Philip. "Introduction: Text and Subject." *Narrative, Apparatus, Ideology.* New York: Columbia University Press, 1986.

Rosenbaum, Jonathan. "Improvisations and Interactions in Altmanville." *Sight and Sound* 44 (1975):90–95.

Rosenzweig, Roy. *Eight Hours for What We Will: Workers and Leisure in an Industrial City, 1870–1920.* New York: Cambridge University Press, 1983.

Rosten, Leo. *Hollywood, the Movie Makers, the Movie Colony.* New York: Harcourt Brace, 1941.

Roth, Philip. *The Counterlife.* New York: Farrar, Straus, Giroux, 1987.

Rourke, Constance. *American Humor: A Study of the National Character.* 1931. Reprint. Garden City: Anchor-Doubleday, 1955.

Rowe, John Carlos. "Eye-Witness: Documentary Styles in the American Representations of Vietnam." *Cultural Critique* 3 (Spring 1986):126–50.

Rowland, Donald. *History of the Office of the Coordinator of Inter-American Affairs.* Washington: Government Printing Office, 1947.

Said, Edward W. *Covering Islam.* New York: Pantheon Books, 1981.

———. *Orientalism.* New York: Random House, 1979.

Saisselin, Remy A. *The Bourgeois and the Bibelot.* New Brunswick: Rutgers University Press, 1984.

Salt, Barry. *Film Style and Technology: History and Analysis.* London: Starword, 1983.

Sanford, Nevitt et al., eds. *Sanctions For Evil.* San Francisco: Jossey-Bass, 1971.

Saxton, C. "The Collective Voice as Cultural Voice." *Cinema Journal* 26 (Fall 1986):19–30.

Schermerhorn, R. A. "Ethnicity in the Perspective of the Sociology of Knowledge." *Ethnicity* 1 (April 1974):1–13.

Schneider, David. *American Kinship: A Cultural Account.* Chicago: University of Chicago Press, 1980.

Schneider, D. J. *Social Psychology.* New York: Harcourt Brace Jovanovich, 1988.

Schneider, D. J., A. H. Hastorf, and P. C. Ellsworth. *Person Perception.* 2d ed. Reading: Addison-Wesley, 1979.

Sedgwick, Eve Kosofsky. *Between Men: English Literature and Male Homosocial Desire.* New York: Columbia University Press, 1985.

Self, Robert. "Robert Altman and the Theory of Authorship." *Cinema Journal* 25 (Fall 1985):3–11.

Sherif, M., and C. Hovland. *Social Judgment.* New Haven: Yale University Press, 1961.

Shils, Edward. *Center and Periphery: Essays in Macrosociology* Chicago: University of Chicago Press, 1975.

———. "Primordial, Personal, Sacred, and Civil Ties." *British Journal of Sociology* 8 (1957):130–45.

Silberman, Charles. *A Certain People: American Jews and Their Lives Today.* New York: Summit Books, 1985.

Siqueira, Servulo. "Tudo e Verdade." *Folka de Sao Paulo,* December 2, 1984.

Sklar, Robert. *Movie-Made America: A Cultural History of American Movies.* New York: Random House, 1975.

———. "Oh Altusser!: Historiography and the Rise of Cinema Studies." *Radical History Review* 41 (1988):11–35.

Sklar, Robert, and Charles Musser, eds. *Resisting Images: Radical Perspectives on Film History.* Philadelphia: Temple University Press, 1990.

Sklare, Marshall. *America's Jews.* New York: Random House, 1971.

Smith, Anthony. *The Geopolitics of Information.* New York: Oxford University Press, 1980.

Smith, Steven B. *Reading Althusser.* Ithaca: Cornell University Press, 1984.

Snyder, Robert. *The Voice of the City.* New York: Oxford University Press, 1989.

Sobchack, Vivian. *Screening Space: The American Science Fiction Film.* 2d ed. New York: Ungar, 1987.

Sollors, Werner. *Beyond Ethnicity: Consent and Descent in American Culture.* New York: Oxford University Press, 1986.

Spelman, Elizabeth V. *Inessential Woman: Problems of Exclusion in Feminist Thought.* Boston: Beacon Press, 1988.

Staiger, Janet. "The Politics of Film Canons." *Cinema Journal* 24 (Spring 1985):4–23.

Stalling, Penny. *Flesh and Fantasy.* New York: St. Martin's Press, 1978.

Stam, Robert. "Orson Welles, Brazil, and the Power of Blackness." *Persistance of Vision,* no. 7 (1989):93–112.

———. *Reflexivity in Film and Literature: From Don Quixote to Jean-Luc Godard.* Ann Arbor: UMI Research Press, 1983.

Stam, Robert, and Ella Shohat. "*Zelig* and Contemporary Theory: Meditation on the Chameleon Text." *Enclitic* 9 (Summer 1987):176–94.

Stam, Robert, and Louise Spence. "Colonialism, Racism and Representation." *Screen* 24, no. 2 (1983):2–20.

Staples, Robert. "Black Male Genocide: A Final Solution to the Race Problem in America." *Black Scholar* 18 (May-June 1987):2–11.

Steinberg, Cobbett. *Reel Facts: The Movie Book of Records.* New York: Vintage Books, 1982.

Steven, Peter, ed. *Jump Cut: Hollywood, Politics, and Counter Cinema.* Toronto: Between the Lines, 1985.

Studlar, Gaylyn, and David Desser. "Never Having to Say You're Sorry: *Rambo's* Rewriting of the Vietnam War." *Film Quarterly* 42 (Fall 1988):9–16.

Suleiman, Susan Rubin. *Authoritarian Fictions.* New York: Columbia University Press, 1983.

————. *The Reader in the Text: Essays on Audience and Interpretation.* Princeton: Princeton University Press, 1980.

Susman, Warren., ed. " 'Personality' and the Making of Twentieth-Century Culture." In *Culture as History: The Transformation of American Society in the Twentieth Century.* New York: Pantheon, 1984.

Swan, W. B., and L. C. Miller. "Why Never Forgetting a Face Matters: Visual Imagery and Social Memory." *Journal of Personality and Social Psychology* 43 (1982):475–80.

Tajfel, H. "Social Psychology of Intergroup Relations." *Annual Review of Psychology* 33 (1982):1–39.

Tajfel, H., and J. Turner. "An Integrative Theory of Intergroup Conflict," In *The Social Psychology of Intergroup Relations.* Edited by W. G. Austin and S. Worchel. Monterey: Brooks-Cole, 1979.

Tarantino, Michael. "Movement as Metaphor: *The Long Goodbye.*" *Sight and Sound* 44 (1975):98–102.

Taylor, Clyde. "Les grands axes et les sources africaines du nouveau cinema noir." *CineAction* 46 (1988).

Thomas, Sari. "Mass Media and the Social Order." In *Inter/Media Interpersonal Communication in a Media World.* Edited by Gary Gumpert and Robert Cathcart. New York: Oxford University Press, 1986.

Thompson, E. P. *People's History and Socialist Theory.* Edited by Rapahel Samuel. London: Routledge and Kegan Paul, 1981.

————. *The Poverty of Theory and Other Essays.* New York and London: Monthly Review Press, 1978.

Todorov, Tzvetan. *The Conquest of America.* Translated by Richard Howard. New York: Harper and Row, 1984.

Tompkins, Jane P. *Reader Response Criticism: From Formalism to Post-Structuralism.* Baltimore: Johns Hopkins University Press, 1980.

Uspensky, Boris. *A Poetics of Composition.* Berkeley: University of California Press, 1973.

Valenti, Peter. *Errol Flynn: A Bio-Bibliography.* Westport: Greenwood Press, 1984.

Vardac, A. Nicholas. *Stage to Screen*. New York: DaCapo Press, 1949.

Weales, Gerald. *Canned Goods as Caviar: American Film Comedies of the 1930s*. Chicago: University of Chicago Press, 1985.

Weber, Max. *Economy and Society*. New York: Bedminster Press, 1968.

——. "The Ethnic Group." In *Theories of Society*. Edited by Talcott Parsons. Glencoe: Free Press, 1961.

Wilden, Anthony. *The Language of the Self*. Baltimore: Johns Hopkins University Press, 1968.

Winokur, Mark. "Improbable Ethnic Hero: William Powell and the Transformation of Ethnic Hollywood." *Cinema Journal* 27 (Fall 1987):5–22.

——. " 'Smile Stranger': Aspects of Immigrant Humor in the Marx Brothers' Humor." *Literature/Film Quarterly* 13, no. 3 (1985):161–71.

Wolfenstein, Martha, and Nathan Leites. *Movies: A Psychological Study*. Glencoe: Free Press, 1950.

Woloch, Nancy. *Women and the American Experience*. New York: Alfred A. Knopf, 1984.

Woll, Allen L. *The Hollywood Musical Goes to War*. Chicago: Nelson Hall, 1983.

——. *The Latin Image in American Film*. Los Angeles: Latin American Center, University of California, 1977.

Woll, Allen L., and Randall M. Miller., eds. *Ethnic and Racial Images in American Film and Television: Historical Essays and Bibliography*. New York: Garland, 1987.

Wong, Eugene Franklin. *On Visual Media Racism: Asians in American Motion Pictures*. New York: Arno Press, 1978.

Wood, Robin. "Hero/Anti-Hero: The Dilemma of *Year of the Dragon*," *Cine-Action!* no. 6 (August 1986):57–61.

——. "Return of the Repressed." *Film Comment* 14 (July-August 1978):24–32.

Yates, Frances. *The Art of Memory*. Chicago: University of Chicago Press, 1966.

Yudice, George. "Bakhtin and the Subject of Postmodernism." In *Bakhtin: Radical Perspectives*. Minneapolis: University of Minnesota Press, in press.

Zangwill, Israel. *The Melting Pot*. In *The Collected Works of Israel Zangwill*. New York: AMS Press, 1969.

——. *King of the Schnorrers*. London: Macmillan, 1893.

Contributors

PAUL S. COWEN is professor agrégé of social psychology and psychology of communication at l'Université du Québec à Montréal. He is the author of several research articles on the role of cognitive processes in the comprehension of film narratives in *Empirical Studies of the Arts* and *Educational Communication and Technology Journal* and is researching the influence of film and television on prejudice in children.

DAVID DESSER, associate professor of cinema studies and speech communication at the University of Illinois at Urbana-Champaign, has written two books on Japanese cinema: *The Samurai Films of Akira Kurosawa* and *Eros Plus Massacre: An Introduction to the Japanese New Wave Cinema*. With Lester Friedman, he has written *In Search of a Tradition: American Jewish Filmmakers and the Jewish Experience in America*.

LESTER D. FRIEDMAN, professor, teaches film at Syracuse University and humanities at the SUNY Health Science Center. He has written extensively about Jewish images in the American cinema, and his book *The Jewish Image in American Film* won the 1988 National Jewish Book Award. He is editing a book on contemporary English cinema.

PAUL GILES has published *Hart Crane: The Contexts of "The Bridge"* as well as articles on Thom Gunn, Charles Dickens, Jane Austen, and other writers. An assistant professor of English at Portland State University (Oregon), he teaches classes in film comedy as well as American literature. He is completing a book on how cultural mythologies of Catholicism have influenced modern American literature and cinema.

SUMIKO HIGASHI teaches history and film at the State University of New York College at Brockport. She is the author of *Virgins, Vamps, and Flappers: The American Silent Movie Heroine* and *Cecil B. DeMille: A Guide to References* and Resources. She is working on a research project about DeMille's early film career.

IAN JARVIE, a product of the London School of Economics and the BFI Film Summer School, teaches philosophy and film at York University, Toronto. His books include *Movies and Society, Movies as Social Criticism,* and *Philosophy of the Film.* His research interests are in the economic history of the film industry.

ANA M. LÓPEZ is assistant professor of communication and an adjunct of the Roger Thayer Stone Center for Latin American Studies at Tulane University. She is preparing a book on Latin American cinema.

GINA MARCHETTI is an assistant professor in the Department of Communication Arts and Theatre, Radio-Television-Film Division, University of Maryland (College Park). She has published articles in *Jump Cut, Journal of Film and Video, Journal of Communication Inquiry, East-West Film Journal, Afterimage, Current Research in Film, Film Reader,* and *Millennium Film Journal.*

CHARLES MUSSER teaches film studies at Columbia University and New York University. He has written a triology on the beginnings of cinema in America: *Before the Nickelodeon: Edwin S. Porter and the Edison Manufacturing Company; High Class Moving Pictures: Lyman H. Howe and the Forgotten Era of Traveling Exhibition;* and *The Emergence of Cinema: The American Screen to 1907.*

ELLA SHOHAT teaches and coordinates the Cinema Studies program of the Department of Performing Arts, The City University of New York, Staten Island. She is on the editorial board of *Social Text* and the author of *Israeli Cinema: East/West and the Politics of Representation.*

VIVIAN SOBCHACK, past president of the Society for Cinema Studies, is professor of theater arts/film studies and director of the arts at the University of California (Santa Cruz). She is co-author of *An Introduction to Film* and author of *Screening Space: The American Science Fiction Film* and *The Address of the Eye: A Phenomenology of Film Experience.*

CLAUDIA SPRINGER is an assistant professor in the English Department and Film Studies Program at Rhode Island College. She has published in *Wide Angle, Jump Cut, Cultural Critique, Literature and Psychology,* and *Genre.*

ROBERT STAM is associate professor in the Cinema Studies Department at New York University. He is the author of *The Interrupted Spectacle, Reflexivity in Film and Literature: From Don Quixote to Jean-Luc Godard,* and *Subversive Pleasures: Bakhtin, Cultural Criticism and Film.* He is co-author of *Brazilian Cinema.*

ROBYN WIEGMAN, assistant professor of English at Syracuse University, teaches courses in feminist theory, American literature and culture, and film. Her articles have appeared in *Criticism* and *American Literary History.* She is working on a book about race and gender in American literature, film, and television.

Mark Winokur, assistant professor, has taught American film and literature at the University of California, Berkeley, and Dickinson College. He has published articles in *Cinema Journal* and *Literature/Film Quarterly* and has written *American Laughter*.